MostUsedWords.com presents

Spanish Frequency Dictionary

Master Vocabulary

7501 - 10000 Most Common Spanish Words

Book 4

First Printing, 2018

MostUsedWords.com
10685-B Hazelhurst Dr. # 22933
HOUSTON, TX 77043
United States

www.MostUsedWords.com

Contents

Why This Book?

Hello, dear reader.

Thank you for purchasing this book. We hope it serves you well on your language learning journey.

Not all words are created equal. The purpose of this frequency dictionary is to list the most common Spanish words in descending order, so you can learn this language as fast and efficiently as possible.

First, we would like to illustrate the value of a frequency dictionary. For the purpose of example, we have combined frequency data from various languages (mainly Romance, Slavic and Germanic languages) and made it into a single chart.

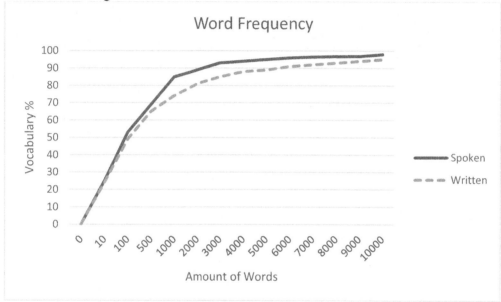

The sweet spots, according to the data seem to be:

Amount of Words	Spoken	Written
• 100	53%	49%
• 1.000	85%	74%
• 2.500	92%	82%
• 5.000	95%	89%
• 7.500	97%	93%
• 10.000	98%	95%

Above data corresponds with Pareto´s law.

Pareto's law, also known as the 80/20 rule, states that, for many events, roughly 80% of the effects come from 20% of the causes.

In language learning, this principle seems to be on steroids. It seems that just 20% of the 20% (95/5) of the most used words in a language account for roughly all the vocabulary you need.

To put this further in perspective: The Collins Spanish Dictionary (August 2016 edition) lists over 310.000 words in current use, while you will only need to know 1.62% (5000 words) to achieve 95% and 89% fluency in speaking and writing. Knowing the most common 10.000 words, or just 3.25%, will net you 98% fluency in spoken language and 95% fluency in written texts.

Keeping this in mind, the value of a frequency dictionary is immense. Study the most frequent words, build your vocabulary and progress quickly. One more frequency asked question needs to be answered.

Well, how many words do you need to know for varying levels of fluency?

While it's important to note that it is impossible to pin down these numbers and statistics with 100% accuracy, these are a global average of multiple sources. According to research, this is the amount of vocabulary needed for varying levels of fluency:

1. 250 words: the essential core of a language. Without these words, you cannot construct any meaningful sentences.
2. 750 words: are used every single day by every person who speaks the language.
3. 2500 words: should enable you to express everything you could possibly want to say, although some creativity might be required.
4. 5000 words: the active vocabulary of native speakers without higher education.
5. 10,000 words: the active vocabulary of native speakers with higher education.
6. 20,000 words: the amount you need to be able to recognize passively to read, understand, and enjoy a work of literature such as a novel by a notable author.

Caveats & Limitations.

1. A frequency list is never "The Definite Frequency List."

Depending on the source material analyzed, you may get different frequency lists. A corpus on spoken word differs from source texts based on a written language.

That is why we chose subtitles as our source, because, according to science, subtitles cover the best of both worlds: they correlate with both spoken and written language.

The frequency list is based on an analysis of roughly 20 gigabytes of Spanish subtitles.

Visualize a book with almost 16 million pages, or 80.000 books of 200 pages each, to get an idea of the number of words that have been analyzed for this book.

If you were to read the source text used for this book, it would take you around 100 years of reading 24/7. A large base text is absolutely vital in order to develop an accurate frequency list.

Since 100 years of simply reading and then trying to process the text is a bit much for one person, we have called in additional power to help us establish the frequency rankings.

The raw data included over 1 million entries, or different "words". The raw data has been lemmatized; words are given in their dictionary form.

2. Creating an accurate frequency list is more complicated than it seems.

Above mentioned method of classification does come with its own complications. Take for example, the word

- **poder(se)**-*vb; m* – be able; power

Obviously, **poder** is most often used as a verb. However, you will see the word rank highly as one of the most common nouns. With our current methods, it is impossible to determine exactly how often **poder** is used as a noun as opposed to the verb.

But while we developed an accurate method of estimating the correct position of "**poder**-*m* – power", (around the 500th most common word in Spanish), we decided we don't want duplicate entries in our frequency dictionaries. Why?

Poder is a single dictionary entry, and it's choosing between either "hey, you have duplicate entries, your list is wrong." and "hey, **poder** isn't the #9 most common noun, your list is wrong." (actual customer feedback, paraphrased.)

Because instances like **poder** are very few and in-between, we kindly ask you to use your common sense while using this dictionary. Decide for yourself on not whether you should learn a translation or not.

Another difficulty is the conjugated verbs. Some conjugated vers can be classified as multiple parts of speech. Take for example **dicho**. It originally ranked somewhere around the 147th most common Spanish word.

As a conjugated verb, **dicho** is the past participle of "**decir**-*vb* – to say" and translates as "said", while as a noun it means "saying, expression".

No way, José, that "saying, expression" is the most 147th most used Spanish word. As previously stated, our words are lemmatized, and **decir** is already listed at place 77.

(Please refer to our upcoming book on Spanish verbs for detailed verb information, all regular and irregular conjugations and bilingual text example sentences.)

We did develop a method to accurately estimate the occurrence of **dicho** as a noun. By the time of writing "**dicho**-*m* – saying, expression" hoovers around the 11.702th place of the most common Spanish words. It is very unlikely that it will enter the 10.000 most common Spanish words, and thus will be out of the scope of our frequency dictionary series.

3. Nouns

We tried our best to keep out proper nouns, such as "**James**, **Ryan**, **Alice** as well as "**Rome**, **Washington**" or "the **Louvre**". Names of countries are an exception to the rule, and are included.

Some common proper nouns have multiple translations. For the ease of explanation, the following example is given in English.

"**Jack**" is a very common first name, but also a noun (a jack to lift up a vehicle) and a verb (to steal something). So is the word "**can**" It is a conjugation of the verb "to be able" as well as a noun (a tin can, or a can of soft drink).

With the current technology, it is unfortunately not possible to precisely identify the correct frequency placements of the above words. We came up with a method to accurately estimate the correct placement of these words.

In example, a competitor's frequency dictionary on the English language listed the noun "**can**", like a can of coke, as the 247th most used word in the English language. Our methods would list it around the 3347th most used word. While not perfect, I *can* tell you that our method is more accurate than theirs.

4. This word doesn't belong there!

Some entries you might find odd in their respective frequency rankings. We were surprised a couple of times ourselves while creating this series. Keep in mind that the frequency list is compiled from a large amount of text, and may include words you wouldn't use yourself. But you might very well encounter them.

In our opinion, it is important you do know these words. Store them somewhere in your passive vocabulary, instead of trying to integrate them into your active vocabulary. But in the end, it's up to you whether you think you should learn a word, or skip it.

5. This is not a Spanish word!

You might find non-Spanish loanwords in this dictionary. We decided to include them, because if they´re being used in subtitle translation, it is safe to assume the word has been integrated into the Spanish general vocabulary.

6. Vulgarities

We also decided to keep out vulgarities, even though these are rather common in daily speech. We wanted to keep this book appropriate for readers of all ages. We tried to imagine what a modern-day middle American woman would take offense to, and drew the line there.

At the same time, some words absolutely needed to be clarified. In rare occasions, the usage of vocabulary items can differ severely between Spanish spoken in Latin America and Spanish spoken in Europe. It could lead to pretty awkward situations if you were not aware of these differences.

These words have been censored in a way that one can still deduce their meaning, if one is already in the know. Kids, ask your parents. In example:

- **coger**-*vb* - to take, f*ck (LA)

7. Parallel text example sentences

Some sentences are easy, some are more difficult. Some are a direct translation, some are more loosely translated. Some mimic spoken language, some mimic written language. Some are more high-brow, some are more colloquial. In short, we tried to include a mix of different types of language, just like you would encounter in real life.

Example sentences are great, because they show you Spanish word usage in context. You get to learn extra vocabulary from the sentences, since they're in parallel text. And since you'll encounter important, common words over and over again, you will ingrain those words faster in your long-term memory.

8. Final thoughts

We are pretty confident our frequency ranking is as solid as it can be, keeping above pitfalls in mind. Still, this frequency list includes 25 extra words to compensate for any irregularities you might encounter. Or you might disagree with the addition of non-Spanish loanwords. So instead of the 5001 – 7500 most common words, you actually get the 5001-7525 most common words.

And one more thing.

The big secret to learning language is this: build your vocabulary, learn basic grammar and go out there and speak. Make mistakes, have a laugh and then learn from your mistakes. Wash, rinse, repeat..

We hope you enjoy this frequency dictionary and that it helps you in your journey of learning Spanish.

How To Use This Dictionary

abbreviation	*abr*	prefix	*pfx*
adjective	*adj*	preposition	*prp*
adverb	*adv*	pronoun	*prn*
article	*art*	suffix	*sfx*
auxiliary verb	*av*	verb	*vb*
conjunction	*con*	verb (reflexive)	*vbr*
contraction	*contr*	singular	*sg*
interjection	*int*	plural	*pl*
noun	*f(eminine), m(asculine)*	(coll)	*colloquial language*
numeral	*num*	(se)	*reflexive verb marker*
particle	*part*	(ES)	*European Spanish*
phrase	*phr*	(LA)	*Latin America Spanish*

Verbs

Some verbs can be used reflexively. Verbs that can be used reflexively are marked by "**(se)**". Only when the verb has a different meaning when used reflexively, we added the qualifier "**vbr**" to indicate the meaning of the reflexive verb.

Word Order

Different parts of speech are divided by "**;**". Generally speaking, the more common translations are given first.

Translations

We made the decision to give the most common translation(s) of a word, and respectively the most common part(s) of speech. It does, however, not mean that this is the only possible translations or the only part of speech the word can be used for.

International Phonetic Alphabet (IPA)

The pronunciation of foreign vocabulary can be tricky. To help you get it right, we added IPA entries for each entry. If you already have a base understanding of the pronunciation, you will find the IPA pronunciation straightforward. For more information, please visit www.internationalphoneticalphabet.org

Spanish English Frequency Dictionary

Rank	Spanish	English Translation(s)
	Part of Speech	Spanish Example Sentences
	[IPA]	-English Example Sentences

7501 urgir — **press**
vb
[ur.ˈxir]
Hemos de urgir el restablecimiento de esta autonomía.
-We must press for the restoration of this autonomy.

7502 chantajear — **blackmail**
vb
[ʧãn̪.ta.xe.ˈar]
Quizás su siguiente movimiento es intentar chantajear al sheriff.
-Maybe his next move is to try to blackmail the sheriff.

7503 bestial — **brutal**
adj
[bɛs.ˈtjal]
Tengo una resaca bestial y se me revuelve el estómago.
-I have a beastly hangover and my bowels are in a tumble.

7504 renombre — **renown**
m
[re.ˈnõm.bre]
Ella es una violinista de cierto renombre.
-She's a violinist of some renown.

7505 frenesí — **frenzy**
m
[fre.ne.ˈsi]
Los tiburones están a punto de unirse al frenesí.
-Next to join the frenzy are the sharks.

7506 heces — **dregs, feces**
fpl
[ˈe.ses]
Puedo llevar las heces yo sola.
-I can transport the feces on my own.

7507 atletismo — **athletics**
m
[at̯.lɛ.ˈtiş.mo]
A mí no me interesaba el atletismo.
-I wasn't interested in athletics.

7508 zurrar — **spank**
vb
[su.ˈrar]
Y te prometemos que nadie te volverá a zurrar otra vez.
-And we promise that no one will ever spank you again.

7509 finalista — **finalist; finalist**
adj; m/f
[fi.na.ˈlis.ta]
Reciban a nuestro primer finalista.
-Please welcome our first finalist.

7510 alegar — **claim**
vb
[a.le.ˈɣar]
Podría alegar que las bombas salvaron vidas.
-So you could claim the bombings saved lives.

7511 estrenar — **use for the first time**
vb
[ɛs.tre.ˈnar]
Será duro, peligroso y una excelente oportunidad de estrenar mis nuevos pantalones.
-It'll be tough, dangerous, and a perfect chance to premiere my new cargo shorts.

7512 poro — **pore**
m
[ˈpo.ro]
Con cada poro de mi cuerpo, tengo miedo.
-With every pore of my body, I'm scared.

7513 indignante — **outrageous**
adj
[ĩn̪.diɣ.ˈnãn̪.te]
Lo que está ocurriendo aquí es, sencillamente, indignante.
-What is happening here is simply outrageous.

7514 catastrófico — **catastrophic**

	adj	Sería un evento catastrófico para el planeta.
	[ka.tas.ˈtro.fi.ko]	-It would be a catastrophic event for the planet.
7515	**canino**	**canine; canine tooth**
	adj; m	Creo que es un diente canino.
	[ka.ˈni.no]	-I think it's a canine tooth.
7516	**dote**	**dowry**
	f	Guárdalo como parte de tu dote.
	[ˈdo.te]	-Keep it as a portion of your dowry.
7517	**radial**	**radio; circular saw**
	adj; f	Nuevamente recibo el sonido radial, señor.
	[ra.ˈðjal]	-I'm getting that radio sound again, sir.
7518	**podio**	**podium**
	m	Todos los candidatos se sentaron en el podio.
	[ˈpo.ðjo]	-All candidates were seated at the podium.
7519	**relevar**	**relieve, substitute**
	vb	Tocar un instrumento puede relevar mucho estrés.
	[re.le.ˈβar]	-Playing an instrument can relieve a lot of stress.
7520	**burócrata**	**bureaucrat**
	m/f	Soy simplemente un burócrata del sistema.
	[bu.ˈro.kra.ta]	-I am merely a bureaucrat of the system.
7521	**intermitente**	**intermittent; blinker**
	adj; m	Parece que se trata de un problema intermitente.
	[ĩn.tɛr.mi.ˈtɛ̃n.te]	-It seems to be an intermittent problem.
7522	**helio**	**helium**
	m	El helio resuena de otra forma en mis cuerdas vocales.
	[ˈe.ljo]	-The helium resonates differently with my vocal chords.
7523	**elixir**	**elixir**
	m	Este café debe ser un elixir de la juventud.
	[e.lik.ˈsir]	-This cafe must be my elixir of youth.
7524	**autonomía**	**autonomy**
	f	Se habla mucho sobre la autonomía personal.
	[au̯.to.no.ˈmi.a]	-Now, we hear a lot of talk about personal autonomy.
7525	**furor**	**fury**
	m	El furor de los cielos puede atacar en cualquier momento.
	[fu.ˈror]	-The fury of heaven may strike at any moment.
7526	**alistar(se)**	**enlist**
	vb	¿Te piensas alistar sin mi permiso?
	[a.lis.ˈtar]	-You intend to enlist without my permission?
7527	**frialdad**	**coldness**
	f	Temo su frialdad con respecto a mi hijo.
	[frjal̪.ˈdað]	-I fear your coldness toward my son.
7528	**barandilla**	**handrail**
	f	Agárrate a la otra barandilla.
	[ba.rã̃n.ˈdi.ja]	-Hold in the other handrail.
7529	**tumbar(se)**	**knock down; lay down**
	vb	Me voy a tumbar por un minuto.
	[tũm.ˈbar]	-I am going to lay down for a minute.
7530	**estudioso**	**studious; scholar**

adj; m
[ɛs.tu.ˈðjo.so]

Tú eres un estudioso, no un guerrero.
-You're a scholar, not a warrior.

7531 innato — **innate**

adj
[ĩn.ˈna.to]

El amor por las pieles no es innato.
-The love of fur is not innate.

7532 municipalidad — **municipality**

f
[mu.ni.si.pa.li.ˈðað]

Ninguna municipalidad ha terminado un plan de desarrollo municipal.
-No municipality has finalized a municipal development plan.

7533 encarnación — **incarnation**

f
[ɛ̃ŋ.kar.na.ˈsjõn]

Me complace verlos en esta encarnación.
-I am glad to see them in this incarnation.

7534 aferrarse — **cling to**

vbr
[a.fɛ.ˈrar.se]

Entiendo la necesidad de aferrarse a todo.
-I understand the need to cling to anything.

7535 rutinario — **routine**

adj
[ru.ti.ˈna.rjo]

Es rutinario cuando hay una investigación.
-It's routine when there's an investigation.

7536 mausoleo — **mausoleum**

m
[mau̯.so.ˈle.o]

Nunca entregaron un ataúd al mausoleo.
-They never delivered a casket to the mausoleum.

7537 cerezo — **cherry tree**

m
[sɛ.ˈre.so]

Un cerezo está floreciendo en la montaña.
-A cherry tree is blooming on the hillside.

7538 ilógico — **illogical**

adj
[i.ˈlo.xi.ko]

Sería ilógico que nos ocultase información.
-It would be illogical for you to withhold information from us.

7539 sodio — **sodium**

m
[ˈso.ðjo]

El sodio se incluye en la lista de nutrientes.
-Sodium is included among the nutrients listed.

7540 esquizofrénico — **schizophrenic**

adj
[ɛs.ki.so.ˈfre.ni.ko]

Encontramos un artista esquizofrénico que cree que es Winslow Homer.
-We found a schizophrenic artist who believes that he's Winslow Homer.

7541 retrospectivo — **retrospective**

adj
[rɛ.tros.pek̚.ˈti.βo]

El sistema retrospectivo es más preciso que el sistema prospectivo.
-The retrospective system is more precise than the prospective system.

7542 asentamiento — **settlement**

m
[a.sɛ̃n.ta.ˈmjɛ̃n.to]

Parece haber un pequeño asentamiento agricultural humano allí.
-It appears there's a small human agricultural settlement there.

7543 contusión — **contusion**

f
[kõn.tu.ˈsjõn]

Tiene una especie de contusión.
-He's got some kind of a contusion.

7544 crematorio — **crematorium**

m
[kre.ma.ˈto.rjo]

Se dejó su bolso en el crematorio.
-She's left her handbag at the crematorium.

7545 trampolín — **springboard**

m
[trãm.po.ˈlĩn]

Ha sido el trampolín de todo lo que hemos hecho.
-It has been the springboard for everything that we have done.

7546	**sociología**	**sociology**
	f	Es licenciado en matemáticas y sociología.
	[so.sjo.lo.ˈxi.a]	-He holds advanced degrees in both mathematics and sociology.
7547	**semi**	**semi**
	pfx	Las cabañas se encontraban en un estado semiarruinado.
	[ˈse.mi]	-The cottages were all in a semi-ruined state.
7548	**embrión**	**embryo**
	m	El primer problema está relacionado con el embrión.
	[ẽm.ˈbrjõn]	-The first problem concerns the embryo.
7549	**activación**	**activation**
	f	El dispositivo de activación, dámelo.
	[ak̚.ti.βa.ˈsjõn]	-The activation device, give it to me.
7550	**ex**	**ex**
	pfx	Mi novio vive con mi hermano.
	[ˈeks]	-My exboyfriend is living with my brother.
7551	**renacuajo**	**tadpole, little kid**
	m	Tengo miedo de perderte, renacuajo.
	[re.na.ˈkwa.xo]	-I'm scared of losing you, tadpole.
7552	**olmo**	**elm**
	m	Había una gran rama de olmo sobre el tejado.
	[ˈol.mo]	-There was a big elm branch over the whole roof.
7553	**invocar**	**invoke**
	vb	Haría lo que fuese por invocar esos sentimientos.
	[ĩm.bo.ˈkar]	-I would do whatever I could to summon those feelings.
7554	**salino**	**saline**
	adj	Necesito un litro de salino.
	[sa.ˈli.no]	-I need a liter of saline.
7555	**acné**	**acne**
	m	El acné es un efecto secundario poco frecuente.
	[ak̚.ˈne]	-Acne is an uncommon side effect.
7556	**desatar**	**untie**
	vb	Me puede desatar. No voy a salir volando.
	[de.sa.ˈtar]	-You can untie me. I'm not going to fly away.
7557	**nitrato**	**nitrate**
	m	Por otra parte, también debería incluirse el nitrato de potasio.
	[ni.ˈtra.to]	-Moreover, potassium nitrate should also be incorporated.
7558	**inca**	**Inca; Incan**
	m/f; adj	En la sociedad inca no existían ni pobres ni mendigos.
	[ˈĩŋ.ka]	-There were no poor or beggars in Inca society.
7559	**exiliar**	**exile**
	vb	No podemos exiliar a la prensa.
	[ɛk.si.ˈljar]	-We can't exile the press.
7560	**sigiloso**	**stealthy**
	adj	Ya me conoces, sigiloso como una sombra.
	[si.xi.ˈlo.so]	-You know me, stealthy as a shadow.
7561	**informático**	**computer; computer expert**
	adj; m	Quería plasmar la mente humana en el lenguaje informático.
	[ĩm.for.ˈma.ti.ko]	-I wanted to capture the human mind in the computer language.

7562	**batuta**	**baton**
	f	Es el momento de pasar la batuta, Laura.
	[ba.ˈtu.ta]	-It's time to pass the baton, Laura.
7563	**gasa**	**chiffon**
	f	Le encantaba su camisón de gasa.
	[ˈga.sa]	-She loved her chiffon nightie.
7564	**engendrar**	**engender**
	vb	Sus plegarias les ayudarán a engendrar un hijo sano.
	[ɛ̃ŋ.xɛ̃n.ˈdrar]	-Their prayers will help you engender a healthy child.
7565	**suspense**	**suspense**
	m	Hermana, no puede mantenerlos en suspense.
	[sus.ˈpɛ̃n.se]	-Sister, you can't keep them in suspense.
7566	**sarta**	**bunch**
	f	¡Sus ideas son una sarta de estupideces!
	[ˈsar.ta]	-Your schemes are a load of old codswallop!
7567	**abordaje**	**approach, boarding**
	m	Con el abordaje adecuado, sin embargo, existe esperanza.
	[a.βor.ˈða.xe]	-With the right approach, however, there is hope.
7568	**candente**	**red-hot**
	adj	Aquí hay una candente declaración del gobernador.
	[kã̃n.ˈdɛ̃n.te]	-Here's a red-hot statement from the governor.
7569	**lucrativo**	**lucrative**
	adj	Esta asociación no tiene un objetivo lucrativo.
	[lu.kra.ˈti.βo]	-This association does not have a lucrative goal.
7570	**voleibol**	**volleyball**
	m	También pasas demasiado tiempo jugando al voleibol.
	[bo.lei̯.ˈβol]	-You also spend too much time playing volleyball.
7571	**puñetero**	**annoyance, damn (coll)**
	m	Intentaba salvar a tu puñetero hijo.
	[pu.ɲɛ.ˈtɛ.ro]	-I was trying to save your damn kid.
7572	**insuficiente**	**insufficient; unsatisfactory**
	adj; m	Además, la cifra propuesta puede resultar insuficiente.
	[ĩn.su.fi.ˈsjɛ̃n.te]	-Moreover, the amount proposed may prove to be insufficient.
7573	**cacerola**	**pan**
	f	Esta es la cacerola que usó.
	[ka.sɛ.ˈro.la]	-This is the pan you used.
7574	**bandada**	**flock**
	f	Vi una bandada de pájaros volando en el aire.
	[bã̃n.ˈda.ða]	-I saw a flock of birds flying aloft.
7575	**afectuoso**	**affectionate**
	adj	Y tú sigues tan afectuoso como siempre.
	[a.fek̚.ˈtwo.so]	-And you're as affectionate as ever.
7576	**mejoría**	**improvement**
	f	Sin embargo, esa mejoría no ha sido uniforme.
	[me.xo.ˈri.a]	-However, this improvement has not been uniform.
7577	**cobijo**	**shelter**
	m	Cuando necesitamos cobijo, construimos rascacielos.
	[ko.ˈβi.xo]	-When we need shelter, we build skyscrapers.

7578	**angular**	**angular**
	adj	Desconocía la idea del tamaño angular.
	[ãŋ.gu.ˈlar]	-I was ignorant of the idea of angular size.
7579	**sencillez**	**simplicity**
	f	Admiro la sencillez de tu moralidad.
	[sɛn.ˈsi.jes]	-I pay homage to the simplicity of your morals.
7580	**abrumador**	**overwhelming**
	adj	Puede resultar abrumador comenzar el instituto.
	[a.βru.ma.ˈðor]	-It can feel overwhelming to start high school.
7581	**caperuza**	**hood**
	f	Una vez, le dio una pequeña caperuza de terciopelo rojo .
	[ka.pɛ.ˈru.sa]	-Once, she gave her a little hood of red velvet.
7582	**tecnológico**	**technological**
	adj	Creo que podemos estar ante algún tipo de problema tecnológico.
	[tek.no.ˈlo.xi.ko]	-I think we might be looking at some kind of technological problem.
7583	**servicial**	**helpful**
	adj	Se esfuerza demasiado por ser servicial.
	[sɛr.βi.ˈsjal]	-She's trying too hard to be helpful.
7584	**frescura**	**freshness**
	f	Las frutas se cogen con hojas para garantizar su frescura.
	[frɛs.ˈku.ra]	-The fruit is picked with its leaves to guarantee freshness.
7585	**anhelar**	**yearn for**
	vb	Tú eres libre de anhelarla.
	[a.ne.ˈlar]	-You're free to yearn for her.
7586	**legua**	**league**
	f	Cambiamos los caballos cada legua, mi señor.
	[ˈle.ɣwa]	-We change horses every league, my lord.
7587	**paternal**	**fatherly**
	adj	Déjame darte un consejo paternal.
	[pa.tɛr.ˈnal]	-Let me give you some fatherly advice.
7588	**gangrena**	**gangrene**
	f	Tienes una infección o gangrena en la pierna.
	[gãŋ.ˈgre.na]	-You have an infection or gangrene on the leg.
7589	**desorientar**	**disorient**
	vb	Se usan para desorientar a tu enemigo.
	[de.so.rjɛ̃n.ˈtar]	-They're used to disorient your enemy.
7590	**redactar**	**write**
	vb	Tienes muchos que reportes que redactar.
	[re.ðak.ˈtar]	-You have a lot of reports to write.
7591	**parentesco**	**kinship**
	m	El derecho a heredar se determina por parentesco.
	[pa.rɛ̃n.ˈtes.ko]	-Rights of inheritance are determined by kinship.
7592	**boina**	**beret**
	f	Esta debe ser la boina que pedí.
	[ˈboi̯.na]	-This must be the beret I ordered.
7593	**estratégico**	**strategic**
	adj	Pero adoptarla sería un grave error estratégico.
	[ɛs.tra.ˈte.xi.ko]	-But to embrace it would be a grave strategic error.

7594	**pasmar**	**astound**
	vb	Me estoy preparando para pasmar al mundo.
	[paş.ˈmar]	-I'm getting ready to astound the world.
7595	**diapositiva**	**slide**
	f	Echemos un vistazo a la primera diapositiva.
	[dja.po.si.ˈti.βa]	-Let's take a look at the first slide.
7596	**vaginal**	**vaginal**
	adj	Encontramos esperma en el área vaginal.
	[ba.xi.ˈnal]	-We've found sperm in the vaginal area.
7597	**encubrimiento**	**concealment**
	m	Bueno, podríamos llamarlo un encubrimiento estratégico.
	[ɛ̃ŋ.ku.βri.ˈmjɛ̃n̯.to]	-Well, we could call it strategic concealment.
7598	**ayunar**	**fast**
	vb	Puedo ayunar cien años y no morir.
	[a.ʝu.ˈnar]	-I can fast a hundred years and not die.
7599	**saliente**	**outgoing; projection**
	adj; m	Debe crear una cuenta saliente antes de realizar un envío.
	[sa.ˈljɛ̃n̯.te]	-You must create an outgoing account before sending.
7600	**riel**	**rail**
	m	Tuve que esposarlo al riel del bar.
	[ˈrjɛl]	-I had to handcuff him to the bar rail.
7601	**comparecer**	**appear**
	vb	El menor debe comparecer en persona.
	[kõm.pa.re.ˈsɛr]	-The juvenile must appear in person.
7602	**indeciso**	**indecisive**
	adj	Puedo parecer indeciso pero no lo soy.
	[ĩn̯.de.ˈsi.so]	-I may seem indecisive, but I'm not.
7603	**súplica**	**plea**
	f	Era una súplica de la madre.
	[ˈsup̚.li.ka]	-It was a plea from the mother.
7604	**persistir**	**persist**
	vb	Esas desigualdades tienden a persistir a lo largo de las generaciones.
	[pɛr.sis.ˈtir]	-Such inequalities tend to persist across generations.
7605	**mordedura**	**bite**
	f	Parece una marca de mordedura humana.
	[mor.ðe.ˈðu.ra]	-It appears to be a human bite mark.
7606	**horrorizar(se)**	**horrify**
	vb	El fiscal quiere horrorizar al jurado.
	[o.ro.ri.ˈsar]	-The prosecutor wants to horrify the jury.
7607	**multiplicar(se)**	**multiply**
	vb	Están tratando de multiplicar, creo.
	[mul̯.tip̚.li.ˈkar]	-They are trying to multiply, I think.
7608	**excluir**	**exclude**
	vb	Debemos excluir a los miembros del parlamento y los senadores.
	[ɛks̯.ˈlwir]	-We must exclude the members of parliament and the senators.
7609	**peña**	**rock, club**
	f	¿Por qué no saltar de esta peña?
	[ˈpe.ɲa]	-Why not jump off this rock?

7610 **adelgazar** — **lose weight**
vb
[a.ðɛl.ɣaˈsar]
Es una lástima que yo no tenga que adelgazar.
-It's too bad that I don't need to lose weight.

7611 **fatalidad** — **fatality**
f
[fa.ta.li.ˈðað]
Están reportando una fatalidad en la escena.
-They're reporting a fatality at the scene.

7612 **tala** — **felling**
f
[ˈta.la]
Eso me permitirá supervisar la tala.
-That will allow me to oversee the felling.

7613 **parto** — **childbirth**
m
[ˈpar.to]
No es necesario intentar un parto natural.
-There's no need to attempt a natural childbirth.

7614 **bulevar** — **boulevard**
m
[bu.le.ˈβar]
Sean bienvenidos a este mágico bulevar de los sueños conocido como Broadway.
-I bid you welcome to the magical boulevard of dreams known as Broadway.

7615 **negociador** — **negotiator**
m
[ne.ɣo.sja.ˈðor]
Sé que es un gran negociador.
-I've heard you're a killer negotiator.

7616 **diabético** — **diabetic; diabetic**
adj; m
[dja.ˈβɛ.ti.ko]
Consígamosle algo de insulina también, es diabético.
-Let's get him some insulin, too, he's diabetic.

7617 **averiguación** — **inquiry**
f
[a.βɛ.ri.ɣwa.ˈsjõn]
Se ha procedido a la averiguación y los resultados son claros.
-The inquiry has been held and the results are clear.

7618 **uniformar** — **standardize**
vb
[u.ni.for.ˈmar]
Esto ayudará a uniformar la calidad de capacitación y sostenerla por un período prolongado.
-This will help in standardizing the quality of training and in sustaining it for a long period.

7619 **vecindad** — **neighborhood**
f
[be.sĩn̪.ˈdað]
Es un día típico en la vecindad.
-It's a typical day in the neighborhood.

7620 **minúsculo** — **tiny**
adj
[mi.ˈnus.ku.lo]
Ahora mataría por solo una minúscula tortita.
-Now I would kill for just one tiny pancake.

7621 **enganchar** — **hook**
vb
[ẽŋ.gãn̪.ˈʧar]
A ver si se puedes enganchar eso.
-See if you can hook that up.

7622 **soldado** — **soldier**
m/f
[sol̪.ˈda.ðo]
Ayer el soldado actuó valientemente.
-The soldier acted bravely yesterday.

7623 **imperativo** — **imperative; imperative**
adj; m
[ĩm.pɛ.ra.ˈti.βo]
Debemos ver esto como un imperativo ético.
-We must see this as an ethical imperative.

7624 **textil** — **textile; textile**

adj; m
[tɛks.ˈtil]

Los primeros inmigrantes se dedicaron al comercio y producción textil.
-The first immigrants went into the textile trade and textile manufacturing.

7625 **deportar** — **deport**
vb
[de.por.ˈtar]

Ellos van a deportar a esos tipos.
-They're going to deport these dudes.

7626 **pacifista** — **pacifist; pacifist**
adj; m/f
[pa.si.ˈfis.ta]

Todo aquel que tenga conciencia es pacifista.
-Anybody of sound mind is a pacifist.

7627 **especificación** — **specification**
f
[ɛs.pe.si.fi.ka.ˈsjõn]

Cualquier descripción o especificación puede resultar restrictiva.
-Any description or specification may be restrictive.

7628 **albatros** — **albatross**
m
[al.ˈβa.tros]

Tiene la colonia de albatros más grande en el mundo.
-It has the largest albatross colony in the world.

7629 **indeseable** — **undesirable; undesirable**
adj; m/f
[ĩn̪.de.se.ˈa.βle]

Esto es totalmente indeseable en cualquier contexto.
-This is entirely undesirable in any framework.

7630 **formular** — **formulate**
vb
[for.mu.ˈlar]

Logró al menos formular un objetivo.
-He was at least able to formulate an objective.

7631 **épico** — **epic**
adj
[ˈe.pi.ko]

Finalmente, puede retomar su épico viaje.
-At last, he can resume his epic journey.

7632 **lúcido** — **lucid**
adj
[ˈlu.si.ðo]

A mí me parece más lúcido que pesimista.
-To me, it seems more lucid than pessimistic.

7633 **triunfal** — **triumphal**
adj
[trjũm̩.ˈfal]

Como si fuese una procesión triunfal.
-As if it were a triumphal procession.

7634 **sobrenombre** — **nickname**
m
[so.βre.ˈnõm.bre]

Cabo, tienes un sobrenombre interesante.
-Corporal, you got an interesting nickname.

7635 **pedante** — **pedantic; pedant**
adj; m/f
[pe.ˈðãn̪.te]

Tu actitud pedante está empezando a molestarme.
-Your pedantic attitude is starting to annoy me.

7636 **calar** — **seep through, sink in**
vb
[ka.ˈlar]

Por fin todo está empezando a calar.
-It's all finally starting to sink in.

7637 **benigno** — **benign**
adj
[be.ˈniɣ.no]

Podría ser benigno en su propio entorno.
-It could be benign in its own environment.

7638 **contrincante** — **opponent**
m/f
[kõn̪.trĩŋ.ˈkãn̪.te]

Esto demuestra que soy una contrincante digna.
-That proves I'm a worthy opponent.

7639 **portería** — **goal**
f
[por.tɛ.ˈri.a]

Jaime avanza lentamente hacia la portería.
-Jaime making her way slowly towards the goal.

7640	**influenciar**		**influence**
	vb		Quiere influenciar el destino del país.
	[ĩɱ.flwɛ̃n.ˈsjar]		-You want to influence the destiny of the country.
7641	**ocupante**		**occupying; occupant**
	adj; m/f		Somos soldados del ejercito del gobierno ocupante.
	[o.ku.ˈpãn̪.te]		-We're soldiers of the occupying government's army.
7642	**equilibrar**		**balance**
	vb		Sí, necesitamos equilibrar nuestros presupuestos.
	[e.ki.li.ˈβrar]		-Yes, we need to balance our budgets.
7643	**astrología**		**astrology**
	f		Ella le dijo que creía en la astrología.
	[as.tro.lo.ˈxi.a]		-She told him that she believed in astrology.
7644	**espasmo**		**spasm**
	m		Probablemente solo sea un espasmo muscular grave.
	[ɛs.ˈpaṣ.mo]		-It's probably just a severe muscle spasm.
7645	**crucifixión**		**crucifixion**
	f		Espero que esté planeando empezar con la crucifixión.
	[kru.si.fik.ˈsjõn]		-I hope he's planning to start with the crucifixion.
7646	**deterioro**		**deterioration**
	m		Esto no constituye un signo de deterioro.
	[dɛ.tɛ.ˈrjo.ro]		-This does not constitute a sign of deterioration.
7647	**asaltante**		**robber**
	m/f		El asaltante quiere escapar con un rehén.
	[a.sal̪.ˈtãn̪.te]		-The robber wants to get away with a hostage.
7648	**inalcanzable**		**unattainable**
	adj		La meta del consenso no era inalcanzable.
	[i.nal.kãn.ˈsa.βle]		-The goal of consensus was not unattainable.
7649	**inferioridad**		**inferiority**
	f		Supongo que es mi complejo de inferioridad, señor.
	[ĩɱ.fɛ.rjo.ri.ˈðað]		-I guess it's my sense of inferiority, sir.
7650	**hinchazón**		**swelling**
	f		Cierta cantidad de hinchazón es perfectamente normal.
	[ĩn̪.ˈtʃa.sõn]		-A certain amount of swelling is perfectly normal.
7651	**perejil**		**parsley**
	m		El perejil se rehoga con mantequilla.
	[pɛ.re.ˈxil]		-The parsley is browned in butter.
7652	**hilera**		**row**
	f		Puede ser una hilera de árboles o incluso otro edificio.
	[i.ˈlɛ.ra]		-It can be a row of trees or even another building.
7653	**consorcio**		**consortium**
	m		Soy miembro de un pequeño consorcio.
	[kõn.ˈsor.sjo]		-I'm a member of a small consortium.
7654	**intensivo**		**intensive**
	adj		Esta superficie generalmente se puede utilizar para el pasto intensivo.
	[ĩn̪.tɛ̃n.ˈsi.βo]		-These areas can normally be used for intensive grazing.
7655	**colegial**		**school; schoolboy**
	adj; m		Estaba actuando como un colegial enamorado.
	[ko.le.ˈxjal]		-He was acting like a schoolboy in love.

7656	**presunción**	**presumption**
	f	No puede haber presunción de infracción.
	[pre.sũn.ˈsjõn]	-There can be no presumption of an infringement.
7657	**respaldar**	**support**
	vb	Me ha parecido razonable respaldar su propuesta.
	[rɛs.pal̺.ˈdar]	-It seemed to me reasonable to support his proposal.
7658	**debilitar**	**weaken**
	vb	Necesitamos dividirnos, debilitar el rastro.
	[de.βi.li.ˈtar]	-We need to split up, weaken the scent.
7659	**chichón**	**bump**
	m	Sobre un objetivo humano, le harías un chichón.
	[tʃi.ˈtʃõn]	-On a human target, you'd get a bump.
7660	**pavor**	**dread**
	m	Tengo pavor de dar ese discurso esta noche.
	[pa.ˈβor]	-I dread making that speech tonight.
7661	**fronterizo**	**border; frontier**
	m; adj	He oído que eres de un pueblo fronterizo... que desapareció hace años tras un aluvión.
	[frõn̺.tɛ.ˈri.so]	-I heard you're from a border village... that was lost years ago in a flood.
7662	**desordenar**	**make a mess of**
	vb	¿Cómo puedes desordenar la casa del gobernador?
	[de.sor.ðe.ˈnar]	-How can you mess up in the governor's house?
7663	**pitar**	**whistle**
	vb	Árbitro, ¿cuándo va a pitar un foul?
	[pi.ˈtar]	-Referee, when are you going to whistle for a foul?
7664	**insistencia**	**insistence**
	f	No entiendo la razón de tu insistencia.
	[ĩn.sis.ˈtẽn.sja]	-I do not understand the reason for your insistence.
7665	**rebeldía**	**rebellion**
	f	Fue mi primer y último acto de rebeldía.
	[re.βɛl̺.ˈdi.a]	-It was my first and last act of rebellion.
7666	**machacar**	**crush**
	vb	Cuidado, no te vayas a machacar un dedo.
	[ma.tʃa.ˈkar]	-Be careful not to crush a finger.
7667	**amplificador**	**amplifying; amplifier**
	adj; m	El medallón actúa como un amplificador espiritual.
	[ãm.pli.fi.ka.ˈðor]	-The medallion acts as a spiritual amplifier.
7668	**ascensión**	**ascension**
	f	Esa ascensión se conoce como mi'raj.
	[as.sẽn.ˈsjõn]	-That ascension is known as the mi'raj.
7669	**novillo**	**heifer, steer**
	m	Vi a un hombre cambiar un novillo por harina.
	[no.ˈβi.jo]	-I saw a man swap a steer for flour.
7670	**versus**	**versus**
	prp	Será atletas versus mineros en una carrera de exhibición.
	[ˈbɛr.sus]	-It will be athletes versus miners in an exhibition race.
7671	**alargar**	**lengthen**

	vb	Tu nariz también se puede alargar un poco.
	[a.lar.ˈɣar]	-Your nose may also lengthen slightly.
7672	**platicar**	**talk (LA)**
	vb	Yo quería platicar más, pero ella me colgó.
	[pla.ti.ˈkar]	-I wanted to talk more, but she just hung up on me.
7673	**confinar**	**confine**
	vb	No podemos confinar nuestros esfuerzos a declaraciones de política.
	[kõɱ.fi.ˈnar]	-We cannot confine our efforts to policy statements.
7674	**maleante**	**criminal**
	m/f	Ese maleante vendería a su propia madre.
	[ma.le.ˈãn̪.te]	-That thug would smuggle his own mama.
7675	**desfilar**	**parade**
	vb	Vamos a desfilar con esta gran escuela de samba.
	[dɛs.fi.ˈlar]	-We are going to parade with this big school of samba.
7676	**maceta**	**pot**
	f	Hay una llave extra debajo de la maceta.
	[ma.ˈsɛ.ta]	-There's a spare key under the flower pot.
7677	**mutilación**	**mutilation**
	f	Creemos que es algún tipo de mutilación simbólica.
	[mu.ti.la.ˈsjõn]	-We're thinking it's some symbolic form of mutilation.
7678	**incendiario**	**incendiary; arsonist**
	adj; m	Tú eres quien quiere al incendiario muerto.
	[ĩn.sɛ̃n̪.ˈdja.rjo]	-You're the one who wants the arsonist dead.
7679	**factible**	**feasible**
	adj	Seguir caminos paralelos puede resultar más factible.
	[fakˈ.ˈti.βle]	-It may be more feasible to pursue parallel tracks.
7680	**perdiz**	**partridge**
	f	He capturado a una perdiz en la llanura.
	[ˈpɛr.ðis]	-I caught a partridge on the plain.
7681	**desmoronar(se)**	**collapse**
	vb	Todo esto se va a desmoronar.
	[dɛʂ.mo.ro.ˈnar]	-This whole thing will fall apart.
7682	**dibujante**	**cartoonist**
	m/f	Buscaré a un dibujante para dibujar a los niños.
	[di.βu.ˈxãn̪.te]	-I'll get a cartoonist to draw the kids.
7683	**subordinar**	**subordinate**
	vb	No pueden subordinar esos intereses al bien público más general.
	[su.βor.ði.ˈnar]	-They can't subordinate those interests to the greater global public good.
7684	**recolección**	**collection**
	f	También tiene que concentrarse más en la recolección y el análisis de datos.
	[re.ko.lɛk.ˈsjõn]	-It must also concentrate more on the collection and analysis of data.
7685	**tampón**	**tampon**
	m	Quizás deba conseguirte un tampón también.
	[tãm.ˈpõn]	-Maybe I should get you a tampon, too.
7686	**narcotraficante**	**drug dealer**
	m/f	Dijo que era un narcotraficante importante.
	[nar.ko.tra.fi.ˈkãn̪.te]	-You said he was a major drug dealer.

7687	**desesperanza**	**despair**
	f	Enséñeme a tolerar una vida de desesperanza.
	[de.sɛs.pɛ.ˈrãn.sa]	-Teach me how to tolerate a life of despair.
7688	**abarcar**	**encompass**
	vb	Evidentemente, tales soluciones duraderas deberán abarcar diversos
	[a.βar.ˈkar]	aspectos.
		-Clearly, such durable solutions would need to encompass several
		aspects.
7689	**divulgar**	**divulge**
	vb	No tengo autorización para divulgarte esta información.
	[di.βul.ˈɣar]	-I'm not at liberty to divulge information to you.
7690	**devastación**	**devastation**
	f	La devastación de la guerra es evidente para todos nosotros.
	[de.βas.ta.ˈsjõn]	-The devastation of war is evident to all of us.
7691	**consagrar**	**enshrine**
	vb	Fue importante consagrar este principio en la legislación.
	[kõn.sa.ˈɣrar]	-It was important to enshrine this principle in the legislation.
7692	**paterno**	**paternal**
	adj	Nuestro corazón paterno sufre, pero no podemos escucharlo.
	[pa.ˈtɛr.no]	-Our paternal heart suffers, but we cannot listen.
7693	**sonata**	**sonata**
	f	Debes aprender su sonata para chelo.
	[so.ˈna.ta]	-You must learn his cello sonata.
7694	**firmamento**	**firmament**
	m	Que el firmamento no caiga sobre él.
	[fir.ma.ˈmẽn.to]	-May the firmament not fall upon him.
7695	**encarcelamiento**	**imprisonment**
	m	Me gustaría hablarle sobre mi encarcelamiento en Andersonville.
	[ẽŋ.kar.se.la.ˈmjẽn.to]	-I would like to tell you about my imprisonment in Andersonville.
7696	**errar**	**err**
	vb	Es mejor errar por ser precavidos.
	[ɛ.ˈrar]	-Rather err on the side of caution.
7697	**arañazo**	**scratch**
	m	Sentirá un ligero arañazo por la aguja.
	[a.ra.ˈɲa.so]	-You'll feel a slight scratch from the needle.
7698	**sentimentalismo**	**sentimentality**
	m	Este no es el lugar para el sentimentalismo.
	[sẽn.ti.mẽn.ta.ˈliṣ.mo]	-This isn't the place for sentimentality.
7699	**regir**	**govern**
	vb	Esto debería regir la formulación de nuestra política en materia de
	[re.ˈxir]	energía en el futuro.
		-This should govern the formulation of our energy policy in the future.
7700	**afán**	**eagerness**
	m	Pero también creo que tiene que ver con un afán de probar cosas
	[a.ˈfãn]	nuevas.
		-But I also think that it has to do with an eagerness to try new things.
7701	**matorral**	**bush**
	m	Quizás tiene un matorral demasiado grande.
	[ma.to.ˈral]	-Maybe she has an abnormally large bush.

7702 **figurar** — **include**
vb
[fi.ɣuˈrar]
Aquí debería figurar todo lo que sea relevante para el consumidor.
-This should include everything of relevance to the consumer.

7703 **fricción** — **friction**
f
[frikˈsjõn]
Es asombroso cuanta fricción causa eso.
-It's amazing how much friction it causes.

7704 **frotar** — **rub**
vb
[froˈtar]
¿Me puedes frotar los hombros?
-Can you rub my shoulders?

7705 **disolver** — **dissolve**
vb
[di.solˈβɛr]
Creo que estás intentando disolver algo más.
-I think you're trying to dissolve something else.

7706 **refrescar** — **refresh**
vb
[re.frɛsˈkar]
Deja que te refresque la memoria.
-Allow me to refresh your memory.

7707 **ruedo** — **arena**
m
[ˈrwe.ðo]
Has pasado buenos momentos en este ruedo.
-You've had some good moments in this arena.

7708 **inmaculado** — **immaculate**
adj
[ĩm.ma.kuˈla.ðo]
A diferencia de tu compañero, tienes un expediente inmaculado.
-Unlike your partner, you've got an immaculate record.

7709 **nutrición** — **nutrition**
f
[nu.triˈsjõn]
No permitirá que recibas la nutrición necesaria.
-It won't allow you to get the nutrition you need.

7710 **negociable** — **negotiable**
adj
[ne.ɣoˈsja.βle]
Ese asunto es negociable hasta cierto punto.
-That matter is, up to a certain point, negotiable.

7711 **consenso** — **consensus**
m
[kõnˈsẽn.so]
Esperamos alcanzar un consenso definitivo en Valencia.
-We hope to reach a final consensus in Valencia.

7712 **carbohidrato** — **carbohydrate**
m
[kar.βo.iˈðra.to]
La lactosa es el único carbohidrato presente.
-Lactose is the only carbohydrate present.

7713 **deparar** — **bring**
vb
[de.paˈrar]
Nunca sabemos lo que nos puede deparar el futuro.
-For we never know what tomorrow may bring.

7714 **maloliente** — **stinking**
adj
[ma.loˈljẽn.te]
Solo queremos que drenen esa agua maloliente.
-All we want is to get that stinking cesspool cleaned up.

7715 **yugo** — **yoke**
m
[ˈɟ͡ʝu.ɣo]
Debemos liberarnos del yugo del dólar.
-We must liberate ourselves from the yoke of the dollar.

7716 **apogeo** — **peak**
m
[a.poˈxe.o]
Roma estaba en el apogeo de su poder.
-Rome was at the peak of its powers.

7717 **lúgubre** — **grim**
adj
[ˈlu.ɣu.βre]
Haces que todo suene muy lúgubre.
-You make it all sound very grim.

7718	**agachar(se)**	**duck**
	vb	Se podría agachar detrás de esos arbustos.
	[a.ɣa.ˈʧar]	-He could duck behind those bushes.
7719	**inaccesible**	**inaccessible**
	adj	Su localización es tan lejana como inaccesible.
	[i.nak.se.ˈsi.βle]	-Her location is as remote as it is inaccessible.
7720	**lesionar**	**injure**
	vb	Hacer los ejercicios de una manera incorrecta puede lesionar su nuevo hombro.
	[le.sjo.ˈnar]	-Doing the exercises in a wrong way can injure your new shoulder.
7721	**quiosco**	**kiosk**
	m	La explosión ocasionó daños materiales en el quiosco.
	[ˈkjos.ko]	-The explosion caused material damage to the kiosk.
7722	**desconfiar**	**distrust**
	vb	No desconfiamos lo suficiente de los hombres.
	[dɛs.kõm̩.ˈfjar]	-We don't distrust men enough.
7723	**mecedora**	**rocking chair**
	f	Estaba pensando en hacer una mecedora.
	[me.se.ˈðo.ra]	-I was thinking I would make a rocking chair.
7724	**incapacitar**	**incapacitate**
	vb	Pueden incapacitar a un objetivo en segundos.
	[ĩŋ.ka.pa.si.ˈtar]	-They can incapacitate a target in seconds.
7725	**consecutivo**	**consecutive**
	adj	Era el quinto mes consecutivo de decline.
	[kõn.se.ku.ˈti.βo]	-That was the fifth consecutive month of decline.
7726	**cronómetro**	**stopwatch**
	m	Si usted está interesado todavía tengo ese cronómetro.
	[kro.ˈno.mɛ.tro]	-If you're interested, I've still got that stopwatch.
7727	**maniobrar**	**maneuver**
	vb	Te estás quedando sin espacio para maniobrar.
	[ma.njo.ˈβrar]	-You're running out of room to maneuver.
7728	**prótesis**	**prosthesis**
	f	Estudio los componentes de sus prótesis.
	[ˈpro.te.sis]	-I'm studying the components in your prosthesis.
7729	**previsión**	**forecast**
	f[pre.βi.ˈsjõn]	No negamos el carácter razonable de su previsión. -We do not question the reasonable nature of your forecast.
7730	**deficiente**	**deficient**
	adj	También puede ser el resultado de un trabajo creativo deficiente.
	[de.fi.ˈsjẽ̩.te]	-It can also reflect poor creative work.
7731	**patinador**	**skater**
	m	Pero el rumor dice que usted es un patinador excepcional.
	[pa.ti.na.ˈðor]	-But the rumor is that you are a superlative skater.
7732	**mole**	**mass**
	f	Si construyeran una mole de cemento, la gente protestaría.
	[ˈmo.le]	-If they built a mass of cement, the people would protest.
7733	**bajista**	**bass player**
	m/f	Sí, hay un nuevo bajista.
	[ba.ˈxis.ta]	-Yes, there's a new bass player.

7734 ejecutor
adj; m
[e.xe.ku.ˈtor]

executing; executor
El productor es simplemente el ejecutor.
-The producer is merely the executor.

7735 inflamable
adj
[ĩm.fla.ˈma.βle]

flammable
Solo quiero evitar una situación claramente inflamable.
-I'm just mindful of avoiding an overtly flammable situation.

7736 merengue
m
[mɛ.ˈrẽŋ.ge]

meringue
Nos quedaremos con el merengue de frambuesa.
-We'll stay with the raspberry meringue.

7737 quijada
f
[ki.ˈxa.ða]

jaw
Ahora dime algo o te rompo la quijada.
-Now you talk to me, or I'll break your jaw.

7738 rareza
f
[ra.ˈre.sa]

rarity
El agua era una rareza en las áridas provincias del Sáhara.
-Water was a rarity in the arid provinces of the Sahara.

7739 furtivo
adj; m
[fur.ˈti.βo]

furtive; poacher
Mi padre ha sido un furtivo por un largo tiempo.
-My father has been a poacher for quite a long time.

7740 penumbra
f
[pe.ˈnũm.bra]

gloom
La región debe transformar la penumbra en esperanza.
-The region must transform gloom into hope.

7741 alquimia
f
[al.ˈki.mja]

alchemy
El secreto de la alquimia descansa en las estrellas.
-The secret of alchemy lies in the stars.

7742 trapecio
m
[tra.ˈpe.sjo]

trapeze
Dijiste que podría morir en el trapecio.
-You said that she could die on the trapeze.

7743 moler
vb
[mo.ˈlɛr]

grind
Mamá usa un molinillo de café para moler los granos de café.
-Mom uses a coffee mill to grind coffee beans.

7744 atributo
m
[a.tri.ˈβu.to]

attribute
Seamos generosos y llamémoslo un atributo.
-Let's be generous and call it an attribute.

7745 arnés
m
[ar.ˈnes]

harness
El perro debe llevar un arnés.
-The dog must be wearing a harness.

7746 exaltado
adj; m
[ɛk.sal̩.ˈta.ðo]

frenzied; hothead
El oficial es un hombre exaltado.
-The officer's a hot-headed man.

7747 derechazo
m
[dɛ.re.ˈtʃa.so]

right
Te va a dar un derechazo.
-He'll hit you with his right.

7748 redada
f
[re.ˈða.ða]

raid
Puedes apostar abiertamente y nunca preocuparte por a una redada.
-You can gamble openly and never worry about a raid.

7749 resbaladizo
adj
[rɛʂ.βa.la.ˈði.so]

slippery
Está un poco resbaladizo por aquí.
-It's a bit slippery round here.

7750	**ilustración**	**illustration**
	f	Es como la ilustración del libro.
	[i.lus.tra.ˈsjõn]	-It's like the illustration in the book.

7751	**tablón**	**plank**
	m	Voy a poner un tablón en la tierra.
	[ta.ˈβlõn]	-I'm going to put a plank on the ground.

7752	**coloso**	**colossus**
	m	Espera a los pies del coloso.
	[ko.ˈlo.so]	-Stand at the foot of the colossus.

7753	**recaer**	**relapse**
	vb	Cuando cesó este conflicto, hubo un intenso temor de recaer.
	[re.ka.ˈɛr]	-When this conflict ended there was an enormous fear of a relapse.

7754	**fideicomiso**	**trust**
	m	Cree que vinimos a crear un fideicomiso.
	[fi.ðei̯.ko.ˈmi.so]	-He thinks that we're here to set up a trust.

7755	**depresivo**	**depressing**
	adj	No puedo imaginar un sitio más depresivo donde estar.
	[de.pre.ˈsi.βo]	-I can't imagine a more depressing place to be.

7756	**varicela**	**chickenpox**
	f	Hasta la fecha, ningún caso de varicela ha sido mortal.
	[ba.ri.ˈse.la]	-To date, no case of chickenpox has been fatal.

7757	**bragueta**	**fly**
	f	Tu bragueta está abierta, Jack.
	[bra.ˈɣɛ.ta]	-Your fly is open, Jack.

7758	**altibajos**	**ups and downs**
	mpl	Ya, supongo que tendrá sus altibajos.
	[al̪.ti.ˈβa.xos]	-Yes, I suppose it has its ups and downs.

7759	**sintético**	**synthetic**
	adj	Es un tipo raro de polímero sintético.
	[sĩn̪.ˈtɛ.ti.ko]	-It's some sort of strange, synthetic polymer.

7760	**colateral**	**collateral**
	adj	La vida es un derecho, no algo colateral o casual.
	[ko.la.tɛ.ˈral]	-Life is a right, not collateral or casual.

7761	**escroto**	**scrotum**
	m	Bueno, el escroto está intacto.
	[ɛs.ˈkro.to]	-Well, his scrotum is intact.

7762	**moderar**	**moderate**
	vb	Su función es moderar e inspirar el debate.
	[mo.ðɛ.ˈrar]	-Its role is to moderate and inspire debate.

7763	**mejillón**	**mussel**
	m	Son un grupo de la familia de mejillón.
	[me.xi.ˈʝõn]	-They are a group of the mussel family.

7764	**soldador**	**welder**
	m	Soy un pastor, no un soldador.
	[sol̪.da.ˈðor]	-I'm a bishop, not a welder.

7765	**tenue**	**faint**
	adj	Un oído sano emite un sonido muy tenue.
	[ˈte.nwe]	-A healthy ear emits a very faint tone.

7766 **aniquilar**
vb
[a.ni.ki.'lar]

annihilate
Si quisiera, os podría aniquilar fácilmente.
-If I want to, I can annihilate you with ease.

7767 **hijastro**
m
[i.'xas.tro]

stepson
Y el hijastro de ella es el padre.
-And that stepson of hers is the father.

7768 **perilla**
f
[pɛ.'ri.ʝa]

goatee
Nunca me ha gustado mucho tu perilla.
-I never really liked your goatee.

7769 **volcar**
vb
[bol.'kar]

dump
Tu madre siempre tiende a volcar todo sobre mí.
-Your mother always tends to dump all over me.

7770 **condecoración**
f
[kõn̪.de.ko.ra.'sjõn]

award
No se siente bien aceptando su condecoración.
-He doesn't feel right accepting his award.

7771 **jeta**
f
['xɛ.ta]

face (coll)
Suéltame un momento para que pueda darle un puñetazo en la jeta.
-Let go a minute, so I can punch him in the face.

7772 **irreversible**
adj
[i.re.βɛr.'si.βle]

irreversible
Sin embargo, en este proceso irreversible, ambas partes tienen exigencias.
-In this irreversible process, though, demands are made of both sides.

7773 **cívico**
adj
['si.βi.ko]

civic
Hay que restablecer el sentido cívico y la idea del servicio público.
-Civic sense and the sense of public service must be restored.

7774 **alameda**
f
[a.la.'me.ða]

avenue
La casa de la que estaba hablando es una con una alameda de nogales.
-The house I was talking about is one with an avenue of walnut trees.

7775 **antidepresivo**
adj
[ãn̪.ti.ðe.pre.'si.βo]

antidepressant
Y puedo darte un antidepresivo leve.
-And I can prescribe a mild antidepressant.

7776 **regatear**
vb; m
[re.ɣa.te.'ar]

haggle; haggling
No estoy en condiciones de regatear.
-I'm not in a position to haggle.

7777 **peseta**
f
[pe.'sɛ.ta]

peseta
Estos son los primeros ejemplos de acuñaciones de nuestra peseta.
-These are the first examples of the mintage of our peseta.

7778 **estornudar**
vb
[ɛs.tor.nu.'ðar]

sneeze
Si necesita estornudar, hágalo con la boca.
-If you need to sneeze, do so with your mouth.

7779 **pelvis**
f
['pɛl.βis]

pelvis
Estoy pegando mi pelvis al suelo.
-I'm putting my pelvis towards the ground.

7780 **almacenamiento**
m
[al.ma.se.na.'mjẽn̪.to]

storage
Traje algunas cosas de mi almacenamiento.
-I brought some of my stuff from storage.

7781 **intrigar**

intrigue

	vb	Sabía que te iba a intrigar.
	[ĩn̪.tri.ˈɣar]	-I knew she would intrigue you.

7782 afección — **condition**

f
[a.fɛk.ˈsjõn]

Al principio me pareció una afección grave.
-At first, it struck me as a serious condition.

7783 neutralizar — **neutralize**

vb
[neu̯.tra.li.ˈsar]

La única forma es neutralizar los factores adversos.
-The only way is to neutralize adverse factors.

7784 originar — **originate**

vb
[o.ri.xi.ˈnar]

Algo así solo se podría originar en Hollywood.
-Something like that could only originate in Hollywood.

7785 duchar(se) — **shower**

vb
[du.ˈtʃar]

Digo, en algún momento se tendrá que duchar.
-I mean, eventually, she has to shower.

7786 parkinson — **parkinson's disease**

m
[par.ˈkĩn.sõn]

El parkinson simplemente le ha robado todo.
-The parkinson's just robbed her of everything.

7787 conciliar — **reconcile**

vb
[kõn.si.ˈljar]

Sería difícil conciliar ambas posiciones.
-It would be difficult to reconcile the two positions.

7788 afgano — **Afghan; Afghan person**

adj; m
[af.ˈɣa.no]

También es un logro del pueblo afgano.
-It is also the accomplishment of the Afghan people.

7789 paramédico — **paramedical; paramedic**

adj; m
[pa.ra.ˈme.ði.ko]

Eres el único paramédico que odia la sangre.
-You are the only paramedic who hates the sign of blood.

7790 articulación — **joint**

f
[ar.ti.ku.la.ˈsjõn]

En realidad deberíamos estar practicando articulación hoy.
-We were actually supposed to work on articulation today.

7791 gotera — **leak**

f
[go.ˈtɛ.ra]

Subiré al ático y arreglaré la gotera.
-I'll go up to the attic and fix the leak.

7792 lapso — **period of time**

m
[ˈlap.so]

No es fácil digerir todo eso en un lapso de tiempo tan breve.
-It is not easy to digest all of that in such a short period of time.

7793 infortunio — **misfortune**

m
[ĩm.for.ˈtu.njo]

Tengo el infortunio de ser profesora de inglés.
-I have the misfortune of being an English instructor.

7794 aplazar — **postpone**

vb
[ap̚.la.ˈsar]

Realmente necesitamos aplazar el debate y la votación hasta noviembre.
-We really need to postpone the debate and the vote until November.

7795 prólogo — **prologue**

m
[ˈpro.lo.ɣo]

No tengo tiempo para el prólogo.
-I don't have time for the prologue.

7796 triunfante — **triumphant**

adj
[trjũm̚.ˈfãn̪.te]

Pero salió triunfante de este momento de crisis.
-But he emerged from this moment of crisis triumphant.

7797 cautivo — **captive; captivity**

adj; m
[kau̯.ˈti.βo]

Siguió siendo libre aun cuando estaba cautivo.
-He remained free even in captivity.

7798 israelita   **Israelite; Israelite person**

adj; m
[iş.ra.e.ˈli.ta]

El nombre divino Yahweh es exclusivo de la antigua religión israelita.
-The divine name Yahweh is unique to ancient Israelite religion.

7799 conciudadano   **fellow citizen**

m
[kõn.sju.ða.ˈða.no]

Quiero decir, francamente, como conciudadano, estoy orgulloso de ti.
-I mean, frankly, as a fellow citizen, I'm proud of you.

7800 quimera   **chimera**

f
[ki.ˈmɛ.ra]

Es una quimera de algún tipo.
-It's a chimera of some kind.

7801 arar   **plow**

vb
[a.ˈrar]

Pensé que necesitaba un caballo para arar, señor Narracot.
-I thought you needed a plow horse, Mr. Narracott.

7802 insurrección   **insurrection**

f
[ĩn.su.rɛk.ˈsjõn]

Tenemos una insurrección entre manos, Alicia.
-We have an insurrection on our hands, Alicia.

7803 alentar   **encourage**

vb
[a.lẽn̪.ˈtar]

Tenemos que alentar estas iniciativas tanto como podamos.
-We need to encourage these initiatives as much as we can.

7804 inflamación   **inflammation**

f
[ĩɱ.fla.ma.ˈsjõn]

También puede presentarse inflamación del tejido muscular.
-There may also be inflammation in the muscle tissue.

7805 escarmentar   **punish severely**

vb
[ɛs.kar.mẽn̪.ˈtar]

Esta es otra forma de tratar de intimidar o escarmentar a los países.
-This is another way of trying to scare countries or punish them.

7806 censo   **census**

m
[ˈsẽn.so]

Simplemente estamos revisando el censo de impuestos.
-We're simply checking the census against the tax rolls.

7807 hornear   **bake**

vb
[or.ne.ˈar]

Adora leerle a niños hambrientos y hornear panecillos caseros.
-She likes to read to starving children and bake homemade scones.

7808 retardar   **slow down**

vb
[rɛ.tar.ˈðar]

Hago un hechizo para retardar tu transformación.
-I cast a spell to slow down your transformation.

7809 racionamiento   **rationing**

m
[ra.sjo.na.ˈmjẽn̪.to]

Espero que no empiecen ese absurdo racionamiento.
-I hope they aren't going to start that rationing nonsense.

7810 tosco   **crude; rough**

adj; m
[ˈtos.ko]

Es tosco, pero funciona bastante bien.
-It's crude, but it works remarkably well.

7811 acústico   **acoustic**

adj
[a.ˈkus.ti.ko]

Las ballenas viven en un entorno acústico asombroso.
-The whales live in an amazing acoustic environment.

7812 tracción   **traction**

f
[trak.ˈsjõn]

Son muy cómodos y me proporcionan tracción.
-They're very comfortable, and they give me traction.

7813 telenovela   **soap opera**

	f	No estoy dirigiendo una telenovela, Milton.
	[te.le.no.ˈβe.la]	-I'm not directing a soap opera, Milton.

7814 desalojo — eviction
m — [de.sa.ˈlo.xo]
Todas sus pertenencias fueron destruidas durante el desalojo.
-All the property they had was destroyed in this eviction.

7815 estirpe — lineage
f — [ɛs.ˈtir.pe]
La estirpe real se extinguirá.
-The royal lineage will die out.

7816 vacilar — tease, hesitate
vb — [ba.si.ˈlar]
No debes vacilar, hijo mío.
-You mustn't hesitate, dear son.

7817 colapsar — collapse
vb — [ko.lap.ˈsar]
La casa parecía estar a punto de colapsar en cualquier momento.
-The house seemed about to collapse at any moment.

7818 aconsejable — advisable
adj — [a.kõn.se.ˈxa.βle]
Sería aconsejable establecer normas firmes a ese respecto.
-It would be advisable to have firm rules in this regard.

7819 comprimir — compress
vb — [kõm.pri.ˈmir]
Otro método consistía en comprimir las colas de una distribución.
-Another method was to compress the tails of a distribution.

7820 difusión — diffusion
f — [di.fu.ˈsjõn]
Debe impedirse o desacreditarse la difusión de propaganda racista en los medios de información locales.
-The diffusion of racist propaganda by local media must be prevented or discredited.

7821 alojar — accommodate
vb — [a.lo.ˈxar]
Se han construido dos hostales para alojar a estos alumnos.
-Two hostels have been built to accommodate these pupils.

7822 lisiado — disabled; disabled person
adj; m — [li.ˈsja.ðo]
Querida, sabes que soy un lisiado.
-Darling, you know that I am a cripple.

7823 garabato — doodle
m — [ga.ra.ˈβa.to]
Puede que sea solo un garabato.
-It might just be a doodle.

7824 invicto — unbeaten
adj — [ĩm.ˈbik̚.to]
Este es un equipo de fútbol que podría resultar invicto.
-This is a football team that could go unbeaten.

7825 latente — latent
adj — [la.ˈtẽn.te]
Estaría feliz con cualquier simple señal de humanidad latente.
-I would be happy with any crude sign of latent humanity.

7826 peatón — pedestrian
m — [pe.a.ˈtõn]
Un policía estaba observando a un peatón sospechoso.
-A policeman was gazing at a suspicious pedestrian.

7827 estimación — estimation
f — [ɛs.ti.ma.ˈsjõn]
Si no existen estadísticas, bastará una estimación.
-If statistics are not available, estimation shall be sufficient.

7828 licenciatura — degree
f — [li.sẽn.sja.ˈtu.ra]
Ni siquiera pueden sacarse una licenciatura.
-They can't even attain the bachelor's degree.

7829	**impresora**		**printer**
	f		Le hice traer una impresora y una plastificadora.
	[ĭm.pre.ˈso.ra]		-I had him bring a printer and a laminating machine.
7830	**emborrachar(se)**		**get drunk**
	vb		Pero, William, te podrías emborrachar.
	[ẽm.bo.ra.ˈʧar]		-But, William, you could get drunk.
7831	**neurótico**		**neurotic; neurotic**
	adj; m		Nunca he conocido a un padre más neurótico.
	[neu̯.ˈro.ti.ko]		-I've never known a more neurotic father.
7832	**caótico**		**chaotic**
	adj		Pronto encontraré la fuerza que regule ese organismo caótico.
	[ka.ˈo.ti.ko]		-Soon I'll find a force to bring order to that chaotic organism.
7833	**marcación**		**marking**
	f		Quienes se encargan del proceso directo de marcación son los fabricantes.
	[mar.ka.ˈsjõn]		-Holders of the direct process of marking are the producers.
7834	**disentería**		**dysentery**
	f		Sus tropas padecen disentería y cólera.
	[di.sẽn̪.ˈtɛ.ri.a]		-His troops are wracked with dysentery and cholera.
7835	**iraní**		**Iranian; Iranian person**
	adj; m/f		Todas las embarcaciones y lanchas llevaban la bandera iraní.
	[i.ra.ˈni]		-All of the vessels and boats flew the Iranian flag.
7836	**degradación**		**degradation**
	f		Las nanosondas compensarán cualquier degradación celular.
	[de.ɣra.ða.ˈsjõn]		-The nanoprobes will compensate for any cellular degradation.
7837	**amenazante**		**threatening**
	adj		Es entendible que me encuentre amenazante.
	[a.me.na.ˈsãn̪.te]		-It's understandable that you would find me threatening.
7838	**seudónimo**		**pseudonym**
	m		Los periodistas a menudo se veían obligados a trabajar utilizando un seudónimo.
	[seu̯.ˈðo.ni.mo]		-Journalists were often forced to work under a pseudonym.
7839	**engranaje**		**gear**
	m		Un engranaje se ha roto y obstruido los contadores.
	[ẽŋ.gra.ˈna.xe]		-A gear has shattered and fouled the counters.
7840	**agrio**		**sour**
	adj		Huele agrio, a carne putrefacta.
	[ˈa.ɣrjo]		-It smells sour, of putrefying flesh.
7841	**sondeo**		**survey**
	m		Nosotros queremos hacer otro sondeo.
	[sõn̪.ˈde.o]		-We want to make another survey.
7842	**jonrón**		**home run**
	m		Era el mejor lugar para capturar una bola de jonrón.
	[xõn.ˈrõn]		-It was the best place to catch a home run ball.
7843	**deudor**		**in debt; debtor**
	adj; m		El deudor siempre podrá impugnar el procedimiento.
	[deu̯.ˈðor]		-The debtor would always be able to disagree with the procedure.
7844	**anexo**		**attached; annex**

	adj; m [a.ˈnɛk.so]	Las disposiciones legales pertinentes figuran en el anexo de este informe. -The relevant legislation articles can be consulted in the annex to this report.
7845	**acortar** vb [a.koɾˈtaɾ]	**shorten** Solo intentamos acortar la película todo cuanto pudimos. -We just tried to shorten the film as much as possible.
7846	**doblado** adj [do.ˈβla.ðo]	**dubbed in, bent** Las películas extranjeras siempre están dobladas. -Foreign films are always dubbed.
7847	**bonificación** f [bo.ni.fi.ka.ˈsjõn]	**bonus** Recibirás una bonificación y un aumento. -You'll get a bonus and a raise.
7848	**pericia** f [pɛ.ˈri.sja]	**expertise** Disculpe si no reverencio su pericia. -Forgive me if I don't bow to your expertise.
7849	**lejía** f [le.ˈxi.a]	**bleach** Deberías empapar eso en lejía y quemarlo. -You should soak that in bleach and burn it.
7850	**sindical** adj [sĩn̠.di.ˈkal]	**union** Querrás hablar con tu delegado sindical. -You'll want to talk to your union delegate.
7851	**intravenoso** adj [ĩn̠.tra.βe.ˈno.so]	**intravenous** Para uso intravenoso después de la reconstitución y de la dilución. -For intravenous use after reconstitution and dilution.
7852	**labrador** m/f [la.βra.ˈðoɾ]	**farmer, lab** Mi padre era labrador y mi madre tendera. -My father was a farmer and my mother a retailer.
7853	**coordinador** m [ko.or.ði.na.ˈðoɾ]	**coordinator** Los hombres habían estado buscando al coordinador de su grupo. -The men had been looking for the coordinator of her group.
7854	**pulsar** vb [pul.ˈsaɾ]	**press** Funciona de forma automática después de pulsar una tecla. -It works automatically after one key press.
7855	**equilibrado** adj [e.ki.li.ˈβra.ðo]	**well-balanced** Yo creo que el proceso está equilibrado. -I believe that the process is well-balanced.
7856	**profundizar** vb [pro.fũn̠.di.ˈsaɾ]	**deepen** Servirá solo para profundizar sus sospechas y además debilitará nuestra relación. -It would only serve to deepen their suspicions and further weaken our relationship.
7857	**ofendido** adj [o.fẽn̠.ˈdi.ðo]	**offended** De hecho, estoy profundamente ofendido. -As a matter of fact, I'm deeply offended.
7858	**desequilibrio** m [de.se.ki.ˈli.βrjo]	**imbalance** Este desequilibrio también da qué pensar. -This imbalance is surely also food for thought.
7859	**hormigueo**	**tingling**

	m	El entumecimiento y el hormigueo deben mejorar o desaparecer.
	[or.mi.ˈɣe.o]	-Numbness and tingling should get better or disappear.
7860	**simulador**	**simulator**
	m	El simulador nunca hubiera sacado eso.
	[si.mu.la.ˈðor]	-The simulator would've never figured that one out.
7861	**relajación**	**relaxation**
	f	Sentí una mezcla de relajación y anticipación.
	[re.la.xa.ˈsjõn]	-I felt a sense of relaxation tempered with anticipation.
7862	**cancelación**	**cancellation**
	f	Siento mucho mi manejo sobre la cancelación.
	[kãn.se.la.ˈsjõn]	-I'm sorry about my handling of the cancellation.
7863	**magnetismo**	**magnetism**
	m	Ahora debemos enfrentarnos al maestro del magnetismo.
	[maɣ.nɛ.ˈtiṣ.mo]	-Now, we must face the master of magnetism.
7864	**ferviente**	**fervent**
	adj	Este es el deseo más ferviente de mi delegación.
	[fɛr.ˈβjẽṇ.te]	-This is my delegation's most fervent hope.
7865	**asesoramiento**	**advice**
	m	Su asesoramiento profesional permitirá mejorar los procedimientos.
	[a.se.so.ra.ˈmjẽṇ.to]	-Your professional advice will enable the improvement of the procedures.
7866	**cuenca**	**basin**
	f	Me refiero a la situación ecológica en la cuenca del Mar de Aral.
	[ˈkwẽŋ.ka]	-I am referring to the ecological situation in the Aral Sea basin.
7867	**conmocionado**	**shocked**
	adj	Estoy realmente conmocionado por la gravedad del caso.
	[kõm.mo.sjo.ˈna.ðo]	-I am genuinely shocked by the seriousness of the case.
7868	**ejercitar**	**exercise**
	vb	Escribía solamente para ejercitar ese músculo.
	[e.xɛr.si.ˈtar]	-I was writing just to exercise that muscle.
7869	**sustancial**	**substantial**
	adj	Por favor, facilite cualquier información sustancial que considere útil.
	[sus.tãn.ˈsjal]	-Please provide any substantial information that you consider useful.
7870	**roncar**	**snore**
	vb	Vos también vas a roncar cuando seas grande.
	[rõŋ.ˈkar]	-You'll snore when you grow up.
7871	**purificación**	**purification**
	m	En ciertas comunidades se percibe como un rito de purificación.
	[pu.ri.fi.ka.ˈsjõn]	-In some communities, it is viewed as a rite of purification.
7872	**pincho**	**spike**
	m	La caja estaba llena de pinchos.
	[ˈpĩṇ.tʃo]	-The box was full of spikes.
7873	**tobogán**	**slide**
	m	Olvidé hacer una salida al final del tobogán.
	[to.βo.ˈɣãn]	-I forgot to make an opening at the end of the slide.
7874	**pomposo**	**pompous**
	adj	Solo estoy intentando, aunque suene pomposo, enseñarle literatura.
	[põm.ˈpo.so]	-I'm just trying, though it may sound pompous, to teach him literature.

7875	**artesano**	**craftsman**
	m	Esta era la vida de un artesano.
	[ar.te.ˈsa.no]	-This was a life as a craftsman.
7876	**envejecimiento**	**aging**
	m	No presenta más señales de envejecimiento prematuro.
	[ẽm.be.xe.si.ˈmjẽn̪.to]	-He's presenting no other signs of premature aging.
7877	**trasplante**	**transplant**
	m	Flannery realizó el trasplante cuando estábamos allí.
	[tras.ˈplãn̪.te]	-Flannery performed the transplant when we were over there.
7878	**marroquí**	**Moroccan; Moroccan person**
	adj; m/f	Descubrieron que su marido era marroquí.
	[ma.ro.ˈki]	-They found out her husband was a Moroccan.
7879	**desquiciar**	**make to despair**
	vb	Si sigues analizando cosas como esa te puedes desquiciar.
	[dɛs.ki.ˈsjar]	-You can lose your mind if you keep analyzing things like that.
7880	**dañino**	**harmful**
	adj	El sacerdote dijo que este libro podría ser dañino para la juventud.
	[da.ˈɲi.no]	-The priest said that this book could be harmful to youth.
7881	**nerviosismo**	**nervousness**
	m	Debes tener un caso grave de nerviosismo crónico.
	[nɛr.βjo.ˈsis̪.mo]	-You must have a very bad case of chronic nervousness.
7882	**sobrevolar**	**fly over**
	vb	Puedes sobrevolar los majestuosos paisajes de Queenstown.
	[so.βre.βo.ˈlar]	-You can fly over the spectacular landscape of Queenstown.
7883	**brea**	**pitch**
	f	Reúne lo que quede de brea y llévasela a Craxus.
	[ˈbre.a]	-Gather the last of the pitch and see it to Crixus.
7884	**aborigen**	**indigenous; aboriginal**
	adj; m/f	La canción de este hombre va sobre el pueblo aborigen.
	[a.βo.ˈri.xẽn]	-This fella song is all about the Aboriginal people.
7885	**televisivo**	**television**
	adj	Prepáreme un guion que pueda utilizar para un reportaje televisivo.
	[te.le.βi.ˈsi.βo]	-Prepare a script I can use for a television news report.
7886	**dramaturgo**	**playwright**
	m	Se supone que tengo que reunirme con el dramaturgo mañana.
	[dra.ma.ˈtur.ɣo]	-I'm supposed to go meet the playwright tomorrow.
7887	**esquivo**	**elusive**
	adj	El sentido común es a veces esquivo para algunos políticos.
	[ɛs.ˈki.βo]	-Common sense is elusive at times for some politicians.
7888	**siquiera**	**at least**
	adv	Es impensable que podamos siquiera permitirlo.
	[si.ˈkjɛ.ra]	-It is unthinkable that we can even allow it.
7889	**exhibir**	**display**
	vb	Tal vez deseas un lugar donde exhibir tus fotografías o publicar tus poesías.
	[ɛk.si.ˈβir]	-Maybe you want a place to display your photographs or poems.
7890	**desplomar(se)**	**collapse**

vb
[dɛs.plo.ˈmar]

¡De esta forma nos vamos a desplomar!
-The way this is going we're going to collapse!

7891 tintar — **dye**
vb
[tĩn̪.ˈtar]

No me voy a tintar el cabello.
-I'm not dying my hair.

7892 prescripción — **prescription**
f
[prɛs.krip.ˈsjõn]

Necesitaba una nueva prescripción, sabe.
-I needed a new prescription, you see.

7893 carabina — **carbine**
f
[ka.ra.ˈβi.na]

Por eso me dio la carabina.
-That's why he gave me the carbine.

7894 hospicio — **hospice**
m
[os.ˈpi.sjo]

Ven inmediatamente al hospicio, te espero allí.
-Come immediately to the hospice; I'll wait there for you.

7895 mediocridad — **mediocre; mediocrity**
m/f; f
[me.ðjo.kri.ˈðað]

Era conmovedor pero recuerdo la total mediocridad.
-It was touching but l remember the sheer mediocrity.

7896 distintivo — **distinctive; emblem**
adj; m
[dis.tĩn̪.ˈti.βo]

Deberías haberle puesto un lazo más distintivo.
-You should've put a more distinctive bow on it.

7897 clavícula — **clavicle**
f
[kla.ˈβi.ku.la]

Una chica vino con una clavícula fracturada.
-A girl came in with a fractured clavicle.

7898 imperialismo — **imperialism**
m
[ĩm.pɛ.rja.ˈliṣ.mo]

Hoy contemplamos el resurgimiento del imperialismo europeo.
-Today, we are seeing the resurgence of European imperialism.

7899 potar — **puke (coll)**
vb
[po.ˈtar]

Creo que voy a potar otra vez.
-I think I'm going to puke again.

7900 presunto — **alleged**
adj
[pre.ˈsũn̪.to]

El personal fue retenido por presunto tráfico ilegal de hidrocarburos.
-The crew was held on charges of alleged illegal trafficking of hydrocarbons.

7901 peregrinación — **pilgrimage**
f
[pɛ.re.ɣri.na.ˈsjõn]

Estoy hasta el cuello organizando esta peregrinación.
-I've been neck deep in organizing this pilgrimage.

7902 postiza — **fake**
adj
[pos.ˈti.sa]

Quizá lleve puesta una barba postiza.
-Maybe he's wearing a false beard.

7903 inquebrantable — **unwavering**
adj
[ĩn.ke.βrãn̪.ˈta.βle]

Nuestra solidaridad con ellos debe ser inquebrantable.
-Our solidarity with them must be unwavering.

7904 carpintería — **carpentry**
f
[kar.pĩn̪.ˈtɛ.ri.a]

Y no sabes nada sobre carpintería.
-And you don't know anything about carpentry.

7905 augurio — **omen**
m
[au̯.ˈɣu.rjo]

No podemos confiar en el augurio.
-We can not rely on omen.

7906	**fallecimiento**	**death**
	m	Hoy es el aniversario de su fallecimiento.
	[fa.je.si.ˈmjẽṉ.to]	-It's the anniversary of his death, today.
7907	**plenitud**	**fullness**
	f	La plenitud de tu dicha, la siento.
	[ple.ni.ˈtuð]	-The fullness of your bliss, I feel it.
7908	**tapiz**	**tapestry**
	m	Lo colgaremos aquí, un precioso tapiz.
	[ˈta.pis]	-We'll hang it here, the beautiful tapestry.
7909	**desgarrar**	**tear**
	vb	Simplemente no puedo desgarrar su corazón.
	[dɛs̝.ɣa.ˈrar]	-I just can't tear his heart out.
7910	**atenerse a**	**abide by**
	vbr	El gobierno tendrá que atenerse a las normas de derecho internacional.
	[a.te.ˈnɛr.se a]	-The government will have to abide by the rule of international law.
7911	**riguroso**	**rigorous**
	adj	Esto será un ejercicio serio, riguroso.
	[ri.ɣu.ˈro.so]	-This will be a serious, rigorous exercise.
7912	**diván**	**divan**
	m	Me había dormido en el diván.
	[di.ˈβãn]	-I'd fallen asleep on the divan.
7913	**oleaje**	**surf**
	m	Aprende a nadar en el oleaje.
	[o.le.ˈa.xe]	-Learn how to swim in the surf.
7914	**deliberar**	**deliberate**
	vb	Probablemente deberíamos deliberar, pero estamos un poco apurados.
	[de.li.βɛ.ˈrar]	-We probably should deliberate, but we're kind of in a hurry.
7915	**rayar**	**scratch**
	vb	Preferiría rayar la pintura de su propio coche.
	[ra.ˈjar]	-He'd rather scratch the paintwork on his own car.
7916	**auge**	**boom**
	m	Lamentablemente, serán víctimas del auge económico venidero.
	[ˈau̯.xe]	-Unfortunately, they'll be the victims of the coming economic boom.
7917	**bis**	**bis; encore**
	adv; m	El artículo 45 bis podría volver a ser formulado apropiadamente.
	[ˈbis]	-Article 45 bis could be reformulated accordingly.
7918	**ranura**	**groove**
	f	Se utiliza un pequeño caudal de lodo por ranura.
	[ra.ˈnu.ra]	-A reduced flow of sludge per groove is used.
7919	**desprevenido**	**unprepared**
	adj	No me pueden pillar desprevenido de nuevo.
	[dɛs.pre.βe.ˈni.ðo]	-I can't be unprepared like that again.
7920	**parpadear**	**blink**
	vb	¿Podría parpadear si me comprende?
	[par.pa.ðe.ˈar]	-Would you blink if you understand me?
7921	**enérgico**	**energetic**
	adj	Ha estado sorprendentemente enérgico hasta ahora.
	[e.ˈnɛr.xi.ko]	-He's been surprising energetic up until now.

7922 desanimar — **discourage**
vb
[de.sa.ni.ˈmar]
Vendrías conmigo para desanimar a los problemas.
-You would come with me to discourage trouble.

7923 cota — **peak**
f
[ˈko.ta]
El mercado americano de originales antiguos está en su cota más alta.
-The American Market in old masters is positively at its peak.

7924 escarabajo — **beetle**
m
[ɛs.ka.ra.ˈβa.xo]
Observen la frecuencia con que el escarabajo danza.
-Watch how often the beetle dances.

7925 asimilar — **assimilate**
vb
[a.si.mi.ˈlar]
Nos ayudará a asimilar esta nave.
-You will assist us to assimilate this vessel.

7926 desesperante — **desperate, maddening**
adj
[de.sɛs.pɛ.ˈrãn̪.te]
He tenido pacientes así antes, y es desesperante.
-I've had patients with it before, and it's maddening.

7927 despistar — **mislead**
vb
[dɛs.pis.ˈtar]
Querían despistar al enemigo y lanzar un ataque sorpresa.
-They wanted to mislead the enemy and launch a surprise attack.

7928 contagio — **contagion**
m
[kõn̪.ˈta.xjo]
Tenéis que amarlos y aceptar el contagio.
-You need to love them and accept the contagion.

7929 resonar — **resonate**
vb
[re.so.ˈnar]
Podrías ver que nuestros argumentos comenzaban a resonar.
-You could see that our arguments were starting to resonate.

7930 masculinidad — **masculinity**
f
[mas.ku.li.ni.ˈðað]
Sería interesante saber si se ha investigado algo sobre la construcción de la masculinidad.
-It would be interesting to know whether any research was being done on the construction of masculinity.

7931 desliz — **slip**
m
[ˈdɛs̪.lis]
Un desliz y podría haberme costado la partida.
-One slip, and it could have cost me the game.

7932 inscribir — **register**
vb
[ĩns.kri.ˈβir]
Ese número de declaraciones bastaba para inscribir su candidatura.
-This number of statements was sufficient to register him as a candidate.

7933 noticiario — **news**
m
[no.ti.ˈsja.rjo]
Quizás acabe como noticia principal de su propio noticiario.
-She might just wind up as the lead story on her own newscast.

7934 lince — **lynx**
m
[ˈlĩn.se]
Sé lo que es un lince.
-I know what a lynx is.

7935 botánico — **botanical; botanist**
adj; m
[bo.ˈta.ni.ko]
El autor era un botánico inglés.
-The author was a British botanist.

7936 espuela — **spur**
f
[ɛs.ˈpwe.la]
Parece la forma de una punta de espuela.
-Looks like the shape of a rowel from a spur.

7937 codorniz — **quail**

	m/f	
	[ko.ˈðor.nis]	Helene está preparando la cena, codorniz o algo así. -Helene is making dinner, quail or something.
7938	**tesorería**	**treasury**
	f	Acabo de hablar con nuestro tipo de tesorería.
	[te.so.rɛ.ˈri.a]	-I just spoke to our guy at treasury.
7939	**antisemita**	**anti-Semitic; anti-Semite**
	adj; m/f	Bueno, él es un antisemita, y está equivocado.
	[ãn̪.ti.se.ˈmi.ta]	-Well, he's an anti-semite, and he is wrong.
7940	**procesador**	**processing; processor**
	adj; m	Este teléfono tiene un procesador de cuatro núcleos.
	[pro.se.sa.ˈðor]	-This phone has a quad-core processor.
7941	**abundar**	**be plentiful, elaborate**
	vb	Trataré de abundar en algunas sugerencias.
	[a.βũn̪.ˈdar]	-I will try to elaborate on some suggestions.
7942	**vincular**	**link**
	vb	No es apropiado vincular estas dos revisiones.
	[bĩŋ.ku.ˈlar]	-It is not appropriate to link these two reviews.
7943	**despegado**	**taken off**
	adj	El avión ya había despegado cuando llegué al aeropuerto.
	[dɛs.pe.ˈɣa.ðo]	-The plane had already taken off when I reached the airport.
7944	**documentar**	**document**
	vb	Debemos aumentar nuestras actividades para documentar y publicar los hechos.
	[do.ku.mẽn̪.ˈtar]	-We must increase our activities to document and to publicize the facts.
7945	**preservación**	**preservation**
	f	Si lo sacamos, su preservación estaría comprometida.
	[pre.sɛr.βa.ˈsjõn]	-If we take him out, his preservation could be compromised.
7946	**estimulación**	**stimulation**
	f	No responde a ninguna estimulación habitual.
	[ɛs.ti.mu.la.ˈsjõn]	-He fails to respond to any normal stimulation.
7947	**detestar**	**loathe**
	vb	Pero antes de que llegaras, estaba empezando a detestar este lugar.
	[dɛ.tɛs.ˈtar]	-But before you got here, I was beginning to loathe this place.
7948	**tapia**	**wall**
	f	La escalada de tapia es algo para los jóvenes.
	[ˈta.pja]	-The climbing wall is something for young people.
7949	**pitido**	**whistle**
	m	Cuando escuchó el pitido, cruzó la calle.
	[pi.ˈti.ðo]	-When he heard the whistle, he crossed the street.
7950	**excusar**	**excuse**
	vb	No trato de excusar mis actos.
	[ɛk.su.ˈsar]	-I'm not trying to excuse my actions.
7951	**decepcionado**	**disappointed**
	adj	Parece liberado y decepcionado al mismo tiempo.
	[de.sɛp.sjo.ˈna.ðo]	-You look relieved and disappointed at the same time.
7952	**tatarabuelo**	**Great-great-grandfather**
	m	Tiene once hijos y ahora ya es tatarabuelo.
	[ta.ta.ra.ˈβwe.lo]	-He has eleven children and is by now great-great-grandfather.

7953	**sistemático**	**systematic**
	adj	Ello provocará un cambio cultural sistemático.
	[sis.te.ˈma.ti.ko]	-That will bring about a systematic change in culture.
7954	**erradicar**	**eradicate**
	vb	Debemos erradicar la geopolítica del hambre.
	[ɛ.ra.ra.ði.ˈkar]	-We must eradicate the geopolitics of hunger.
7955	**intimidación**	**intimidation**
	f	Estos profesionales deben estar protegidos contra la intimidación.
	[ĩn̪.ti.mi.ða.ˈsjõn]	-Those professionals must be protected from intimidation.
7956	**envasar**	**package**
	vb	Queríamos envasar el aroma del café.
	[ẽm.ba.ˈsar]	-We wanted to package the aroma of coffee.
7957	**labia**	**gift of the gab**
	f	Le dije que tienes una labia tremenda.
	[ˈla.βja]	-I told him you had terrific chatter.
7958	**hernia**	**hernia**
	f	Es infrecuente que una hernia reaparezca.
	[ˈɛr.nja]	-It is rare for a hernia to come back.
7959	**mueca**	**grin**
	f	Esa mueca tuya está a punto de cortarte la cabeza.
	[ˈmwe.ka]	-That grin of yours is about to cut the top of your head off.
7960	**avioneta**	**plane**
	f	Esa avioneta de ahí arriba probablemente sea de la policía.
	[a.βjo.ˈnɛ.ta]	-That airplane up there, it probably belongs to the police.
7961	**regulador**	**regulator; regulating**
	m; adj	Actúa como organismo asesor y regulador.
	[re.ɣu.la.ˈðor]	-It acts as an advisory and regulatory body.
7962	**chévere**	**great (LA) (coll); cool (LA) (coll)**
	int; adj	Yo pienso que es muy chévere.
	[ˈtʃe.βɛ.re]	-I think it is pretty cool.
7963	**quehacer**	**chore**
	m	Algunas personas dicen que esto es una carga y un quehacer.
	[ke.a.ˈsɛr]	-Some people say that this is a burden and a chore.
7964	**bazo**	**spleen**
	m	Ni siquiera he comprobado el bazo todavía.
	[ˈba.so]	-I haven't even checked the spleen yet.
7965	**entablar**	**enter into**
	vb	No propongo entablar debate alguno.
	[ẽn̪.ta.ˈβlar]	-I do not propose to enter into any kind of debate.
7966	**forjado**	**wrought**
	adj	Voy hacia lo que sea que el destino tenga forjado para mí.
	[for.ˈxa.ðo]	-I'm going towards whatever destiny I have wrought for myself.
7967	**nacionalista**	**nationalist; nationalist**
	adj; m/f	Lo siento si he ofendido su simpatía nacionalista.
	[na.sjo.na.ˈlis.ta]	-I'm sorry if I've offended your nationalist sympathy.
7968	**rosca**	**thread**
	f	Se puede usar para reparar cualquier rosca dañada.
	[ˈros.ka]	-It can be used to repair any damaged thread.

7969	**consumar**	**consummate**	
	vb	Tal vez solo quiera consumar el divorcio.	
	[kõn.su.ˈmar]	-Maybe she just wants to consummate the divorce.	
7970	**suavizar**	**soften**	
	vb	Intenté suavizar los ojos un poco.	
	[swa.βi.ˈsar]	-I tried to soften the eyes a little.	
7971	**brotar**	**sprout**	
	vb	Si solo le pudieran brotar las alas.	
	[bro.ˈtar]	-If only it could sprout wings.	
7972	**estrofa**	**stanza**	
	f	Lo verás en la segunda estrofa.	
	[ɛs.ˈtro.fa]	-You will see it in the second stanza.	
7973	**trazado**	**outline**	
	m	Verán que he trazado varias contramedidas.	
	[tra.ˈsa.ðo]	-You'll see that I've outlined several countermeasures.	
7974	**armenio**	**Armenian; Armenian person**	
	adj; m	El idioma oficial de Armenia es el armenio.	
	[ar.ˈme.njo]	-The official State language of Armenia is Armenian.	
7975	**despecho**	**spite**	
	m	Lo echas todo a perder por despecho hacia mí.	
	[dɛs.ˈpe.tʃo]	-You throw everything away to spite me.	
7976	**cepa**	**strain**	
	f	Necesito saber que cepa del virus tienes.	
	[ˈse.pa]	-I need to know what strain of the virus you have.	
7977	**marítimo**	**maritime**	
	adj	Deseo destacar la importancia de un espacio marítimo sin fronteras.	
	[ma.ˈri.ti.mo]	-I wish to stress the importance of a maritime space without barriers.	
7978	**invernal**	**wintry**	
	adj	Abotonen sus abrigos en la brisa invernal.	
	[ĩm.bɛr.ˈnal]	-Button up your overcoat in the wintry breeze.	
7979	**validez**	**validity**	
	f	Fue preciso revisar la validez del método.	
	[ba.ˈli.ðes]	-It became necessary to revisit the validity of the method.	
7980	**espesor**	**thickness**	
	m	El vial se suministra en un blindaje de plomo del espesor adecuado.	
	[ɛs.pe.ˈsor]	-The vial is supplied in a lead pot of appropriate thickness.	
7981	**almacenar**	**store**	
	vb	No almacenar comidas por prolongados periodos de tiempo.	
	[al.ma.se.ˈnar]	-Do not store food for a prolonged period of time.	
7982	**privación**	**deprivation**	
	f	Cuatro de cada diez personas sufren intensa privación.	
	[pri.βa.ˈsjõn]	-Four out of 10 persons are subject to intense deprivation.	
7983	**antiaéreo**	**anti-aircraft**	
	adj	A los dos regímenes separatistas se les proporcionó armamento antiaéreo.	
	[ãn̪.ˈtja.ɛ.re.o]	-Anti-aircraft equipment was provided to both separatist regimes.	
7984	**cristiandad**	**Christianity**	

f
[kris.tjãn̩.ˈdað]

Otros se han convertido a la cristiandad plenamente.
-Others have converted entirely to Christianity.

7985 panorámico

adj
[pa.no.ˈra.mi.ko]

panoramic

El almuerzo será servido en el panorámico restaurante Uma Kollu.
-Lunch will be served at the panoramic Uma Kollu restaurant.

7986 desplegar

vb
[dɛs.ple.ˈɣar]

deploy

Puede también desplegar expertos de su propio personal.
-It may also deploy experts from among its own staff.

7987 fraternal

adj
[fra.tɛr.ˈnal]

fraternal

Sencillamente hoy te veo con piedad fraternal.
-It's just that I see you today with fraternal pity.

7988 idear

vb
[i.ðe.ˈar]

devise

Lo volveremos contra él y le dejaremos idear su propia caída.
-We will turn it on him and let him devise his own downfall.

7989 mongol

adj; m
[mõŋ.ˈgol]

Mongolian; Mongol

Nunca mereció ocupar el trono mongol.
-He never deserved to occupy the Mongol throne.

7990 proeza

f
[pro.ˈe.sa]

feat

Su última proeza fue hace unos días.
-His last feat was a few days ago.

7991 flexibilidad

f
[flɛk.si.βi.li.ˈðað]

flexibility

Debemos proceder con cautela y flexibilidad.
-We have to proceed with caution and with flexibility.

7992 nominar

vb
[no.mi.ˈnar]

nominate

Por ahora, tenemos que votar y nominar a nuestro jinete.
-For now, we have to cast our votes and nominate our rider.

7993 perjudicado

adj
[pɛr.xu.ði.ˈka.ðo]

harmed

O peor, pude haberte perjudicado.
-Or worse, I could have harmed you.

7994 flagrante

adj
[fla.ˈɣrãn̩.te]

flagrant

Este es resultado de la violación intencionada y flagrante de las normas vigentes.
-This is the outcome of the intentional and flagrant violation of existing norms.

7995 veintiséis

num
[bein̩.ti.ˈseis]

twenty-six

Ya he llevado a veintiséis personas a salvo al barco.
-I have led twenty-six people safely by now to the ferry.

7996 incomodidad

f
[ĩŋ.ko.mo.ði.ˈðað]

discomfort

Deberías sentir incomodidad, no dolor.
-You should be feeling discomfort, not pain.

7997 camaradería

f
[ka.ma.ra.ðɛ.ˈri.a]

camaraderie

He terminado compartiendo una extraña camaradería con él.
-I've ended up sharing a strange camaraderie with him.

7998 sepultar

vb
[se.pul̩.ˈtar]

bury

Estos no son residuos que debamos sepultar o quemar.
-This is not waste that we should bury or burn.

7999 hereditario

adj
[ɛ.re.ði.ˈta.rjo]

hereditary

No, pero a menudo es hereditario.
-No, but it is often hereditary.

8000	**vulgaridad**	**vulgarity**
	f	Es un evidente signo de vulgaridad.
	[bul.ɣa.ri.ˈðað]	-It's a sure sign of vulgarity.
8001	**ocurrencia**	**idea**
	f	Es solo una ocurrencia, no tienes que hacerlo.
	[o.ku.ˈrẽn.sja]	-It's just an idea, you don't have to.
8002	**comestible**	**edible**
	adj	Aquí, prácticamente no hay vegetación comestible.
	[ko.mɛs.ˈti.βle]	-Here, there is virtually no edible vegetation at all.
8003	**narcotráfico**	**drug trafficking**
	m	También se aplica a los delitos de narcotráfico.
	[nar.ko.ˈtra.fi.ko]	-It is also meant for the offenses of drug trafficking.
8004	**posteridad**	**posterity**
	f	Esa será nuestra contribución a la posteridad.
	[pos.tɛ.ri.ˈðað]	-This will be our contribution to posterity.
8005	**turbina**	**turbine**
	f	Tengo que alejarme de la turbina.
	[tur.ˈβi.na]	-I need to move away from the turbine.
8006	**toma**	**socket**
	f	De hecho, ni siquiera puedo ver una toma de teléfono allí abajo.
	[ˈto.ma]	-In fact, I can't even see a telephone socket down there.
8007	**deportación**	**deportation**
	f	Evitará la deportación cuanto sea posible.
	[de.por.ta.ˈsjõn]	-You'll avoid deportation as long as possible.
8008	**engañoso**	**misleading**
	adj	Seguir haciéndolo en este momento parecería engañoso.
	[ɛ̃ŋ.ga.ˈɲo.so]	-To continue such usage at this time seems misleading.
8009	**premisa**	**premise**
	f	No se reconocieron mutuamente como premisa elemental.
	[pre.ˈmi.sa]	-They did not take recognition of the other as a basic premise.
8010	**dispersión**	**dispersion**
	f	Debe evitarse la dispersión de estos esfuerzos.
	[dis.pɛr.ˈsjõn]	-The dispersion of these efforts must be overcome.
8011	**medicinal**	**medicinal**
	adj	Parece estar creando algún tipo de compuesto medicinal.
	[me.ði.si.ˈnal]	-He seems to be creating some sort of medicinal compound.
8012	**ceremonial**	**ceremonial**
	adj	Incluso puedo conseguir una lanza ceremonial si están interesados.
	[sɛ.re.mo.ˈnjal]	-I can even get a ceremonial spear if you're interested.
8013	**duplicar**	**double**
	vb	Te diré cómo pueden duplicar la ganancia.
	[dup̚.li.ˈkar]	-I will tell you how they could double their profits.
8014	**listado**	**list**
	m	Hicimos un listado de nuestras fortalezas y debilidades.
	[lis.ˈta.ðo]	-We've made a list of our strengths and weaknesses.
8015	**afrenta**	**affront**
	f	Sería una afrenta contra la gente.
	[a.ˈfrẽn̪.ta]	-It would be an affront against the people.

8016	**degradar**	**degrade**
	vb	Nunca dejaría que un hombre me degradara así.
	[de.ɣra.ˈðar]	-I would never let a guy degrade me like that.
8017	**parrillada**	**barbecue**
	f	Esta noche vamos a hacer una parrillada.
	[pa.ri.ˈja.ða]	-We're having a barbecue tonight.
8018	**supersticioso**	**superstitious**
	adj	Ahora nunca haces copias porque eres supersticioso.
	[su.pɛrs.ti.ˈsjo.so]	-Now you never make copies because you're superstitious.
8019	**reclusión**	**imprisonment**
	f	Es preciso reconocer los aspectos raciales de la violencia y la reclusión.
	[re.klu.ˈsjõn]	-The racial aspects of violence and imprisonment shall be recognized.
8020	**comillas**	**quotation marks**
	fpl	Como dije, no había comillas.
	[ko.ˈmi.jas]	-As I said, there were no quotation marks.
8021	**prosa**	**prose**
	f	Podría refinar su prosa pero lo entendemos.
	[ˈpro.sa]	-His prose could use refinement but we get the point.
8022	**encariñarse**	**grow fond of**
	vbr	No puedes encariñarte con ese perro.
	[ẽŋ.ka.ri.ˈɲar.se]	-You can't get attached to that dog.
8023	**autocontrol**	**self-control**
	m	Dice que tendré más confianza y autocontrol.
	[au̯.to.kõn̪.ˈtrol]	-It says I'll have more confidence and self-control.
8024	**aberración**	**aberration**
	f	El bloqueo es una aberración jurídica.
	[a.βɛ.ra.ˈsjõn]	-The blockade is a legal aberration.
8025	**meticuloso**	**meticulous**
	adj	Él no es un tipo muy meticuloso.
	[mɛ.ti.ku.ˈlo.so]	-He's not a very meticulous guy.
8026	**rentar**	**rent**
	vb	Buscaré un lugar barato para rentar.
	[r̃ẽn̪.ˈtar]	-I'll just look for a cheap place to rent.
8027	**ensuciar(se)**	**mess**
	vb	Quien ha escrito la carta solo quiere ensuciar nuestro nombre.
	[ẽn.su.ˈsjar]	-Whoever posted the letter, just wants to mess our name.
8028	**hipotéticamente**	**hypothetically**
	adv	Digamos, hipotéticamente, que le hice un libro.
	[i.po.ˈtɛ.ti.ka.mẽn̪.te]	-Let's say, hypothetically, that I made a book for him.
8029	**aparador**	**sideboard**
	m	Tengo un aparador muy valioso que deben recoger.
	[a.pa.ra.ˈðor]	-I have a very valuable sideboard that has to be picked up.
8030	**electrón**	**electron**
	m	En la naturaleza hay una cosa llamada electrón.
	[e.lek.ˈtrõn]	-In nature, there's a thing called the electron.
8031	**subestimar**	**underestimate**
	vb	Tampoco debemos subestimar las ventajas económicas.
	[su.βes.ti.ˈmar]	-We must not underestimate the economic advantages either.

8032	**perfeccionar**	**perfect**
	vb	Intentaba perfeccionar mi programa médico.
	[pɛr.fɛk.sjo.ˈnar]	-I was trying to perfect my medical program.
8033	**antropología**	**anthropology**
	f	Creo que dijo que era licenciada en antropología.
	[ãn̪.tro.po.ˈlo.xi.a]	-I think she said her degree was in anthropology.
8034	**currículum**	**curriculum vitae**
	m	Rellene el siguiente formulario y envíenos su currículum.
	[ku.ˈri.ku.lũm]	-Fill in the form here below and send Your Curriculum Vitae.
8035	**retrovisor**	**rear-view mirror**
	m	Tienes un calcetín sucio colgando del retrovisor de tu coche.
	[rɛ.tro.βi.ˈsor]	-You have a dirty sock hanging from the rearview mirror of your car.
8036	**apego**	**attachment**
	m	Puedes entender el apego a nuestros clientes.
	[a.ˈpe.ɣo]	-You can understand our attachment to our clients.
8037	**suplemento**	**supplement**
	m	Pretende ser un suplemento del informe inicial.
	[sup̚.le.ˈmẽn̪.to]	-It is intended to serve as a supplement to the initial report.
8038	**hospitalario**	**hospitable**
	adj	Dudo que encuentres ese ambiente mas hospitalario.
	[os.pi.ta.ˈla.rjo]	-I doubt you'll find that environment any more hospitable.
8039	**ampliación**	**extension**
	f	Ahora hay una ampliación en construcción.
	[ãm.plja.ˈsjõn]	-An extension is currently under construction.
8040	**contienda**	**contest**
	f	Deberán enfrentarse en la contienda final.
	[kõn̪.ˈtjẽn̪.da]	-They are to face each other in the final contest.
8041	**galera**	**galley**
	f	Ser un esclavo de galera no tiene ningún encanto para mí.
	[ga.ˈlɛ.ra]	-Being a galley slave holds no appeal for me.
8042	**caballerosidad**	**chivalry**
	f	No me hable de caballerosidad en Italia.
	[ka.βa.je.ro.si.ˈðað]	-Don't talk to me about chivalry in Italy.
8043	**limpiaparabrisas**	**wiper**
	m	Necesito un copiloto para usar el limpiaparabrisas.
	[lĩm.pja.pa.ra.ˈβri.sas]	-I need a copilot to turn on the windshield wiper.
8044	**anemia**	**anemia**
	f	Tenemos un severo caso de anemia.
	[a.ˈne.mja]	-We're lookin' at a severe case of anemia.
8045	**planificar**	**plan**
	vb	Vamos a planificar nuestro siguiente movimiento.
	[pla.ni.fi.ˈkar]	-We are going to plan our next move.
8046	**propicio**	**conductive**
	adj	Me parece propicio trabajar de esta manera.
	[pro.ˈpi.sjo]	-I find it conducive to work in this way.
8047	**balanceo**	**rocking**
	m	Estaba mareado por el balanceo del barco.
	[ba.lãn̪.ˈse.o]	-I was seasick from the rocking of the boat.

8048 **macabro**

adj
[ma.ˈka.βro]

macabre

Lamentablemente, esto tiene un trasfondo macabro.
-Unfortunately, there is a macabre background to that.

8049 **torniquete**

m
[tor.ni.ˈkɛ.te]

tourniquet

Necesita un torniquete, o morirá.
-She needs a tourniquet or she's going to die.

8050 **obscenidad**

f
[oβs.se.ni.ˈðað]

obscenity

Parecemos estar paralizados ante esta obscenidad.
-We seem paralyzed in the face of this obscenity.

8051 **disminución**

f
[diṣ.mi.nu.ˈsjõn]

decrease

Esta disminución no produjo signos clínicos.
-This decrease did not result in clinical signs.

8052 **masón**

m
[ma.ˈsõn]

mason

¿Afirma ser un compañero masón?
-You claim to be a fellow Mason?

8053 **afinidad**

f
[a.fi.ni.ˈðað]

affinity

Siento algo de afinidad con él.
-I feel a bit of affinity with him.

8054 **acontecer**

vb
[a.kõn̪.te.ˈsɛr]

happen

Y aún así su humanismo es precisamente el por qué la guerra debe acontecer.
-And yet your humanism is precisely why war must happen.

8055 **configuración**

f
[kõɱ.fi.ɣu.ra.ˈsjõn]

configuration

Esto es probablemente por una configuración errónea.
-This is most likely due to a wrong configuration.

8056 **subversivo**

adj
[suβ.βɛr.ˈsi.βo]

subversive

Pero si quiere saberlo, estamos buscando material subversivo.
-But if you want to know, we're looking for subversive materials.

8057 **camaleón**

m
[ka.ma.le.ˈõn]

chameleon

Tenemos que descubrir quien es el camaleón.
-We need to figure out who the chameleon is.

8058 **cómic**

m
[ˈko.mik]

comic

Todos nos quedaremos con el cómic.
-We'll all stay with the comic book.

8059 **lagartija**

f
[la.ɣar.ˈti.xa]

lizard

Parece olvidar que es solo una pequeña lagartija.
-You seem to forget you're just one little lizard.

8060 **espiritualidad**

f
[ɛs.pi.ri.twa.li.ˈðað]

spirituality

Tu hijo tiene anhelo de espiritualidad.
-Your son's got a yearning for spirituality.

8061 **analogía**

f
[a.na.lo.ˈxi.a]

analogy

Pero la analogía no funciona sociológicamente.
-But the analogy doesn't hold up sociologically.

8062 **desmayo**

m
[dɛṣ.ˈma.jo]

fainting

Eso explica el ahogo y el desmayo.
-That explains the choking and fainting.

8063 **distorsión**

distortion

f
[dis.tor.ˈsjõn]

Esto supondría una clara distorsión del mercado.
-This would be a clear distortion of the market.

8064 rosal — **rosebush**

m
[ro.ˈsal]

Es una espina de un rosal.
-It's a thorn from a rosebush.

8065 costear — **finance**

vb
[kos.te.ˈar]

Sus puertos no han generado suficientes ingresos para costear nuevas mejoras.
-Its ports had not been generating enough money to finance new developments.

8066 girasol — **sunflower**

m
[xi.ra.ˈsol]

No puedes casarte con esa semilla de girasol.
-You can't marry that sunflower seed.

8067 metamorfosis — **metamorphosis**

f
[mɛ.ta.mor.ˈfo.sis]

En el proceso de la metamorfosis hay cuatro fases.
-In the process of metamorphosis, there are four stages.

8068 ciclón — **cyclone**

m
[si.ˈklõn]

Nargis fue el ciclón más devastador que jamás haya afectado a Myanmar.
-Nargis was the most devastating cyclone ever to hit Myanmar.

8069 entrometerse — **interfere**

vbr
[ɛ̃n̪.tro.mɛ.ˈtɛr.se]

Justo a tiempo de entrometerse en la inauguración.
-Just in time to interfere with the opening.

8070 financiamiento — **financing**

m
[fi.nãn.sja.ˈmjɛ̃n̪.to]

Incluso pueden traerse algo de financiamiento.
-They even can bring with them some financing.

8071 reescribir — **rewrite**

vb
[re.ɛs.kri.ˈβir]

Pueden reescribir esto en un momento.
-They can rewrite this stuff in a shot.

8072 bravucón — **cocky; bully**

adj; m
[bra.βu.ˈkõn]

Solo eres un bravucón grande y azul.
-You're just a big, blue bully.

8073 funda — **cover**

f
[ˈfũn̪.da]

Noté que tu otra funda estaba bastante deteriorada.
-I noticed that your other cover was pretty beat up.

8074 estancar(se) — **stall**

vb
[ɛs.tãŋ.ˈkar]

Sin embargo, las dificultades actuales no deben estancar la aplicación de la hoja de ruta.
-But current setbacks must not stall the implementation of the roadmap.

8075 municipal — **municipal**

adj
[mu.ni.si.ˈpal]

Aquí es donde encontrará la reserva municipal.
-This is where you'll find the municipal reservoir.

8076 comparable — **comparable**

adj
[kõm.pa.ˈra.βle]

Es comparable a la invención del microscopio.
-It's comparable to the invention of the microscope.

8077 jurídico — **legal**

adj
[xu.ˈri.ði.ko]

Es parte sagrada de nuestro patrimonio jurídico.
-It is a sacred part of our legal heritage.

8078	**sílaba**	**syllable**
	f	Después de esto, no pronunciaré otra sílaba.
	[ˈsi.la.βa]	-After this, I won't utter another syllable.
8079	**rotundo**	**resounding**
	adj	Nuestra respuesta es un no rotundo.
	[ro.ˈtũn̪.do]	-Our answer is a resounding no.
8080	**parejo**	**even**
	adj	El desempeño fue relativamente parejo en todas las prácticas.
	[pa.ˈre.xo]	-Performance across practices was relatively even.
8081	**audífono**	**hearing aid**
	m	Si alguien pregunta, di que es tu nuevo audífono.
	[au̯.ˈði.fo.no]	-If anybody asks, tell them it's your new hearing aid.
8082	**bombear**	**pump**
	vb	El corazón sirve para bombear sangre.
	[bõm.be.ˈar]	-The heart serves to pump blood.
8083	**refrigeración**	**refrigeration**
	f	Imagina los problemas que tienen en la jungla sin refrigeración.
	[re.fri.xɛ.ra.ˈsjõn]	-Imagine the problems they have in the jungle without refrigeration.
8084	**bucal**	**oral**
	adj	Es importante cuidar todos los elementos que componen la cavidad bucal.
	[bu.ˈkal]	-Taking care of all the elements that make up the oral cavity is very important.
8085	**congelación**	**freezing**
	f	Deberá evitarse evitará la congelación de estas muestras.
	[kõŋ.xe.la.ˈsjõn]	-Freezing of those samples shall be avoided.
8086	**flamante**	**brand-new**
	adj	Prosperaremos y triunfaremos en nuestra flamante oficina.
	[fla.ˈmãn̪.te]	-May we be healthy and successful in our brand-new suite.
8087	**notificar**	**notify**
	vb	Porque fue mi idea notificar al ejército.
	[no.ti.fi.ˈkar]	-Because it was my idea to notify the military.
8088	**inmensidad**	**immensity**
	f	La revelación de esta inmensidad era como enamorarse.
	[ĩm.mẽn.si.ˈðað]	-The revelation of this immensity was like falling in love.
8089	**afable**	**affable**
	adj	Siempre me ha parecido un joven afable y franco.
	[a.ˈfa.βle]	-I've always found him to be an affable and forthright young man.
8090	**hundimiento**	**sinking**
	m	El hundimiento del Erika tuvo un efecto totalmente nuevo y sorprendente.
	[ũn̪.di.ˈmjẽn̪.to]	-The sinking of the Erika had a completely new and surprising effect.
8091	**previsible**	**foreseeable**
	adj	Otras complicaciones guardan relación con la reacción previsible del personal.
	[pre.βi.ˈsi.βle]	-Other complications will have to do with the foreseeable reaction of the staff.
8092	**locutor**	**announcer**

	m	Obviamente sonará mejor con la voz del locutor.
	[lo.ku.'tor]	-Obviously, it'll sound better with the announcer's voice.
8093	**catalizador**	**catalyst**
	m	Sharon actuó como catalizadora del último episodio de violencia.
	[ka.ta.li.sa.'ðor]	-Sharon acted as a catalyst of this latest occurrence of violence.
8094	**declive**	**decline**
	m	Hay evidencia de declive en su nivel de función mental.
	[de.'kli.βe]	-There is evidence of the decline in your level of mental function.
8095	**vándalo**	**vandal**
	m/f	El vándalo destrozó bien tu moto.
	['bãn̦.da.lo]	-The vandal really wrecked your bike.
8096	**deseoso**	**keen**
	adj	Mi país está deseoso de continuar cumpliendo con su cometido.
	[de.se.'o.so]	-My country is eager to continue doing its part.
8097	**promocionar**	**promote**
	vb	Es imposible promocionar algo que no existe.
	[pro.mo.sjo.'nar]	-There's no way to promote something that doesn't exist.
8098	**borrón**	**smudge**
	m	Un diminuto borrón que parece una huella.
	[bo.'rõn]	-A little tiny smudge that's like a fingerprint.
8099	**relatividad**	**relativity**
	f	Pocos científicos entienden la teoría de la relatividad.
	[re.la.ti.βi.'ðað]	-Few scientists understand the theory of relativity.
8100	**preservativo**	**condom**
	m	Pero sabes que utilizaste un preservativo.
	[pre.sɛr.βa.'ti.βo]	-But you know that you used a condom.
8101	**retina**	**retina**
	f	La imagen que se proyecta en la retina está invertida.
	[rɛ.'ti.na]	-The image projected in the retina is inverted.
8102	**elector**	**elector**
	m	Las elecciones son por mayoría simple y cada elector puede emitir dos votos.
	[e.lek̚.'tor]	-Elections are by simple majority, and each elector can cast two votes.
8103	**celibato**	**celibacy**
	m	El celibato en algunas culturas es visto como una señal de fuerza.
	[se.li.'βa.to]	-Celibacy in some cultures is seen as a sign of strength.
8104	**conspirar**	**conspire**
	vb	Eddie y yo tenemos que conspirar.
	[kõns.pi.'rar]	-Eddie and I need to conspire.
8105	**verter**	**pour**
	vb	Ahora van a verter el agua.
	[bɛr.'tɛr]	-Now they'll pour the water.
8106	**venerable**	**venerable**
	adj	La reforma de una institución tan venerable no es nunca una tarea fácil.
	[be.nɛ.'ra.βle]	-Reform of such a venerable institution is never easy.
8107	**contiguo**	**adjacent**
	adj	El edificio contiguo tiene una vista panorámica de la oficina.
	[kõn̦.'ti.ɣwo]	-The adjacent building has an unobstructed view into the office.

8108	**inaugurar**		**inaugurate**
	vb		Tengo el honor de inaugurar esta comisaría.
	[i.nau̯.ɣu.ˈrar]		-It's my honor to inaugurate this police station.
8109	**salvoconducto**		**pass**
	m		Tengo un salvoconducto para todo ello.
	[sal.βo.kõn̪.ˈduk̚.to]		-I have a pass to all.
8110	**insensatez**		**folly**
	f		Si no es insensatez, sin duda es irresponsabilidad.
	[ĩn.sẽn.ˈsa.tes]		-If it is not folly, it is certainly irresponsibility.
8111	**aeroplano**		**airplane**
	m		Nunca antes había visto un aeroplano.
	[a.ɛ.rop̚.ˈla.no]		-I had never seen an airplane before.
8112	**preventivo**		**preventive**
	adj		Necesitamos un enfoque cautelar pero no preventivo.
	[pre.βẽn̪.ˈti.βo]		-We need a precautionary approach but not a preventive one.
8113	**utensilio**		**utensil**
	m		Pica las hierbas utilizando un utensilio adecuado.
	[u.tẽn.ˈsi.ljo]		-Chop the herbs using a suitable utensil.
8114	**zapatería**		**shoe shop**
	f		Los dos trabajáis en la zapatería.
	[sa.pa.tɛ.ˈri.a]		-You both work in the shoe shop.
8115	**indiscutible**		**indisputable**
	adj		El compromiso de Nueva Zelanda para con la familia es indiscutible.
	[ĩn̪.dis.ku.ˈti.βle]		-New Zealand's commitment to the family is indisputable.
8116	**melodramático**		**melodramatic**
	adj		Era demasiado melodramático y las heroínas son bidimensionales.
	[me.lo.ðra.ˈma.ti.ko]		-It was too melodramatic and his heroines are so two-dimensional.
8117	**novedoso**		**novel**
	adj		Alojamiento con spa, qué novedoso.
	[no.βe.ˈðo.so]		-A lodge with a spa, how novel.
8118	**contagiar**		**infect**
	vb		Vas a contagiar a todos.
	[kõn̪.ta.ˈxjar]		-You're going to infect everybody.
8119	**triplicar**		**triple**
	vb		Puede triplicar su inversión revendiendo armas de fuego en México.
	[trip̚.li.ˈkar]		-He can triple his investment by reselling firearms in Mexico.
8120	**reabrir**		**reopen**
	vb		Esto obligó a las autoridades a reabrir el procedimiento de expropiación.
	[re.a.ˈβrir]		-This forced the authorities to reopen the expropriation procedure.
8121	**hispano**		**Hispanic; Hispanic**
	adj; m		Esas medidas buscan, claramente, limitar el voto hispano.
	[is.ˈpa.no]		-These measures are clearly intended to limit the Hispanic vote.
8122	**espinal**		**spinal**
	adj		Tiene una fractura espinal y hemorragia interna severa.
	[ɛs.pi.ˈnal]		-She's got a spinal fracture and massive internal bleeding.
8123	**subsuelo**		**subsoil**

m
[suβ.ˈswe.lo]

En los demás casos, las riquezas del subsuelo son propiedad de la nación.
-In other cases, the subsoil resources belonged to the nation.

8124 **discapacidad**

f
[dis.ka.pa.si.ˈðað]

disability

Se reconocen el primer, segundo y tercer grado de discapacidad.
-First, second and third degrees of disability are recognized.

8125 **planetario**

adj; m
[pla.nɛ.ˈta.rjo]

planetary; planetarium

No puedo creer que recurran al bombardeo planetario.
-I can't believe they'd resort to planetary bombardment.

8126 **pediatra**

m/f
[pe.ˈðja.tra]

pediatrician

Entonces la llevaré a su pediatra.
-Then I'll take her to her pediatrician.

8127 **televidente**

m/f
[te.le.βi.ˈðɛ̃n̪.te]

viewer

Este televidente hace acusaciones muy serias.
-This viewer is making some pretty serious allegations.

8128 **fatigar**

vb
[fa.ti.ˈɣar]

exhaust

¿Cómo va a fatigarlo un afeitado?
-How can a shave tire him?

8129 **exceptuar**

vb
[ɛk.sep̚.ˈtwar]

exclude

No quiero exceptuar productos que en realidad podrían cumplir los requisitos.
-I don't want to exempt products which in reality could meet the requirements.

8130 **astrónomo**

m
[as.ˈtro.no.mo]

astronomer

Este efecto fue descubierto por el astrónomo alemán Carl Pulfrich.
-This effect was discovered by the German astronomer Carl Pulfrich.

8131 **lentejuela**

f
[lɛ̃n̪.te.ˈxwe.la]

sequin

Sí, y no te dejes ni una lentejuela.
-Yes, and do not leave out a sequin.

8132 **frac**

m
[ˈfrak]

tuxedo

No voy a ponerme una bufanda con el frac.
-I'm not wearing a scarf with a tuxedo.

8133 **extinguir**

vb
[ɛks.tĩŋ.ˈgir]

extinguish

Aunque moramos en este mundo, solo vivimos para extinguir la luz.
-Though we walk in this world, we live only to extinguish the light.

8134 **féretro**

m
[ˈfɛ.rɛ.tro]

coffin

Hay mucho tiempo para llenar otro féretro mañana.
-There's plenty of time to fill another coffin tomorrow.

8135 **indagar**

vb
[ĩn̪.da.ˈɣar]

investigate

Tenemos que indagar en el problema juntos.
-We have to investigate the problem together.

8136 **destierro**

m
[dɛs.ˈtjɛ.ro]

exile

Tu destierro parece algo más cómodo de lo que recuerdo.
-Your exile seems a bit more comfortable than I remember.

8137 **peldaño**

m
[pɛl̪.ˈda.ɲo]

step

Miren, el tercer peldaño está muy suelto.
-Look, the third step is very loose.

8138 **reconfortar**

comfort

vb
[re.kõɱ.for.ˈtar]

No sabía a quien de los dos reconfortar.
-I didn't know which one of us to comfort.

8139 ganadero — **farmer**

m
[ga.na.ˈðɛ.ro]

Nunca serás un ganadero de vacas.
-You'll never be a dairy farmer.

8140 aplastante — **overwhelming**

adj
[ap̚.las.ˈtãn̪.te]

Una mayoría aplastante de Estados comparten este punto de vista.
-An overwhelming majority of states share this view.

8141 venidero — **coming**

adj
[be.ni.ˈðe.ro]

El año venidero será fundamental para el desarrollo.
-The coming year is crucial in terms of development.

8142 trópico — **tropic; tropic**

adj; m
[ˈtro.pi.ko]

Otro huracán se dirige al trópico.
-Another hurricane is headed for the tropics.

8143 causante — **responsible; cause**

adj; m
[kau̯.ˈsãn̪.te]

Todos sabemos quién fue el causante de la violencia.
-We all know who caused the violence.

8144 idealismo — **idealism**

m
[i.ðe.a.ˈliṣ.mo]

Dejamos nuestro idealismo en el taxi, espero.
-We left our idealism in the taxi, I hope.

8145 lenteja — **lentil**

f
[lẽn̪.ˈte.xa]

¡Había una lenteja en tu vientre!
-There was a lentil on your belly!

8146 tez — **complexion**

f
[ˈtes]

No estoy seguro que este tono combine con mi tez.
-I'm not sure this shade matches my complexion.

8147 franela — **flannel**

f
[fra.ˈne.la]

Es la misma franela roja.
-It's the same red flannel.

8148 envoltorio — **wrapper**

m
[ẽm.bol̩.ˈto.rjo]

El envoltorio se veía igual a lo que había adentro.
-The wrapper looked like what was inside.

8149 cojear — **limp**

vb
[ko.xe.ˈar]

Hace días que no lo veo cojear.
-I haven't seen him limp in days.

8150 perdurar — **endure**

vb
[pɛr.ðu.ˈrar]

Nuestros corazones están rotos, pero nuestra fe debe perdurar.
-Our hearts may be broken, but our faith must endure.

8151 desocupado — **unoccupied**

adj
[de.so.ku.ˈpa.ðo]

Necesito una habitación en un piso desocupado.
-I need a room on an unoccupied floor.

8152 pectoral — **chest; chest**

adj; m
[pek̚.to.ˈral]

Eva, ponle un tubo pectoral en la izquierda.
-Eva, place a chest tube on the left.

8153 manzanilla — **chamomile**

f
[mãn.sa.ˈni.ja]

Dice manzanilla pero huele a menta.
-It says chamomile, but it smells like peppermint.

8154 atajo — **shortcut**

m
[a.ˈta.xo]
Tomó un atajo a través del bosque.
-He took a shortcut through the forest.

8155 **imperfecto**
adj
[ĩm.pɛr.ˈfek̚.to]
imperfect
No importa cuan imperfecto resultó ser ese héroe.
-No matter how imperfect that hero turned out to be.

8156 **diócesis**
f
[ˈdjo.se.sis]
diocese
La diócesis presentó una moción de sobreseimiento.
-The diocese has filed the motion to dismiss.

8157 **imaginativo**
adj
[i.ma.xi.na.ˈti.βo]
imaginative
Quiero que sea imaginativo y original.
-I want it to be imaginative and original.

8158 **infrarrojo**
adj
[ĩm.fra.ˈro.xo]
infrared
Añadiré eso a su trazado infrarrojo.
-I'll add that to your infrared layout.

8159 **contradecir**
vb
[kõn̪.tra.ðe.ˈsir]
contradict
Cómo te atreves a contradecir a tu padre.
-How dare you contradict your father.

8160 **manjar**
m
[mãŋ.ˈxar]
delicacy
Un manjar de tamaño extra grande.
-A delicacy in size extra large.

8161 **ajuar**
m
[a.ˈxwar]
trousseau
Está trabajando conmigo en el ajuar.
-She is working with me on the trousseau.

8162 **meseta**
f
[me.ˈsɛ.ta]
plateau
Pensamos que están en la meseta.
-We think that they are in the plateau.

8163 **inepto**
adj
[i.ˈnep̚.to]
inept
Admito que es algo inepto socialmente.
-I will admit he is somewhat socially inept.

8164 **magnesio**
m
[maɣ.ˈne.sjo]
magnesium
Quitó la mitad del magnesio del pedernal.
-He shaved half the magnesium off the flint.

8165 **brasa**
f
[ˈbra.sa]
ember
Hay una brasa ardiendo detrás de ti.
-There is a burning ember behind you.

8166 **concluyente**
adj
[kõŋ.klu.ˈɟẽn̪.te]
conclusive
Necesitaré una muestra para tener un resultado concluyente.
-I'll need a sample to get a conclusive result.

8167 **malicioso**
adj
[ma.li.ˈsjo.so]
malicious
Fuimos víctimas de un ataque malicioso.
-We were the victim of a malicious hack.

8168 **servil**
adj
[sɛr.ˈβil]
servile
Querían que fuese inofensivo y servil.
-They wanted him to be harmless and servile.

8169 **enrollar**
vb
[ẽn.ro.ˈʝar]
roll
Bueno, supongo que iré a enrollar calcetines.
-Well, I guess I'll go roll socks.

8170 **irritación**
irritation

		f
		[i.ri.ta.ˈsjõn]

Los efectos frecuentes incluyen dolor, quemazón, irritación o enrojecimiento.
-Common effects include pain, burning, irritation or redness.

8171 cablear — **wire**
vb
[ka.βle.ˈar]
Van a cablear el mundo entero.
-They'll wire the whole world.

8172 verruga — **wart**
f
[bɛ.ˈru.ɣa]
Cubra la verruga con un vendaje para evitar su propagación.
-Cover the wart with a bandage to prevent it from spreading.

8173 conmemorar — **commemorate**
vb
[kõm.me.mo.ˈrar]
Podemos conmemorar este momento con una foto.
-We can commemorate this moment in a photo.

8174 domiciliario — **home**
adj
[do.mi.si.ˈlja.rjo]
Aún tienes fisioterapia, y cuidado domiciliario.
-You've still got physical therapy, and home care.

8175 sátira — **satire**
f
[ˈsa.ti.ra]
Solo puedo describirlo como una sátira de la vida real.
-This I can describe only as real-life satire.

8176 neutrón — **neutron**
f
[neu̯.ˈtrõn]
Para empezar la reacción en cadena, solo necesitamos un neutrón.
-To start the chain reaction, all we need is one neutron.

8177 concretar — **specify**
vb
[kõŋ.krɛ.ˈtar]
La reforma también fue la ocasión para concretar ciertos aspectos.
-The reform was also the occasion to specify certain aspects.

8178 similitud — **similarity**
f
[si.mi.li.ˈtuð]
Hay una gran similitud entre las víctimas.
-There's a terrible similarity about all the victims.

8179 cacho — **piece**
m
[ˈka.tʃo]
Me siento como un cacho de carne en esta cosa.
-I feel like a piece of meat in this thing.

8180 emisor — **sender; emitting**
m; adj
[e.mi.ˈsor]
Esta pantalla muestra las conexiones entre el emisor y el receptor.
-This screen displays the connections between the sender and the receiver.

8181 beneficioso — **beneficial**
adj
[be.ne.fi.ˈsjo.so]
Este arreglo demostró ser mutuamente beneficioso.
-This arrangement has proven to be mutually beneficial.

8182 transcurrir — **elapse**
vb
[trãns.ku.ˈrir]
Hasta que se cumpla esta condición puede transcurrir mucho tiempo.
-Until this criterion is satisfied, a long time may elapse.

8183 timonel — **helmsperson**
m/f
[ti.mo.ˈnɛl]
Él es el timonel de este barco pesquero.
-He is the helmsman of this fishing boat.

8184 atormentado — **tormented**
adj
[a.tor.mẽn̪.ˈta.ðo]
El tímido soldado era atormentado por terribles pesadillas.
-The timid soldier was tormented by terrible nightmares.

8185 percusión — **percussion**
f
[pɛr.ku.ˈsjõn]
Los pulmones suenan huecos a la percusión porque están llenos de aire.
-Lungs sound hollow on percussion because they are filled with air.

8186	**crisma**	**neck (coll)**
	f	Espero que no se rompa la crisma.
	[ˈkris̱.ma]	-I hope she doesn't break her neck.
8187	**hidráulico**	**hydraulic**
	adj	Mi gato hidráulico no resistió tanta presión.
	[i.ˈðɾaṷ.li.ko]	-My hydraulic jack didn't stand up to the pressure.
8188	**criadero**	**hatchery**
	m	Los mineros deben haber entrado en el criadero.
	[krja.ˈðɛ.ro]	-Miners must have broken into the hatchery.
8189	**catecismo**	**Catechism**
	m	Aprender el catecismo requiere gran diligencia.
	[ka.te.ˈsis̱.mo]	-To learn your catechism requires great diligence.
8190	**objetividad**	**objectivity**
	f	Lo importante es informar con objetividad.
	[oβ.xɛ.ti.βi.ˈðað]	-The important thing is to report with objectivity.
8191	**cancillería**	**chancellery**
	f	Llévate a este pequeñajo a la cancillería.
	[kãn.si.ʝɛ.ˈri.a]	-Take this little guy to the chancellery.
8192	**reuma**	**rheumatism**
	m	No, no padezco de reuma.
	[ˈreṷ.ma]	-No, I'm not troubled with rheumatism.
8193	**cesárea**	**C-section**
	f	Te dije que no quería una cesárea.
	[se.ˈsa.re.a]	-I told you I didn't want a C-section.
8194	**recolector**	**collector**
	m	En realidad hay un recolector de basura a un lado.
	[re.ko.lek̚.ˈtor]	-There's actually a debris collector on the side.
8195	**yugular**	**jugular**
	adj	Cuando estés aquí, vas a la yugular.
	[ɟʝu.ɣu.ˈlar]	-When you're here, you go for the jugular.
8196	**nebuloso**	**foggy**
	adj	Desapareció lentamente en el nebuloso bosque.
	[ne.βu.ˈlo.so]	-She slowly disappeared into the foggy forest.
8197	**oficinista**	**office worker**
	m/f	Eres el oficinista que puede distorsionar el espacio y tiempo.
	[o.fi.si.ˈnis.ta]	-You are the office worker who can bend space and time.
8198	**imaginable**	**imaginable**
	adj	Hemos intentado analizarla, usando todo dispositivo imaginable.
	[i.ma.xi.ˈna.βle]	-We've tried analyzing it, using every device imaginable.
8199	**desequilibrar**	**unbalance**
	vb	Su peso podría desequilibrar todo.
	[de.se.ki.li.ˈβrar]	-His weight could unbalance everything.
8200	**inestabilidad**	**instability**
	f	Todo esto produjo cierta sensación de inestabilidad.
	[i.nɛs.ta.βi.li.ˈðað]	-All this led to a certain feeling of instability.
8201	**retroceso**	**setback**
	m	No quiero arriesgarnos a un retroceso.
	[rɛ.tro.ˈse.so]	-I don't want to risk a setback.

8202	**innovación**	**innovation**
	f	Necesitan innovación en nuestros procedimientos, pero tampoco bastará.
	[ĩn.no.βa.ˈsjõn]	-They need innovation in our procedures, but it will not be enough.
8203	**monogamia**	**monogamy**
	f	La ley reconoce la monogamia y la poligamia.
	[mo.no.ˈɣa.mja]	-The law recognizes monogamy and polygamy.
8204	**nailon**	**nylon**
	m	Este nailon no deja pasar el aire.
	[ˈnai̯.lõn]	-You can't get much air through this nylon.
8205	**contraatacar**	**fight back**
	vb	Quiere mantenernos débiles para que nadie pueda contraatacar.
	[kõn.tra.a.ta.ˈkar]	-He wants to keep us weak so no one can fight back.
8206	**instrumental**	**instrumental; instrument**
	adj; m	Tengo el instrumental preciso para ayudarle.
	[ĩns.tru.mẽn.ˈtal]	-I have the very instrument to help you.
8207	**masticar**	**chew**
	vb	Por eso son difíciles de masticar.
	[mas.ti.ˈkar]	-That's why they're so hard to chew.
8208	**laptop**	**laptop**
	f	Dejé la laptop en el apartamento.
	[lap̚.ˈtop]	-I left my laptop back at the apartment.
8209	**riego**	**irrigation**
	m	La salinización de los suelos es resultado de un riego inapropiado.
	[ˈrje.ɣo]	-Soil salinization results from improper irrigation.
8210	**clamor**	**cry**
	m	Nuestro clamor colectivo pidiendo pan para quienes padecen hambre no puede quedar sin respuesta.
	[kla.ˈmor]	-Our common cry for bread on behalf of all who are suffering from hunger must not fail to be heard.
8211	**canibalismo**	**cannibalism**
	m	No tendremos que recurrir al canibalismo.
	[ka.ni.βa.ˈliṣ.mo]	-We will not have to resort to cannibalism.
8212	**beneficiario**	**beneficiary**
	m	Pensaba que su beneficiario tendría un motivo potencial.
	[be.ne.fi.ˈsja.rjo]	-I was thinking your beneficiary would have a potential motive.
8213	**irrefutable**	**irrefutable**
	adj	Su lógica parece irrefutable, pero...
	[i.re.fu.ˈta.βle]	-Your logic seems irrefutable, but...
8214	**localidad**	**town**
	f	El olor se extendió hasta las casas cercanas a la localidad de Duhayrah.
	[lo.ka.li.ˈðað]	-The smell spread to the homes near Duhayrah town.
8215	**oportunista**	**opportunistic; opportunist**
	adj; m/f	Fue un interno oportunista intentando conseguir dinero.
	[o.por.tu.ˈnis.ta]	-It was some opportunistic intern trying to get a payday.
8216	**predestinar**	**predestine**
	vb	Esta actividad puede predestinar tu futuro.
	[pre.ðɛs.ti.ˈnar]	-This activity can predestine your future.
8217	**ultravioleta**	**ultraviolet**

adj
[ul̪.tra.ˈβjo.ˈlɛ.ta]
No emiten luces ultravioleta ni infrarrojas.
-They do not emit ultraviolet or infrared light.

8218 **horquilla** — **hairpin**
f
[or.ˈki.ja]
Francamente, no necesito otra horquilla.
-Frankly, I don't need another hairpin.

8219 **enfriamiento** — **cooling**
m
[ẽm.frja.ˈmjẽn̪.to]
En otros casos, el enfriamiento mediante aire no está restringido.
-In other cases cooling air is not restricted.

8220 **minería** — **mining**
f
[mi.nɛ.ˈri.a]
Mi colega trabajaba en la minería.
-My colleague worked in mining.

8221 **tacho** — **container (LA)**
m
[ˈta.tʃo]
Agarra un tacho y limpia arriba.
-Get a bucket and clean up there.

8222 **alarde** — **boast**
m
[a.ˈlar.ðe]
Pero lo mío no es solo un alarde.
-But mine is not just boasting.

8223 **manso** — **tame**
adj
[ˈmãn.so]
Algunas personas dicen que el oso es manso.
-Some people say the bear is tame.

8224 **exceder** — **exceed**
vb
[ɛk.se.ˈðɛr]
El trabajo semanal no podrá exceder las treinta horas.
-The working week must not exceed thirty hours.

8225 **laca** — **lacquer**
f
[ˈla.ka]
Normalmente se reconocen por su aroma a disolvente o laca.
-They can usually be recognized by their solvent or lacquer aromas.

8226 **vibrante** — **vibrant**
adj
[bi.ˈβrãn̪.te]
Podría encontrarte algo vibrante y alegre para la hacienda.
-I could find you something vibrant and cheerful for the estate.

8227 **escama** — **scale**
f
[ɛs.ˈka.ma]
Es una escama de pterodáctilo de verdad.
-This is a real pterodactyl scale.

8228 **asimismo** — **also**
adv
[a.si.ˈmis̝.mo]
Necesitamos asimismo pensar más a escala regional.
-We also need to think more in terms of regions.

8229 **festejo** — **feast**
m
[fɛs.ˈte.xo]
Como sea, es un festejo.
-Either way, it's a feast.

8230 **rebotar** — **bounce**
vb
[re.βo.ˈtar]
Ahora este chico puede rebotar una pelota de fútbol en su cabeza.
-Now, this boy can bounce a soccer ball on his head.

8231 **casaca** — **coat**
f [ka.ˈsa.ka]
Oí que llevabas la casaca azul. -I heard you were wearing the blue coat.

8232 **libreto** — **script**
m
[li.ˈβrɛ.to]
Debe atenerse al libreto, Gobernadora.
-You must stick to the script, Governor.

8233 **impropio** — **inappropriate**

		adj	

adj
[ĩm.ˈpro.pjo]

Nada en esta casa es impropio.
-Nothing in this house is inappropriate.

8234 movilidad — **mobility**

f
[mo.βi.li.ˈðað]

Tiene una buena probabilidad de recuperar la movilidad.
-He's got a good chance of recovering mobility.

8235 radioactividad — **radioactivity**

f
[ra.ðjo.akˈ.ti.βi.ˈðað]

Es cierto que todos estamos bañados en radioactividad natural.
-It is true to say that we are all bathed in natural radioactivity.

8236 estructural — **structural**

adj
[es.trukˈ.tu.ˈral]

Tomemos como ejemplo la política estructural y de cohesión.
-Let us take the structural and cohesion policy as an example.

8237 pasa — **raisin**

f
[ˈpa.sa]

Tienes cuatro galletas y una pasa.
-You have four crackers and a raisin.

8238 oval — **oval**

adj
[o.ˈβal]

Servirlos en la mesita oval de cobre.
-Serve it in the copper oval tableside.

8239 imperialista — **imperialistic; imperialist**

adj; m/f
[ĩm.pɛ.rja.ˈlis.ta]

Están luchando para vencer al sistema imperialista.
-They are fighting to defeat the imperialist system.

8240 casto — **chaste**

adj
[ˈkas.to]

No me digas que has sido casto.
-Don't tell me you've been chaste.

8241 sacerdocio — **priesthood**

m
[sa.sɛr.ˈðo.sjo]

Estoy aprendiendo mucho sobre el sacerdocio, Don.
-I'm learning a lot about the priesthood, Don.

8242 dolencia — **disease**

f
[do.ˈlɛ̃n.sja]

No murió de una dolencia respiratoria.
-He didn't die of any breathing disease.

8243 remolcador — **tugboat**

m
[re.mol.ka.ˈðor]

No quieres pasar el resto de tu vida en un remolcador.
-You don't want to spend the rest of your life on a tugboat.

8244 mediador — **mediator**

m
[me.ðja.ˈðor]

Me pidió que actuara como mediador imparcial.
-He asked me to act as an impartial mediator.

8245 desarme — **disarmament**

m
[de.ˈsar.me]

Es indudable que este desarme necesita tiempo.
-There is no doubt that such disarmament will take time.

8246 oca — **goose**

f
[ˈo.ka]

Es una oca, salta a la vista.
-It's a goose, as anyone can plainly see.

8247 filial — **subsidiary; filial**

f; adj
[fi.ˈljal]

Nos comunicamos frecuentemente con nuestra filial en Kiev.
-We frequently communicate with our branch in Kiev.

8248 inexperto — **inexperienced**

adj
[i.nɛks.ˈpɛr.to]

Es un poco inexperto, quizás.
-He's a little inexperienced, maybe.

8249 unanimidad — **unanimity**

	f	Esta unanimidad de opinión ya no existe.
	[u.na.ni.mi.ˈðað]	-This unanimity of opinion no longer exists.
8250	**insolación**	**sunstroke**
	f	Eso que habla es la insolación.
	[ĭn.so.la.ˈsjõn]	-That's the sunstroke talking.
8251	**reparo**	**objection**
	m	Mi grupo político no alberga reparo alguno en cuanto a la energía nuclear.
	[re.ˈpa.ro]	-My group has no objection in principle to nuclear energy.
8252	**cutis**	**skin**
	m	Tenían el cutis malo y usaban mucho maquillaje.
	[ˈku.tis]	-They had bad skin and wore too much makeup.
8253	**mecenas**	**patron**
	m/f	No es fácil ser un mecenas del arte.
	[me.ˈse.nas]	-Not easy being a patron of the arts.
8254	**medicar**	**medicate**
	vb	No puedes medicar a una persona y marcharte a los cinco minutos.
	[me.ði.ˈkar]	-You can't just medicate someone and leave in five minutes.
8255	**babear**	**drool**
	vb	Intente no babear sobre los mandos.
	[ba.βe.ˈar]	-Try not to drool on the controls.
8256	**manzano**	**apple tree**
	m	Teníamos un manzano en el patio.
	[mãn.ˈsa.no]	-We had an apple tree in the backyard.
8257	**procedencia**	**origin**
	f	Los fondos sean de procedencia lícita.
	[pro.se.ˈðɛ̃n.sja]	-The funds are legal in origin.
8258	**aparear**	**mate**
	vb	Solo la morsa más fuerte se podrá aparear.
	[a.pa.re.ˈar]	-Only the strongest walrus will be able to mate.
8259	**polémico**	**controversial**
	adj	El proyecto será tan difícil como polémico.
	[po.ˈle.mi.ko]	-The project will be as difficult as it will be controversial.
8260	**geología**	**geology**
	f	Estudié geología un par de años.
	[xe.o.lo.ˈxi.a]	-I studied geology for a couple of years.
8261	**innegable**	**undeniable**
	adj	Eso siempre existe y es innegable.
	[ĭn.ne.ˈɣa.βle]	-That's always there and it's undeniable.
8262	**ochocientos**	**eight hundred**
	num	La gente paga setecientos u ochocientos dólares por un pájaro que habla.
	[o.ʧo.ˈsjɛ̃n̪.tos]	-People will pay seven or eight hundred bucks for a talking bird.
8263	**camada**	**litter**
	f	De esta camada nacieron cuatro machos y una hembra.
	[ka.ˈma.ða]	-There are four males and one female in this litter.
8264	**arribar**	**arrive**
	vb	Eres el último de nuestros pacientes en arribar.
	[a.ri.ˈβar]	-You're the last of our patients to arrive.

8265	**enganche**	**coupling**
	m	Cualquier enganche mecánico debe ir acompañado por unas
	[ɛ̃ŋ.ˈgãn̪.tʃe]	instrucciones de empleo facilitadas por el fabricante del mismo.
		-All mechanical couplings must be accompanied by the manufacturer's instructions for use.

8266	**alegación**	**allegation**
	f	El tribunal considera acertada dicha alegación.
	[a.le.ɣa.ˈsjõn]	-The court considered that allegation to be correct.

8267	**integrado**	**integrated**
	adj	Se han integrado de vuelta en la comunidad.
	[ĩn̪.te.ˈɣra.ðo]	-They have been integrated back into the community.

8268	**sicario**	**hitman**
	m	Un sicario llamaría demasiado la atención.
	[si.ˈka.rjo]	-A hitman would draw too much attention.

8269	**hipotermia**	**hypothermia**
	f	Nadie resistiría este grado de hipotermia.
	[i.po.ˈtɛr.mja]	-No one could withstand this degree of hypothermia.

8270	**desempeñar**	**perform**
	vb	No hay capacidad permanente para desempeñar esa función.
	[de.sẽm.pe.ˈɲar]	-There is no standing capacity to perform this function.

8271	**epiléptico**	**epileptic; epileptic**
	adj; m	Tu padre tuvo otro ataque epiléptico.
	[e.pi.ˈlep̚.ti.ko]	-Your father has had another epileptic fit.

8272	**austriaco**	**Austrian; Austrian person**
	adj; m	El tribunal austriaco había formulado dos preguntas.
	[au̯s.ˈtrja.ko]	-The Austrian court submitted two questions.

8273	**canon**	**canon**
	m	El canon musical evoluciona lentamente.
	[ˈka.nõn]	-The musical canon evolves slowly.

8274	**canoa**	**canoe**
	f	Me gustaría ir en canoa también.
	[ka.ˈno.a]	-I'd like to go canoeing too.

8275	**calvario**	**ordeal (coll)**
	m	No pareces haberte recuperado de tu calvario.
	[kal.ˈβa.rjo]	-You do not seem to have recovered from your ordeal.

8276	**agüero**	**omen**
	m	No dije que fuera de buen agüero.
	[a.ˈɣwɛ.ro]	-I didn't say it was a good omen.

8277	**perito**	**expert; expert**
	m/f; adj	A cada caso se asigna un perito supervisor.
	[pɛ.ˈri.to]	-An expert supervisor is assigned to each case.

8278	**consistencia**	**consistency**
	f	La consistencia es el último refugio del poco imaginativo.
	[kõn.sis.ˈtẽn.sja]	-Consistency is the last refuge of the unimaginative.

8279	**ratero**	**pickpocket**
	m	Shakespeare dijo que la víctima era un ratero.
	[ra.ˈtɛ.ro]	-Shakespeare said the victim was a pickpocket.

8280	**arrodillar(se)**	**kneel**

	vb	No te debes arrodillar ante nadie.
	[a.ro.ði.ˈxar]	-You mustn't kneel down for anybody.
8281	**enjaular**	**cage**
	vb	Tengo que enjaular a este gato.
	[ẽŋ.xau̯.ˈlar]	-I have to cage this cat.
8282	**setecientos**	**seven hundred**
	num	Su número no excederá de setecientos cincuenta.
	[se.te.ˈsjẽn̪.tos]	-They shall not exceed seven hundred and fifty in number.
8283	**apreciación**	**appreciation**
	f	No sé cómo expresar mi apreciación.
	[a.pre.sja.ˈsjõn]	-I don't know how to express my appreciation.
8284	**autobiografía**	**autobiography**
	f	Vamos a trabajar en mi autobiografía.
	[au̯.to.βjo.ɣra.ˈfi.a]	-We are going to work in my autobiography.
8285	**traste**	**fret**
	m	Vale, este traste está roto.
	[ˈtras.te]	-Okay, this fret is cracked.
8286	**sutileza**	**subtlety**
	f	Supongo que debemos darte las gracias por esa sutileza jurídica.
	[su.ti.ˈle.sa]	-I presume we have you to thank for that legal subtlety.
8287	**podrir**	**rot**
	vb	Yo habría dejado que te pudrieras allí.
	[po.ˈðrir]	-I'd have left you there to rot.
8288	**aderezar**	**season**
	vb	Tienes que aderezar la ensalada.
	[a.ðɛ.re.ˈsar]	-You have to season the salad.
8289	**balancear(se)**	**balance**
	vb	Ni siquiera sé balancear mi chequera.
	[ba.lãn.se.ˈar]	-I don't even know how to balance a checkbook.
8290	**obrar**	**act**
	vb	Debemos obrar con rapidez y decisión.
	[o.ˈβrar]	-We must act rapidly and with resolve.
8291	**cala**	**cove**
	f	Hay una trucha que vive en esta cala.
	[ˈka.la]	-There's a trout living in this cove.
8292	**filosófico**	**philosophical**
	adj	No sabía que estaba siendo filosófico.
	[fi.lo.ˈso.fi.ko]	-I didn't know I was being philosophical.
8293	**prestigioso**	**prestigious**
	adj	Era prestigioso ser elegido para mi desfile.
	[pres.ti.ˈxjo.so]	-It was prestigious to be selected for my show.
8294	**desplazamiento**	**displacement**
	m	El desplazamiento acabó con sus medios de vida.
	[des.pla.sa.ˈmjẽn̪.to]	-Their means of livelihood has been destroyed by the displacement.
8295	**coraza**	**shell**
	f	Pon una coraza entre tú y el resto de la humanidad.
	[ko.ˈra.sa]	-Put a shell between yourself and the rest of humanity.
8296	**discordia**	**discord**

f

[dis.ˈkor.ðja]

Quiero sofocar cualquier rumor de discordia.
-I want to put to rest any rumor of discord.

| 8297 | **alfabético** | **alphabetical** |

adj

[al.fa.ˈβɛ.ti.ko]

Quiero una lista alfabética de licencias, permisos y registros ordenada por nombre o tipo.
-I want an alphabetical listing of licenses, permits, and registrations by name or type.

| 8298 | **progresista** | **progressive; progressive** |

adj; m/f

[pro.ɣre.ˈsis.ta]

Es un colegio rural y son muy progresistas.
-It's a farm college, and they're very progressive.

| 8299 | **monotonía** | **monotony** |

f

[mo.no.to.ˈni.a]

La monotonía de esa frase tiene cierto encanto.
-The monotony of this sentence has the grace.

| 8300 | **artimaña** | **trick** |

f

[ar.ti.ˈma.ɲa]

Su artimaña era sembrar la duda entre sus clientes.
-Her trick was to create doubt in a client's mind.

| 8301 | **irrigación** | **irrigation** |

f

[i.ri.ɣa.ˈsjõn]

Tenemos que promover la agricultura, incluida la irrigación.
-We have to promote agriculture, including irrigation.

| 8302 | **fotocopiar** | **photocopy** |

vb

[fo.to.ko.ˈpjar]

Tienen que fotocopiar textos de libros.
-You have to photocopy texts from books.

| 8303 | **suspirar** | **sigh** |

vb

[sus.pi.ˈrar]

Hace rato que perdí la energía para suspirar.
-I have long lost the energy to sigh.

| 8304 | **desenlace** | **outcome** |

m

[de.sɛ̃n.ˈla.se]

Nunca hubo ninguna duda del desenlace.
-There was never any doubt in the outcome.

| 8305 | **ardid** | **scheme** |

m

[ar.ˈðið]

Son todos una fachada para su ardid.
-They are all a facade for his scheme.

| 8306 | **rancio** | **rancid** |

adj

[ˈrãn.sjo]

Liz intenta evitar ese olor a rancio.
-Liz is trying to avoid that rancid smell.

| 8307 | **caballeroso** | **gentlemanly** |

adj

[ka.βa.ʝɛ.ˈro.so]

Fue muy caballeroso de tu parte.
-That was very gentlemanly of you.

| 8308 | **suministrar** | **supply** |

vb

[su.mi.nis.ˈtrar]

Necesitamos suministrar una infraestructura de emergencia con gran rapidez.
-We need to be able to supply very rapidly an emergency infrastructure.

| 8309 | **hospitalizar** | **hospitalize** |

vb

[os.pi.ta.li.ˈsar]

Me van a hospitalizar.
-They're going to hospitalize me.

| 8310 | **legalidad** | **legality** |

f

[le.ɣa.li.ˈðað]

Se trata del principio de legalidad.
-This is the principle of legality.

| 8311 | **bellaco** | **coward** |

	adj	¡Me llamaron bellaco delante de María!
	[be.ˈja.ko]	-I was called a coward in front of Maria!
8312	**sanción**	**sanction**
	f	La sanción solo puede aplicarse con consentimiento del médico.
	[sãn.ˈsjõn]	-The sanction may only be applied with the doctor's advice.
8313	**autismo**	**autism**
	m	La causa del autismo todavía se desconoce.
	[au̯.ˈtiş.mo]	-The cause of autism is yet to be known.
8314	**incalculable**	**incalculable**
	adj	El costo humano de la guerra es incalculable.
	[ĩŋ.kal.ku.ˈla.βle]	-The human cost of war is incalculable.
8315	**artesanía**	**craftwork**
	f	Su gastronomía, artesanía y urbanismo se ven determinados por su
	[ar.te.sa.ˈni.a]	glorioso pasado histórico.
		-The gastronomy, craftwork and urban planning are influenced by its
		glorious past.
8316	**emancipación**	**emancipation**
	f	Lo siento, pero su emancipación ha sido denegada.
	[e.mãn.si.pa.ˈsjõn]	-I'm sorry, but his emancipation is denied.
8317	**embolia**	**embolism**
	f	Me temo que usted ha sufrido una embolia esquizoide.
	[ẽm.ˈbo.lja]	-I'm afraid you're suffering a schizoid embolism.
8318	**finlandés**	**Finnish; Finnish person**
	adj; m	Pronto me voy al frente finlandés.
	[fĩn.lãn̪.ˈdes]	-Soon I'm off to the Finnish front.
8319	**mercadeo**	**marketing**
	m	Estamos hablando de estrategias de mercadeo.
	[mɛr.ka.ˈðe.o]	-We're talking about marketing strategies.
8320	**autista**	**autistic; autistic person**
	adj; m/f	Tiene un hijo autista al que adora completamente.
	[au̯.ˈtis.ta]	-He's got this autistic son that he absolutely adores.
8321	**finalidad**	**purpose**
	f	La finalidad de esa disposición es acelerar el procedimiento.
	[fi.na.li.ˈðað]	-The purpose of that provision is to speed up the procedure.
8322	**corretear**	**run around**
	vb	Tienen toda la sala para corretear.
	[ko.rɛ.te.ˈar]	-You got the whole room to run around in.
8323	**recambio**	**replacement**
	m	Este es el nuevo recambio de Pagani.
	[re.ˈkãm.bjo]	-This is the new replacement for it from Pagani.
8324	**forzoso**	**forced**
	adj	El matrimonio de menores de edad y forzoso ya es ilegal en Nueva
	[for.ˈso.so]	Zelanda.
		-Underage and forced marriage is already illegal in New Zealand.
8325	**envoltura**	**wrapper**
	f	Encontré una envoltura de dulce vacía en el mostrador.
	[ẽm.bol̪.ˈtu.ra]	-I found an empty dessert wrapper on the counter.
8326	**fragata**	**frigate**

	f	Llamaré para informarte sobre la fragata.
	[fra.ˈɣa.ta]	-I'll call to inform you about the frigate.
8327	**linchamiento**	**lynching**
	m	No seas parte de un linchamiento.
	[lĩn̯.ʧa.ˈmjẽn̯.to]	-Don't be part of a lynching.
8328	**artilugio**	**gadget**
	m	Es un artilugio aparatoso pero no le será incómodo.
	[ar.ti.ˈlu.xjo]	-It is an ostentatious gadget but you will not be uncomfortable.
8329	**ciclista**	**cyclist**
	m/f	Justo esta mañana, un ciclista me cortó el paso.
	[si.ˈklis.ta]	-Just this morning a cyclist cut me off.
8330	**simetría**	**symmetry**
	f	Personalmente, me gusta su simetría.
	[si.mɛ.ˈtri.a]	-Personally, I like the symmetry of it.
8331	**acidez**	**heartburn**
	f	Este reflujo puede causar síntomas de acidez gástrica.
	[a.ˈsi.ðes]	-Reflux may cause symptoms of heartburn.
8332	**desgaste**	**wear**
	m	El desgaste es otro problema que conduce a la necesidad de sustituir el dispositivo.
	[dɛṣ.ˈɣas.te]	-Wear is another problem that leads to the need to replace the device.
8333	**frívolo**	**frivolous**
	adj	Yo no soy un hombre frívolo.
	[ˈfri.βo.lo]	-I am not a frivolous man.
8334	**setiembre**	**September**
	m	El circuito finalizará a finales de setiembre.
	[sɛ.ˈtjẽm.bre]	-The circuit will be dying down at the end of September.
8335	**brío**	**verve**
	m	En nuestra universidad tienes que tener brío y carisma.
	[ˈbri.o]	-At our university, you have to have verve and charisma.
8336	**brincar**	**jump**
	vb	Puedes brincar en mi cama cuando gustes.
	[brĩŋ.ˈkar]	-You can jump on my mattress any time.
8337	**damisela**	**damsel**
	f	No soy una damisela en apuros que necesita ser rescatada.
	[da.mi.ˈse.la]	-I'm not some damsel in distress that needs rescuing.
8338	**encubierto**	**undercover**
	adj	Quería disculparme por mentirte mientras estaba encubierto.
	[ẽŋ.ku.ˈβjɛr.to]	-I wanted to apologize for lying to you while I was undercover.
8339	**fisura**	**fissure**
	f	Una fisura ha sido descubierta en el flanco opuesto.
	[fi.ˈsu.ra]	-A fissure has been detected on the opposite pitch.
8340	**polución**	**pollution**
	f	La polución del aire en nuestras ciudades requiere una acción inmediata.
	[po.lu.ˈsjõn]	-Air pollution in our cities requires urgent action.
8341	**globalización**	**globalization**
	f	Sin embargo, también hay desafíos asociados con la globalización.
	[glo.βa.li.sa.ˈsjõn]	-There are, however, also challenges associated with globalization.

8342	**infinidad**	**infinity**
	f	Este es el símbolo para la infinidad.
	[ĩm.fi.ni.ˈðað]	-That's the symbol for infinity.
8343	**catolicismo**	**Catholicism**
	m	Allí comenzó la mayor conversión al catolicismo de la historia.
	[ka.to.li.ˈsis̬.mo]	-There, she began the greatest conversion to Catholicism in history.
8344	**baranda**	**railing**
	f	Ponga las manos sobre la baranda que tiene enfrente.
	[ba.ˈrãn̪.da]	-Put your hands on the railing in front of you.
8345	**vigésimo**	**twentieth**
	num	Los recapitulamos en nuestro vigésimo aniversario.
	[bi.ˈxe.si.mo]	-We recalled it on our twentieth anniversary.
8346	**entrometer(se)**	**interfere**
	vb	Su intención es observarnos y entrometerse.
	[ɛ̃n̪.tro.me.ˈtɛr]	-Their intention is to observe us and meddle.
8347	**puf**	**beanbag; ugh**
	m; int	Creí que era el puf.
	[ˈpuf]	-I thought it was the beanbag.
8348	**resaltar**	**highlight**
	vb	Me gustaría resaltar algunas cosas de este ejercicio fiscal.
	[re.sal̪.ˈtar]	-I would like to highlight a few points from this financial year.
8349	**grosor**	**thickness**
	m	Tengo el grosor perfecto de la pasta.
	[gro.ˈsor]	-I've got the perfect thickness of the pasta.
8350	**desalojar**	**evict**
	vb	No pueden desalojar a las personas sin más.
	[de.sa.lo.ˈxar]	-They can't just evict people.
8351	**armazón**	**frame**
	m	El armazón de metal se está helando ahora.
	[ar.ma.ˈsõn]	-The metal frame is icing now.
8352	**caritativo**	**charitable**
	adj	Eso parece caritativo, pero es inapropiado.
	[ka.ri.ta.ˈti.βo]	-This sounds charitable but is inappropriate.
8353	**nómada**	**nomadic; Nomad**
	adj; m/f	Somos una civilización nómada de artesanos.
	[ˈno.ma.ða]	-We are a nomad civilization of artisans.
8354	**premiar**	**reward**
	vb	No vamos a premiar esta agresión.
	[pre.ˈmjar]	-We are not going to reward this aggression.
8355	**barniz**	**varnish**
	m	El barniz todavía no estaba seco.
	[ˈbar.nis]	-The varnish was not dry yet.
8356	**callado**	**quiet**
	adj	Es muy callado pero nunca se enfada.
	[ka.ˈja.ðo]	-He's very quiet, but never angry.
8357	**reprochar**	**reproach**
	vb	De momento, eso no es posible y no quiero reprochar nada a nadie.
	[re.pro.ˈtʃar]	-That is not possible at the moment, and it is not a reproach to anyone.

8358	**bobina**	**coil**
	f	Vamos a robar una bobina.
	[bo.ˈβi.na]	-We're going to steal a coil.
8359	**confidencia**	**confidence**
	f	Te dije esas cosas sobre mí en estricta confidencia.
	[kõm̩.fi.ˈðɛ̃n.sja]	-I told you those things about me in strictest confidence.
8360	**bíceps**	**biceps**
	m	Debí haber sabido que estaría aquí, trabajando esos bíceps.
	[ˈbi.seps]	-I should have known you were here buffing those biceps.
8361	**liberador**	**liberating**
	adj	Fue aterrador pero liberador a la vez.
	[li.βɛ.ra.ˈðor]	-It was terrifying, yet liberating all at the same time.
8362	**indoloro**	**painless**
	adj	Es completamente indoloro para la mayoría de la gente.
	[ĩn̩.do.ˈlo.ro]	-It's completely painless for most people.
8363	**hardware**	**hardware**
	m	Esto también es muy diferente al hardware anterior.
	[ar.ˈðwa.re]	-That, too, is quite different from previous hardware.
8364	**peinar(se)**	**comb your hair**
	vb	Puedes peinarte con las manos, así.
	[pei̯.ˈnar]	-You can just comb your hair with the hands, like that.
8365	**fardo**	**bundle**
	m	Te llevo el fardo en la bici.
	[ˈfar.ðo]	-I'll take your bundle on my bike.
8366	**paréntesis**	**parentheses**
	m	Pedí que utilizaran paréntesis, no corchetes.
	[pa.ˈrɛ̃n̩.te.sis]	-I told them to use parenthesis, not brackets.
8367	**nazismo**	**Nazism**
	m	El día 8 de mayo, Europa celebra la victoria sobre el nazismo.
	[na.ˈsis̪.mo]	-On 8 May, Europe celebrates victory over Nazism.
8368	**bioquímico**	**biochemical; biochemist**
	adj; m	Sé lo que es un bioquímico.
	[bjo.ˈki.mi.ko]	-I know what a biochemist is.
8369	**promiscuidad**	**promiscuity**
	f	Todo el mundo sabe lo peligrosa que es la promiscuidad.
	[pro.mis.kwi.ˈðað]	-Everyone knows how dangerous promiscuity is.
8370	**antisocial**	**anti-social**
	adj	El abuso de esta confianza es un acto antisocial.
	[ã̩n̩.ti.so.ˈsjal]	-An abuse of this trust is an anti-social act.
8371	**biopsia**	**biopsy**
	f	Estoy esperando los resultados de una biopsia.
	[ˈbjop.sja]	-I'm waiting for the results of a biopsy.
8372	**estereotipar**	**stereotype**
	vb	Mamá, no deberías estereotipar así a la gente.
	[ɛs.tɛ.re.o.ti.ˈpar]	-Mom, you shouldn't stereotype people like that.
8373	**contemporáneo**	**contemporary; contemporary**
	adj; m	Pero creo que tiene un barniz muy contemporáneo.
	[kõn̩.tẽm.ˈpo.ra.ne.o]	-But I think it's got a very contemporary veneer.

8374	**cazuela**	**pot**
	f	Los va metiendo dentro de la cazuela.
	[ka.ˈswe.la]	-She's putting them into the pot.
8375	**disperso**	**dispersed**
	adj	El resto ha sido disperso por todo el orbe.
	[dis.ˈpɛr.so]	-The rest have been dispersed throughout the world.
8376	**monótono**	**monotonous**
	adj	El uniforme de preso es monótono.
	[mo.ˈno.to.no]	-The uniform of a prisoner is monotonous.
8377	**conmocionar**	**shake profoundly**
	vb	Están hechas para conmocionar, provocar.
	[kõm.mo.sjo.ˈnar]	-They're meant to shock, provoke.
8378	**ímpetu**	**impetus**
	m	Necesitamos una fuerza o un ímpetu de este tipo en las regiones.
	[ˈĩm.pɛ.tu]	-We need a driving force or an impetus of this kind in the regions.
8379	**fonógrafo**	**phonograph**
	m	Enciende el fonógrafo cuando te digamos.
	[fo.ˈno.ɣra.fo]	-Turn on the phonograph when we tell you.
8380	**respirador**	**inhaling; respirator**
	adj; m	Le retiraron el respirador esta mañana.
	[rɛs.pi.ra.ˈðor]	-They took him off the respirator this morning.
8381	**crecida**	**flood**
	f	Allí el río es fantástico cuando está en crecida.
	[kre.ˈsi.ða]	-There the river is fantastic when in flood.
8382	**peligrar**	**endanger**
	vb	Si lo haces, estarás haciendo peligrar la paz mundial.
	[pe.li.ˈɣrar]	-If you do that, you'll be endangering world peace.
8383	**resfriarse**	**catch a cold**
	vbr	La gente no suele resfriarse en pleno verano.
	[rɛs.ˈfrjar.se]	-People don't usually catch a cold in midsummer.
8384	**propenso**	**prone**
	adj	Entonces sabrá que será propenso a delinquir.
	[pro.ˈpẽn.so]	-Then you know he'll be prone to delinquency himself.
8385	**analfabeto**	**illiterate; illiterate**
	adj; m	Cuando fue a prisión, era analfabeto.
	[a.nal.fa.ˈβɛ.to]	-When he went to prison, he was illiterate.
8386	**perjuicio**	**damage**
	m	Ese país ha sufrido ya un enorme perjuicio económico.
	[pɛr.ˈxwi.sjo]	-That country has already suffered enormous economic damage at this point.
8387	**pertinente**	**relevant**
	adj	La duración del servicio tampoco constituye un criterio pertinente.
	[pɛr.ti.ˈnẽn.te]	-The duration of the service is not a relevant criterion, either.
8388	**síntesis**	**synthesis**
	f	Esta cuestión se examinará en mayor detalle en la síntesis definitiva.
	[ˈsĩn.te.sis]	-That subject will be developed in the final synthesis.
8389	**reaccionario**	**reactionary; reactionary**

adj; m
[re.ak.sjo.ˈna.rjo]

Es reaccionario permitir una relación como ésta.
-It's reactionary to tolerate a relationship like this.

8390 **craneal** — **cranial**

adj
[kra.ne.ˈal]

Veamos qué tiene que decir la cavidad craneal.
-Well, let's see what the cranial cavity has to say.

8391 **disfunción** — **dysfunction**

f
[dis.fũn.ˈsjõn]

Tomaré una foto de tu disfunción.
-I'm going to take a picture of your dysfunction.

8392 **realizador** — **producer**

m
[re.a.li.sa.ˈðor]

Concertaré una audición con nuestro experto realizador.
-I'll set up an audition with our ace producer.

8393 **radioactivo** — **radioactive**

adj
[ra.ðjo.ak̚.ˈti.βo]

Tiene razón. No soy radioactivo.
-She's right. I'm not radioactive.

8394 **térmico** — **thermal**

adj
[ˈtɛr.mi.ko]

Esto se ha hecho mediante pinturas de control térmico.
-This has been done by thermal control paints.

8395 **menopausia** — **menopause**

f
[me.no.ˈpau̯.sja]

Me siento como si tuviera menopausia.
-I feel like I'm hitting menopause.

8396 **clonación** — **cloning**

f
[klo.na.ˈsjõn]

Dejemos la clonación para los investigadores.
-Let us leave cloning in the realm of research.

8397 **ligereza** — **lightness**

f
[li.xɛ.ˈre.sa]

La ligereza de esta penitencia me angustió.
-The lightness of this penance overwhelmed me.

8398 **prórroga** — **extension**

f
[ˈpro.ro.ɣa]

También es apropiado estudiar su posible prórroga futura.
-It is also appropriate to examine its possible future extension.

8399 **deambular** — **wander**

vb
[de.ãm.bu.ˈlar]

¿Solo tengo que deambular por este mundo?
-Do I have to wander through this world?

8400 **mísero** — **measly**

adj
[ˈmi.sɛ.ro]

Hay mucho más en juego que un mísero subsidio.
-There is way more at stake than some measly grant.

8401 **corpulento** — **corpulent**

adj
[kor.pu.ˈlẽn̪.to]

Parece ser que soy un tipo corpulento.
-I seem to be a corpulent fellow.

8402 **férreo** — **iron**

adj
[ˈfɛ.re.o]

Sí, parece ejercer un férreo control sobre la máquina política de Londres.
-Yes, he seems to exert an iron grip over London's political machine.

8403 **narrativo** — **narrative; narrative**

adj; f
[na.ra.ˈti.βo]

Todo va de controlar el hilo narrativo.
-It's all about controlling the narrative.

8404 **polizón** — **stowaway**

m/f
[po.li.ˈsõn]

El pasajero del tiburón azul es un polizón.
-The blue shark's passenger is a stowaway.

8405	**complexión**		**complexion**
	f		Esta luz no le va bien a su complexión.
	[kõm.plɛk.ˈsjõn]		-This light is really unflattering for his complexion.
8406	**residencia**		**residence**
	f		Admitió que tenía residencia en dos lugares.
	[re.si.ˈðɛ̃n.sja]		-He admitted to having a residence in two places.
8407	**veintinueve**		**twenty-nine**
	num		Tiene veintinueve, es su última oportunidad.
	[bei̯n.ti.ˈnwe.βe]		-He's twenty-nine, this is his last shot.
8408	**dorso**		**back**
	m		Hay una breve traducción en el dorso.
	[ˈdor.so]		-There's a short translation on the back.
8409	**solapar**		**overlap**
	vb		Solapó las capas para demostrarlo.
	[so.la.ˈpar]		-He overlapped the layers to demonstrate it.
8410	**habituar(se)**		**get in the habit of**
	vb		Solo tengo que habituarme al frío.
	[a.βi.ˈtwar]		-I just need to get used to the cold.
8411	**glóbulo**		**globule**
	m		Quedó un pequeño glóbulo verde en su batería.
	[ˈglo.βu.lo]		-There was a little green globule on his drum seat.
8412	**azulejo**		**tile**
	m		Hay una posible marca de quemadura en el azulejo.
	[a.su.ˈle.xo]		-There is a possible burn mark on the tile.
8413	**conformidad**		**accordance**
	f		Se debe impartir justicia en estricta conformidad con las normas internacionales del proceso debido.
	[kõɱ.for.mi.ˈðað]		-Justice must be served in strict accordance with international standards of due process.
8414	**insurgente**		**insurgent; rebel**
	adj; m/f		Pensaron que era un insurgente.
	[ĭn.sur.ˈxẽn.te]		-They thought he was an insurgent.
8415	**fluidez**		**fluency**
	f		La fluidez en inglés, el acento y el dominio gramatical no se evaluarían.
	[ˈflwi.ðes]		-English fluency, accent, and grammatical proficiency would not be evaluated.
8416	**brevedad**		**brevity**
	f		Se apreció la claridad y brevedad de este resumen.
	[bre.βe.ˈðað]		-The clarity and brevity of this synthesis were appreciated.
8417	**esterilización**		**sterilization**
	f		La esterilización solo estaba autorizada por razones médicas.
	[ɛs.te.ri.li.sa.ˈsjõn]		-Sterilization was allowed only on medical grounds.
8418	**fichero**		**filing cabinet**
	m		Tengo un fichero en lugar de un cerebro.
	[fi.ˈʧɛ.ro]		-I have a filing cabinet instead of a mind.
8419	**miope**		**short-sighted**
	adj		Este enfoque es esencialmente erróneo e incluso miope.
	[ˈmjo.pe]		-This approach is fundamentally flawed and even short-sighted.
8420	**sacacorchos**		**corkscrew**

| | m | Qué pena que no tengamos un sacacorchos. |
| | [sa.ka.ˈkor.ʧos] | -It's a shame we don't have a corkscrew. |

8421 péndulo — **pendulum**
m
[ˈpẽn̪.du.lo]
La superficie del péndulo estará limpia y seca.
-The surface of the pendulum shall be clean and dry.

8422 mordaz — **scathing**
adj
[ˈmor.ðas]
Alessandra dijo que no es tan mordaz.
-Alessandra said it isn't that scathing.

8423 aneurisma — **aneurysm**
adj
[a.neu̯.ˈriş.ma]
Podría haber nacido con un aneurisma.
-He could have been born with an aneurysm.

8424 caucásico — **Caucasian; Caucasian person**
adj; m
[kau̯.ˈka.si.ko]
El paladar es de aspecto caucásico.
-The palate has a Caucasian aspect to it.

8425 operacional — **operational**
adj
[o.pɛ.ra.sjo.ˈnal]
Ahora es necesario pasar a una fase operacional eficaz.
-It is now necessary to move to an effective operational phase.

8426 reciclaje — **recycling**
m
[re.si.ˈkla.xe]
Tenemos reciclaje en todas nuestras escuelas.
-We have recycling in all of our schools.

8427 cercanía — **closeness**
f
[sɛr.ka.ˈni.a]
No quiere tener esa cercanía ni confianza con la gente.
-He doesn't want to have that closeness and rapport with people.

8428 lucidez — **lucidity**
f
[lu.ˈsi.ðes]
Se necesitará mucha lucidez y valentía.
-A great deal of lucidity and courage will be required.

8429 maya — **Mayan; Mayan person**
adj; m
[ˈma.ja]
Un sacerdote maya me dio esto.
-A Mayan priest gave this to me.

8430 savia — **sap**
f
[ˈsa.βja]
La laca sale de la savia del árbol.
-Lacquer comes from the tree sap.

8431 apresar — **apprehend**
vb
[a.pre.ˈsar]
Él es el hombre al que vamos a apresar.
-He is the man we're going to apprehend.

8432 ilegítimo — **illegitimate**
adj
[i.le.ˈxi.ti.mo]
Han sido tomados como rehenes de un régimen ilegítimo.
-They are held hostage by an illegitimate regime.

8433 butaca — **armchair**
f
[bu.ˈta.ka]
Siéntate en la butaca y tranquilízate un minuto.
-Take a seat in the armchair and calm down a while.

8434 traspasar — **cross, hand over**
vb
[tras.pa.ˈsar]
Sabes que hay límites que no voy a traspasar.
-You know there are lines I won't cross.

8435 clandestinidad — **underground**
f
[klãn̪.dɛs.ti.ni.ˈðað]
En cierto sentido ha pasado a la clandestinidad.
-In a sense, it has gone underground.

8436 ficticio — **fictional**

	adj	Es ficticio, pero no puedes tenerlo todo.
	[fikˈti.sjo]	-He's fictional, but you can't have everything.
8437	**programador**	**programmer**
	m	Jim es un programador de computadores.
	[pro.ɣra.maˈðor]	-Jim is a computer programmer.
8438	**abrigar(se)**	**shelter, keep warm**
	vb	¿Tienen cosas con las que abrigarse?
	[a.βriˈɣar]	-Do you have things for shelter?
8439	**croqueta**	**croquette**
	f	¡Es la ganadora de la competición de croquetas!
	[kroˈkɛ.ta]	-She is the winner of the croquette contest!
8440	**camarote**	**cabin**
	m	Estará más cómodo en mi camarote.
	[ka.ma.ˈro.te]	-He'd be more comfortable in my cabin.
8441	**pringar(se)**	**drizzle (LA), work hard (coll), stain**
	vb	Ese vino pringará tu camiseta.
	[prĩŋ.ˈgar]	-That wine will stain your shirt.
8442	**clarín**	**bugle**
	m	Tenemos que conseguir un clarín chino.
	[kla.ˈrĩn]	-We've got to get a Chinese bugle.
8443	**íntegro**	**entire**
	adj	Es importante retirar el contenido íntegro del vial.
	[ˈĩn.te.ɣro]	-It is important to withdraw the entire contents of the vial.
8444	**incorporar**	**incorporate**
	vb	He logrado incorporar varias de sus enmiendas.
	[ĩŋ.kor.po.ˈrar]	-I have managed to incorporate a number of their amendments.
8445	**patrocinio**	**patronage**
	m	El patrocinio debe ser limitado en el tiempo.
	[pa.tro.ˈsi.njo]	-Patronage must be limited in time.
8446	**apatía**	**apathy**
	f	Había algo convincente en tu apatía.
	[a.pa.ˈti.a]	-Well, there was something compelling about your apathy.
8447	**supremacía**	**supremacy**
	f	Permitirles vencer sería aceptar la supremacía del mal.
	[su.pre.ma.ˈsi.a]	-To allow them to win would be to accept the supremacy of evil.
8448	**anestésico**	**anesthetic**
	adj	El anestésico puede arder o picar apenas se inyecta.
	[a.nɛs.ˈte.si.ko]	-The anesthetic will sting or burn when first injected.
8449	**hoz**	**sickle**
	f	Yo creo que es una hoz.
	[ˈos]	-I believe it's a sickle.
8450	**embudo**	**funnel**
	m	Sería como entrar en un embudo.
	[ẽm.ˈbu.ðo]	-It'd be like going through a funnel.
8451	**refinería**	**refinery**
	f	Quiero comprar su refinería y usted necesita venderla.
	[re.fi.nɛ.ˈri.a]	-I want to buy your refinery, and you need to sell it.
8452	**marxista**	**marxist; Marxist**

adj; m/f
[mark.ˈsis.ta]

Si fuera un verdadero marxista no estaría aquí acusándonos.
-If you were a true Marxist you wouldn't be here accusing us.

8453 logística — logistics

f
[lo.ˈxis.ti.ka]

Y no tenía formación ni experiencia en logística.
-And he had no training or background in logistics.

8454 intercepción — interception

f
[ĩn̪.tɛɾ.sep.ˈsjõn]

Tenemos un informe de una posible intercepción.
-We got a report of a possible interception.

8455 menstruación — menstruation

f
[mẽns.trwa.ˈsjõn]

La menstruación es algo muy normal.
-Menstruation is a pretty normal thing.

8456 enzima — enzyme

f
[ẽn.ˈsi.ma]

Nos interesa porque segrega una enzima especial.
-We were interested in it because of a special enzyme it secretes.

8457 óvulo — ovum

m
[ˈo.βu.lo]

Señora, puedo ver solo un óvulo en el derecho.
-Madame, I can see only one ovum on the right.

8458 coliflor — cauliflower

f
[ko.li.ˈflor]

Compra una coliflor y un kilo de cebollas.
-Get a cauliflower and a kilo of onion.

8459 vid — vine

f
[ˈbið]

Está hecho de fruta fresca directamente desde la vid.
-It's made with fresh fruit right off the vine.

8460 adiestramiento — training

m
[a.ðjɛs.tra.ˈmjẽn̪.to]

Lo consideramos un método de adiestramiento satisfactorio.
-We find it a successful method of training.

8461 suscripción — subscription

f
[sus.krip.ˈsjõn]

Quiero cancelar mi suscripción al boletín.
-I would like to cancel my subscription to the newsletter.

8462 sota — jack

f
[ˈso.ta]

Eso es una sota de trébol.
-That's a Jack of clubs.

8463 incitar — incite

vb
[ĩn.si.ˈtar]

Ello solo sirve para incitar al conflicto en lugar de atenuar las diferencias.
-This serves only to incite conflict rather than to bridge differences.

8464 bombo — bass drum

m
[ˈbõm.bo]

Papá, el bombo no es como los violines.
-Papa, the bass drum is not like the violins.

8465 islamista — Islamist

adj
[iş.la.ˈmis.ta]

Los islamistas insurgentes se sumaron luego a la refriega.
-Islamist insurgents subsequently joined the fray.

8466 capote — cape

m
[ka.ˈpo.te]

Ha visto el capote de tu hijo.
-He has seen your son's cape.

8467 compresión — compression

f
[kõm.pre.ˈsjõn]

Es una especie de compresión del cerebro.
-It's a form of compression on the brain.

8468	**coartada**	**alibi**
	f	Pero parece tener una coartada sólida.
	[ko.ar.ˈta.ða]	-But she seems to have a solid alibi.
8469	**simplificar**	**simplify**
	vb	Sí, tenemos que simplificar el sistema.
	[sĩm.pli.fi.ˈkar]	-Yes, we have to simplify the system.
8470	**escolta**	**bodyguard**
	m/f	Yo quiero ser escolta como papá.
	[ɛs.ˈkol̪.ta]	-I want to be a bodyguard like Dad.
8471	**chinchar**	**tease**
	vb	¡Ella me chinchará todo el día!
	[tʃĩn.ˈtʃar]	-She will tease me all day!
8472	**aislante**	**insulation; insulator**
	adj; m	Esto es como el aislante de mi ático.
	[ais̞.ˈlãn̪.te]	-This is like the insulation in my attic.
8473	**amparar**	**protect**
	vb	Se han introducido protecciones administrativas y jurídicas para amparar a los niños.
	[ãm.pa.ˈrar]	-Administrative and legal protections have been instituted to protect children.
8474	**boquilla**	**mouthpiece**
	f	No, vine por mi boquilla.
	[bo.ˈki.ja]	-No, I came for my mouthpiece.
8475	**irrazonable**	**unreasonable**
	adj	Esa observación no parece ser irrazonable.
	[i.ra.so.ˈna.βle]	-That does not seem to be an unreasonable observation.
8476	**resina**	**resin**
	f	Es la resina fosilizada de antiguos pinos.
	[re.ˈsi.na]	-It is the fossilized resin of ancient pine trees.
8477	**reanudar**	**resume**
	vb	Damas y caballeros, podemos reanudar la sesión.
	[re.a.nu.ˈðar]	-Ladies and gentlemen, we can resume the sitting.
8478	**contrabajo**	**double bass**
	m	Este es el puente de su contrabajo.
	[kõn̪.tra.ˈβa.xo]	-This is the bridge from his double bass.
8479	**albergar**	**host**
	vb	Italia se ha mostrado dispuesta a albergar una conferencia de paz.
	[al.βɛr.ˈɣar]	-Italy has declared its willingness to host a peace conference.
8480	**planeador**	**glider**
	m	Pero usted iba en el planeador sola.
	[pla.ne.a.ˈðor]	-But you went in the glider alone.
8481	**irreparable**	**unrepairable**
	adj	Si lo destruyes puede ser irreparable.
	[i.re.pa.ˈra.βle]	-If you destroy that it may be irreparable.
8482	**descalificar**	**disqualify**
	vb	Voy a tener que descalificar a este muchacho.
	[dɛs.ka.li.fi.ˈkar]	-I'll have to disqualify this boy.
8483	**coacción**	**coercion**

	f	Nunca se ha recurrido a la coacción.
	[ko.ak.ˈsjõn]	-Coercion has never been resorted to.
8484	**propagar**	**spread**
	vb	Él es quien puede propagar la enfermedad.
	[pro.pa.ˈɣar]	-He's the one who can spread the disease.
8485	**clamar**	**clamour for**
	vb	Entonces podremos clamar como campeones, si tenemos fuerzas para ello.
	[kla.ˈmar]	-Then we can clamor like champions if we have the spittle for it.
8486	**llamamiento**	**call**
	m	Permítaseme renovar y ampliar ese llamamiento.
	[ʎa.ma.ˈmjẽn̪.to]	-Allow me to renew and amplify that call.
8487	**golondrina**	**swallow**
	f	Un pequeño broche con la forma de una golondrina.
	[go.lõn̪.ˈdri.na]	-A little brooch in the shape of a swallow.
8488	**espino**	**hawthorn**
	m	También me dio bayas de espino.
	[ɛs.ˈpi.no]	-He also gave me hawthorn berries.
8489	**sobresalir**	**excel**
	vb	Ahí fue cuando empezaste a sobresalir.
	[so.βre.sa.ˈlir]	-That's when you started to excel.
8490	**cordillera**	**mountain range**
	f	Huyeron a una cordillera cercana.
	[kor.ði.ˈʝɛ.ra]	-They fled to a nearby mountain range.
8491	**disciplinado**	**disciplined**
	adj	Su programa de trabajo era sumamente disciplinado.
	[dis.sip̚.li.ˈna.ðo]	-His work schedule was extremely disciplined.
8492	**gratificación**	**gratification**
	f	Aquel que busque el orden encontrará gratificación.
	[gra.ti.fi.ka.ˈsjõn]	-He who seeks order shall find gratification.
8493	**recurrente**	**recurrent**
	adj	La participación fue un tema recurrente durante el debate.
	[re.ku.ˈrẽn̪.te]	-Participation was a recurrent topic during the discussion.
8494	**inhibición**	**inhibition**
	f	Se calculan luego los diversos grados de inhibición.
	[i.ni.βi.ˈsjõn]	-The various degrees of inhibition are then calculated.
8495	**minucioso**	**thorough**
	adj	Solo trato de ser minucioso e imparcial.
	[mi.nu.ˈsjo.so]	-I'm just trying to be thorough and impartial.
8496	**encoger**	**shrink**
	vb	Pero entonces, la caja se empieza a encoger.
	[ẽŋ.ko.ˈxɛr]	-But then, the box begins to shrink.
8497	**cúbico**	**cubic**
	adj	Estos datos describen, literalmente, cada centímetro cúbico del sector.
	[ˈku.βi.ko]	-This data describes, literally, every cubic centimeter in this sector.
8498	**rifar**	**raffle**
	vb	Entonces decidimos rifar el piano.
	[ri.ˈfar]	-Then we decide to raffle off the piano.

8499 **notorio** — **notorious**
adj
[no.ˈto.rjo]
Bueno, probablemente sea el más notorio.
-Well, he's probably the most notorious.

8500 **bujía** — **spark plug**
f
[bu.ˈxi.a]
Dice que tiene una bujía nueva.
-He says he has the new spark plug.

8501 **electrodoméstico** — **domestic appliance**
m
[e.lek̚.tro.ðo.ˈmɛs.ti.ko]
Los cargadores electrónicos son ya un electrodoméstico imprescindible en cualquier hogar.
-Electronic chargers are now an essential domestic appliance in any home.

8502 **retención** — **retention**
f
[rɛ.tẽn.ˈsjõn]
Las tasas de escolarización y retención escolar han mejorado.
-Enrolment and retention rate has improved.

8503 **discutible** — **questionable**
adj
[dis.ku.ˈti.βle]
El momento elegido también es muy discutible.
-The timing of this is also highly questionable.

8504 **controversial** — **controversial**
adj
[kõn.tro.βɛr.ˈsjal]
Escuché que usted es muy controversial.
-I've heard that you are very controversial.

8505 **DNI** — **identity card**
abr
[ˈd.ni]
Tienes que enseñarle tu DNI a esa persona.
-You have to show your identity card to that person.

8506 **faceta** — **facet**
f
[fa.ˈsɛ.ta]
No deberíamos temer esta nueva faceta democrática.
-We should not be afraid of this new facet of democracy.

8507 **resignación** — **resignation**
f
[re.siɣ.na.ˈsjõn]
He ofrecido mi resignación al obispo.
-I've tendered my resignation with the bishop.

8508 **simpatizante** — **sympathetic to; sympathizer**
adj; m/f
[sĩm.pa.ti.ˈsãn.te]
Probablemente sepa que lo han mencionado como simpatizante comunista.
-You probably know that you've been named a Communist sympathizer.

8509 **caoba** — **mahogany**
adj
[ka.ˈo.βa]
Debemos comprarle una cruz de caoba.
-We ought to buy a cross of mahogany.

8510 **preludio** — **prelude**
m
[pre.ˈlu.ðjo]
Piense en ello como un preludio de todas las cosas buenas que ocurrirán.
-Think of it as a prelude to all good things to happen.

8511 **intemperie** — **weather**
f
[ĩn.tẽm.ˈpɛ.rje]
El cofre compacto protege la lona recogida de la suciedad y de la intemperie.
-The compact protective casing shelters the rolled-up cover against dirt and the weather.

8512 **apoplejía** — **stroke**
f
[a.pop̚.le.ˈxi.a]
Tu madre ha sufrido una apoplejía.
-Your mother's had a stroke.

8513 **regata**

f

[re.ˈɣa.ta]

regatta

Como en todas las competiciones de velocidad, una regata es cuestión de precisión.

-As in any contest of speed, precision is of the essence in a regatta.

8514 **gustoso**

adj

[gus.ˈto.so]

delicious, gladly

Cuando eso esté hecho, moriré gustoso.

-When that's done, I'll die gladly.

8515 **hidalgo**

m

[i.ˈðal.ɣo]

nobleman

Un hidalgo no se asusta ante nada.

-A nobleman is afraid of nothing.

8516 **inactivo**

adj

[i.nakˈti.βo]

inactive

El consejo estuvo inactivo durante el año 2006.

-The council was inactive during the year 2006.

8517 **maza**

f

[ˈma.sa]

mace

Podría haber usado mi maza si me hubieses dejado.

-I could have used my mace on it If you'd given me a chance.

8518 **inyectar**

vb

[ĩn.ɟjekˈtar]

inject

Va a inyectar nanobots para reparar tus heridas.

-She's going to inject nanobots to repair your injuries.

8519 **lumbre**

f

[ˈlũm.bre]

fire

Perdóname, pero tengo el arroz en la lumbre.

-Forgive me, but I have the rice on the fire.

8520 **caballeriza**

f

[ka.βa.ʝɛ.ˈri.sa]

stable

Solo hay un caballo en mi caballeriza.

-There's only one horse in my stable.

8521 **cabida**

f

[ka.ˈβi.ða]

room

No hay cabida para explicaciones ni excusas.

-There is no room for explanations or excuses.

8522 **incansable**

adj

[ĩŋ.kãn.ˈsa.βle]

tireless

La búsqueda de la paz debe ser incansable.

-The search for peace must be tireless.

8523 **velorio**

m

[be.ˈlo.rjo]

wake

Escucha, quiero organizar un velorio.

-Listen, I want to have a wake.

8524 **enema**

m

[e.ˈne.ma]

enema

De todas formas, aquí tienes tu enema.

-I used that for an emergency enema.

8525 **inerte**

adj

[i.ˈnɛr.te]

inert

En este estado es completamente inerte.

-In its present state, it's completely inert.

8526 **individualidad**

f

[ĩn.di.βi.ðwa.li.ˈðað]

individuality

Esta individualidad y diversidad no tiene que dividirnos.

-This individuality and diversity do not have to divide us.

8527 **simbolismo**

m

[sĩm.bo.ˈliș.mo]

symbolism

Era más una cuestión de simbolismo.

-It was much more a matter of symbolism.

8528 **posguerra**

post-war era

f
[poʂ.ˈɣɛ.ra]

Nuestra conclusión es que es un espía especial basado en tecnología posguerra.
-Our conclusion is that he's a special spy based on postwar tech.

8529 **severidad** — **severity**

f
[se.βɛ.ri.ˈðað]

La violación de este principio es sancionada con toda severidad.
-Violation of this principle is punished with the utmost severity.

8530 **asentar(se)** — **settle**

vb
[a.sẽn.ˈtar]

Deme un caramelo de menta para asentar el estómago.
-I'll have a peppermint to settle my stomach.

8531 **socializar** — **socialize**

vb
[so.sja.li.ˈsar]

Ellen prefería socializar conmigo y mi círculo.
-Ellen preferred to socialize with me and my circle.

8532 **docente** — **educational; teacher**

adj; m/f
[do.ˈsẽn.te]

Su institución docente podrá darle más información sobre este tema.
-Your educational institution can provide more information on this subject.

8533 **traumático** — **traumatic**

adj
[trau̯.ˈma.ti.ko]

Creo que ha experimentado algo traumático.
-I think that he's experienced something traumatic.

8534 **sutura** — **stitch**

f
[su.ˈtu.ra]

He sacado la bala, solo tienes que suturarlo.
-I took the bullet out, you just need to stitch it up.

8535 **risco** — **crag**

m
[ˈris.ko]

El pueblo está localizado a los pies de un risco.
-The village is located at the foot of a crag.

8536 **plagiar** — **plagiarise**

vb
[pla.ˈxjar]

He intentado plagiar a un artista japonés del siglo XVII.
-I tried to plagiarize Japanese artist of the 17th century.

8537 **pelón** — **bald (coll)**

adj
[pe.ˈlõn]

¡Yo ya soy pequeño y no creo que pudiera soportar quedarme pelón también!
-I'm already small and I don't think I could handle being bald!

8538 **urbanización** — **urbanisation**

f
[ur.βa.ni.sa.ˈsjõn]

Existe una relación directa entre urbanización y desarrollo.
-There is a positive correlation between urbanization and development.

8539 **tibetano** — **Tibetan; Tibetan person**

adj; m
[ti.βɛ.ˈta.no]

Este era un lago tibetano sagrado y muy especial.
-This was a very special and holy Tibetan lake.

8540 **secuela** — **sequel**

f
[se.ˈkwe.la]

Vamos a guardarlo para la secuela.
-Let's save it for the sequel.

8541 **paradigma** — **paradigm**

m
[pa.ra.ˈðiɣ.ma]

El reto es cambiar el paradigma.
-The challenge is to shift the paradigm.

8542 **tortillera** — **dyke (coll)**

adj
[tor.ti.ˈjɛ.ra]

Sé que es una tortillera.
-I know she's a dyke.

8543 **encomendar** — **entrust**

	vb	No podemos encomendar la seguridad del mundo a un perro.
	[ẽŋ.ko.mẽn̪.ˈdar]	-We can't entrust the security Of the entire world to one dog.
8544	**dividendo**	**dividend**
	m	El desarrollo es un dividendo de la paz.
	[di.βi.ˈðẽn̪.do]	-Development is a dividend of peace.
8545	**atestiguar**	**testify**
	vb	Tengo un doctor que desea atestiguar.
	[a.tɛs.ti.ˈɣwar]	-I've got a doctor who wants to testify.
8546	**agridulce**	**bittersweet**
	adj	Fue un momento agridulce porque tenía miedo.
	[a.ɣri.ˈðul.se]	-It was a bittersweet moment because she was scared.
8547	**erotismo**	**eroticism**
	m	Hubiese dedicado más tiempo al erotismo.
	[ɛ.ro.ˈtis̪.mo]	-I'd have devoted more time to eroticism.
8548	**agilidad**	**agility**
	f	Este dinamismo y agilidad también hacen falta a escala mundial.
	[a.xi.li.ˈðað]	-This dynamism and agility are also required at the global level.
8549	**sagaz**	**sharp**
	adj	Nunca le pareció muy sagaz o agudo.
	[ˈsa.ɣas]	-He never thought he was very shrewd or sharp.
8550	**cátedra**	**professorship**
	f	Durante años, Tim trabajó 14 horas diarias para conseguir la cátedra.
	[ˈka.te.ðra]	-For years, Tim worked 14 hours a day for that professorship.
8551	**óleo**	**oil painting**
	m	Estamos haciendo un poco de pintura al óleo.
	[ˈo.le.o]	-We're doing a little oil painting.
8552	**dificultar**	**hinder**
	vb	Esto va a dificultar el matrimonio de Yukiko.
	[di.fi.kul̪.ˈtar]	-This will hinder Yukiko's marriage.
8553	**regadera**	**watering can, shower (LA)**
	f	Tengo tina, quería una regadera.
	[re.ɣa.ˈðɛ.ra]	-I have a bathroom, I wanted a shower.
8554	**gruñido**	**growl**
	m	Tenemos que trabajar en ese gruñido.
	[gru.ˈɲi.ðo]	-We got to work on that growl.
8555	**amapola**	**poppy**
	f	La amapola es una planta muy resistente.
	[a.ma.ˈpo.la]	-The poppy is a very sturdy flower.
8556	**toldo**	**awning**
	m	Pusieron un toldo en la tienda nueva.
	[ˈtol̪.do]	-There's an awning on the new store.
8557	**dedicatoria**	**dedicatory; dedication**
	adj; f	Una bonita dedicatoria de Joan Alder.
	[de.ði.ka.ˈto.rja]	-A nice little dedication by Joan Alder.
8558	**inherente**	**inherent**
	adj	Hemos señalado la deficiencia inherente a este enfoque.
	[i.nɛ.ˈrẽn̪.te]	-We have pointed out the inherent shortcomings of this approach.
8559	**terapéutico**	**therapeutic**

adj
[tɛ.ra.ˈpeu̯.ti.ko]

Estoy intentando conducir un proceso terapéutico.
-I am trying to conduct a therapeutic process.

8560 vivero — **nursery**

m
[bi.ˈβɛ.ro]

El vivero, aquí, es muy diferente.
-The nursery, in here, is quite different.

8561 epicentro — **epicenter**

m
[e.pi.ˈsɛ̃n.tro]

Normalmente no es tan difícil hallar el epicentro.
-It's not normally this hard to find the epicenter.

8562 ecografía — **ultrasound**

f
[e.ko.ɣra.ˈfi.a]

He estado preocupada por la ecografía.
-I've been concerned because of the ultrasound.

8563 murmurar — **murmur**

vb
[mur.mu.ˈrar]

¡Los vecinos están empezando a murmurar!
-The neighbors are starting to murmur!

8564 camillero — **stretcher-bearer**

m
[ka.mi.ˈjɛ.ro]

Se supone que el camillero salve vidas.
-The stretcher-bearer is supposed to save lives.

8565 archiduque — **archduke**

m
[ar.tʃi.ˈðu.ke]

El archiduque es un hombre piadoso.
-The Archduke is a pious man.

8566 glotón — **glutton; gluttonous**

m; adj
[glo.ˈtõn]

Me siento como un glotón total.
-I feel like a total glutton.

8567 rebajar — **reduce**

vb
[re.βa.ˈxar]

Es necesario rebajar la edad de votar.
-The voting age needs to be reduced.

8568 estigma — **stigma**

m
[ɛs.ˈtiɣ.ma]

Sencillamente no tiene el mismo estigma.
-It simply does not carry the same stigma.

8569 penetrante — **penetrating**

adj
[pe.nɛ.ˈtrã̃n.te]

El dióxido de azufre es un gas incoloro con un olor penetrante y asfixiante.
-Sulfur dioxide is a colorless gas with a penetrating, choking odor.

8570 desfigurar — **disfigure**

vb
[dɛs.fi.ɣu.ˈrar]

Tú me vas a desfigurar.
-You are going to disfigure me.

8571 merecedor — **worthy**

adj
[mɛ.re.se.ˈðor]

El informe es más que merecedor de apoyo.
-The report is more than worthy of support.

8572 tontear — **flirt (coll), fool around (coll)**

vb
[tõ̃n.te.ˈar]

¿Te parece normal tontear así con ella?
-Do you think it's okay to flirt with her like that?

8573 compasivo — **compassionate**

adj
[kõm.pa.ˈsi.βo]

Seré un tipo compasivo, encantador.
-I'll be a compassionate, lovely guy.

8574 actualizar — **update**

vb
[ak̚.twa.li.ˈsar]

Era necesario actualizar las referencias en el documento.
-There was a need to update references in the paper.

8575	**jovial**	**jovial**
	adj	Mostraos jovial entre vuestros invitados esta noche.
	[xo.ˈβjal]	-Be jovial among your guests tonight.
8576	**menear**	**shake**
	vb	Es hora de menear un poco las cosas.
	[me.ne.ˈar]	-It's time to shake things up a little bit.
8577	**asfixiar**	**choke**
	vb	Podrías asfixiar a una docena de burros con eso.
	[as.fik.ˈsjar]	-You could choke a dozen donkeys on that.
8578	**privar**	**deprive**
	vb	Necesitamos privar a la tormenta de su fuente de energía.
	[pri.ˈβar]	-We need to deprive the storm of its energy source.
8579	**derroche**	**waste**
	m	No hay orgullo en el derroche.
	[dɛ.ˈro.tʃe]	-There's no pride in wastefulness.
8580	**quirúrgico**	**surgical**
	adj	Si hay algo quirúrgico, puedo ayudar.
	[ki.ˈrur.xi.ko]	-If there's anything surgical, I can help.
8581	**deficiencia**	**deficiency**
	f	Quizás necesite suplir su deficiencia química para sobrevivir.
	[de.fi.ˈsjɛ̃n.sja]	-Maybe he needs to replenish this chemical deficiency to survive.
8582	**destrozo**	**heavy damage**
	m	¿Eso es lo que ha causado todo el destrozo?
	[dɛs.ˈtro.so]	-That's what caused all the damage?
8583	**asignatura**	**subject**
	f	Él me explicó cómo debía abordar la asignatura.
	[a.siɣ.na.ˈtu.ra]	-He enlightened me on how I should attack the subject.
8584	**alcázar**	**fortress**
	m	Estamos prisioneros en este alcázar y no os dais cuenta.
	[al.ˈka.sar]	-We are prisoners in this fortress and you do not realize it.
8585	**finito**	**finite**
	adj	No pretendemos que el proceso de reforma sea fácil o finito.
	[fi.ˈni.to]	-We do not pretend the process of reform is easy or finite.
8586	**emigrar**	**emigrate**
	vb	Mi amigo quiere emigrar a Sudáfrica.
	[e.mi.ˈɣrar]	-My friend wants to emigrate to South Africa.
8587	**pueblerino**	**hick (coll)**
	adj	No me digas que ese pueblerino te contagió sarna.
	[pwe.βlɛ.ˈri.no]	-Don't tell me that hick gave you scabies.
8588	**atónito**	**stunned**
	adj	Ocurrió todo tan deprisa, supongo que estaba atónito...
	[a.ˈto.ni.to]	-It happened so fast, I guess I was stunned...
8589	**varonil**	**manly**
	adj	No quería herir tu orgullo varonil.
	[ba.ro.ˈnil]	-I didn't want to hurt your manly pride.
8590	**haba**	**bean**
	f	¿Cómo consiguen sacar leche de un haba?
	[ˈa.βa]	-How do you get milk from a bean?

8591	**colibrí**	**hummingbird**
	m	No, están viendo ese colibrí.
	[ko.li.ˈβri]	-No, they're watching that hummingbird.
8592	**vivaz**	**vivacious**
	adj	Jennifer es amable, es vivaz.
	[ˈbi.βas]	-Jennifer is friendly, she's vivacious.
8593	**rubor**	**blush**
	m	El blanco le ha dado un nuevo rubor a tus mejillas.
	[ru.ˈβor]	-The white has brought a new blush to your cheeks.
8594	**jarro**	**mug**
	m	No puedes beber de mi jarro.
	[ˈxa.ro]	-You can't drink from my mug.
8595	**monzón**	**monsoon**
	m	Atacaremos la isla cuando termine el monzón.
	[mõn.ˈsõn]	-We will attack the island when the monsoon ends.
8596	**adición**	**addition**
	f	Serán una encantadora adición al jardín.
	[a.ði.ˈsjõn]	-They'll be a lovely addition to the garden.
8597	**glucosa**	**glucose**
	f	Le daré inmediatamente la solución de glucosa.
	[glu.ˈko.sa]	-I will give him the glucose solution right now.
8598	**grupal**	**group**
	adj	Estoy intentando mandar un mensaje grupal.
	[gru.ˈpal]	-I'm trying to send a group text.
8599	**precintar**	**seal**
	vb	Finalmente, precinte el paquete con la pegatina.
	[pre.sĩn.ˈtar]	-Finally, seal the package with the sticker.
8600	**despojo**	**dispossession**
	m	Pakistán sigue estando profundamente preocupado por el prolongado sufrimiento y el despojo del que es víctima el pueblo palestino.
	[dɛs.ˈpo.xo]	-Pakistan remains deeply concerned by the protracted suffering and dispossession of the Palestinian people.
8601	**logotipo**	**logo**
	m	Incluso llevan el logotipo al frente.
	[lo.ɣo.ˈti.po]	-They've even got the logo on the front.
8602	**absorto**	**absorbed**
	adj	Él está absorto en su investigación.
	[aβ.ˈsor.to]	-He is absorbed in his research.
8603	**forjar**	**forge**
	vb	Elijo forjar mi destino con usted.
	[for.ˈxar]	-I choose to forge my fate with you.
8604	**abusivo**	**abusive**
	adj	El funcionario tenía también un comportamiento errático, abusivo y amenazante.
	[a.βu.ˈsi.βo]	-The staff member also engaged in erratic, abusive and threatening behavior.
8605	**coágulo**	**clot**
	m	Un coágulo impide que la sangre fluya.
	[ko.ˈa.ɣu.lo]	-A clot is preventing blood flow.

8606	**marginal**		**marginal**
	adj		Estamos estimando dónde estaría el error marginal.
	[mar.xi.ˈnal]		-We are estimating where the marginal error would be.
8607	**redoblar**		**redouble**
	vb		No hará otra cosa más que redoblar su esfuerzo nuclear.
	[re.ðo.ˈβlar]		-He'll do nothing but redouble his nuclear efforts.
8608	**instruido**		**instructed**
	adj		Les he instruido a todos ellos.
	[ĩns.ˈtrwi.ðo]		-I've instructed all of them.
8609	**reverso**		**reverse**
	m		Elige entre las distintas plantillas disponibles para el reverso.
	[re.ˈβɛr.so]		-Choose from different templates for the reverse.
8610	**productividad**		**productivity**
	f		Como consecuencia, aumentó su productividad.
	[pro.ðuk̚.ti.βi.ˈðað]		-As a result, their productivity had increased.
8611	**canapé**		**canape**
	m		¿Quiere un canapé, caballero?
	[ka.na.ˈpe]		-Would you like a canape, sir?
8612	**pisotear**		**trample**
	vb		¡Tenemos que ir porque nos quieren pisotear!
	[pi.so.te.ˈar]		-We have to go because they want to trample on us!
8613	**olivo**		**olive tree**
	m		Bajo el olivo en el jardín.
	[o.ˈli.βo]		-Under the olive tree in the garden.
8614	**territorial**		**territorial**
	adj		Creo que apoyamos la integridad territorial del país.
	[tɛ.ri.to.ˈrjal]		-We support the territorial integrity of the country, or so I believe.
8615	**panteón**		**pantheon**
	m		Seguramente entrará en el panteón de los héroes latinoamericanos.
	[pãn̪.ˈte.õn]		-He is sure to enter the pantheon of Latin American heroes.
8616	**fomentar**		**foster**
	vb		Tenemos que asegurarnos de fomentar la estabilidad e invertir en crecimiento.
	[fo.mẽn̪.ˈtar]		-We need to ensure that we foster stability and invest for growth.
8617	**abolir**		**abolish**
	vb		El problema no es abolir la muerte.
	[a.βo.ˈlir]		-The problem is not to abolish death.
8618	**autodefensa**		**self-defence**
	f		Quiero decir que parece autodefensa.
	[au̯.to.ðe.ˈfɛ̃n.sa]		-I mean, that just sounds like self-defense.
8619	**golfista**		**golfer**
	m/f		Mi hijo quiere ser un golfista profesional.
	[gol.ˈfis.ta]		-My son wants to be a professional golfer.
8620	**lámina**		**sheet**
	f		La lámina de plástico no incluye microprocesadores electrónicos.
	[ˈla.mi.na]		-The plastic sheet does not contain electronic chips.
8621	**carencia**		**lack**

f   Todos sufren por la carencia de luz.
[ka.ˈr̃en.sja]   -Everybody is suffering from the lack of light.

8622 **parpadeo**   **blink**

m   La frecuencia del parpadeo no se puede modificar.
[par.pa.ˈðe.o]   -You cannot change the blink frequency.

8623 **remolque**   **trailer**

m   Quiero alquilar un remolque para dos.
[re.ˈmol.ke]   -I want to rent a trailer for 2.

8624 **estereotipo**   **stereotype**

m   Solo digo que es un estereotipo ofensivo.
[es.te.re.o.ˈti.po]   -I'm just saying it's an offensive stereotype.

8625 **marxismo**   **Marxism**

m   El marxismo es una versión del determinismo económico.
[mark.ˈsiş.mo]   -Marxism is a version of economic determinism.

8626 **espontaneidad**   **spontaneity**

f   Debería estar lleno de sorpresa y espontaneidad.
[es.põn̪.ta.nei̯.ˈðað]   -It should be full of surprise and spontaneity.

8627 **profano**   **profane**

adj   Como si Dios se hubiese vuelto profano.
[pro.ˈfa.no]   -As if God's become profane.

8628 **dicción**   **diction**

f   Nunca nadie ha tenido ningún problema con mi dicción.
[dik.ˈsjõn]   -No one's ever had a problem with my diction before.

8629 **conocedor**   **knowledgeable; connoisseur**

adj; m   Sucede que soy un conocedor impresionista.
[ko.no.se.ˈðor]   -I happen to be an impressionistic connoisseur.

8630 **triunfador**   **winner; winning**

m; adj   Nadie diría que un triunfador y un fracasado podrían ser amigos.
[trjũm̩.fa.ˈðor]   -You wouldn't think a winner and a loser could be friends.

8631 **gallardo**   **dashing; gallant**

adj; m   Es el joven más gallardo de Japón.
[ga.ˈjar.ðo]   -He's the most dashing young man in Japan.

8632 **disolución**   **dissolution**

f   La disolución del matrimonio se lleva practicando muchos siglos.
[di.so.lu.ˈsjõn]   -The dissolution of marriage has been in practice for countless
                           centuries.

8633 **sinfónico**   **symphonic**

adj   Recuerda que mi debut sinfónico falló estrepitosamente.
[sĩm̩.ˈfo.ni.ko]   -Remember, my symphonic debut failed resoundingly.

8634 **pana**   **corduroy**

f   Pero no le pediría que me prestara su chaqueta de pana.
[ˈpa.na]   -But I wouldn't ask to borrow his corduroy jacket.

8635 **pagaré**   **promissory note**

m   Entonces trae el pagaré firmado por tu padre.
[pa.ɣa.ˈre]   -Then bring me that promissory note signed by your father.

8636 **contorno**   **contour**

m   Aplica el contorno al objeto seleccionado.
[kõn̪.ˈtor.no]   -Applies the contour to the selected object.

8637	**rascar**	**scratch**
	vb	No me tienes que rascar la espalda.
	[ras.ˈkar]	-You don't have to scratch my back.
8638	**nicho**	**niche**
	m	A veces cuesta encontrar tu nicho.
	[ˈni.ʧo]	-Sometimes it's hard to find your niche.
8639	**unificación**	**unification**
	f	Aprendamos del proceso alemán de unificación.
	[u.ni.fi.ka.ˈsjõn]	-Let us learn from the German unification process.
8640	**fármaco**	**drug**
	m	No se ha investigado el efecto de la cirugía gastrointestinal previa sobre la absorción del fármaco.
	[ˈfar.ma.ko]	-The effect of prior gastrointestinal surgery on drug absorption has not been investigated.
8641	**delator**	**informer**
	m	¡Debo encontrar a ese delator!
	[de.la.ˈtor]	-I have to find that informer!
8642	**imperfección**	**imperfection**
	f	No debería tener la más mínima imperfección.
	[ĩm.pɛr.fɛk.ˈsjõn]	-It should not have the slightest imperfection in it.
8643	**libertino**	**licentious; libertine**
	adj; m	El hombre era un libertino reconocido.
	[li.βɛr.ˈti.no]	-The man is a confirmed libertine.
8644	**regeneración**	**regeneration**
	f	Habló sobre leer mentes y la regeneración espontánea.
	[re.xe.nɛ.ra.ˈsjõn]	-He was talking about mind reading and spontaneous regeneration.
8645	**contrarrestar**	**counter**
	vb	Nuestro objetivo es prevenir y contrarrestar los actos terroristas.
	[kõn̪.tra.rɛs.ˈtar]	-Our objective is to prevent and counter terrorist acts.
8646	**converso**	**converted; convert**
	adj; m	Creedme, estáis predicando al converso.
	[kõm.ˈbɛr.so]	-Believe me, you're preaching to the converted.
8647	**zinc**	**zinc**
	m	El óxido de zinc se utiliza como medicamento.
	[ˈsĩŋk]	-Zinc oxide is used as a medicament.
8648	**monóxido**	**monoxide**
	m	Había una fuga en la tubería así que se mezcló oxígeno con el monóxido.
	[mo.ˈnok.si.ðo]	-There was a leak in the pipes, so oxygen mixed with the monoxide.
8649	**epitafio**	**epitaph**
	m	Tal vez eso será mi epitafio.
	[e.pi.ˈta.fjo]	-Perhaps that will be my epitaph.
8650	**pistón**	**piston**
	m	El pistón está diseñado para operar automáticamente la compuerta.
	[pis.ˈtõn]	-The piston is designed to operate the gate automatically.
8651	**gruñir**	**growl**
	vb	Déjame oír al oso polar gruñir.
	[gru.ˈɲir]	-Let me hear a polar bear growl.
8652	**sobriedad**	**sobriety**

f
[so.βrje.ˈðað]

Estoy tratando de recuperar la sobriedad.
-I'm trying to get my sobriety back.

8653 exclusividad — **exclusivity**

f
[ɛks̪.lu.si.βi.ˈðað]

Deberíamos crear un aire de exclusividad.
-We need to create an air of exclusivity.

8654 libido — **libido**

f
[li.ˈβi.ðo]

Tu libido está fuera de control.
-Your libido is out of control.

8655 quejido — **whimper, sigh**

m
[ke.ˈxi.ðo]

Ese quejido que has oído era de mi cartera.
-That sigh you just heard was my wallet.

8656 purificar — **purify**

vb
[pu.ri.fi.ˈkar]

Arrojan sal para purificar el ring.
-They are throwing salt to purify the ring.

8657 benévolo — **benevolent**

vb
[be.ˈne.βo.lo]

Esto es de lo más benévolo por tu parte.
-That's most benevolent of you.

8658 cataclismo — **cataclysm**

m
[ka.ta.ˈklis̪.mo]

Solo cambiaré si hay un cataclismo.
-I'll only change if there is a cataclysm.

8659 enriquecer(se) — **enrich**

vb
[ɛ̃n.ri.ke.ˈsɛr]

Queremos enriquecer esta asociación mucho más que en el pasado.
-We want to enrich this partnership much more than it has been in the past.

8660 relicario — **reliquary**

m
[re.li.ˈka.rjo]

Supongo que este relicario está roto.
-I guess this reliquary's broken.

8661 paria — **outcast**

m/f
[ˈpa.rja]

Tengo que llamar a la puerta como un paria.
-I have to bang on the door like an outcast.

8662 talonario — **checkbook**

m
[ta.lo.ˈna.rjo]

Tengo un talonario en el escritorio.
-I've got a checkbook on that desk.

8663 neurólogo — **neurologist**

m
[neu̯.ˈro.lo.ɣo]

Necesitas que te examine un neurólogo.
-You need to be cleared by a neurologist.

8664 inexistente — **nonexistent**

adj
[i.nɛk.sis.ˈtẽ̪n.te]

Confías demasiado en la inexistente solidaridad racial.
-You rely too much on a nonexistent racial solidarity.

8665 patológico — **pathological**

adj
[pa.to.ˈlo.xi.ko]

Lo más probable es que sea patológico.
-He'll most likely be pathological.

8666 abarrotar — **pack**

vb
[a.βa.ro.ˈtar]

Verás, podríamos abarrotar el sitio.
-See, we could pack this joint.

8667 cúspide — **top**

f
[ˈkus.pi.ðe]

Al final, el jefe alcanza la cúspide.
-In the end, the boss reaches the top.

8668	**atraco**	**robbery**
	m	Está detenida por homicidio y atraco.
	[a.ˈtra.ko]	-You're under arrest for homicide and robbery.
8669	**pronunciación**	**pronunciation**
	f	Me gustaría mejorar mi pronunciación del inglés.
	[pro.nũn.sja.ˈsjõn]	-I would like to improve my English pronunciation.
8670	**escarcha**	**frost**
	f	Pensé que la escarcha había arrasado con ellos.
	[ɛs.ˈkar.ʧa]	-I thought the frost wipe them all out.
8671	**vigente**	**existing**
	adj	La legislación vigente está siendo revisada actualmente.
	[bi.ˈxẽn̪.te]	-A review of existing legislation is currently underway.
8672	**pastar**	**graze**
	vb	Tengo que sacar los caballos a pastar.
	[pas.ˈtar]	-I have to let the horses out to graze.
8673	**góndola**	**gondola**
	f	Y podrías pasear en góndola conmigo.
	[ˈgõn̪.do.la]	-And you would ride a gondola with me.
8674	**bolos**	**bowling**
	mpl	Creo que es altamente improbable que Tom vaya a jugar bolos.
	[ˈbo.los]	-I think it's highly unlikely that Tom will go bowling.
8675	**roer**	**gnaw**
	vb	Bueno, vamos a la tienda y compramos algo para roer.
	[ro.ˈɛr]	-Well, let's go to the store and get them something to gnaw on.
8676	**agredir**	**assault**
	vb	No tenía ningún derecho a agredir a un policía.
	[a.ɣre.ˈðir]	-You had no right whatsoever to assault a police officer.
8677	**erosión**	**erosion**
	f	En Jamaica se formuló un programa de lucha contra la erosión de los suelos.
	[ɛ.ro.ˈsjõn]	-A soil erosion control programme was formulated in Jamaica.
8678	**semifinal**	**semi-final**
	f	Tenemos un ganador de la segunda semifinal.
	[se.mi.fi.ˈnal]	-We have a winner of the second semi-final.
8679	**carismático**	**charismatic; charismatic**
	adj; m	Él trabajó duro para parecer carismático.
	[ka.ris̺.ˈma.ti.ko]	-He worked hard to try and appear charismatic.
8680	**ambiguo**	**ambiguous**
	adj	No busquen ningún horizonte político ambiguo.
	[ãm.ˈbi.ɣwo]	-Do not look for any ambiguous political horizon.
8681	**columnista**	**columnist**
	m/f	Quiere advertirte de que soy columnista de chismes.
	[ko.lũm.ˈnis.ta]	-She wants to warn you that I'm a gossip columnist.
8682	**reparador**	**comforting; repairman**
	adj; m	Es un genio reparador de cafeteras.
	[re.pa.ra.ˈðor]	-He's a genius coffee repairman.
8683	**retribución**	**payment**

	f	Debería haber una retribución equitativa por el mismo trabajo.
	[rɛ.tri.βu.ˈsjõn]	-There should be equal pay for equal work.
8684	**reluciente**	**shiny**
	adj	Yo quiero también una espada reluciente.
	[re.lu.ˈsjẽn̪.te]	-I want a shiny sword, too.
8685	**disección**	**dissection**
	f	Diles que sigan con la disección.
	[di.sɛk.ˈsjõn]	-Tell them to go ahead with the dissection.
8686	**tórax**	**thorax**
	m	Ejercitas los brazos y el tórax.
	[ˈto.raks]	-You exercise the arms and the thorax.
8687	**ascendente**	**rising**
	adj	Clasifica el contenido del campo en orden ascendente.
	[as.sẽn̪.ˈdẽn̪.te]	-It sorts the field contents in ascending order.
8688	**desnudar(se)**	**undress**
	vb	Tendrías que desnudar a todo el mundo.
	[dɛs̪.nu.ˈðar]	-You'll have to strip everyone.
8689	**atenuante**	**mitigating**
	adj	Los conflictos militares no puede ser un factor atenuante.
	[a.te.ˈnwãn̪.te]	-Military conflicts cannot be a mitigating factor.
8690	**contrata**	**contract**
	f	Esta previsión comprende la reparación local por contrata.
	[kõn̪.ˈtra.ta]	-This provision includes local contract repairs.
8691	**desintoxicación**	**detoxification**
	f	Ella no cuenta con clínicas de desintoxicación.
	[de.sĩn̪.tok.si.ka.ˈsjõn]	-She does not have detoxification clinics.
8692	**movilizar**	**mobilize**
	vb	Era crucial movilizar recursos adecuados para alcanzar esos objetivos.
	[mo.βi.li.ˈsar]	-It is crucial to mobilize adequate resources to achieve these goals.
8693	**reseña**	**review**
	f	Volveré enseguida con la verdadera reseña.
	[re.ˈse.ɲa]	-I'll be right back with the real review.
8694	**correspondiente**	**corresponding**
	adj	Esperamos obtener el respaldo correspondiente de la comunidad internacional.
	[ko.rɛs.põn̪.ˈdjẽn̪.te]	-We hope to obtain the corresponding support of the world community.
8695	**estratega**	**strategist**
	m/f	Tú eres un tremendo estratega.
	[ɛs.tra.ˈte.ɣa]	-You're a hell of a strategist.
8696	**almidón**	**starch**
	m	Está constituido principalmente por fibra interna y almidón.
	[al.mi.ˈðõn]	-It is mainly composed of internal fiber and starch.
8697	**subvención**	**grant**
	f	Consiste en elementos de préstamo y subvención.
	[suβ.βẽn.ˈsjõn]	-It consists of both loan and grant elements.
8698	**prestación**	**provision**
	f	Hay muchas complejidades en la prestación de asesoramiento.
	[pɾɛs.ta.ˈsjõn]	-There are many complexities to the provision of counseling.

8699	**convivencia**	**coexistence**
	f	La igualdad de género es un principio esencial de convivencia.
	[kõm.bi.ˈβẽn.sja]	-Gender equality is an essential principle for coexistence.
8700	**abolición**	**abolition**
	f	No hay consenso internacional a favor de su abolición.
	[a.βo.li.ˈsjõn]	-There is no international consensus on its abolition.
8701	**alimentario**	**food**
	adj	Descubrí el lado oscuro del sistema alimentario industrial.
	[a.li.mẽn̪.ˈta.rjo]	-I discovered the dark side of the industrialized food system.
8702	**afinar**	**tune**
	vb	Esto es muy difícil de afinar.
	[a.fi.ˈnar]	-This is very difficult to tune.
8703	**matiz**	**nuance**
	m	No se trata de un simple cambio de matiz.
	[ˈma.tis]	-This is not a mere change of nuance.
8704	**patrocinar**	**sponsor**
	vb	Es un placer para Australia patrocinar estos textos.
	[pa.tro.si.ˈnar]	-Australia is pleased to sponsor these texts.
8705	**infiltración**	**infiltration**
	f	La infiltración es nuestra mejor oportunidad.
	[ĩɱ.fil̪.tra.ˈsjõn]	-Infiltration is our best chance.
8706	**protón**	**proton**
	m	Es como tomar una instantánea muy rápida del protón.
	[pro.ˈtõn]	-It's like taking a very sudden snapshot of the proton.
8707	**aleatorio**	**random**
	adj	Supuse que fue un crimen aleatorio.
	[a.le.a.ˈto.rjo]	-I assumed that it was a random crime.
8708	**diagnosticar**	**diagnose**
	vb	Debemos diagnosticar las causas del terrorismo para erradicarlo.
	[djaɣ.nos.ti.ˈkar]	-We should diagnose the causes of terrorism in order to eradicate it.
8709	**sensorial**	**sensory**
	adj	Estoy incapacitada, por afasia sensorial.
	[sẽn.so.ˈrjal]	-I'm incapacitated, it's sensory aphasia.
8710	**provincial**	**provincial**
	adj	La policía provincial está administrada por el gobernador.
	[pro.βĩn.ˈsjal]	-The provincial police are administered by the governor.
8711	**economista**	**economist**
	m/f	Para un economista, la recuperación de Argentina no es una sorpresa.
	[e.ko.no.ˈmis.ta]	-To an economist, Argentina's recovery is no surprise.
8712	**escenografía**	**scenography**
	f	No hubiera sido una escenografía tan inspiradora sin este teatro.
	[ɛs.se.no.ɣra.ˈfi.a]	-It wouldn't be such an inspiring scenography without this theater.
8713	**farola**	**lamppost**
	f	Necesitas una farola en la calle.
	[fa.ˈro.la]	-You need a lamppost out in the street.
8714	**ferocidad**	**ferocity**
	f	Los espantamos con nuestra feroz ferocidad.
	[fɛ.ro.si.ˈðað]	-We scared them off with our fierce ferocity.

8715	**infestar**	**infest**
	vb	Podrían escaparse e infestar mi apartamento.
	[ĩm.fɛs.ˈtar]	-They could escape and infest my apartment.

8716	**acompañamiento**	**accompanying**
	m	Cualquier otro paso no puede ser más que una medida de acompañamiento.
	[a.kõm.pa.ɲa.ˈmjẽ̞.to]	-Anything else can be nothing more than an accompanying measure.

8717	**progresión**	**progression**
	f	Conviene supervisar la progresión de la escoliosis.
	[pro.ɣre.ˈsjõn]	-They should be monitored for progression of their scoliosis.

8718	**fortuito**	**fortuitous**
	adj	¿Sabes? Esto podría ser bastante fortuito.
	[for.ˈtwi.to]	-You know, this could be rather fortuitous.

8719	**desconcertar**	**perplex**
	vb	Pero creo que la historia está a punto de desconcertar a los escépticos.
	[dɛs.kõn.sɛr.ˈtar]	-But I believe history is about to confound the skeptics.

8720	**tambalearse**	**stagger**
	vbr	¡Olvídate de la danza, ni siquiera puede tambalearse!
	[tãm.ba.le.ˈar.se]	-Forget dancing, he can't even stagger!

8721	**renombrado**	**renowned**
	adj	Allá en Europa, él fue un renombrado concertista.
	[re.nõm.ˈbra.ðo]	-Back in Europe, he was a renowned recitalist.

8722	**biólogo**	**biologist**
	m	Y Max quiere ser biólogo marino.
	[ˈbjo.lo.ɣo]	-And Max wants to be a marine biologist.

8723	**palpitación**	**pounding**
	f	¿Por qué hay una palpitación en mi corazón?
	[pal.pi.ta.ˈsjõn]	-Why is there a pounding in my heart?

8724	**bastión**	**bastion**
	m	Bolivia es un bastión de la vida silvestre.
	[bas.ˈtjõn]	-Bolivia is a bastion of the wildlife.

8725	**bronquitis**	**bronchitis**
	f	Llamé a la biblioteca y les dije que tenías bronquitis.
	[brõŋ.ˈki.tis]	-I called the library and said you had bronchitis.

8726	**asemejar(se)**	**resemble**
	vb	Incluso muchos aspectos de su comportamiento se asemejan a los nuestros.
	[a.se.me.ˈxar]	-Even many aspects of their behavior resemble our own.

8727	**contingente**	**contingent; possible**
	m; adj	Habla otro miembro del contingente rico.
	[kõ̞n.tĩŋ.ˈxẽ̞n.te]	-Another member of the wealthy contingent is speaking.

8728	**piquete**	**picket**
	m	Creí que eran pilotos montándote un piquete.
	[pi.ˈkɛ.te]	-I thought they were pilots picketing you.

8729	**sobrepeso**	**overweight**
	m	Si tienes sobrepeso, te descalificaré.
	[so.βre.ˈpe.so]	-If you're overweight I'll disqualify you.

| 8730 | **interino** | **interim; caretaker** |

	adj; m	Servirá como alcalde interino mientras me estoy recuperando.
	[ĩn̪.tɛ.ˈri.no]	-He'll serve as interim mayor while I'm recovering.
8731	**minimizar**	**minimise**
	vb	Lo importante es minimizar esos riesgos.
	[mi.ni.mi.ˈsar]	-The important point is to minimize those risks.
8732	**especializar**	**specialize**
	vb	German se quiere especializar en ciencias forenses con la Policía Nacional Haitiana.
	[ɛs.pe.sja.li.ˈsar]	-German wants to specialize in forensic sciences with the Haitian National Police.
8733	**vinilo**	**vinyl**
	m	Invirtió en el equipo y comenzó a mezclar las pistas a través de vinilo.
	[bi.ˈni.lo]	-He invested in equipment and started mixing tracks via vinyl.
8734	**ovario**	**ovary**
	m	El procedimiento se repite para el otro ovario.
	[o.ˈβa.rjo]	-The procedure is repeated for the other ovary.
8735	**multinacional**	**multinational; multinational**
	f; adj	Necesitamos un enfoque multinacional para los problemas globales.
	[mul̪.ti.na.sjo.ˈnal]	-We need to have a multinational approach to global problems.
8736	**provechoso**	**fruitful**
	adj	Espero que su estadía sea provechosa y relajante.
	[pro.βe.ˈʧo.so]	-I hope his stay will be fruitful and relaxing.
8737	**marimacho**	**tomboy (coll)**
	m	No pienso en ella como una marimacho.
	[ma.ri.ˈma.ʧo]	-I don't think of her as a tomboy.
8738	**compactar**	**compact**
	vb	Necesitamos compactar lo más que podamos.
	[kõm.pak̚.ˈtar]	-We need to compact the most we can.
8739	**insuperable**	**unbeatable**
	adj	Te garantizo un precio insuperable para mis visitantes.
	[ĩn.su.pɛ.ˈra.βle]	-I guarantee you unbeatable prices for my visitors.
8740	**requerimiento**	**requirement**
	m	No me di cuenta de que era un requerimiento.
	[re.kɛ.ri.ˈmjẽn̪.to]	-I didn't realize that was a requirement.
8741	**exterminación**	**extermination**
	f	La exterminación de los cristianos no debe continuar.
	[ɛks.tɛr.mi.na.ˈsjõn]	-The extermination of Christians must not continue.
8742	**saltador**	**jumper**
	m	Tengo noticias nuevas de nuestro saltador.
	[sal̪.ta.ˈðor]	-Got some news on our jumper.
8743	**vulnerabilidad**	**vulnerability**
	f	Somos sensibles debido a nuestra vulnerabilidad.
	[bul.nɛ.ra.βi.li.ˈðað]	-We're sensitive because of our vulnerability.
8744	**flautista**	**flutist**
	m/f	Las ostras no llegan y el flautista tiene gripe.
	[flau̯.ˈtis.ta]	-The oysters don't arrive and the flutist has the ague.
8745	**derivar**	**derive**
	vb	Podríamos derivar una estructura que la computadora reconozca.
	[dɛ.ri.ˈβar]	-We may be able to derive a pattern the computer would recognize.

8746	**colación**	**collation**
	f	Es un poco más compleja que una colación binaria.
	[ko.la.ˈsjõn]	-It is a little more complex than a binary collation.
8747	**frecuentar**	**frequent**
	vb	Suena como una discoteca que solía frecuentar en Berlín.
	[fre.kwẽ̯.ˈtar]	-Sounds like a disco I used to frequent in Berlin.
8748	**víscera**	**entrails**
	f	No me gusta comer vísceras de animales.
	[ˈbis.sɛ.ra]	-I don't like eating animal entrails.
8749	**inmueble**	**building**
	m	El inmueble, sin embargo, sufrió considerables daños.
	[ĩm.ˈmwe.βle]	-The building was, however, severely damaged.
8750	**provocador**	**provocative; troublemaker**
	adj; m	Nadie sabe lo que significa, pero es provocador.
	[pro.βo.ka.ˈðor]	-No one knows what it means, but it's provocative.
8751	**bellota**	**acorn**
	f	Lo hallé bajo un árbol, cual bellota caída.
	[be.ˈʝo.ta]	-I found him under a tree like a dropped acorn.
8752	**tardío**	**late**
	adj	Su marido quería sorprenderla con un almuerzo tardío.
	[tar.ˈði.o]	-Your husband wanted to surprise you with a late lunch.
8753	**pasador**	**pin**
	m	Solo tengo que hacer de nuevo el pasador de seguridad.
	[pa.sa.ˈðor]	-I just have to redo the safety pin.
8754	**elástico**	**elastic; elastic**
	m; adj	Pero también analicé el pelo del elástico.
	[e.ˈlas.ti.ko]	-But I also ran the hair from the elastic.
8755	**polluelo**	**chick**
	m	Quizás quede algo para el polluelo.
	[po.ˈʝwe.lo]	-Maybe there will be some for the chick.
8756	**categórico**	**categorical**
	adj	Hay un mensaje categórico e irrevocable para todos.
	[ka.te.ˈʝo.ri.ko]	-There's one categorical, irrevocable message for all.
8757	**eliminatoria**	**heat**
	f	Eso suena como el comienzo de la próxima eliminatoria.
	[e.li.mi.na.ˈto.rja]	-That sounds the start of the next heat.
8758	**centenario**	**centenary; centennial**
	adj; m	Tengo grandes planes para el centenario.
	[sẽ̯.te.ˈna.rjo]	-I've got big plans for the centennial.
8759	**polio**	**polio**
	f	No se han confirmado casos de polio desde 1997.
	[ˈpo.ljo]	-No polio cases have been confirmed since 1997.
8760	**exprimir**	**squeeze**
	vb	Vamos a exprimir a la prensa local.
	[ɛks.pri.ˈmir]	-We're going to squeeze the local press.
8761	**diagonal**	**diagonal; diagonal**
	adj; f	Se accede a ellos por este elevador diagonal.
	[dja.ɣo.ˈnal]	-They are accessed through this diagonal elevator.

8762	**avistar**	**sight**
	vb	Acaban de avistar a nuestra escuadra.
	[a.βis.ˈtar]	-They've just sighted our squadron.
8763	**betún**	**shoe polish**
	m	A veces toma prestado mi betún.
	[bɛ.ˈtũn]	-Sometimes he borrows my shoe polish.
8764	**colonización**	**colonization**
	f	Esto constituye una nueva colonización directa de la región.
	[ko.lo.ni.sa.ˈsjõn]	-This is a new direct colonization of the region.
8765	**refrigerio**	**snack**
	m	Serán un buen refrigerio para febrero.
	[re.fri.ˈxɛ.rjo]	-It'll be a nice snack for February.
8766	**acusador**	**prosecutor**
	m	El acusador le espera fuera.
	[a.ku.sa.ˈðor]	-The prosecutor is waiting for you outside.
8767	**mundano**	**mundane**
	adj	Fuera de contexto, es un detalle absolutamente mundano.
	[mũn̪.ˈda.no]	-Out of context, it's an utterly mundane detail.
8768	**póstumo**	**posthumous**
	adj	Debemos asegurarnos de que sus muertes tengan un significado póstumo.
	[ˈpos.tu.mo]	-We must make sure that their deaths have posthumous meaning.
8769	**margarina**	**margarine**
	f	Tienes muchísima margarina en tu cabello.
	[mar.ɣa.ˈri.na]	-You have so much margarine in your hair.
8770	**ahijado**	**godson**
	m	Marcus estaba hablando sobre tu ahijado.
	[a.i.ˈxa.ðo]	-Marcus was telling me about your godson.
8771	**neutralidad**	**neutrality**
	f	Cualquier violación de la neutralidad repercutiría en el capitán.
	[neu̯.tra.li.ˈðað]	-Any violation of neutrality would reflect on the captain.
8772	**batidora**	**blender**
	m	Las pasé por la batidora ya que él no tiene dientes.
	[ba.ti.ˈðo.ra]	-I put them in the blender since he has no teeth.
8773	**majestuoso**	**majestic**
	adj	Estás delante de este majestuoso edificio.
	[ma.xɛs.ˈtwo.so]	-You're in front of this majestic building.
8774	**aeronáutica**	**aerospace; aviation**
	adj; f	Hay nuevas tecnologías desarrollándose rápidamente en la aeronáutica.
	[a.ɛ.ro.ˈnau̯.ti.ka]	-New technology is developing rapidly in aviation.
8775	**glacial**	**glacial**
	adj	Reinaba un silencio glacial, como de tumba.
	[gla.ˈsjal]	-A glacial silence reigned, as in a tomb.
8776	**disquete**	**diskette**
	m	También se proporcionan a solicitud copias de la base de datos en disquete.
	[dis.ˈkɛ.te]	-Copies of the database on diskette are also provided as required.
8777	**boludez**	**nonsense (LA) (coll)**

	f	Es una boludez, querido mío.
	[bo.ˈlu.ðes]	-That's nonsense, my dear.
8778	**impersonal**	**impersonal**
	adj	Bueno, uno trata de ser impersonal sobre estas cosas.
	[ĩm.pɛr.so.ˈnal]	-Well, you try and be impersonal about these things.
8779	**barbarie**	**barbarism**
	f	Estoy seguro de que la barbarie y sus acólitos serán vencidos.
	[bar.ˈβa.rje]	-I am sure that barbarism and its acolytes will be defeated.
8780	**cartelera**	**billboard**
	f	Llamó cuando vio nuestra nota en una cartelera electrónica.
	[kar.te.ˈlɛ.ra]	-She called when she spotted our note on an electronic billboard.
8781	**recomendable**	**advisable**
	adj	También es recomendable evitar ropas pesadas.
	[re.ko.mẽn̪.ˈda.βle]	-It is also advisable to avoid heavy garments.
8782	**mica**	**mica**
	f	Le puse mica en el pigmento.
	[ˈmi.ka]	-I put mica in the pigment.
8783	**chasis**	**chassis**
	m	Analicé cada fibra del chasis del autobús.
	[ˈtʃa.sis]	-I analyzed every strip of fabric from the bus' chassis.
8784	**centralita**	**switchboard**
	f	La centralita de aquí es terrible, así que vine directamente.
	[sẽn̪.tra.ˈli.ta]	-The switchboard here is appalling, so I came directly.
8785	**descerebrado**	**brainless**
	adj	Solo un ternero descerebrado se quedaría atascado en el barro.
	[dɛs.sɛ.re.ˈβra.ðo]	-Only a brainless calf would get himself stuck in the mud.
8786	**filtrar**	**filter**
	vb	Puedo filtrar algunas de las interferencias.
	[fil̪.ˈtrar]	-I can filter out some of the interference.
8787	**protagonizar**	**star in**
	vb	Tu papi debió dejarte protagonizar sus películas.
	[pro.ta.ɣo.ni.ˈsar]	-Your daddy should have left you to star in his movies.
8788	**estupefaciente**	**narcotic**
	m	Necesita añadirse muy poco para convertirlo en un estupefaciente.
	[ɛs.tu.pe.fa.ˈsjẽn̪.te]	-Very little needs to be added to convert it into a narcotic.
8789	**acumulación**	**accumulation**
	f	Es solo una acumulación de fluidos.
	[a.ku.mu.la.ˈsjõn]	-That is just an accumulation of fluid.
8790	**matricular(se)**	**enroll**
	vb	Puedes matricularle a él en Harvard.
	[ma.tri.ku.ˈlar]	-You can enroll him at Harvard.
8791	**albanés**	**Albanian; Albanian person**
	adj; m	La televisión estatal difunde también las noticias en albanés.
	[al.βa.ˈnes]	-News in Albanian is also broadcast on State television.
8792	**acoplamiento**	**coupling**
	m	Pasas demasiado tiempo leyendo el acoplamiento.
	[a.kop̚.la.ˈmjẽn̪.to]	-You spent too much time reading the coupling.
8793	**libanés**	**Lebanese; Lebanese person**

adj; m
[li.βa.ˈnes]

Un soldado libanés resultó herido en el ataque.
-A Lebanese soldier was wounded in the attack.

8794 moralista — **moralist; moralistic**

m/f; adj
[mo.ra.ˈlis.ta]

No tienes derecho a ponerte moralista.
-You have no right to get moralistic.

8795 descarte — **discard**

m
[dɛs.ˈkar.te]

El descarte no supone conservación, sino un despilfarro.
-Discarding is not conservation, it is waste.

8796 ovación — **ovation**

f
[o.βa.ˈsjõn]

Escuchen la ovación que la gente le tributa.
-Listen to the ovation the crowd is giving him.

8797 precario — **precarious**

adj
[pre.ˈka.rjo]

La salud de la población es extremadamente precaria.
-The health of the population is extremely precarious.

8798 mítico — **mythical**

adj
[ˈmi.ti.ko]

Hay también un aspecto mítico y cósmico de su enseñanza.
-There is also a cosmic and mythical aspect to his teaching.

8799 sucumbir — **succumb**

vb
[su.kũm.ˈbir]

No vamos a sucumbir al dolor.
-We will not succumb to grief.

8800 fauces — **maw**

fpl
[ˈfau̯.ses]

Se autodenominan las fauces de Fenris.
-They call themselves the maw of Fenris.

8801 desigual — **unequal**

adj
[de.si.ˈɣwal]

El problema del desigual acceso afecta también a otros vendedores y productos.
-The problem of unequal access also affects other sellers and products.

8802 enemistad — **enmity**

f
[e.ne.mis.ˈtað]

Podemos vivir con esa enemistad o buscar una forma de cambiarla.
-We can choose to live with that enmity or seek a way to change it.

8803 estepa — **steppe**

f
[ɛs.ˈte.pa]

La estepa es común en el oeste de Andalucía y Levante.
-The steppe is a common feature in the west of Andalusia and Levante.

8804 pita — **pita**

f
[ˈpi.ta]

Tienes que doblar el pan de pita.
-You need to fold that pita.

8805 parienta — **wife (coll)**

f
[pa.ˈrjẽn̯.ta]

Es la parienta otra vez, por supuesto.
-It's the wife again, of course.

8806 archivar — **file**

vb
[ar.ʧi.ˈβar]

¿Qué hago con un tipo que solía archivar documentos?
-What do I do with a guy who used to file papers?

8807 mote — **nickname**

m
[ˈmo.te]

Incluso nos llamaba con el mismo mote.
-He even gave us both the same nickname.

8808 bosquejar — **sketch**

vb
[bos.ke.ˈxar]

Pero ella dijo que podría bosquejar algunas botellas de gin.
-But she said I could sketch some gin bottles.

8809	**operario**	**operator**
	m	Ahora hay una máquina con un operario.
	[o.pɛˈra.rjo]	-Now it is one machine with one operator.
8810	**originalidad**	**originality**
	f	Esta amplia habitación ofrece tanto confort como originalidad.
	[o.ri.xi.na.liˈðað]	-This very spacious room offers at the same time comfort and originality.
8811	**terminación**	**termination**
	f	En este contexto, su país exige la terminación de ambos mandatos.
	[tɛr.mi.naˈsjõn]	-In that context, his country called for the termination of both mandates.
8812	**pupitre**	**desk**
	m	Bueno, este pupitre parece estar desocupado.
	[puˈpi.tre]	-Well, this desk appears to be unoccupied.
8813	**gaita**	**bagpipe**
	f	Tenemos que hacer esto, a menos que Leon pueda tocar la gaita.
	[ˈgai̯.ta]	-We have to do this unless Leon can play the bagpipe.
8814	**marginar**	**marginalize**
	vb	Las religiones no deben utilizarse como un pretexto para marginar o excluir a los demás.
	[mar.xiˈnar]	-Religion should not be used as a pretext to marginalize or exclude others.
8815	**ápice**	**apex**
	m	El ápice del triángulo estará orientado hacia arriba.
	[ˈa.pi.se]	-The apex of the triangle shall be directed upwards.
8816	**anfibio**	**amphibious; amphibian**
	adj; m	Siempre tienes razón, mi hermoso príncipe anfibio.
	[ãɱˈfi.βjo]	-You are always right, my beautiful amphibian prince.
8817	**teorema**	**theorem**
	m	Como el teorema de Fermat, es un rompecabezas que quizá no resolvamos nunca.
	[te.o.ˈre.ma]	-Like Fermat's theorem, it's a puzzle we may never solve.
8818	**giratorio**	**rotating**
	adj	Como puede ver, esto es un campo magnético giratorio.
	[xi.ra.ˈto.rjo]	-As you can see, this is a rotating magnetic field.
8819	**conjunción**	**conjunction**
	f	Ejercen sus derechos individualmente y en conjunción con otros.
	[kõŋ.xũn.ˈsjõn]	-They exercise their rights individually and in conjunction with others.
8820	**remolacha**	**beet**
	f	También se obtuvieron aumentos moderados en la producción de leguminosas, patatas y remolacha azucarera.
	[re.mo.ˈla.tʃa]	-Moderate increases were also realized in the production of pulses, potatoes, and sugar beet.
8821	**autónomo**	**autonomous; independent**
	adj; m	Se trata de un territorio autónomo pero no de una formación nacional.
	[au̯.ˈto.no.mo]	-This is an autonomous territorial, but not national, formation.
8822	**incinerador**	**incinerating; incinerator**
	adj; m	El incinerador fue devuelto a las autoridades.
	[ĩn.si.nɛ.ra.ˈðor]	-The incinerator has been given back to the authorities.

8823 **obeso** — **obese**
adj
[o.ˈβe.so]
Somos el país más obeso del mundo.
-We're the most obese country in the world.

8824 **soportable** — **bearable**
adj
[so.por.ˈta.βle]
Cuanto menos me resistiera, sería más soportable.
-The less I resisted, it would be more bearable.

8825 **regresión** — **regression**
f
[re.ɣre.ˈsjõn]
Esta regresión tomará tiempo, pero llegará.
-This regression will take time, but it will happen.

8826 **sobrellevar** — **endure**
vb
[so.βre.ɟe.ˈβar]
He intentado sobrellevar mi desgracia a solas.
-I have tried to endure my misfortune in silence.

8827 **plástica** — **acrylic; plastic**
adj; f
[ˈplas.ti.ka]
En el interior hay una pieza ovalada de espuma plástica.
-On the inside, there is an oval-shaped piece of plastic foam.

8828 **volátil** — **volatile; volatility**
adj; m
[bo.ˈla.til]
Se trata de una situación insostenible y extremadamente volátil.
-It is a situation that is both unsustainable and extremely volatile.

8829 **segregación** — **segregation**
f
[se.ɣre.ɣa.ˈsjõn]
También observa niveles persistentemente elevados de segregación ocupacional.
-It also notes the persistence in the high levels of occupational segregation.

8830 **páncreas** — **pancreas**
m
[ˈpãŋ.kre.as]
Podemos ver mucho líquido en el páncreas.
-We can see lots of fluid in the pancreas.

8831 **ecosistema** — **ecosystem**
m
[e.ko.sis.ˈte.ma]
Tenemos que velar por el ecosistema.
-We have to look out for the ecosystem.

8832 **descontaminación** — **decontamination**
f
[dɛs.kõn̪.ta.mi.na.ˈsjõn]
Se ha efectuado una operación de descontaminación de algunos lugares contaminados.
-A decontamination operation was carried out on certain polluted sites.

8833 **contestación** — **reply**
f
[kõn̪.tɛs.ta.ˈsjõn]
No tuve respuesta, ni contestación.
-I've had no response or a reply.

8834 **despojar(se)** — **strip**
vb
[dɛs.po.ˈxar]
Sin embargo, también es necesario despojar al terrorismo de su motivación.
-But terrorism also needs to be stripped of its motivation.

8835 **apremiar** — **hurry**
vb
[a.pre.ˈmjar]
¿Podemos apremiar el informe del laboratorio?
-Can we push the lab report?

8836 **frenético** — **frantic**
adj
[fre.ˈnɛ.ti.ko]
El consejo de administración está frenético.
-The board of director is frantic.

8837 **brebaje** — **concoction**
m
[bre.ˈβa.xe]
Toma, es un sabroso brebaje.
-Here, it's a tasty concoction.

8838	**agitador**		**agitator**
	m		Dijeron que querían ver a su hermano, el agitador.
	[a.xi.ta.ˈðor]		-They said they wanted to see her brother, the agitator.
8839	**caudillo**		**leader**
	m		No hay hogar para un caudillo que traiciona a su pueblo.
	[kau̯.ˈði.jo]		-There's no home for a leader who fails his people.
8840	**obstinación**		**obstinacy**
	f		Si aceptas, mi obstinación terminará.
	[oβs.ti.na.ˈsjõn]		-If you agree, my obstinacy will end.
8841	**atañer**		**concern**
	vb		Este problema os atañe a todos vosotros.
	[a.ta.ˈɲɛr]		-This issue concerns all of you.
8842	**arrendamiento**		**lease**
	m		Rompimos después de que firmara el arrendamiento.
	[a.rẽn̪.da.ˈmjẽn̪.to]		-We broke up after I already signed the lease.
8843	**despachar**		**dispatch**
	vb		Tengo que despachar el camión grande.
	[dɛs.pa.ˈʧar]		-I must dispatch the great truck.
8844	**rigidez**		**rigidity**
	f		El acero se utiliza para aportar rigidez y resistencia a los neumáticos.
	[ri.ˈxi.ðes]		-Steel is used to provide rigidity and strength in the tires.
8845	**gaceta**		**gazette**
	f		Es cierto, no había terminado la gaceta.
	[ga.ˈsɛ.ta]		-That's right, I didn't finish my gazette.
8846	**esguince**		**sprain**
	m		Llegó a casa con un esguince de tobillo.
	[ɛs̠.ˈɣĩn.se]		-She came home with a sprained ankle.
8847	**certero**		**accurate**
	adj		Es más certero que un reloj.
	[sɛr.ˈtɛ.ro]		-He's more accurate than any clock.
8848	**bifurcación**		**fork**
	f		Encontrarás una bifurcación en el camino.
	[bi.fur.ka.ˈsjõn]		-You'll find a fork in the road.
8849	**jauría**		**pack**
	f		Parecen una jauría de perros hambrientos.
	[xau̯.ˈri.a]		-They're like a pack of hungry dogs.
8850	**anfiteatro**		**amphitheater**
	m		Sí, es el anfiteatro en Roma.
	[ãm̩.fi.te.ˈa.tro]		-Yes, it is the amphitheater in Rome.
8851	**empaquetar**		**pack**
	vb		No se me ocurrió empaquetar uno.
	[ẽm.pa.kɛ.ˈtar]		-I didn't think to pack one.
8852	**natalidad**		**birth rate**
	f		En primer lugar, hablaremos de la tasa de natalidad.
	[na.ta.li.ˈðað]		-First of all, we will talk about the birth rate.
8853	**instructivo**		**instructive**
	adj		Será instructivo para ella observar un matrimonio feliz.
	[ĩns.truk̚.ˈti.βo]		-It will be instructive for her to observe a happy marriage.

8854 **termal** **thermal**

adj

[tɛr.ˈmal]

Usamos imagen termal para ver qué actividad había dentro del edificio. -We used thermal imagery to see what activity there was inside the buildings.

8855 **mixto** **mixed**

adj

[ˈmiks.to]

No hay un sistema de encarcelamiento mixto en Paraguay. -Paraguay does not have a system of mixed incarceration.

8856 **meteorólogo** **meteorologist**

m

[mɛ.te.o.ˈro.lo.ɣo]

Puedes ser un meteorólogo toda tu vida... -You could be a meteorologist all your life...

8857 **triciclo** **tricycle**

m

[tri.ˈsi.klo]

Sería como una hormiga empujando un triciclo. -It would be like an ant pushing a tricycle.

8858 **semental** **stud; stallion**

adj; m

[se.mẽn.ˈtal]

Parecen un semental y cuatro yeguas. -It looks like a stallion and four mares.

8859 **clarividente** **clairvoyant; psychic**

adj; m/f

[kla.ri.βi.ˈðẽn.te]

Quiero presentarte al clarividente más divino. -I want to show you the most divine clairvoyant.

8860 **trituradora** **crusher**

f

[tri.tu.ra.ˈðo.ra]

Siempre he querido montar una trituradora. -I've always wanted to ride a crusher.

8861 **frustrado** **frustrated**

adj

[frus.ˈtra.ðo]

No sabes lo que es sentirse completamente frustrado. -You don't know what it's like to feel completely frustrated.

8862 **materialista** **materialistic; materialist**

adj; m/f

[ma.tɛ.rja.ˈlis.ta]

No sabía que era tan materialista. -I didn't know you were this materialistic.

8863 **primate** **primate**

m

[pri.ˈma.te]

Ese fue el primer primate erguido. -That was the first upright primate.

8864 **tridimensional** **three-dimensional**

adj

[tri.ði.mẽn.sjo.ˈnal]

Solo estoy intentando crear el personaje más tridimensional que pueda. -I'm just trying to build the most three-dimensional character I can.

8865 **anticonceptivo** **contraceptive; birth control**

adj; m

[ãn.ti.kõn.sep̚.ˈti.βo]

Cualquier tipo de anticonceptivo puede fallar. -Any type of birth control can fail.

8866 **bipolar** **bipolar**

adj

[bi.po.ˈlar]

El sobrediagnóstico del desorden bipolar tiene sus costes. -Over-diagnosis of bipolar disorder has costs.

8867 **diminutivo** **diminutive; diminutive**

adj; m

[di.mi.nu.ˈti.βo]

El diminutivo de Nicola es Nicky más que Nick. -The diminutive of Nicola is Nicky, rather than Nick.

8868 **baza** **asset**

f

[ˈba.sa]

El buen nombre de un hombre puede ser su mayor baza. -A man's good name can be his greatest asset.

8869 **atestar** **attest**

	vb	Al atestar, el testigo declara y confirma que la persona a la que ha
	[a.tɛs.ˈtar]	observado firmar el documento efectivamente lo hizo.
		-By attesting, the witness states and confirms that the person whom he or she watched sign the document in fact did so.

8870 **anticuario**   **antique dealer**

m

[ãn̯.ti.ˈkwa.rjo]

Jérome, el anticuario, me lo regaló.

-Jérome, the antique dealer, gave it to me.

8871 **infusión**   **infusion**

f

[ĩɱ.fu.ˈsjõn]

Bebí una infusión de hierbas.

-I drank an herbal infusion.

8872 **austríaco**   **Austrian; Austrian person**

adj; m

[aṵs.ˈtri.a.ko]

Un ciudadano portugués es ciudadano austríaco.

-A Portuguese citizen is an Austrian citizen.

8873 **huelguista**   **striker**

m/f

[wɛl.ˈɣis.ta]

Fui a ver a la mujer de ese huelguista.

-I went to see that striker's wife.

8874 **navegador**   **browser, navigator**

m

[na.βe.ɣa.ˈðor]

Puedes probarlo ahora en tu navegador.

-You can test it now in your browser.

8875 **encabezar**   **lead**

vb

[ẽŋ.ka.βe.ˈsar]

Tenemos que encabezar los esfuerzos para intentar frenar el cambio climático.

-We must lead the way in trying to slow down climate change.

8876 **trascendental**   **momentous**

adj

[tras.sẽn̯.dẽn̯.ˈtal]

Doctor, podríamos estar ante un descubrimiento trascendental.

-Doctor, we could be on the verge of a momentous discovery.

8877 **jacinto**   **hyacinth**

m

[xa.ˈsĩn̯.to]

Ella usa un perfume con jacinto que huele como los de verdad.

-She uses a perfume with hyacinth that smells just like real ones.

8878 **magnolia**   **magnolia**

f

[maɣ.ˈno.lja]

No voy a ver florecer la magnolia.

-I won't see the magnolia blossom.

8879 **desenmascarar**   **unmask**

vb

[de.sẽm.mas.ka.ˈrar]

Los cuales están resultando muy difíciles de desenmascarar.

-All of whom are proving extremely difficult to unmask.

8880 **cauce**   **channel**

m

[ˈkaṵ.se]

El cauce monetario presenta problemas semejantes.

-The currency channel is similarly impaired.

8881 **gardenia**   **gardenia**

f

[gar.ˈðe.nja]

Y luego te entregaría una gardenia.

-And then he might hand you a gardenia.

8882 **quid**   **crux**

m

[ˈkið]

Siempre vas directamente al quid de la cuestión.

-You always come directly to the crux of the matter.

8883 **inoxidable**   **stainless**

adj

[i.nok.si.ˈða.βle]

Es suave, elegante, con un acabado inoxidable.

-It is smooth, elegant, with a stainless finish.

8884 **desguazar**   **scrap**

	vb	No obligamos a nadie a desguazar su buque o a dejar su actividad pesquera.
	[dεṣ.ɣwa.ˈsar]	-We are not forcing anyone to scrap their vessel or give up fishing as a career.
8885	**narciso**	**daffodil**
	m	Esto es una curraca amarilla bebiendo de un narciso.
	[nar.ˈsi.so]	-This is a yellow warbler drinking out of a daffodil.
8886	**insuficiencia**	**insufficiency**
	f	A menudo se señalaba la insuficiencia de servicios y medios docentes.
	[ĩn.su.fi.ˈsjẽn.sja]	-The insufficiency of educational services and facilities was often pointed out.
8887	**poderío**	**power**
	m	Se necesita algo más que poderío y fuerza militar.
	[po.ðε.ˈri.o]	-Something other than power and military strength is needed.
8888	**sumario**	**summary; investigation**
	adj; m	Puedo mandarte un sumario en cuanto termine.
	[su.ˈma.rjo]	-I can send you a summary when I'm m finished.
8889	**cuña**	**wedge**
	f	Dentro de este dibujó una cuña circular.
	[ˈku.ɲa]	-Inside this, he drew a circular wedge.
8890	**insatisfecho**	**dissatisfied**
	adj	Estoy insatisfecho con devolver la misma cantidad.
	[ĩn.sa.tis.ˈfe.ʧo]	-I'm dissatisfied with giving back the same amount.
8891	**constructivo**	**constructive**
	adj	Será bien acogido todo asesoramiento constructivo.
	[kõns.truk̚.ˈti.βo]	-Any constructive advice will, of course, be most welcome.
8892	**conmemorativo**	**memorial**
	adj	Quiero ofrecer un servicio conmemorativo por mamá.
	[kõm.me.mo.ra.ˈti.βo]	-I want to have a memorial service for mom.
8893	**deteriorar**	**deteriorate**
	vb	Ello sugiere que su situación ya se empezó a deteriorar antes de la crisis.
	[dε.tε.rjo.ˈrar]	-This suggested that their situation started to deteriorate already before the crisis.
8894	**vértebra**	**vertebra**
	f	Entre cada vértebra se encuentra un disco intervertebral.
	[ˈbεr.te.βra]	-Between each vertebra is an intervertebral disk.
8895	**traumatismo**	**trauma**
	m	Miren los diferentes matices del traumatismo.
	[trau̯.ma.ˈtiṣ.mo]	-Look at the different hues from the trauma.
8896	**ascendencia**	**ancestry**
	f	Son individuos únicos que comparten un respeto profundo por su ascendencia irlandesa.
	[as.sẽn̪.ˈdẽn.sja]	-They're unique individuals who share a deep respect for their Irish ancestry.
8897	**anticuerpo**	**antibody**
	m	Nuestro doctor podría ayudarle a sintetizar el anticuerpo.
	[ãn̪.ti.ˈkwεr.po]	-Our doctor could assist you with synthesizing the antibody.
8898	**azafrán**	**saffron**

	m	Para empezar, reemplazó el romero con azafrán.
	[a.sa.ˈfrãn]	-He replaced the rosemary with saffron, for one thing.
8899	**cachetada**	**slap**
	f	Yo diría que fue más bien una cachetada.
	[ka.tʃɛ.ˈta.ða]	-I'd say it was more like a slap.
8900	**tartamudo**	**stutterer**
	m/f	El tartamudo habló de un informante.
	[tar.ta.ˈmu.ðo]	-The stutterer spoke of an informer.
8901	**metafórico**	**metaphorical**
	adj	Es un sistema metafórico impreciso. Está abierto a interpretaciones.
	[mɛ.ta.ˈfo.ri.ko]	-It's an imprecise metaphorical system. It's open to interpretation.
8902	**abridor**	**opener**
	m	Hay un abridor eléctrico en la estantería de la cocina.
	[a.βri.ˈðor]	-There's an electric opener on the shelf in the kitchen.
8903	**pornográfico**	**pornographic**
	adj	Y no queríamos vender nada que fuera pornográfico.
	[por.no.ˈɣra.fi.ko]	-And we didn't want to sell anything that was pornographic.
8904	**curador**	**healing; curator**
	adj; m	Su curador es un hombre llamado Lupo Mercuri.
	[ku.ra.ˈðor]	-Its curator is a man called Lupo Mercuri.
8905	**plática**	**talk (LA)**
	f	Estás escuchando la mejor plática de Texas.
	[ˈpla.ti.ka]	-You're listening to the best talk in Texas.
8906	**decodificador**	**decoder**
	m	Perdóname. He perdido mi anillo decodificador secreto.
	[de.ko.ði.fi.ka.ˈðor]	-Forgive me. I've lost my secret decoder ring.
8907	**fotocopiadora**	**photocopier**
	f	Entonces podremos saber qué fotocopiadora utilizaron.
	[fo.to.ko.pja.ˈðo.ra]	-Then we'll be able to tell what photocopier they used.
8908	**rectoría**	**rectory**
	f	Tengo que volver a la rectoría.
	[rek̚.to.ˈri.a]	-I have to get back to the rectory.
8909	**triangular**	**triangular; triangulate**
	adj; vb	Esta es una formación triangular también.
	[trjãŋ.gu.ˈlar]	-This is in a triangular formation as well.
8910	**festividad**	**festivity**
	f	El 7 de julio es la festividad de San Fermín.
	[fɛs.ti.βi.ˈðað]	-July 7th is the festivity of San Fermín.
8911	**circunstancial**	**circumstantial**
	adj	Hay mucha evidencia circunstancial para apoyar la teoría.
	[sir.kũns.tãn.ˈsjal]	-There's a lot of circumstantial evidence to support the theory.
8912	**estremecer(se)**	**shudder**
	vb	La simple mención de la sangre me hace estremecer.
	[ɛs.tre.me.ˈsɛr]	-The mere mention of blood makes me shudder.
8913	**fanatismo**	**fanaticism**
	m	Provocan brotes de radicalismo, fanatismo y extremismo.
	[fa.na.ˈtiṣ.mo]	-They cause an outbreak of radicalism, fanaticism, and extremism.
8914	**desprender**	**detach, release**

	vb	Golpea ligeramente el frasco para desprender el polvo.
	[dɛs.prɛ̃n̩.ˈdɛr]	-Tap the bottle to release the powder.
8915	**proclamación**	**proclamation**
	f	La proclamación no fue modificada, revocada, ni terminada.
	[pro.kla.ma.ˈsjõn]	-The proclamation was not amended, revoked or denounced.
8916	**plebeyo**	**commoner; peasant**
	m; adj	Me siento bien compartiéndolo con un plebeyo.
	[ple.ˈβe.jo]	-It feels good to share it with a commoner.
8917	**percance**	**mishap**
	m	Tuve un pequeño percance con un pájaro.
	[pɛr.ˈkãn.se]	-I had a small mishap with a bird.
8918	**anclar**	**anchor**
	vb	Los piratas solían anclar en esa ensenada.
	[ã̃ŋ.ˈklar]	-Pirate ships used to anchor in that cove.
8919	**libertador**	**liberator; liberator**
	m; adj	Yo seré su libertador esta tarde.
	[li.βɛr.ta.ˈðor]	-I'll be your liberator this evening.
8920	**pirueta**	**pirouette**
	f	En este mismo momento vi el secreto de su pirueta.
	[pi.ˈrwɛ.ta]	-At this very moment, I saw the secret of his pirouette.
8921	**costal**	**bag**
	m	Ese costal no te va a golpear de vuelta.
	[kos.ˈtal]	-That bag's not going to hit you back.
8922	**letrado**	**counsel; learned**
	m; adj	El autor está representado por un letrado.
	[lɛ.ˈtra.ðo]	-The author is represented by counsel.
8923	**donativo**	**donation**
	m	Nunca lamentará este generoso donativo de 3.000$.
	[do.na.ˈti.βo]	-You'll never regret this generous donation of $3,000.
8924	**pliegue**	**crease**
	m	No puedo ver nada en el pliegue.
	[ˈplje.ɣe]	-I can't make out anything in the crease.
8925	**lucero**	**bright star**
	m	Si fuera un lucero les diría que juntos nos trajeran la fortuna.
	[lu.ˈsɛ.ro]	-If I was a bright star, I'd tell them to bring us luck, both of them altogether.
8926	**cacique**	**cacique**
	m/f	España tuvo que enviar a un embajador para negociar con el cacique.
	[ka.ˈsi.ke]	-Spain had to send an ambassador to meet with the Cacique.
8927	**yema**	**yolk**
	f	Cuidado. No rompas la yema.
	[ˈɟje.ma]	-Careful. Don't break the egg yolk.
8928	**charca**	**pond**
	f	Vendrán aquí para comer en la charca.
	[ˈtʃar.ka]	-They'll be coming down here to the pond to feed.
8929	**ecológico**	**ecological**
	adj	Podríamos destruir el equilibrio ecológico del río.
	[e.ko.ˈlo.xi.ko]	-We could upset the ecological balance of the river.

8930 **culminación** — **culmination**
f
[kul.mi.na.ˈsjõn]
Esta amenaza es la culminación de dos tendencias inquietantes.
-This threat is the culmination of two worrying trends.

8931 **comentarista** — **commentator**
m/f
[ko.mẽn̯.ta.ˈris.ta]
Saluden a nuestro nuevo comentarista invitado.
-Say hello to our new guest commentator.

8932 **garza** — **heron**
f
[ˈgar.sa]
Te has transformado en una garza.
-You've turned into a heron.

8933 **inercia** — **inertia**
f
[i.ˈnɛr.sja]
Tenemos competidores que no muestran esa inercia.
-We have competitors who do not show that inertia.

8934 **embalaje** — **packaging**
m
[ẽm.ba.ˈla.xe]
No queríamos un embalaje de adorno.
-We did not want any cosmetic packaging.

8935 **cardiólogo** — **cardiologist**
m
[kar.ˈðjo.lo.ɣo]
Necesito a un cardiólogo aquí.
-I need a cardiologist in here.

8936 **irresponsabilidad** — **irresponsibility**
f
[i.rɛs.põn.sa.βi.li.ˈðað]
Esto no es pacifismo, esto es demagogia e irresponsabilidad.
-This is not pacifism, it is demagoguery and irresponsibility.

8937 **placenta** — **placenta**
f
[pla.ˈsẽn̯.ta]
La placenta crece dentro del útero.
-The placenta's grown into the uterus wall.

8938 **orégano** — **oregano**
m
[o.ˈre.ɣa.no]
Es cordero preparado lentamente al orégano.
-It's lamb cooked very, very slowly in oregano.

8939 **casete** — **cassette**
m/f
[ka.ˈsɛ.te]
Creo que es mejor decirles sobre el casete.
-I think it's better to tell them about the cassette.

8940 **desechar** — **discard**
vb
[de.se.ˈtʃar]
Quite y deseche el protector transparente de plástico que cubre el adhesivo.
-Remove and discard the clear plastic liner covering the adhesive.

8941 **tilde** — **accent**
f
[ˈtil̯.de]
Tienes que añadir una tilde a esa palabra.
-You have to add an accent to that word.

8942 **caducar** — **expire**
vb
[ka.ðu.ˈkar]
La oferta del lanzamiento gratis está por caducar.
-The free introductory offer is about to expire.

8943 **pesticida** — **pesticide**
m
[pɛs.ti.ˈsi.ða]
Después traed tanto pesticida como podáis cargar.
-Then bring back as much pesticide as you can carry.

8944 **surtir(se)** — **supply**
vb
[sur.ˈtir]
Apenas podíamos surtir a todos.
-We could barely supply everybody.

8945 **destituir** — **remove**

	vb	No quiero destituir a mi marido.
	[dɛs.ti.ˈtwir]	-I do not want to impeach my husband.
8946	**pecaminoso**	**sinful**
	adj	Es pecaminoso no dar oportunidad de absolución.
	[pe.ka.mi.ˈno.so]	-It is sinful to offer no chance of absolution.
8947	**satánico**	**satanic; satanist**
	adj; m	Es miembro de éste culto satánico y perverso.
	[sa.ˈta.ni.ko]	-She's a member of this evil and satanic cult.
8948	**asador**	**grill**
	m	Todo el asador está en llamas.
	[a.sa.ˈðor]	-The whole grill is on fire.
8949	**elegía**	**elegy**
	f	Es donde Gray escribió su elegía.
	[e.le.ˈxi.a]	-It's where Gray wrote his elegy.
8950	**cántico**	**chant**
	m	Nunca es bueno cuando escucho ese cántico.
	[ˈkãn̪.ti.ko]	-It's never good when I hear that chant.
8951	**perdigón**	**pellet**
	m	Le inyectaron un minúsculo perdigón envenenado.
	[pɛr.ði.ˈɣõn]	-He was injected with some sort of tiny poison pellet.
8952	**pastoral**	**pastoral**
	adj	Intenté mantenerla bajo mi vigilancia pastoral.
	[pas.to.ˈral]	-I tried to keep a pastoral eye on her.
8953	**ucraniano**	**Ukrainian; Ukrainian person**
	adj; m	Me sorprendió oír un acento ucraniano.
	[u.kra.ˈnja.no]	-I was surprised to hear a Ukrainian accent.
8954	**marejada**	**tidal wave**
	f	Fue como una marejada que venía hacia mí.
	[ma.re.ˈxa.ða]	-It was like a tidal wave coming at me.
8955	**feligrés**	**parishioner**
	m	Tengo un problema con un colega feligrés.
	[fe.li.ˈɣres]	-I have an issue with a fellow parishioner.
8956	**parra**	**vine**
	f	Comimos uvas directamente de la parra.
	[ˈpa.ra]	-We ate grapes right off the vine.
8957	**taquigrafía**	**shorthand**
	f	No la contrataste por su taquigrafía.
	[ta.ki.ɣra.ˈfi.a]	-You didn't hire her for her shorthand.
8958	**tanda**	**batch**
	f	Y envié una última tanda de postales.
	[ˈtãn̪.da]	-And I sent out one last batch of postcards.
8959	**estampa**	**stamp**
	f	A estos efectos, se estampa un sello en sus pasaportes.
	[ɛs.ˈtãm.pa]	-A stamp to this effect is affixed on their passports.
8960	**brocha**	**brush**
	f	La próxima vez que alguien vaya a la ciudad puede comprar una brocha.
	[ˈbro.tʃa]	-Next time anybody is in town they can pick up a paintbrush.
8961	**quinina**	**quinine**

	f	Necesitamos toda la quinina que tenemos.
	[ki.ˈni.na]	-We need all the quinine we have.
8962	**edredón**	**quilt**
	m	Todas las camas disponen de almohada y edredón.
	[e.ðre.ˈðõn]	-All beds are equipped with a pillow and quilt.
8963	**nacionalismo**	**nationalism**
	m	Existía el nacionalismo y era fuerte.
	[na.sjo.na.ˈliṣ.mo]	-Nationalism did exist, and it was a powerful force.
8964	**fundamentalista**	**fundamentalist; fundamentalist**
	adj; m/f	Le hemos clasificado como algo llamado justiciero fundamentalista.
	[fũn.da.mẽn.ta.ˈlis.ta]	-We're classifying him as something called a fundamentalist vigilante.
8965	**ocioso**	**idle**
	adj	Veo que no ha estado ocioso en mi ausencia.
	[o.ˈsjo.so]	-I see that he has not been idle in my absence.
8966	**estabilizar(se)**	**stabilize**
	vb	Es tarea del gobierno estabilizar las expectativas.
	[ɛs.ta.βi.li.ˈsar]	-It is the government's job to stabilize expectations.
8967	**emanar**	**emanate**
	vb	Las leyes deben emanar de la Constitución.
	[e.ma.ˈnar]	-Laws must emanate from the Constitution.
8968	**rasgar**	**rip**
	vb	Pensé que una bolsa de basura se rasgaría.
	[raṣ.ˈɣar]	-I thought a trash bag would rip.
8969	**capar**	**castrate**
	vb	¡Yo te voy a capar!
	[ka.ˈpar]	-I'm going to have you neutered!
8970	**neutro**	**neutral**
	adj	Por esta razón debería elegirse un logotipo neutro.
	[ˈneu̯.tro]	-For this reason, a neutral logo should be chosen.
8971	**nexo**	**nexus**
	m	Así pues, hay un nexo estrecho entre vida y medios de subsistencia.
	[ˈnɛk.so]	-There is thus a close nexus between life and means of livelihood.
8972	**integrar**	**integrate**
	vb	Debemos continuar nuestro trabajo e integrar nuestras economías.
	[ĩn.te.ˈɣrar]	-We must carry on our work and integrate our economies.
8973	**escayolar**	**put in a cast**
	vb	El tipo llevaba el brazo escayolado.
	[ɛs.ka.jo.ˈlar]	-The guy's arm was in a cast.
8974	**desacreditar**	**discredit**
	vb	Creo que alguien está intentando desacreditar la campaña.
	[de.sa.kre.ði.ˈtar]	-I think someone's trying to discredit the campaign.
8975	**eufórico**	**euphoric**
	adj	El efecto de esta variedad es potente y eufórico.
	[eu̯.ˈfo.ri.ko]	-The effect of this variety is powerful and euphoric.
8976	**empanada**	**pie**
	f	Haz una empanada para tu madre.
	[ɛ̃m.pa.ˈna.ða]	-Make a pie for your mother.
8977	**inmunológico**	**immune**

adj
[ĩm.mu.no.ˈlo.xi.ko]

Ambos tienen un saludable sistema inmunológico.
-You both have healthy immune systems.

8978 **espermatozoide**

spermatozoon

m
[ɛs.per.ma.to.ˈsoi̯.ðe]

No te voy a preguntar de quién es el espermatozoide victorioso.
-I won't ask whose victorious spermatozoon it is.

8979 **cromosoma**

chromosome

m
[kro.mo.ˈso.ma]

Queríamos construir el cromosoma bacteriano entero.
-We wanted to build the entire bacterial chromosome.

8980 **telecomunicaciones**

telecommunications

fpl
[te.le.ko.mu.ni.ka.ˈsjo.nes]

Las telecomunicaciones cambian nuestra vida con rapidez.
-Telecommunications are changing our lives at a fast pace.

8981 **étnico**

ethnic

adj
[ˈɛt̚.ni.ko]

Esos comentarios se consideraron incitación al odio étnico.
-Those remarks were considered to be an incitement to ethnic hatred.

8982 **discográfico**

recording

adj
[dis.ko.ˈɣra.fi.ko]

Quiero tener un contrato discográfico.
-I want to have a recording deal.

8983 **física**

physical; physics

adj; f
[ˈfi.si.ka]

Como de costumbre, el profesor de física llegó tarde a clase.
-As usual, the physics teacher was late for class.

8984 **cinematografía**

cinematography

f
[si.ne.ma.to.ɣra.ˈfi.a]

Gran parte de la cinematografía europea ha desaparecido.
-A lot of European cinematography has disappeared.

8985 **escasear**

be scarce

vb
[ɛs.ka.se.ˈar]

Espere unas pocas semanas hasta que sus recursos comiencen a escasear.
-Wait a few weeks until your resources start to run out.

8986 **prolongado**

prolonged

adj
[pro.lõŋ.ˈga.ðo]

No tienen temple para un conflicto prolongado.
-They do not have the stomach for a prolonged conflict.

8987 **cepo**

trap

m
[ˈse.po]

Haré un cepo mañana en la fundición.
-I'll make a trap tomorrow in the forge.

8988 **inestimable**

invaluable

adj
[i.nɛs.ti.ˈma.βle]

La contribución del voluntariado a la sociedad es inestimable.
-The contribution volunteering makes to society is invaluable.

8989 **superhombre**

superman

m
[su.pɛ.ˈrõm.bre]

No trates de ser un superhombre aquí.
-Don't try to be a superman here.

8990 **torácico**

thoracic; thoracic duct

adj; m
[to.ˈra.si.ko]

No tendrán un cirujano torácico disponible.
-They wouldn't have a thoracic surgeon on call.

8991 **junco**

reed

m
[ˈxũŋ.ko]

¿Era un junco temblando con el viento?
-Was it a reed trembling in the wind?

8992 **desplazar**

displace

vb
[dɛs.pla.ˈsar]

El segundo enfoque consiste en desplazar completamente al deudor.
-The second approach was to displace the debtor altogether.

8993	**pancarta**	**banner**
	f	Haré una pancarta con algunas mujeres del pueblo.
	[pãŋ.ˈkar.ta]	-I'll make a banner with some of the women from the village.
8994	**filtrado**	**filtering; filter**
	adj; m	El medio de filtrado debe limpiarse o cambiarse periódicamente.
	[fiḻ.ˈtra.ðo]	-The filtering medium needs to be cleaned or exchanged periodically.
8995	**revocar**	**revoke**
	vb	No me obligues a revocar tus privilegios de estacionamiento.
	[re.βo.ˈkar]	-Don't force me to revoke your parking privileges.
8996	**prevalecer**	**prevail**
	vb	El imperio del derecho debe prevalecer en todo momento.
	[pre.βa.le.ˈsɛr]	-The rule of law must always prevail.
8997	**neurológico**	**neurological**
	adj	Significa que hay algún tipo de problema neurológico.
	[neu̯.ro.ˈlo.xi.ko]	-Means there's some sort of neurological problem.
8998	**entonar**	**sing**
	vb	Estoy pensando en una canción que mi nodriza solía entonarme.
	[ɛ̃n.to.ˈnar]	-I'm thinking of a song my nursemaid used to sing to me.
8999	**sintonizar**	**tune**
	vb	Donna, yo no obligo a nadie a conectarse y sintonizar.
	[sĩn.to.ni.ˈsar]	-Donna, I'm not forcing anybody to log on and tune in.
9000	**mirlo**	**blackbird**
	m	¿Pero te gusta mi mirlo?
	[ˈmir.lo]	-But do you like my blackbird?
9001	**fornido**	**strapping**
	adj	Lamento molestar, pero pareces bastante fornido.
	[for.ˈni.ðo]	-Sorry to intrude, but you seem rather strapping.
9002	**acatar**	**abide by**
	vb	Nos gustaría mucho acatar sus instrucciones.
	[a.ka.ˈtar]	-We would like very much to abide by your instructions.
9003	**agobiar(se)**	**overwhelm**
	vb	Las culturas incipientes de aprendizaje e innovación suelen agobiar a las
	[a.ɣo.ˈβjar]	culturas de acatamiento existentes.
		-Emerging cultures of learning and innovation frequently overwhelm existing cultures of compliance.
9004	**amputar**	**amputate**
	vb	Anoche tuve que amputar una pierna.
	[ãm.pu.ˈtar]	-Last night I had to amputate a leg.
9005	**balde**	**bucket**
	m	Yo llené el balde con agua.
	[ˈbaḻ.de]	-I filled the bucket with water.
9006	**perturbación**	**disturbance**
	f	Solo recuerden informar de cualquier signo de perturbación.
	[pɛr.tur.βa.ˈsjõn]	-Just remember to report the least sign of a disturbance.
9007	**remisión**	**remission**
	f	Esta mujer parece haber estado en remisión.
	[re.mi.ˈsjõn]	-This woman seems to have been in remission.
9008	**imposición**	**imposition**

f

Espero que no te importe la imposición.
-I hope you don't mind the imposition.

9009 **permanencia**

permanence

f

La permanencia es el polo opuesto de la rendición de cuentas.
-Permanence is the polar opposite of accountability.

[pɛr.ma.ˈnɛn.sja]

9010 **trotar**

trot

vb

Llevo robando aves como método de subsistencia desde antes de aprender a trotar.
-I've been stealing birds for a living since before I could trot.

[tro.ˈtar]

9011 **níquel**

nickel

m

Dame algo relajante que valga un níquel.
-Give me a nickel's worth of anything soothing.

[ˈni.kɛl]

9012 **bidón**

drum

m

Vamos, échame una mano con este bidón.
-Come on, give me a hand with this drum.

[bi.ˈðõn]

9013 **condimento**

seasoning

m

No necesitan ningún tipo de condimento porque tienen su propio aroma picante.
-They need no sort of seasoning because they have their own kind of pungent aroma.

[kõn.di.ˈmẽn.to]

9014 **arbitrar**

arbitrate

vb

Aquí no hay nada que arbitrar.
-There's nothing here to arbitrate.

[ar.βi.ˈtrar]

9015 **instintivo**

instinctive

adj

Este país volvió a su aislacionismo instintivo.
-This country reverted to its instinctive isolationism.

[ĩns.tĩn.ˈti.βo]

9016 **dogma**

dogma

m

Disiento del dogma de la Iglesia establecida.
-I dissent from the dogma of the established Church.

[ˈdoɣ.ma]

9017 **culebra**

snake

f

Ahora tengo que conseguir una culebra.
-Now I have to get a snake.

[ku.ˈle.βra]

9018 **promiscuo**

promiscuous

adj

La mayoría de las cosas se agotan por el uso promiscuo.
-Most things become exhausted by promiscuous use.

[pro.ˈmis.kwo]

9019 **cifrar**

encrypt

vb

Existen diferentes formas de cifrar sus datos.
-There are different ways to encrypt your data.

[si.ˈfrar]

9020 **curvatura**

curvature

f

Notará la curvatura del horizonte.
-You'll notice the curvature of the horizon.

[kur.βa.ˈtu.ra]

9021 **inmigración**

immigration

f

Dicha inmigración ha enriquecido a nuestro continente y continuará haciéndolo.
-Such immigration has enriched our continent and will continue to do so.

[ĩm.mi.ɣra.ˈsjõn]

9022 **quilombo**

mess

m

No sé cómo puede vivir en este quilombo.
-I don't know how he can live in this mess.

[ki.ˈlõm.bo]

9023	**modelar**	**model**
	vb	Necesitan modelar su matrimonio como uno perfecto.
	[mo.ðe.ˈlar]	-You two need to model your marriage after a perfect one.
9024	**tembloroso**	**trembling**
	adj	Has convertido a un tipo duro en un chico tembloroso.
	[tẽm.blo.ˈro.so]	-You turned a hard-core felon into a trembling teenager.
9025	**alfalfa**	**alfalfa**
	f	Aquí planté alfalfa, mi niño.
	[al.ˈfal.fa]	-Here I have planted alfalfa, my boy.
9026	**epílogo**	**epilogue**
	f	Me gustaría añadir un epílogo final.
	[e.ˈpi.lo.ɣo]	-I want to add a final epilogue.
9027	**venerar**	**worship**
	vb	Cada uno decide cómo venerar a Dios.
	[be.nɛ.ˈrar]	-We decide how we worship God.
9028	**inquietar**	**unsettle**
	vb	Rodean a la manada, tratando de inquietarla y separarla.
	[ĩŋ.kjɛ.ˈtar]	-They circle the herd, trying to unsettle it and split it up.
9029	**patriarca**	**patriarch**
	m	La oración del patriarca comenzará en breve.
	[pa.ˈtrjar.ka]	-The Patriarch's prayer will start any minute.
9030	**isleño**	**island; islander**
	adj; m	En realidad, buscamos a un isleño.
	[iş.ˈle.ɲo]	-Actually, it's an Islander we're looking for.
9031	**reorganizar**	**reorganize**
	vb	Tenemos que fortalecer y reorganizar las fronteras de la comunidad.
	[re.or.ɣa.ni.ˈsar]	-We have to strengthen and reorganize the external borders of the community.
9032	**rencoroso**	**spiteful**
	adj	Fue deliberado, el acto rencoroso de un niño neurótico.
	[rẽŋ.ko.ˈro.so]	-It was deliberate, the spiteful act of a neurotic child.
9033	**vigoroso**	**vigorous**
	adj	Serás más vigoroso si te ejercitas.
	[bi.ɣo.ˈro.so]	-You will be more vigorous if you exercise.
9034	**barítono**	**baritone**
	m	Es el barítono que estábamos buscando.
	[ba.ˈri.to.no]	-He's just the baritone we've been looking for.
9035	**aval**	**guarantee**
	m	En el acuerdo de suscripción figuraba una cláusula compromisoria, pero no en el aval.
	[a.ˈβal]	-There was an arbitration clause in the subscription agreement, but not the guarantee.
9036	**cuestionable**	**questionable**
	adj	Excederse con un hombre desarmado siempre es cuestionable.
	[kwɛs.tjo.ˈna.βle]	-Escalating force with an unarmed subject is always questionable.
9037	**nogal**	**walnut**
	m	Sus propiedades son similares a las del nogal europeo.
	[no.ˈɣal]	-Its properties are similar to those of European walnut.
9038	**acequia**	**ditch**

f
[a.ˈse.kja]
Ha ido a sacar un coche de una acequia.
-He is away to get out a car from a ditch.

9039 zanja ditch

f
[ˈsãŋ.xa]
Podría tener la zanja inundada en pocos días.
-I could have the ditch flooded in a few days.

9040 bochorno embarrassment

m
[bo.ˈʧor.no]
Es prácticamente un bochorno para todos nosotros.
-He's pretty much an embarrassment to all of us.

9041 aparejo rig

m
[a.pa.ˈre.xo]
Este aparejo estaba bien cuando hice mi comprobación de seguridad.
-This rigging was secure when I did my safety check.

9042 bilis bile

f
[ˈbi.lis]
La excreción tiene lugar en la bilis.
-Excretion takes place in the bile.

9043 sumiso submissive

adj
[su.ˈmi.so]
El otro es sumiso y muestra tendencias obsesivo-compulsivas.
-The other is submissive and displays obsessive-compulsive tendencies.

9044 habichuela bean

f
[a.βi.ˈʧwe.la]
Y este es mi famoso guisado de habichuela.
-And this is my green bean casserole.

9045 andamio scaffold

m
[ãn̪.ˈda.mjo]
Usa el andamio para subir al techo.
-Use the scaffold to get to the roof.

9046 chutar shoot

vb
[ʧu.ˈtar]
Está a punto de chutar.
-She is about to shoot.

9047 incompatible incompatible

adj
[ĩŋ.kõm.pa.ˈti.βle]
Esto sería incompatible con el texto del Tratado.
-This would be incompatible with the wording of the Treaty.

9048 minusválido disabled; disabled person

adj; m
[mi.nuş.ˈβa.li.ðo]
El antiguo propietario estuvo minusválido sus últimos años de vida.
-The previous owner was disabled the last years of his life.

9049 viral viral

adj
[bi.ˈral]
Eso es bastante común con una infección viral.
-That's actually quite common with a viral infection.

9050 prefijo prefix

m
[pre.ˈfi.xo]
Introduzca aquí el prefijo que quiera usar.
-Enter the prefix you wish to use here.

9051 ecología ecology

f
[e.ko.lo.ˈxi.a]
La sociedad humana forma parte de una ecología más amplia.
-The human society is part of the wider ecology.

9052 saudí Saudi; Saudi person

adj; m/f
[sau̯.ˈði]
Estoy aquí para recibir al embajador saudí.
-I'm here to welcome the Saudi ambassador.

9053 carnívoro carnivore

adj
[kar.ˈni.βo.ro]
La mordida del carnívoro ha hecho su trabajo.
-The carnivore's bite has done its job.

9054 abrelatas can opener

	f	No necesitas un abrelatas eléctrico para comer.
	[a.βre.ˈla.tas]	-You don't need an electric can opener to feed yourself.

9055 legislador — **legislative; legislator**

adj; m
[le.xiş.la.ˈðor]

Es prerrogativa del legislador actuar así.
-It is the legislator's prerogative to do so.

9056 cupo — **quota**

m
[ˈku.po]

Ya he cubierto el cupo de empleados discapacitados para este año.
-I've already filled our quota of handicapped employees for the year.

9057 encantado — **delighted**

adj
[ɛ̃ŋ.kã̠n.ˈta.ðo]

No, estoy segura de que él estaría encantado.
-No, I'm sure he'd be delighted.

9058 atemorizar — **terrify**

vb
[a.te.mo.ri.ˈsar]

Así, sin ningún motivo, para atemorizar a los demás.
-Just like that, for no reason, to scare the others.

9059 sedición — **sedition**

f
[se.ði.ˈsjõn]

Fue acusada de daños a la propiedad y sedición.
-She was accused of damaging property and sedition.

9060 dolido — **hurt**

adj
[do.ˈli.ðo]

Porque estaba dolido y enfadado y demasiado borracho.
-Because I was hurt and angry and way too drunk.

9061 inmovilizar — **immobilize**

vb
[ĩm.mo.βi.li.ˈsar]

Te tengo que inmovilizar este brazo.
-I have to immobilize this arm.

9062 pirarse — **bait (ES) (coll)**

vbr
[pi.ˈrar.se]

Pero aun así tenemos que pirarnos.
-But we still got to bail.

9063 fantasmal — **ghostly**

adj
[fã̠n.taş.ˈmal]

Yo no creo que haya nada fantasmal en eso.
-I don't think there's anything ghostly about that.

9064 vestigio — **vestige**

m
[bɛs.ˈti.xjo]

Ciertamente ese es un vestigio del sistema jurídico colonial.
-That was surely a vestige of the colonial legal system.

9065 periferia — **periphery**

f
[pɛ.ri.ˈfɛ.rja]

Producen un impacto en las regiones rurales y en su periferia inmediata.
-They impact on rural regions and the immediate periphery.

9066 enagua — **petticoat**

f
[e.ˈna.ɣwa]

Debería encontrar alguna forma de arreglar esta enagua.
-I ought to find some way to mend this petticoat.

9067 impuro — **impure**

adj
[ĩm.ˈpu.ro]

Será puro quién purifique a un impuro.
-It'll be pure who purifies an impure.

9068 pamplinas — **nonsense**

fpl
[pã̠m.ˈpli.nas]

Se cree de verdad que me asusta con sus pamplinas.
-She actually believes she scares me with that nonsense.

9069 anaconda — **anaconda**

f
[a.na.ˈkõ̠n.da]

De acuerdo, ve a por la anaconda.
-Okay, go for the anaconda.

9070 irrevocable — **irrevocable**

	adj	Lo consideraré como una promesa irrevocable.
	[i.re.βo.ˈka.βle]	-I will regard that as an irrevocable promise.
9071	**electrodo**	**electrode**
	m	El electrodo puede usarse como ánodo en una pila de combustible.
	[e.lek̚.ˈtro.ðo]	-The electrode can be used as an anode in a fuel cell.
9072	**auditoría**	**audit**
	f	Una auditoría puede ser muy motivadora.
	[au̯.ði.to.ˈri.a]	-An audit can be highly motivating.
9073	**relajo**	**relax**
	m	Sabes que así es como me relajo.
	[re.ˈla.xo]	-You know this is how I relax.
9074	**carente**	**lacking**
	adj	Su cerebro ya está carente de emoción.
	[ka.ˈrẽn̪.te]	-His brain is already lacking excitement.
9075	**frutilla**	**strawberry (LA)**
	f	Tenemos galletitas de frutilla y de chocolate.
	[fru.ˈti.ʝa]	-We have strawberry and chocolate cookies.
9076	**espora**	**spore**
	f	Tiene que ser algún tipo de ameba o espora.
	[ɛs.ˈpo.ra]	-It has to be some type of amoeba or spore.
9077	**rústico**	**rustic**
	adj	El restaurante te da la bienvenida en un entorno rústico y acogedor.
	[ˈrus.ti.ko]	-The restaurant welcomes you in a rustic and convivial setting.
9078	**estampar**	**stamp**
	vb	Los bancos siempre usan sellos para estampar las fechas.
	[ɛs.tãm.ˈpar]	-Banks always use hand-stamps for the dates.
9079	**clausura**	**closing**
	f	Ayer fue la ceremonia de clausura del colegio.
	[klau̯.ˈsu.ra]	-Yesterday was the school closing ceremony.
9080	**anotador**	**notepad (LA)**
	m	Pueden traer un anotador y una lapicera.
	[a.no.ta.ˈðor]	-They can bring one pad and one pen.
9081	**opositor**	**opponent**
	m	Y tú eres el opositor más digno.
	[o.po.si.ˈtor]	-And you are the most worthy opponent.
9082	**laringe**	**larynx**
	f	He implantado un microchip en su laringe.
	[la.ˈrĩŋ.xe]	-I've implanted a microchip on your larynx.
9083	**embotellar**	**bottle**
	vb	Deberías embotellar ese amor ya que cura problemas mentales.
	[ẽm.bo.te.ˈʝar]	-You should bottle that love since it cures mental problems.
9084	**planeamiento**	**planning**
	m	En particular, es esencial un planeamiento integrado.
	[pla.ne.a.ˈmjẽn̪.to]	-In particular, integrated planning is essential.
9085	**desperfecto**	**flaw**
	m	Pero hubo un desperfecto en el diseño.
	[dɛs.pɛr.ˈfek̚.to]	-But there was a design flaw.
9086	**refutar**	**refute**

	vb	El segundo malentendido general es más difícil de refutar.
	[re.fu.ˈtar]	-The second general misunderstanding is more difficult to refute.
9087	**paladín**	**paladin**
	m	Quiten el cuerpo del paladín de aquí.
	[pa.la.ˈðĩn]	-Remove the paladin body from here.
9088	**sindicalista**	**union; trade unionist**
	adj; m/f	Mi padre ha sido siempre sindicalista.
	[sĩn̪.di.ka.ˈlis.ta]	-Dad's always been a union man.
9089	**prioritario**	**critical**
	adj	Este área también debe considerarse prioritaria.
	[prjo.ri.ˈta.rjo]	-This should also be considered a priority area.
9090	**puertorriqueño**	**Puerto Rican; Puerto Rican person**
	adj; m	No tiene nada que ver con ser puertorriqueño.
	[pwɛr.to.ri.ˈke.ɲo]	-It has nothing to do with being a Puerto Rican.
9091	**islámico**	**Islamic**
	adj	Pakistán es un país islámico y debemos respetarlo.
	[iş.ˈla.mi.ko]	-Pakistan is an Islamic country and we must respect that.
9092	**interfaz**	**interface**
	f	También necesita saber cómo configurar la nueva interfaz.
	[ĩn̪.ˈtɛr.fas]	-You also need to know how to configure the new interface.
9093	**feudal**	**feudal**
	adj	En la época feudal existían miles de enclaves en Europa.
	[feu̯.ˈðal]	-In feudal time, thousands of enclaves existed in Europe.
9094	**voraz**	**voracious**
	adj	Resulta que tienen un apetito voraz por los gusanos.
	[ˈbo.ras]	-They happen to have a voracious appetite for webworms.
9095	**sobrecargar**	**overburden**
	vb	Debemos tener cuidado de no sobrecargar este importante sector.
	[so.βre.kar.ˈɣar]	-We must be careful not to overburden this important industry.
9096	**penuria**	**hardship**
	f	El conflicto ha causado gran penuria para la gente.
	[pe.ˈnu.rja]	-The conflict has caused much hardship for people.
9097	**apodar**	**nickname**
	vb	Él usa nombres de famosos para apodar a sus amigos.
	[a.po.ˈðar]	-He uses famous nicknames for his friends.
9098	**argelino**	**Algerian; Algerian person**
	adj; m	Después está este problema en el frente argelino.
	[ar.xe.ˈli.no]	-Then, there's this situation on the Algerian front.
9099	**ducado**	**duchy**
	m	Tiene derecho al ducado de Milán.
	[du.ˈka.ðo]	-He has a claim to the duchy of Milan.
9100	**domesticado**	**domesticated**
	adj	Quizás no estás tan domesticado como pensé.
	[do.mɛs.ti.ˈka.ðo]	-Maybe you're not as domesticated as I thought.
9101	**estaño**	**tin**
	m	El bronce está compuesto de cobre y estaño.
	[ɛs.ˈta.ɲo]	-Bronze is composed of copper and tin.
9102	**incesante**	**incessant**

adj
[ĭn.se.ˈsãn̪.te]

Requiere el esfuerzo incesante del Estado y la sociedad civil.
-It required incessant effort by the State and by civil society.

9103 subsistir — **subsist**

vb
[suβ.sis.ˈtir]

Al menos él será capaz de subsistir.
-At least he'll be able to subsist.

9104 báltico — **Baltic**

adj
[ˈbal̪.ti.ko]

El bacalao es importante para el ecosistema báltico en su conjunto.
-The cod is important for the Baltic ecosystem as a whole.

9105 cónyuge — **spouse**

m/f
[ˈkõn̪.ɟ͡ʝu.xe]

Alguien aquí engañó a su cónyuge anoche.
-Someone in here cheated on their spouse last night.

9106 atmosférico — **atmospheric**

adj
[at̪.mos.ˈfɛ.ri.ko]

Lo que yo propongo es que creemos un escudo atmosférico.
-What I propose is we create an atmospheric shield.

9107 secular — **secular**

adj
[se.ku.ˈlar]

Siria es también un régimen secular.
-Syria is also a secular regime.

9108 incinerar — **incinerate**

vb
[ĭn.si.nɛ.ˈrar]

No podría incinerar a una mosca.
-I couldn't incinerate a fly.

9109 procrear — **procreate**

vb
[pro.kre.ˈar]

Nos dijeron que no podemos procrear con humanos.
-They told us that we could not procreate with humans.

9110 fiambre — **meat**

m
[ˈfjãm.bre]

Vine porque se perdieron partes del fiambre.
-I came because parts of the meat are missing.

9111 quilla — **keel**

f
[ˈki.ja]

Hemos encontrado el cuerpo de Alistair en la quilla.
-We found Alistair's body in the keel.

9112 conjuro — **spell**

m
[kõŋ.ˈxu.ro]

Dicen que conoces un conjuro para provocar celos.
-They say that you know a spell for provoking jealousy.

9113 evocar — **evoke**

vb
[e.βo.ˈkar]

Solo las soluciones nuevas pueden evocar una grandeza igual a la del pasado.
-Only new solutions can evoke a grandeur equal to the past.

9114 fontanería — **plumbing**

f
[fõn̪.ta.ˈnɛ.ri.a]

Estamos demasiado ocupados intentando perfeccionar la fontanería interior universal.
-We are too busy trying to perfect universal indoor plumbing.

9115 banqueta — **stool**

f
[bãŋ.ˈkɛ.ta]

Hay una banqueta justo a tu derecha.
-There's a stool just to your right.

9116 recetar — **prescribe**

vb
[re.sɛ.ˈtar]

No puedo recetar medicamentos a un pariente.
-I can't prescribe meds to a family member.

9117 intestinal — **intestinal**

adj
[ĭn̪.tɛs.ti.ˈnal]

Su hemorragia intestinal puede solucionarse con una simple cirugía.
-Your intestinal bleeding can be fixed with a very simple surgery.

9118 levar — **weigh**
vb
[le.ˈβar]
Reconozco que es hora de levar anclas.
-I reckon it's time to weigh anchor.

9119 abreviar — **shorten**
vb
[a.βre.ˈβjar]
Como el tiempo es escaso, voy a abreviar mi declaración.
-Given the time constraints, I will shorten my statement.

9120 cojera — **limp**
f
[ko.ˈxɛ.ra]
Tengo una cojera permanente pero sigo andando.
-I got a permanent limp but I'm walking.

9121 carabinero — **policeman**
m
[ka.ra.βi.ˈnɛ.ro]
No deje que toque a este carabinero.
-Do not let me touch this policeman.

9122 momentáneo — **momentary**
adj
[mo.mẽn̪.ˈta.ne.o]
Perdóname, ha sido un momentáneo lapsus en mis buenos modales.
-Please pardon me, I just had a momentary lapse of good manners.

9123 sulfurar(se) — **get angry**
vb
[sul.fu.ˈrar]
No tienes que sulfurarte por eso.
-You don't have to get angry about that.

9124 albornoz — **bathrobe**
m
[al.ˈβor.nos]
Incluye un cuarto de baño en mármol provisto de zapatillas y albornoz.
-It includes a marbled bathroom with bathrobe and slippers.

9125 laborista — **Labour; Labor Party member**
adj; m
[la.βo.ˈris.ta]
El nuevo gobierno laborista se mostrará igualmente resuelto.
-The new Labour government will be equally resolute.

9126 propagación — **spreading**
f
[pro.pa.ɣa.ˈsjõn]
Esto es lo único que detiene esta propagación.
-This is the only thing that stops it from spreading.

9127 bisagra — **hinge**
f
[bi.ˈsa.ɣra]
Pon una gota de aceite en cada bisagra.
-You put a drop of oil on each hinge.

9128 estrangulación — **strangulation**
f
[ɛs.trãŋ.gu.la.ˈsjõn]
Su cuerpo presentaba marcas de estrangulación y un brazo fracturado.
-Her body bore scars of strangulation and a broken arm.

9129 progresivo — **progressive**
adj
[pro.ɣre.ˈsi.βo]
En 2013 podría discutirse el cierre progresivo del programa humanitario.
-The progressive closure of the humanitarian agenda may be discussed in 2013.

9130 rehabilitar — **rehabilitate**
vb
[re.a.βi.li.ˈtar]
También se proyecta rehabilitar los centros de asistencia veterinaria.
-It is also planned to rehabilitate veterinarian welfare centers.

9131 amplitud — **extent**
f
[ãm.pli.ˈtuð]
La amplitud de las reasignaciones varió mucho de un programa a otro.
-The scope for reallocations varied widely among programmes.

9132 gimnasta — **gymnast**
m/f
[xĩm.ˈnas.ta]
He oído que la española es una gimnasta.
-I hear the Spaniard is a gymnast.

9133 criminalidad — **criminality**

f
[kri.mi.na.li.ˈðað]

El centro se ocupa de las encuestas sobre criminalidad.
-The center deals with surveys of criminality.

9134 bombeo

m
[bõm.ˈbe.o]

pumping

Las bombas hidráulicas que constituyen partes de sistemas de motor eléctrico son fundamentales en diversos procedimientos de bombeo.
-Water pumps forming parts of electric motor systems are essential in various pumping processes.

9135 bengalí

adj; m/f
[bẽŋ.ga.ˈli]

Bengali; Bengali person

Te entenderá aunque hables en bengalí.
-He'll understand even if you speak in Bengali.

9136 lineal

adj
[li.ne.ˈal]

linear

La relación lineal debe determinarse mediante un método estadístico adecuado.
-The linear relationship is to be determined by a suitable statistical approach.

9137 existencial

adj
[ɛk.sis.tẽn.ˈsjal]

existential

Se trata de un dilema verdaderamente existencial.
-This is a genuine existential dilemma.

9138 asesoría

f
[a.se.so.ˈri.a]

advice

Y debería contar con mucha asesoría local experimentada.
-And it should have plenty of experienced, local advice.

9139 corroborar

vb
[ko.ro.βo.ˈrar]

corroborate

Puede con seguridad corroborar los eventos previos a eso.
-He can most certainly corroborate events prior to that.

9140 prehistórico

adj
[pre.is.ˈto.ri.ko]

prehistoric

También corrobora que el hombre prehistórico llegó a Europa procedente de África a través del Cáucaso.
-It also confirms that prehistoric humans entered Europe from Africa via the Caucasus.

9141 inducir

vb
[ĩn̠.du.ˈsir]

induce

Estaba intentando inducir un estado meditativo.
-I was trying to induce a meditative state.

9142 ciudadela

f
[sju.ða.ˈðe.la]

citadel

Derribé sus defensas y asedié la ciudadela.
-I broke down her defenses and stormed the citadel.

9143 fechoría

f
[fe.tʃo.ˈri.a]

piece of mischief

Es decir, me asombró su fechoría.
-I mean, I was shocked by his wrongdoing.

9144 energético

adj
[e.nɛr.ˈxe.ti.ko]

energetic

Pero tienes que ser un poco más energético.
-But you have to be a little bit more energetic.

9145 caracterizar

vb
[ka.rak̚.tɛ.ri.ˈsar]

characterize

Este es un estudio para caracterizar los tipos de suelo.
-This is an investigation to characterize types of soils.

9146 esbozo

m
[ɛs̺.ˈβo.so]

outline

Se acogió con satisfacción la presentación oportuna del esbozo.
-The timely submission of the outline was welcomed.

9147 mirador

viewpoint

m

[mi.ra.ˈðor]

Cuenta con dos observatorios de aves y un mirador para los visitantes.

-There are two bird observatories and a viewpoint for visitors.

9148 **apalear** **beat**

vb

[a.pa.le.ˈar]

Muchos de ellos tienen órdenes de apalear a los cabecillas.

-Many of them are under orders to beat up the leaders.

9149 **debutante** **debut; debutante**

adj; m/f

[de.βu.ˈtãn̪.te]

¿Ha sido la carrera muy desalentadora para este debutante?

-Has the run been too daunting for this debutant?

9150 **voltereta** **somersault**

f

[bol̪.tɛ.ˈrɛ.ta]

Rompí el escenario con una voltereta.

-I broke the stage with a somersault.

9151 **escarbar** **dig**

vb

[ɛs.kar.ˈβar]

Podría escarbar en las crónicas si quieres.

-I could dig in the chronicles if you like.

9152 **difteria** **diphtheria**

f

[dif.ˈtɛ.rja]

Varios países han notificado brotes de tuberculosis, difteria y cólera.

-A number of countries have reported outbreaks of tuberculosis, diphtheria, and cholera.

9153 **ricachón** **rich man (coll)**

f

[ri.ka.ˈtʃõn]

Es lo que trato de decirte, ricachón.

-That's what I'm trying to say, rich man.

9154 **metodista** **Methodist; Methodist**

adj; m/f

[mɛ.to.ˈðis.ta]

Me criaron como metodista, si es un problema, puedo irme.

-I was raised Methodist, so if that's a problem, I can go.

9155 **conmemoración** **commemoration**

f

[kõm.me.mo.ra.ˈsjõn]

Muchos de esos asociados ya están preparando actividades para la conmemoración.

-Activities for the commemoration are already being planned by many of these partners.

9156 **poblado** **populated; village**

adj; m

[po.ˈβla.ðo]

Este es un pequeño poblado de alrededor 130 habitantes de origen precolombino.

-This is a little village of around 130 inhabitants of pre-columbine origins.

9157 **aguacate** **avocado**

m

[a.ɣwa.ˈka.te]

No sé cómo escoger un aguacate.

-I don't know how to pick out an avocado.

9158 **bonanza** **bonanza**

f

[bo.ˈnãn.sa]

Esta bonanza se ha debido principalmente a un ambiente internacional extraordinariamente positivo.

-This bonanza has largely been the result of an extraordinarily positive international environment.

9159 **rectificar** **rectify**

vb

[rek̚.ti.fi.ˈkar]

Creo que primero debemos rectificar esas cuestiones.

-I feel that we have to rectify those matters first.

9160 **iluso** **gullible, deluded**

adj

[i.ˈlu.so]

Pero es tan iluso como tú.

-But he's as deluded as you are.

9161 **hormonal** **hormonal**

adj
[or.mo.'nal]

Bueno, entiendo las necesidades hormonales de un adolescente.
-Well, I understand a teenage boy's hormonal urges.

9162 **obstruir** **obstruct**

vb
[oβs.'trwir]

Espero que no pretenda obstruir esas instrucciones.
-I hope you don't intend to obstruct that brief.

9163 **fatídico** **fateful**

adj
[fa.'ti.ði.ko]

Es mucho lo que ha ocurrido desde ese fatídico diciembre.
-So much has happened since that fateful December.

9164 **incomunicar** **isolate**

vb
[ĩŋ.ko.mu.ni.'kar]

¿Tú puedes incomunicar esa estación?
-Can you isolate the workstation?

9165 **digestivo** **digestive**

adj
[di.xɛs.'ti.βo]

Esperemos que tenga un proceso digestivo lento.
-Let's hope it has a slow digestive process.

9166 **periodístico** **journalistic**

adj
[pɛ.rjo.'ðis.ti.ko]

Quiere que escriba sobre el mundo periodístico.
-She wants me to write about the journalistic world.

9167 **noquear** **knock out**

vb
[no.ke.'ar]

Me gustaría noquear el resto de sus dientes.
-I'd like to knock out the rest of her teeth.

9168 **amoníaco** **ammonia; ammonia**

m; adj
[a.mo.'ni.a.ko]

El problema del amoníaco debe solucionarse en el ámbito local y nacional.
-The problem of ammonia must be solved at a local and national level.

9169 **exhaustivo** **comprehensive**

adj
[ɛk.saṵs.'ti.βo]

Además se dispondrá un régimen de supervisión exhaustivo.
-Moreover, a comprehensive supervisory regime will be put in place.

9170 **concesionario** **concessionaire**

m
[kõn.se.sjo.'na.rjo]

Además, ningún otro concesionario potencial se ha mostrado interesado por explotar la terminal de carga seca.
-In addition, no other potential concessionaire has expressed an interest to operate the dry bulk terminal.

9171 **afiche** **poster**

m
[a.'fi.tʃe]

Así que este es el afiche de la discordia.
-So this is the disputed poster.

9172 **albahaca** **basil**

f
[al.βa.'a.ka]

Separa las hojas de la albahaca del tronco.
-Remove the basil leaves from the stem.

9173 **transportación** **transportation**

f
[trãns.por.ta.'sjõn]

Necesito transportación esperándome en la esquina.
-I need transportation to meet me on the corner.

9174 **penitenciario** **penitentiary; prison**

adj; m
[pe.ni.tẽn.'sja.rjo]

Se considera que esto contribuye a normalizar el ambiente penitenciario.
-It is considered that this adds to the normalization of the prison environment.

9175 **transformador** **transformer**

m
[trãns.for.ma.'ðor]

Hay cerca un transformador que interfiere en sus tansmisiones.
-There's a transformer nearby that jams its transmissions.

9176 **posgrado** **postgraduate degree; postgraduate**

m; adj
[poṣ.ˈɣra.ðo]

El estudiante crónico necesita terapia, no un posgrado.
-Chronic students need therapy, not a postgraduate course.

9177 **atrio** **atrium**

m
[ˈa.trjo]

El atrio es solo una prueba para mi gran proyecto.
-The atrium is just a dry run for my first big project.

9178 **alinear** **align**

vb
[a.li.ne.ˈar]

Estas guías te ayudan a alinear objetos.
-These guides help you align objects.

9179 **integrante** **integral; member**

adj; m/f
[ĩn.te.ˈɣrãn.te]

Muchachos, saluden a nuestro nuevo integrante.
-Fellows, say hello to our newest member.

9180 **genealógico** **genealogical**

adj
[xe.ne.a.ˈlo.xi.ko]

Brandy vino a ayudar con mi informe genealógico.
-Brandy came to help me with my genealogy report.

9181 **bocanada** **breath**

f
[bo.ka.ˈna.ða]

Cada bocanada de viento está llena de mar.
-Every breath of wind is full of the sea.

9182 **persistencia** **persistence**

f
[pɛr.sis.ˈtẽn.sja]

Tu persistencia es realmente increíble, Miyamoto.
-Your persistence is really incredible, Miyamoto.

9183 **ilustrar** **illustrate**

vb
[i.lus.ˈtrar]

Permítaseme ilustrar estas ideas con tres ejemplos.
-Allow me to illustrate these points through three examples.

9184 **infringir** **infringe**

vb
[ĩɱ.frĩŋ.ˈxir]

No debe invocarse esta diversidad para infringir los derechos humanos.
-Such diversity should not be invoked in order to infringe human rights.

9185 **mellar** **chip**

vb
[me.ˈʝar]

Unas pocas flechas no son suficientes para mellar su fe, soldado.
-A few arrows aren't enough to pierce your faith, soldier.

9186 **varilla** **rod**

f
[ba.ˈri.ja]

Quisiera examinar esa varilla de datos.
-I'd like to examine that data rod.

9187 **silenciar** **silence**

vb
[si.lẽn.ˈsjar]

Amenazó con venir y silenciar el ruido.
-She threatened to come over and silence the noise.

9188 **adjudicar** **award**

vb
[að.xu.ði.ˈkar]

Esto también se debería tener en cuenta al adjudicar contratos públicos.
-This should also be taken into account in the award of public contracts.

9189 **deshielo** **thaw**

m
[de.ˈsje.lo]

Lo encontraremos después del primer deshielo.
-We'll find him after the first thaw.

9190 **evaporar** **evaporate**

vb
[e.βa.po.ˈrar]

Debes tener cuidado, ya que se empezará a evaporar rápidamente.
-You must use caution, as it will begin to evaporate quickly.

9191 **rodillo** **roller**

m
[ro.ˈði.jo]

Disfruten de mi invención, el rodillo para pintar.
-Enjoy my invention, the paint roller.

9192 preferente — **preferential**

adj
[pre.fɛ.ˈrẽn̪.te]

Concretamente, procede establecer plazos para el uso preferente del material digitalizado.
-In particular, it is necessary to set time limits for the preferential use of the digitized material.

9193 prepotente — **arrogant**

adj
[pre.po.ˈtẽn̪.te]

Sí, pero tú eres tacaña y prepotente.
-Yes, but you're greedy and arrogant.

9194 cristalino — **crystalline**

adj
[kris.ta.ˈli.no]

La melamina es un polvo cristalino de color blanco que se obtiene de la urea.
-Melamine is a white crystalline powder obtained from urea.

9195 quebrantar — **break**

vb
[ke.βrãn̪.ˈtar]

Me exiliaron para quebrantar mi espíritu.
-They have exiled me to break my spirit.

9196 tópico — **cliche; topical**

m; adj
[ˈto.pi.ko]

Esta historia no es más que un gran tópico.
-This story is nothing more than a big cliche.

9197 trazo — **stroke**

m
[ˈtra.so]

Un trazo de esa pluma y miles de millones de vidas serán salvadas.
-One stroke of this pen and billions of lives will be saved.

9198 complemento — **complement**

m
[kõm.ple.ˈmẽn̪.to]

Tienen el mismo complemento de armas que nosotros.
-They have the same complement of weapons as we do.

9199 hipotético — **hypothetical**

adj
[i.po.ˈtɛ.ti.ko]

Parece demasiado trabajo hipotético, entrenador.
-Sounds like a lot of hypothetical work, coach.

9200 burdo — **crude**

adj
[ˈbur.ðo]

Este es un instrumento burdo.
-This is a crude instrument.

9201 hule — **oilcloth**

m
[ˈu.le]

Lleva un paquete envuelto en hule y atado con una cuerda gruesa.
-He carries a parcel wrapped in oilcloth and tied with thick string.

9202 envergadura — **scale**

f
[ẽm.bɛr.ɣa.ˈðu.ra]

Las estadísticas nos dan una idea de la envergadura de este problema.
-Statistics give an idea of the scale of this issue.

9203 enjuague — **rinse**

m
[ẽŋ.ˈxwa.ɣe]

Dale a eso un enjuague, por favor.
-Give that a rinse, please.

9204 visualizar — **visualize**

vb
[bi.swa.li.ˈsar]

Trataba de visualizar nuestra próxima toma.
-I was trying to visualize our next score.

9205 imposibilidad — **impossibility**

f
[ĩm.po.si.βi.li.ˈðað]

Entiendo el cinismo. Entiendo el sentimiento de imposibilidad.
-I get this cynicism. I get this sense of impossibility.

9206 exclusión — **exclusion**

	f	Casi siempre conlleva exclusión social de los débiles.
	[ɛkṣ.lu.ˈsjõn]	-It almost always leads to the social exclusion of the weak.
9207	**binario**	**binary**
	adj	Este tipo de archivo es mas grande que un binario.
	[bi.ˈna.rjo]	-This file type is larger than a binary.
9208	**chileno**	**Chilean; Chilean person**
	adj; m	Es considerado el parque más bello del litoral chileno.
	[tʃi.ˈle.no]	-It is considered the most beautiful park of the Chilean coast.
9209	**transparencia**	**transparency**
	f	Todos sabemos que no hay democracia sin transparencia.
	[trãns.pa.ˈrẽn.sja]	-We all of us know that there is no democracy without transparency.
9210	**garrapata**	**tick**
	f	Tuviste una convulsión cuando intentamos quitarte la garrapata.
	[ga.ra.ˈpa.ta]	-You got a jolt when we tried to remove the tick.
9211	**cabezazo**	**header**
	m	Y de golpe, de un cabezazo atravesó la ventana.
	[ka.βe.ˈsa.so]	-And boom, a header right through the window.
9212	**kurdo**	**Kurdish; Kurdish person**
	adj; m	Hay una loable excepción, y es el sector kurdo.
	[ˈkur.ðo]	-There is one laudable exception, and that is the Kurdish sector.
9213	**piropo**	**compliment**
	m	Y te iba a dar las gracias por el piropo.
	[pi.ˈro.po]	-And I was going to thank you for the compliment.
9214	**revestimiento**	**coating**
	m	La calidad del revestimiento mejora a medida que se reduce la espumación.
	[re.βɛs.ti.ˈmjẽn.to]	-Coating quality is improved as foaming is reduced.
9215	**sumir**	**plunge**
	vb	Está demostrado que la mala política económica y las condiciones internacionales desfavorables pueden sumir a poblaciones enteras en la pobreza.
	[su.ˈmir]	-It had been demonstrated that bad economic policy and unfavorable international conditions could plunge whole populations into poverty.
9216	**alzado**	**raised**
	adj	El regimiento se ha alzado contra el poder soviético.
	[al.ˈsa.ðo]	-The regiment has been raised against Soviet power.
9217	**esmero**	**care**
	m	Nos hemos preparado para esto con redoblado esmero.
	[ɛṣ.ˈmɛ.ro]	-We have prepared ourselves for this with redoubled care.
9218	**vagabundear**	**roam**
	vb	Si un perro no tiene dueño, empezará a vagabundear.
	[ba.ɣa.βũn.de.ˈar]	-If a dog doesn't have an owner, he'll start roaming about.
9219	**relatar**	**recount**
	vb	Pero no vine para relatar la trágica historia de mi familia.
	[re.la.ˈtar]	-But I didn't come over to recount my family's tragic history.
9220	**punzante**	**sharp**
	adj	La original fue hecha con algo punzante.
	[pũn.ˈsãn.te]	-The original one was done with something sharp.
9221	**folclore**	**folklore**

	m	
	[fol.ˈklo.re]	Mayormente suena a antiguo folclore y fábulas.
		-Mostly it sounds like old folklore and fables.

9222 supresión — **suppression**

f

[su.pre.ˈsjõn]

Intenta relajar un poco tu supresión emocional.
-Try to relax your emotional suppression just a little.

9223 náufrago — **castaway**

m/f

[ˈnau̯.fra.ɣo]

Su actuación de náufrago es muy convincente.
-His castaway performance is very convincing.

9224 apañar — **fix**

vb

[a.pa.ˈɲar]

Tengo que apañar esa puerta.
-I have to fix that door.

9225 inusualmente — **unusually**

adv

[i.nu.swal.ˈmẽn̪.te]

Tus latidos cardíacos son inusualmente lentos.
-Your heart rate is unusually slow.

9226 conferir — **confer**

vb

[kõɱ.fɛ.ˈrir]

No debemos conferir demasiada distinción a Huntington.
-We need not confer too much distinction on Huntington.

9227 boicot — **boycott**

m

[boi̯.ˈkot]

No participaremos, ordenaré un boicot.
-We won't take part, I'll call for a boycott.

9228 disciplinario — **disciplinary**

adj

[dis.sip̚.li.ˈna.rjo]

La discriminación es punible como delito disciplinario.
-Discrimination is punishable as a disciplinary offense.

9229 comitiva — **motorcade**

f

[ko.mi.ˈti.βa]

La comitiva estará allí en menos de 20 minutos.
-The motorcade will be there in less than 20 minutes.

9230 camuflar — **camouflage**

vb

[ka.mu.ˈflar]

Tenemos que camuflar el interior del coche.
-We need to camouflage the interior of the car.

9231 adornar — **decorate**

vb

[a.ðor.ˈnar]

Si te interesa, nos gustaría que vinieras a ayudarnos a adornar la casa.
-If you're interested, we'd love to have you come help decorate the house.

9232 pulcro — **neat**

adj

[ˈpul.kro]

Quiero decir, este apartamento está pulcro como una patena.
-I mean, this apartment is neat as a pin.

9233 emplazamiento — **site**

m

[ẽm.pla.sa.ˈmjẽn̪.to]

Necesitamos inspeccionar el emplazamiento otra vez.
-We need to check out the site again.

9234 consolidar — **consolidate**

vb

[kõn.so.li.ˈðar]

Es necesario consolidar las dimensiones sociales del mercado interior.
-It is necessary to consolidate the social dimensions of the internal market.

9235 nauseabundo — **nauseating**

adj

[nau̯.se.a.ˈβũn̪.do]

Otros filmes muestran el exceso como algo nauseabundo.
-Other films cast excess as nauseating.

9236 encuadre — **framing**

m

[ẽŋ.ˈkwa.ðre]

Eres muy bueno en el encuadre.
-You're so good at framing.

9237	**rematar**	**conclude**
	vb	Para rematar, destruyes mi relación.
	[re.ma.ˈtar]	-To conclude, you ruin my relationship.
9238	**metafísico**	**metaphysical**
	adj	Estoy en el mundo de lo metafísico.
	[mɛ.ta.ˈfi.si.ko]	-I am in the realms of the metaphysical.
9239	**cazatalentos**	**talent scout**
	m/f	De hecho, soy un cazatalentos.
	[ka.sa.ta.ˈlɛ̃n̪.tos]	-In fact, I'm a headhunter.
9240	**navegante**	**navigator**
	m/f	Era navegante de un carguero espacial.
	[na.βe.ˈɣã̪n̪.te]	-He was a navigator on a spice freighter.
9241	**fisiología**	**physiology**
	f	No sabes nada sobre fisiología jordaniana.
	[fi.sjo.lo.ˈxi.a]	-You don't know anything about Jordanian physiology.
9242	**esternón**	**sternum**
	m	Tengo que atravesar el esternón primero.
	[ɛs.tɛr.ˈnõn]	-I got to get through the sternum first.
9243	**acupuntura**	**acupuncture**
	f	Algunos seguros médicos cubren tratamientos como quiropráctica o acupuntura.
	[a.ku.pũn̪.ˈtu.ra]	-Some health insurance plans pay for therapies such as chiropractic or acupuncture.
9244	**simposio**	**symposium**
	m	El primer simposio se inició con un grupo de cuatro expertos.
	[sĩm.ˈpo.sjo]	-The first symposium was launched with a panel of four experts.
9245	**urbanismo**	**town planning**
	m	Sheffield marca la pauta del urbanismo.
	[ur.βa.ˈnis̠.mo]	-Sheffield leads the way in town planning.
9246	**reciclar**	**recycle**
	vb	Todo lavado y listo para reciclar.
	[re.si.ˈklar]	-All rinsed and ready to recycle.
9247	**magma**	**magma**
	m	El magma llegara al pueblo si avanza más.
	[ˈmaɣ.ma]	-The magma'll reach the village if it advances any further.
9248	**exagerado**	**exaggerated**
	adj	Otro aspecto que se ha exagerado son las transferencias de dinero.
	[ɛk.sa.xɛ.ˈra.ðo]	-Another thing that is exaggerated is the transfers of money.
9249	**subsecretario**	**undersecretary**
	m	El subsecretario se había ido a la cama.
	[suβ.se.krɛ.ˈta.rjo]	-The undersecretary had gone to bed.
9250	**radiactivo**	**radioactive**
	adj	El uranio es un metal pesado y radiactivo.
	[ra.ðjak̚.ˈti.βo]	-Uranium is both radioactive and a heavy metal.
9251	**reconciliar**	**reconcile**
	vb	De verdad que no puedo reconciliar esto.
	[re.kõn.si.ˈljar]	-I really can't reconcile this.
9252	**centígrado**	**centigrade**

	adj	Un seis por ciento por grado centígrado.
	[sɛ̞n.ˈti.ɣra.ðo]	-Six percent per degree centigrade.
9253	**febril**	**febrile**
	adj	Ya sabes, mareada y febril y con náuseas.
	[fe.ˈβril]	-You know, dizzy and feverish and nauseous.
9254	**superfluo**	**superfluous**
	adj	Cualquier otro mecanismo de investigación es, por tanto, superfluo.
	[su.ˈpɛr.flwo]	-Any other inquiry mechanism was, therefore, superfluous.
9255	**despilfarro**	**waste**
	m	Es un despilfarro económico y humano inadmisible.
	[dɛs.pil.ˈfa.ro]	-It all amounts to an intolerable economic and human waste.
9256	**valoración**	**assessment**
	f	Hoy hemos escuchado una valoración alentadora.
	[ba.lo.ra.ˈsjõn]	-Today, we have heard an encouraging assessment.
9257	**degollar**	**cut someone's throat**
	vb	Tal vez decida degollar a otra persona.
	[de.ɣo.ˈjar]	-He may decide to cut the throat of someone else.
9258	**degeneración**	**degeneration**
	f	Está sufriendo una forma de rápida degeneración celular.
	[de.xe.nɛ.ra.ˈsjõn]	-He's suffering from a form of rapid cellular degeneration.
9259	**inmoralidad**	**immorality**
	f	Ya hay suficiente inmoralidad en el mundo.
	[ĭm.mo.ra.li.ˈðað]	-There's enough immorality in the world already.
9260	**tenencia**	**possession**
	f	Lo detuvieron por tenencia de narcóticos.
	[te.ˈnɛ̃n.sja]	-He got picked up for possession of narcotics.
9261	**celuloide**	**celluloid**
	m	Esas están hechas de celuloide, es muy inflamable.
	[se.lu.ˈloi̯.ðe]	-Those are made of celluloid, highly flammable.
9262	**escepticismo**	**skepticism**
	m	Tienes que tener escepticismo y humildad.
	[ɛs.sep̚.ti.ˈsis̝.mo]	-You've got to have skepticism and humility.
9263	**catedral**	**cathedral**
	f	Eso es una catedral con aspecto de fortaleza militar.
	[ka.te.ˈðral]	-That is a cathedral with the appearance of a military fortress.
9264	**desbordar**	**overflow**
	vb	Apúrate, se va a desbordar el agua.
	[dɛs̝.βor.ˈðar]	-Hurry, it's going to overflow.
9265	**escaramuza**	**skirmish**
	f	Tuvimos una escaramuza con él.
	[ɛs.ka.ra.ˈmu.sa]	-We were engaged in a skirmish with him.
9266	**coreógrafo**	**choreographer**
	m	No sabía que fueras un coreógrafo.
	[ko.re.ˈo.ɣra.fo]	-I didn't know you were a choreographer.
9267	**calza**	**wedge**
	f	En cuanto la bisagra reviente, calza la puerta abierta.
	[ˈkal.sa]	-The moment that hinge pops, you wedge that door open.
9268	**inflar**	**inflate**

	vb	No, me parece que lo tenemos que inflar más.
	[ĩɱ.ˈflar]	-No, I feel like we need to inflate it more.
9269	**galeón**	**galleon**
	m	Un galeón se hundió a tres millas de aquí.
	[ga.le.ˈõn]	-A galleon went down 3 miles from here.
9270	**berenjena**	**eggplant**
	f	La berenjena está lista para cortarse.
	[bɛ.rẽɲ.ˈxe.na]	-Eggplant's just about ready to be picked.
9271	**tablilla**	**clipboard**
	f	Tercero, prohibido tocar mi tablilla.
	[ta.ˈβli.ja]	-Third, no touchin' my clipboard.
9272	**alusión**	**allusion**
	f	Esta duplicidad de la alusión invalida, por tanto, la acusación.
	[a.lu.ˈsjõn]	-This twofold manner of allusion thus invalidates the accusation.
9273	**presentimiento**	**feeling**
	m	Tengo el presentimiento de que encontraré algo.
	[pre.sẽn.ti.ˈmjẽn.to]	-I just have a feeling I'll find something.
9274	**pescadería**	**fish market**
	f	Puedes conseguirlas en cualquier pescadería o tienda de comestibles.
	[pɛs.ka.ðɛ.ˈri.a]	-You can get them at any fish market or grocery store.
9275	**canalizar**	**channel**
	vb	Dale algo para canalizar su energía.
	[ka.na.li.ˈsar]	-Give him something to channel his energy into.
9276	**comandar**	**command**
	vb	Quieren contratarme para comandar su rebelión.
	[ko.mãn.ˈdar]	-They want to hire me to command their rebellion.
9277	**panal**	**honeycomb**
	m	Este lugar es como un panal de miel.
	[pa.ˈnal]	-This place is like a honeycomb.
9278	**surco**	**groove**
	m	Hay, se podría decir, un surco en un lateral.
	[ˈsur.ko]	-There's a, you might say, a groove to one side.
9279	**inadvertido**	**unnoticed**
	adj	El daño inicial puede en ocasiones pasar relativamente inadvertido debido a su lenta progresión.
	[i.nað.βɛr.ˈti.ðo]	-Original damage can sometimes go relatively unnoticed due to its slow progression.
9280	**arrollar**	**run down**
	vb	No puedo simplemente arrollar a la vieja.
	[a.ro.ˈjar]	-I can't just run the old lady down.
9281	**venéreo**	**venereal**
	adj	No hay nada de venéreo en ello.
	[be.ˈnɛ.re.o]	-There's nothing venereal about it.
9282	**jesuita**	**Jesuit; Jesuit**
	adj; m/f	El tercer ganador fue un teólogo jesuita.
	[xe.ˈswi.ta]	-The third winner was a Jesuit theologian.
9283	**decaer**	**decay**
	vb	El bosque comenzó bruscamente a decaer.
	[de.ka.ˈɛr]	-The forest started suddenly to decay.

9284	**aorta**	aorta
	f	Este es un modelo de mi aorta.
	[a.ˈor.ta]	-This is a model of my aorta.

9285	**comadre**	**close friend (coll) (LA), midwife (coll) (ES)**
	f	Hoy mataron al hijo de su comadre.
	[ko.ˈma.ðre]	-Today they killed the son of her godmother.

9286	**especificar**	**specify**
	vb	Me gustaría especificar exactamente lo que acepto.
	[ɛs.pe.si.fi.ˈkar]	-I should like to specify exactly what I accept.

9287	**experimentación**	**experimentation**
	f	Inventé estas seis oraciones luego de mucha experimentación.
	[ɛks.pe.ri.mẽn̪.ta.ˈsjõn]	-I came up with these six sentences after much experimentation.

9288	**vegetar**	**vegetate**
	vb	¡No quiero vegetar aquí para siempre!
	[be.xɛ.ˈtar]	-I don't want to vegetate here forever!

9289	**tríada**	**triad**
	f	Hay una tríada de sol, lago y montañas en el corazón de Suiza.
	[ˈtri.a.ða]	-There is a triad of sun, lake, and mountains in the heart of Switzerland.

9290	**papal**	**papal**
	adj	Asumiré el trono papal de inmediato.
	[pa.ˈpal]	-I shall assume the papal throne at once.

9291	**lactosa**	**lactose**
	f	Este medicamento contiene lactosa y sacarosa.
	[lak̚.ˈto.sa]	-This medicinal product contains lactose and sucrose.

9292	**maña**	**skill**
	f	Solo necesitas tener maña para volver a restaurarlas.
	[ˈma.ɲa]	-You just need the skill to put it back together.

9293	**cuaresma**	**Lent**
	f	Renuncié a la dieta por cuaresma.
	[kwa.ˈrɛş.ma]	-I gave up my diet for Lent.

9294	**aplacar**	**placate**
	vb	Los chinos están haciendo casi todo lo posible para aplacar los temores rusos.
	[ap̚.la.ˈkar]	-The Chinese are doing almost everything possible to placate Russian concerns.

9295	**púlpito**	**pulpit**
	m	No usaré ese púlpito para anuncios públicos.
	[ˈpul.pi.to]	-I won't use that pulpit for public announcements.

9296	**ultramar**	**overseas**
	m	En tiempos de prosperidad económica se ha atraído a los trabajadores desde ultramar.
	[ul̪.tra.ˈmar]	-In times of economic prosperity, laborers have been attracted from overseas.

9297	**escénico**	**scenic**
	adj	Y si lo acepta, quiere que me vaya con ella como su artista escénico.
	[ɛs.ˈse.ni.ko]	-And if she accepts it, she wants me to go with her as her scenic artist.

| 9298 | **esclerosis** | **sclerosis** |

f
[ɛs.klɛ.ˈro.sis]

La esclerosis tuberosa no causa fiebre.
-Tuberous sclerosis doesn't cause fever.

9299 tintura — **dye**

f
[tĩn̪.ˈtu.ra]

Esta es toda la tintura que pude encontrar.
-This is all the dye I could find.

9300 traspaso — **transfer**

m
[tras.ˈpa.so]

El traspaso se realiza de conformidad con el plan para la transición.
-The transfer is proceeding in accordance with the transition plan.

9301 fragilidad — **fragility**

f
[fra.xi.li.ˈðað]

He mencionado la fragilidad del mundo actual.
-I have mentioned the fragility of today's world.

9302 purga — **purge**

f
[ˈpur.ɣa]

Estas técnicas reducen el volumen de purga de salmuera.
-These techniques reduce the brine purge volume.

9303 lamentación — **lamentation**

f
[la.mẽn̪.ta.ˈsjõn]

Hay algunos motivos de lamentación.
-There are some reasons for regret.

9304 abastecer — **supply**

vb
[a.βas.te.ˈsɛr]

No pretendemos abastecer a la grandes empresas minoristas.
-We're not looking to supply the big retailers.

9305 carretero — **chimney**

m
[ka.rɛ.ˈtɛ.ro]

Tengo un amigo que fuma como un carretero.
-I have a friend that smokes like a chimney.

9306 idóneo — **suitable**

adj
[i.ˈðo.ne.o]

El producto será idóneo para su finalidad.
-The product shall be suitable for its purpose.

9307 pesimismo — **pessimism**

m
[pe.si.ˈmis̪.mo]

Estoy intentando tapar mi pesimismo con optimismo.
-I'm trying to overwhelm my pessimism with optimism.

9308 microchip — **microchip**

m
[mi.kro.ˈʧip]

Mi cuerpo está bien afinado como un microchip.
-My body is finely tuned, like a microchip.

9309 empalmar(se) — **connect; overlap (LA), get a hard-on (ES) (coll)**

vb; vbr
[ẽm.pal.ˈmar]

¿Sabes cómo empalmar este cable?
-Do you know how to connect this wire?

9310 incoherente — **incoherent**

adj
[ĩŋ.ko.ɛ.ˈrẽn̪.te]

La policía intento interrogarla, pero era incoherente.
-The police tried to question her, but she was incoherent.

9311 ventajoso — **advantageous**

adj
[bẽn̪.ta.ˈxo.so]

Eso sería muy ventajoso para su padre.
-That would be greatly advantageous for your father.

9312 repugnancia — **disgust**

f
[re.puɣ.ˈnãn.sja]

Quisiera expresar mi consternación y repugnancia por dichas actuaciones.
-I wish to express my dismay and disgust at those actions.

9313 sofocar(se) — **suffocate; get embarrassed, get upset**

vb; vbr
[so.fo.ˈkar]

Te vas a sofocar hasta morir.
-You're going to suffocate to death.

9314 **ego**
m
[ˈe.ɣo]

ego
Tengo mi ego para mantenerme caliente.
-I have my ego to keep me warm.

9315 **flotación**
f
[flo.ta.ˈsjõn]

flotation
Te buscaré un dispositivo de flotación.
-I will seek you a device of flotation.

9316 **troyano**
adj; m
[tro.ˈja.no]

Trojan; Trojan horse
Creo que sé cómo podemos deshacernos del troyano.
-I think I know how we can get rid of the trojan.

9317 **colocado**
adj
[ko.lo.ˈka.ðo]

placed, stoned
Cuando estaba colocado, hice algo.
-When I was high, I did something.

9318 **aleación**
f
[a.le.a.ˈsjõn]

alloy
Esa cosa está hecha de una aleación mágica.
-That thing is made out of a magical alloy.

9319 **bronceador**
m
[brõn.se.a.ˈðor]

tanning lotion
Le presté a Dean un poco de tu bronceador.
-I let Dean borrow some of your tanning lotion.

9320 **anterioridad**
f
[ãn̪.tɛ.rjo.ri.ˈðað]

previous
No se aceptan reservas con una anterioridad a 72 horas a la fecha del servicio.
-No reservations are accepted before 72 hours previous to the requested service.

9321 **intencionado**
adj
[ĩn̪.tẽn.sjo.ˈna.ðo]

deliberate
Parece ser un asunto muy intencionado.
-It seems to be a very deliberate affair.

9322 **alejamiento**
m
[a.le.xa.ˈmjẽn̪.to]

removal
El alejamiento de la familia debería ser el último recurso.
-Removal from the family should be a last resort.

9323 **diana**
f
[ˈdja.na]

target
La flecha cayó junto a la diana.
-The arrow fell short of the target.

9324 **legislatura**
f
[le.xis̪.la.ˈtu.ra]

legislature
Esto fue aprobado aquí en la legislatura pasada.
-This was approved here during the last legislature.

9325 **portuario**
adj
[por.ˈtwa.rjo]

port
El sector portuario se está expandiendo rápidamente.
-The port sector is expanding rapidly.

9326 **floral**
adj
[flo.ˈral]

floral
Eso podría ser demasiado floral para el inframundo.
-That might be too much floral for the underworld.

9327 **recelo**
m
[re.ˈse.lo]

suspicion
El recelo nos mantuvo vivos todos estos años.
-The suspicion has kept us alive all these years.

9328 **veracidad**
f
[bɛ.ra.si.ˈðað]

veracity
Estoy explorando la veracidad de esa afirmación.
-I'm exploring the veracity of that determination.

9329 **oruga**

caterpillar

	f	La criatura parece ser una oruga gigante.
	[o.ˈru.ya]	-The creature is reported to be a large caterpillar.
9330	**morro**	**snout**
	m	Mantén su morro fuera del agua.
	[ˈmo.ro]	-Keep his snout out of the water.
9331	**inconstante**	**inconstant**
	adj	Tal vez sea una mujer mala, inconstante.
	[ĩŋ.kõns.ˈtãn̪.te]	-Perhaps I am a bad, inconstant woman.
9332	**mosaico**	**mosaic; mosaic**
	adj; m	Vamos, es solo un mosaico. No puede hacerte daño.
	[mo.ˈsai̯.ko]	-Come on, it is just a mosaic. It cannot harm you.
9333	**ciclismo**	**cycling**
	m	Iré a hacer ciclismo aunque llueva.
	[si.ˈklis̬.mo]	-I will go cycling even if it rains.
9334	**estratagema**	**stratagem**
	f	El finge que es una estratagema.
	[ɛs.tra.ta.ˈxe.ma]	-He pretends it is a stratagem.
9335	**subsistencia**	**subsistence**
	f	La subsistencia de los fotógrafos depende de su trabajo.
	[suβ.sis.ˈtẽn.sja]	-Photographers' subsistence depends on their work.
9336	**arbitrario**	**arbitrary**
	adj	Debo decir que esto parece caprichoso y arbitrario.
	[ar.βi.ˈtra.rjo]	-I have to say, this seems capricious and arbitrary.
9337	**vocalista**	**vocalist**
	m/f	Básicamente soy vocalista, pero estudio interpretación.
	[bo.ka.ˈlis.ta]	-I'm basically a vocalist, but I am studying acting.
9338	**dislocar(se)**	**dislocate**
	vb	Esto se va a dislocar inmediatamente.
	[dis̬.lo.ˈkar]	-This is going to dislocate immediately.
9339	**indebido**	**improper**
	adj	No se debe producir ningún retraso indebido.
	[ĩn̪.de.ˈβi.ðo]	-There should not be any undue delay.
9340	**pantorrilla**	**calf**
	f	Ese calambre en la pantorrilla vino de la nada.
	[pãn̪.to.ˈri.ʝa]	-That calf cramp came out of nowhere.
9341	**pegajoso**	**sticky**
	adj	No quiero estar pegajoso antes del ensayo.
	[pe.ɣa.ˈxo.so]	-I don't want to get sticky before rehearsal.
9342	**deposición**	**deposition**
	f	Estaba leyendo la transcripción de su deposición.
	[de.po.si.ˈsjõn]	-I was reading from the transcript of her deposition.
9343	**tendón**	**tendon**
	m	En algún momento, el tendón se desgasta y se rompe.
	[tẽn̪.ˈdõn]	-At some point, the tendon wears down and tears.
9344	**reservado**	**reserved**
	adj	Si tiene parking reservado, nosotros les acompañaremos.
	[re.sɛr.ˈβa.ðo]	-If you have reserved parking, we will accompany you.
9345	**perico**	**parakeet**

m

[pɛ.ˈri.ko]

Tiene la cabeza de un perico.

-He has the head of a parakeet.

9346 comunal — **communal**

adj

[ko.mu.ˈnal]

Podrías llamarlo una granja comunal, supongo.

-You could call it a communal farm, I suppose.

9347 implementar — **implement**

vb

[ĭm.ple.mẽn̪.ˈtar]

Algunos lectores podrán implementar este método luego de leerlo.

-Some readers will be able to implement this approach after they read about it.

9348 sangría — **indentation, sangria**

f

[sãŋ.ˈgri.a]

Bueno, voy a traer el coñac para hacer la sangría.

-Well, I'll bring the brandy to make sangria.

9349 reanimación — **revival**

f

[re.a.ni.ma.ˈsjõn]

Tú siempre dices que el amor es la reanimación de tu propio narcisismo.

-You always said love is a revival of your own narcissism.

9350 candela — **candle**

f

[kãn̪.ˈde.la]

No, es a mí a la que le toca soplar la candela.

-No, I'm the one that gets to blow out the candle.

9351 látex — **latex**

m

[ˈla.teks]

Durante el primer mes recomendaría llevar guantes de látex.

-For the first month, I would recommend wearing latex gloves.

9352 diálisis — **dialysis**

f

[ˈdja.li.sis]

Está en diálisis porque bebió demasiado.

-You're on dialysis because you drank too much.

9353 sinapsis — **synapse**

f

[si.ˈnap.sis]

Daría mi última sinapsis por una jugosa manzana.

-I'd give my last synapse for a juicy apple.

9354 ADN — **DNA**

abr

[ˈaðn]

Estarán familiarizados con la doble hélice del ADN.

-You'll be familiar with the double helix of DNA.

9355 disfuncional — **dysfunctional**

adj

[dis.fũn.sjo.ˈnal]

Estoy hablando de un matrimonio muy disfuncional.

-I'm talking about a very dysfunctional marriage.

9356 vaivén — **swinging**

m

[bai̯.ˈβẽn]

La única forma de detener el vaivén es arrojarlo al agua.

-The only way to stop it swinging is to drop it back in the water.

9357 designio — **plan**

m

[de.ˈsiɣ.njo]

Diles que ese es el designio del Señor.

-Tell them that is the Lord's plan.

9358 fulgor — **brightness**

m

[ful.ˈɣor]

Y ella tenía ese fulgor como tiene ahora.

-And she had that radiance as she does now.

9359 descontar — **discount**

vb

[dɛs.kõn̪.ˈtar]

Es una teoría que puedes descontar.

-That's one theory you can discount.

9360 perecer — **perish**

vb

[pɛ.re.ˈsɛr]

Estoy condenado a perecer en las rocas.

-I am doomed to perish upon the rocks.

9361 **decretar** **decree**

vb
[de.kɾɛ.ˈtar]

Pero todo salió mal y ahora debo decretar.
-But it all went wrong and now I must decree.

9362 **sustitución** **substitution**

f
[sus.ti.tu.ˈsjõn]

Haría lo que se llama sustitución.
-I'd do what they call a substitution.

9363 **biombo** **screen**

m
[ˈbjõm.bo]

Ponte detrás del biombo y pulsa el botón de grabar.
-Get behind that screen and hit record.

9364 **yunque** **anvil**

m
[ˈɟ͡ʝũŋ.ke]

El martillo nunca golpeará el yunque.
-The hammer will never meet the anvil.

9365 **tachar** **cross out**

vb
[ta.ˈt͡ʃar]

Bueno, podemos tachar eso de la lista.
-Well, we can scratch that off the list.

9366 **selectivo** **selective**

adj
[se.lek̚.ˈti.βo]

Existe además el peligro de ser selectivo.
-And there is also the danger of being selective.

9367 **discrepancia** **discrepancy**

f
[dis.kɾe.ˈpãn.sja]

Sabían de la discrepancia del reporte.
-They knew about the discrepancy in the report.

9368 **concienzudo** **conscientious**

adj
[kõn.sjẽn.ˈsu.ðo]

Demostró ser un trabajador honesto, concienzudo y meticuloso.
-He showed himself to be an honorable, conscientious and meticulous worker.

9369 **explícito** **explicit**

adj
[ɛks.ˈpli.si.to]

El texto del acuerdo es detallado y explícito.
-The text of the understanding itself is detailed and explicit.

9370 **arrebato** **outburst**

m
[a.re.ˈβa.to]

Me gustaría disculparme por el arrebato anterior.
-I'd like to apologize for the previous outburst.

9371 **sumergible** **submersible**

adj
[su.mɛɾ.ˈxi.βle]

Llegamos hasta ellas con nuestro sumergible.
-We went up to them with our submersible.

9372 **meteorología** **meteorology**

f
[mɛ.te.o.ro.lo.ˈxi.a]

No tienes una licenciatura en meteorología.
-You don't have a degree in meteorology.

9373 **precipitación** **precipitation**

f
[pɾe.si.pi.ta.ˈsjõn]

Necesitamos dirigirnos a aquellas áreas con la mayor precipitación.
-We need to head into those areas with the most precipitation.

9374 **malversación** **embezzlement**

f
[mal.βɛɾ.sa.ˈsjõn]

Estos números no bastan para probar la malversación.
-These numbers aren't enough to prove embezzlement.

9375 **recio** **tough**

adj
[ˈre.sjo]

No buscamos a un tipo recio.
-We aren't looking for a tough guy.

9376 **croata** **Croatian; Croatian person**

adj; m/f
[kro.ˈa.ta]

El caso croata puede ser un buen ejemplo.
-The Croatian case may be a good example.

9377 sabandija — **bug, scoundrel (coll)**

f
[sa.βãn̪.ˈdi.xa]

Casi perdemos esto por culpa de esa sabandija.
-We almost lost this to that scoundrel.

9378 confrontar — **confront**

vb
[kõɱ.frõn̪.ˈtar]

Me gustaría verte confrontar a alguien.
-I'd like to see you confront someone.

9379 temporario — **temporary**

adj
[tẽm.po.ˈra.rjo]

Esperaba que el trastorno fuera temporario.
-He hoped that the disruption would be temporary.

9380 relieve — **importance, topography**

m
[re.ˈlje.βe]

También se pone de relieve el desarrollo del registro.
-The development of the registry is also given prominence.

9381 tiritar — **shiver**

vb
[ti.ri.ˈtar]

Si estás tiritando arrópate con las mantas.
-If you're shivering, put your blankets up.

9382 hermético — **airtight**

adj
[ɛr.ˈmɛ.ti.ko]

Esta comida se conservará por una semana en un contenedor hermético.
-This food will keep for a week in an airtight container.

9383 acuñar — **coin**

vb
[a.ku.ˈɲar]

Con oro uno puede acuñar dinero.
-With gold, one can coin money.

9384 nutritivo — **nutritious**

adj
[nu.tri.ˈti.βo]

Este es un almuerzo muy nutritivo.
-This is a very nutritious lunch.

9385 oceánico — **oceanic**

adj
[o.se.ˈa.ni.ko]

Esas boyas son el equivalente oceánico de las radiosondas que utilizan los meteorólogos para elaborar perfiles de la atmósfera.
-These floats are oceanic analogs to the radiosondes used by meteorologists to profile the atmosphere.

9386 distorsionar — **distort**

vb
[dis.tor.sjo.ˈnar]

No distorsiones la marca de ningún modo.
-Do not distort the mark in any way.

9387 rating — **rating**

m
[ra.ˈtĩŋg]

Este programa tendrá un gran rating.
-This show's going to get a great rating.

9388 remodelación — **remodeling**

f
[re.mo.ðe.la.ˈsjõn]

Quiere vengarse de mí por la remodelación.
-She's trying to get even with me for the remodeling.

9389 ecologista — **ecologist; environmental**

m/f; adj
[e.ko.lo.ˈxis.ta]

Una de ellas era una ecologista de la selva.
-One of them was a rainforest ecologist.

9390 ambigüedad — **ambiguity**

f
[ãm.bi.ɣwe.ˈðað]

No creemos que esta ambigüedad se haya esclarecido suficientemente.
-We do not believe that this ambiguity has been sufficiently clarified.

9391 embriagar — **get drunk**

vb
[ẽm.brja.ˈɣar]

Nosotros nos vamos a embriagar.
-We're going to get drunk.

9392 fulminante — **fulminant**

adj
[ful.mi.ˈnãn̪.te]

El terrorismo es una infección fulminante en el cuerpo de nuestra sociedad.
-Terrorism is a fulminant infection in the body of our society.

9393 simpatizar — **sympathize**

vb
[sĩm.pa.ti.ˈsar]

¿Tengo que simpatizar contigo ahora?
-Do I have to sympathize with you now?

9394 plausible — **plausible**

adj
[plau̯.ˈsi.βle]

Suena plausible cuando lo explicas así.
-Sounds plausible when you put it like that.

9395 enfatizar — **emphasize**

vb
[ẽɱ.fa.ti.ˈsar]

Nos gustaría simplemente enfatizar algunos puntos.
-We would simply like to emphasize a few points.

9396 salpicar — **splash**

vb
[sal.pi.ˈkar]

Es un pecado salpicar con leche.
-It's a sin to splash milk.

9397 malabarista — **juggler**

m/f
[ma.la.βa.ˈris.ta]

Es como un malabarista en la cuerda floja.
-It's like a juggler on a tightrope.

9398 incubadora — **incubator**

f
[ĩŋ.ku.βa.ˈðo.ra]

No podemos simplemente sacar la incubadora.
-It's not like we can just take the incubator out.

9399 veranear — **spend the summer in**

vb
[bɛ.ra.ne.ˈar]

Solía veranear aquí con mi familia cuando era un niño.
-I used to summer here with my family when I was a kid.

9400 losa — **slab**

f
[ˈlo.sa]

Jefe, necesitamos reforzar esa losa.
-Chief, we need to reinforce that slab.

9401 carrocería — **bodywork**

f
[ka.ro.sɛ.ˈri.a]

En cambio, su color proviene de manchas de cristal integrado en la carrocería.
-Instead, its color comes from flecks of crystal embedded in the bodywork.

9402 insertar — **insert**

vb
[ĩn.sɛr.ˈtar]

Voy a insertar el catéter ahora.
-I'm going to insert the catheter now.

9403 árido — **arid**

adj
[ˈa.ri.ðo]

Su territorio, grande como una provincia, es árido y desolado.
-Their territory, as big as a province, is arid and desolated.

9404 índole — **nature**

f
[ˈĩn̪.do.le]

Asimismo, hay dos causas de índole intercontinental.
-In addition, there are two cases of an intercontinental nature.

9405 trascender — **transcend**

vb
[tras.sẽn̪.ˈdɛr]

Tales operaciones podrán trascender la noción de localización geográfica.
-Such operations may transcend the concept of geographic location.

9406 reclutador — **recruiter**

	m	Soy un reclutador corporativo que se especializa en trabajadores nucleares.
	[re.klu.ta.ˈðor]	-I'm a corporate recruiter who specializes in nuclear workers.
9407	**felino**	**feline; feline**
	adj; m	El tigre es un gran felino carnívoro del Sureste de Asia.
	[fe.ˈli.no]	-The tiger is a large carnivorous feline of Southeast Asia.
9408	**agrupación**	**group**
	f	Es miembro de una agrupación ilegal que realiza actividades clandestinas.
	[a.ɣru.pa.ˈsjõn]	-He is a member of an illegal group that engages in clandestine activities.
9409	**retar**	**challenge**
	vb	Ahora todo lo que tenemos que hacer es retar a un campeón.
	[rɛ.ˈtar]	-Now, all we got to do is challenge a champion.
9410	**desenterrar**	**dig up**
	vb	Lo necesitaba para desenterrar la maleta.
	[de.sẽn.tɛ.ˈrar]	-I needed him to dig up the suitcase.
9411	**impasible**	**impassive**
	adj	El gobierno estaba intentando no permanecer impasible.
	[ĩm.pa.ˈsi.βle]	-The government was trying not to remain impassive.
9412	**oleoducto**	**pipeline**
	m	Quieren la tierra para su oleoducto.
	[o.le.o.ˈðuk̚.to]	-They want the land for their pipeline.
9413	**directriz**	**guideline**
	f	Esa cuestión, sin embargo, podría tratarse en una directriz aparte.
	[di.ˈrek̚.tris]	-That question, however, could be dealt with in a separate guideline.
9414	**dispersar**	**disperse**
	vb	Van a dispersar el virus sobre Berlín.
	[dis.pɛr.ˈsar]	-They're going to disperse the virus over Berlin.
9415	**guijarro**	**pebble**
	m	Por la noche parece un guijarro en el suelo.
	[gi.ˈxa.ro]	-By evening it looks like a pebble on the ground.
9416	**meningitis**	**meningitis**
	f	Recibimos los resultados y no es meningitis.
	[me.nĩŋ.ˈxi.tis]	-We have received the results and it's not meningitis.
9417	**saturación**	**saturation**
	f	Las técnicas de saturación permite optimizar los recursos escasos.
	[sa.tu.ra.ˈsjõn]	-The saturation techniques allow optimizing the limited resources.
9418	**dimensional**	**dimensional**
	adj	Estamos a minutos del portal dimensional.
	[di.mẽn.sjo.ˈnal]	-We're minutes away from the dimensional gateway.
9419	**ebriedad**	**drunkenness**
	f	Por supuesto, aceptamos la ebriedad.
	[e.βrje.ˈðað]	-Of course, we accept drunkenness.
9420	**expirar**	**expire**
	vb	El contrato está a punto de expirar.
	[ɛks.pi.ˈrar]	-The contract's about to expire.
9421	**tedio**	**tedium**

	m	Sí, mi tedio tiene un límite.
	['te.ðjo]	-Yes, my tedium is limitless.
9422	**norteño**	**northern; northerner**
	adj; m	Eso no será necesario, norteño.
	[nor.'te.ɲo]	-No need for that, Northerner.
9423	**justiciero**	**tough; vigilante**
	adj; m	Era más un justiciero que un periodista.
	[xus.ti.'sjɛ.ro]	-He was more of a vigilante than a journalist.
9424	**provinciano**	**provincial; provincial**
	adj; m	Me ven como un provinciano, trabajador.
	[pro.βĭn.'sja.no]	-They see me as provincial, hard-working.
9425	**mortífero**	**lethal**
	adj	No se utilizará para el suministro de material mortífero.
	[mor.'ti.fɛ.ro]	-It will not be used for the provision of lethal equipment.
9426	**retratar**	**portray**
	vb	Y él siente que no puedes retratar ese realismo.
	[rɛ.tra.'tar]	-And he feels you can't portray that realism.
9427	**evangelista**	**evangelist**
	m/f	Solía atrapar serpientes para un evangelista.
	[e.βãŋ.xe.'lis.ta]	-I used to trap snakes for this evangelist.
9428	**asunción**	**assumption**
	f	Antes de hacerlo, desearía felicitarle por la asunción de la presidencia.
	[a.sũn.'sjõn]	-Before I do that, I would like to congratulate you on your assumption of the presidency.
9429	**entrelazar**	**weave together, interlock**
	vb	Ella entrelazó sus dedos con los míos.
	[ɛ̃n.tre.la.'sar]	-She interlocked her fingers with mine.
9430	**flotador**	**float**
	m	Sin contar que entre sus cosas encontramos un sedal y un flotador.
	[flo.ta.'ðor]	-Not to mention that among his things find a line and a float.
9431	**reglamentario**	**regulation**
	adj	Es reglamentario, debo preguntarle estas cosas.
	[re.ɣla.mẽn.'ta.rjo]	-It's regulation, I have to ask you these things.
9432	**desgastar**	**wear out**
	vb	Tarde o temprano, me voy a desgastar.
	[dɛs̠.ɣas.'tar]	-Eventually, I'm going to wear out.
9433	**gala**	**gala**
	f	Habrá prensa en la gala mañana.
	['ga.la]	-There'll be press at the gala tomorrow.
9434	**despampanante**	**stunning**
	adj	Una mujer despampanante viene en camino.
	[dɛs.pãm.pa.'nãn̪.te]	-There's a stunning woman on her way over here.
9435	**saturar**	**saturate**
	vb	Podríamos saturar los colores, hacerlos resaltar.
	[sa.tu.'rar]	-We could saturate the colors, make them pop.
9436	**acalorar**	**heat up; get worked up**
	vb; vbr	No tiene sentido acalorarse y molestarse.
	[a.ka.lo.'rar]	-No sense in getting all hot and bothered.

9437	**especialización**	**specialization**
	f	Existe además una pauta de especialización en este sector.
	[ɛs.pe.sja.li.sa.ˈsjõn]	-There is also a pattern of specialization in this industry.
9438	**esclavizar**	**enslave**
	vb	Es una gran conspiración para esclavizar al hombre común.
	[ɛs.kla.βi.ˈsar]	-It's a vast conspiracy to enslave the common man.
9439	**forraje**	**forage**
	m	Es un forraje sumamente adecuado para numerosas especies animales.
	[fo.ˈra.xe]	-It is an extremely suitable forage for many species of animals.
9440	**tolerable**	**tolerable**
	adj	Por eso hablamos de riesgo tolerable.
	[to.lɛ.ˈra.βle]	-That is why we speak of a tolerable risk.
9441	**puchero**	**pot**
	m	Tuvo un accidente con un puchero de agua hirviendo.
	[pu.ˈʧɛ.ro]	-She had an accident with a pot of scalding water.
9442	**ídem**	**likewise; ditto**
	prn; adv	Dices "ídem", y eso no es lo mismo que "te quiero".
	[ˈi.ðɛ̃m]	-You say "ditto", and that's not the same as "I love you".
9443	**descolgar**	**take down**
	vb	No quería levantar ninguna bandera que no pudiera descolgar.
	[dɛs.kol.ˈɣar]	-I didn't want to raise any flags that I couldn't take down.
9444	**corroer**	**corrode**
	vb	Podría corroer la salud de ella.
	[ko.ro.ˈɛr]	-It may corrode her health.
9445	**feudo**	**fief**
	m	Este no es tu feudo personal.
	[ˈfeu̯.ðo]	-This isn't your personal fiefdom.
9446	**langostino**	**prawn**
	m	Hay tempura de langostino y ensalada de algas.
	[lãŋ.gos.ˈti.no]	-We got prawn tempura and seaweed salad.
9447	**vencimiento**	**expiration**
	m	Las tres fechas de vencimiento conocidas ya han pasado.
	[bɛ̃n.si.ˈmjɛ̃n.to]	-The three known expiry dates have now passed.
9448	**contaminante**	**pollutant; contaminant**
	adj; m	El mercurio es un importante contaminante del medio ambiente.
	[kõn.ta.mi.ˈnãn.te]	-Mercury is an important environmental contaminant.
9449	**remontar**	**overcome; date back**
	vb; vbr	No se puede remontar a un momento dado.
	[re.mõn.ˈtar]	-It can't be traced to any one moment.
9450	**dialéctica**	**dialectic**
	f	Ya ha comenzado una nueva dialéctica.
	[dja.ˈlek.ti.ka]	-A new dialectic has already begun.
9451	**unificar**	**unify**
	vb	No pretende unificar los sistemas de seguridad social.
	[u.ni.fi.ˈkar]	-It does not aim to unify social security systems.
9452	**fémur**	**femur**
	m	Eso explicaría el misterio del fémur destrozado.
	[ˈfe.mur]	-That would explain the mystery of the shattered femur.

9453	**reprobar**	**fail**
	vb	Temo que vayas a reprobar mi clase.
	[re.pro.ˈβar]	-I'm worried you're going to fail my class.
9454	**deshidratar**	**dehydrate**
	vb	Puede deshidratar a su oponente con solo tocarlo.
	[de.si.ðra.ˈtar]	-He can dehydrate his opponent with a single touch.
9455	**examinador**	**examiner**
	m	Los registros de formación deberán estar a disposición del examinador.
	[ɛk.sa.mi.na.ˈðor]	-The training records shall be made available to the examiner.
9456	**interactuar**	**interact**
	vb	No serán capaces de interactuar con nadie.
	[ĩn̪.tɛ.rak̚.ˈtwar]	-You won't be able to interact with anyone.
9457	**congestión**	**congestion**
	f	Tengo esta terrible congestión en el pecho.
	[kõŋ.xɛs.ˈtjõn]	-I've got this awful congestion in my chest.
9458	**liposucción**	**liposuction**
	f	Las complicaciones significativas de la liposucción son poco frecuentes.
	[li.po.suk̚.ˈsjõn]	-Significant liposuction complications are few.
9459	**parlamentario**	**parliamentary; Member of Parliament**
	adj; m	Pero nuestro régimen no es parlamentario.
	[par.la.mẽn̪.ˈta.rjo]	-But we are not under a parliamentary regime.
9460	**presumible**	**likely, alleged**
	adj	Estás diciendo que Ethan murió de las heridas de esta presumible pelea.
	[pre.su.ˈmi.βle]	-You're saying Ethan died of injuries from this presumed fight.
9461	**convocatoria**	**call**
	f	La primera convocatoria constituyó un verdadero éxito.
	[kõm.bo.ka.ˈto.rja]	-The first call was a complete success.
9462	**boticario**	**apothecary**
	m	Me di cuenta de que olvidaste tus píldoras en el boticario.
	[bo.ti.ˈka.rjo]	-I noticed you forgot your pills at the apothecary.
9463	**purgar**	**purge**
	vb	Debes purgar todo eso que fue acumulándose.
	[pur.ˈɣar]	-You need to purge all this stuff that's been building up.
9464	**consternar**	**shock**
	vb	¡Deja de intentar consternar a esos niños!
	[kõns.tɛr.ˈnar]	-Stop trying to shock all those kids!
9465	**marchitar**	**wither**
	vb	Pero la soledad solo te hace marchitar.
	[mar.tʃi.ˈtar]	-But solitude only makes you wither.
9466	**lastimoso**	**pitiful**
	adj	Es que a veces es muy lastimoso.
	[las.ti.ˈmo.so]	-It's just that sometimes it's so pitiful.
9467	**contratación**	**recruitment**
	f	La contratación de sus miembros se completará pronto.
	[kõn̪.tra.ta.ˈsjõn]	-The recruitment of its members will be completed very soon.
9468	**barómetro**	**barometer**
	m	Las elecciones actúan como un barómetro en cualquier democracia.
	[ba.ˈro.mɛ.tro]	-Elections act as a barometer in any democracy.

9469	**achicoria**	**chicory**
	f	Puedes agregarle un poco de achicoria a su café.
	[a.tʃi.ˈko.rja]	-You can add a little chicory to his coffee.

9470	**intendencia**	**quartermaster**
	f	Nuestra intendencia te ofrecerá su cooperación total.
	[ĩn̪.tẽn̪.ˈdẽn.sja]	-Our quartermaster will give you his fullest co-operation.

9471	**censor**	**censorial; censor**
	adj; m	No puedes robarle al censor.
	[sẽn.ˈsor]	-You can't steal from the censor.

9472	**referí**	**referee**
	m	Y quería que yo fuera el referí.
	[re.fɛ.ˈri]	-And he wanted me to be the referee.

9473	**predisposición**	**predisposition**
	f	Gracias a mí, tienes una predisposición genética al alcoholismo.
	[pre.ðis.po.si.ˈsjõn]	-Thanks to me, you have a genetic predisposition to alcoholism.

9474	**conciso**	**concise**
	adj	Habla un inglés excelente y conciso cuando quiere.
	[kõn.ˈsi.so]	-You speak an excellent and concise English when you wish.

9475	**medición**	**measurement**
	f	Podrá realizarse una medición antes o después del ensayo.
	[me.ði.ˈsjõn]	-One measurement may be performed prior to or after the test.

9476	**fogoso**	**ardent**
	adj	Cielos, qué carácter más fogoso.
	[fo.ˈɣo.so]	-My, what a fiery nature.

9477	**catedrático**	**professor**
	m	Ha sido catedrático universitario de derecho procesal desde 1985.
	[ka.te.ˈðra.ti.ko]	-He has been a university professor in procedural law since 1985.

9478	**refinamiento**	**refinement**
	m	Todas nuestras habitaciones conjugan buen gusto, refinamiento y confort.
	[re.fi.na.ˈmjẽn̪.to]	-All our comfortable rooms feature refinement combined with good taste.

9479	**ascuas**	**embers**
	fpl	¡Se han vuelto a encender las ascuas de su amor!
	[ˈas.kwas]	-The embers of their love have been rekindled!

9480	**canjear**	**exchange**
	vb	Puedes canjear 500 puntos por un código de activación.
	[kãn.xe.ˈar]	-You can exchange 500 points for an activation code.

9481	**cautivar**	**captivate**
	vb	Se trata de lo que puedes hacer para cautivarme.
	[kau̯.ti.ˈβar]	-It's about what you can do to captivate me.

9482	**estanco**	**watertight; shop**
	adj; m	Esta es la eslora del correspondiente compartimiento estanco.
	[ɛs.ˈtãŋ.ko]	-This is the length of the watertight compartment in question.

9483	**afiliar**	**enrol**
	vb	Ha organizado también reuniones para afiliar a nuevos miembros.
	[a.fi.ˈljar]	-It has also held meetings to enroll new members.

9484	**lanzar**	**throw**

	vb	Fue muy fácil lanzar ese strike.
	[lãn.ˈsar]	-It was very easy to throw that strike.
9485	**optar**	**choose**
	vb	No obstante, el testigo podrá optar por hacer esa declaración.
	[op̚.ˈtar]	-However, the witness may choose to make such statement.
9486	**disecar**	**dissect**
	vb	No podría disecar una rana en secundaria.
	[di.se.ˈkar]	-I couldn't dissect a frog in high school.
9487	**mercantil**	**commercial**
	adj	Hay transacciones de naturaleza mercantil, industrial o profesional.
	[mɛr.kã̠n.ˈtil]	-There are transactions of a commercial, industrial or professional nature.
9488	**cronograma**	**timeline**
	m	No hay cambios en el cronograma del proyecto.
	[kro.no.ˈɣra.ma]	-There are no changes in the project timeline.
9489	**aclamar**	**hail**
	vb	Nos complace tener esta oportunidad de aclamar sus progresos.
	[a.kla.ˈmar]	-We are pleased to have this occasion to hail its progress.
9490	**recreativo**	**recreational**
	adj	El zoológico es un lugar recreativo, alberga una gran cantidad de animales.
	[re.kre.a.ˈti.βo]	-A zoo is a recreational place; it has a great number of animals.
9491	**antropólogo**	**anthropologist**
	m	Me dio la receta un antropólogo.
	[ã̠n.ˈtro.po.lo.ɣo]	-The recipe was given to me by an anthropologist.
9492	**recluir**	**detain**
	vb	Se exige este documento para recluir al detenido.
	[re.ˈklwir]	-This document is required for confining the detainee.
9493	**sacristía**	**sacristy**
	F	A la izquierda se encuentra la sacristía.
	[sa.kris.ˈti.a]	-To the left is the sacristy.
9494	**mediación**	**mediation**
	f	Asimismo pueden solicitar mediación del colectivo.
	[me.ðja.ˈsjõn]	-They could also request mediation by the collective.
9495	**membrana**	**membrane**
	f	Está cubierta de una membrana mucosa.
	[mẽm.ˈbra.na]	-It's covered by this mucous membrane.
9496	**colocación**	**placement**
	f	Por lo general no se evalúa la colocación.
	[ko.lo.ka.ˈsjõn]	-There is usually no evaluation of placement.
9497	**abrupto**	**abrupt**
	adj	Perdón, eso fue un poco abrupto.
	[a.ˈβrup̚.to]	-I'm sorry, that was a little abrupt.
9498	**interestelar**	**interstellar**
	adj	Van a empezar una guerra interestelar.
	[ĩn̠.te.rɛs.te.ˈlar]	-He's going to start an interstellar war.
9499	**castración**	**castration**

f
[kas.tra.ˈsjõn]

En el mismo artículo se prohíben la psicocirugía y la castración.
-The same article does not permit application of psychosurgery and castration.

9500 laburar — **work (LA)**

vb
[la.βu.ˈrar]

¿Te gustaría laburar para Núñez?
-Do you want to work for Núñez?

9501 hebilla — **buckle**

f
[e.ˈβi.ja]

Ninguna otra parte de la hebilla podrá ser de este color.
-No other part of the buckle shall be of this color.

9502 inanición — **starvation**

f
[i.na.ni.ˈsjõn]

Se siguen denunciando casos de muertes de inanición.
-Deaths from starvation continue to be reported.

9503 cedro — **cedar**

m
[ˈse.ðro]

Dicen que tendrán que derribar el viejo cedro cualquier día de estos.
-They say the old cedar will have to come down one of these days soon.

9504 sotavento — **leeward**

m
[so.ta.ˈβẽn̪.to]

Están en la zona de sotavento.
-They're on the leeward side.

9505 inagotable — **inexhaustible**

adj
[i.na.ɣo.ˈta.βle]

La riqueza de la humanidad es inagotable.
-The wealth of humankind is inexhaustible.

9506 repulsión — **repulsion**

f
[re.pul.ˈsjõn]

Eso podría ser repulsión o disgusto.
-That could be repulsion or disgust.

9507 perpetuar — **perpetuate**

vb
[pɛr.pɛ.ˈtwar]

Pero no podemos perpetuar soluciones excepcionales.
-But we cannot perpetuate exceptional arrangements.

9508 parábola — **parable**

f
[pa.ˈra.βo.la]

No necesito sentarme y escuchar otra parábola.
-I do not need to sit and listen to another parable.

9509 jornalero — **day laborer**

m
[xor.na.ˈlɛ.ro]

Mi tío Juan era un jornalero.
-My Uncle Juan was a day laborer.

9510 inexcusable — **inexcusable**

adj
[i.nɛk.su.ˈsa.βle]

Ocultarme un asunto de seguridad nacional es inexcusable.
-Keeping me in the dark on a matter of national security is inexcusable.

9511 deslizamiento — **slide**

m
[dɛʂ.li.sa.ˈmjẽn̪.to]

Significa que hubo un deslizamiento hace una o dos semanas.
-It means there was a slide a week or two ago.

9512 alumbrar — **light**

vb
[a.lũm.ˈbrar]

Necesitamos a dirigentes para alumbrar el camino.
-We need leaders to light the way.

9513 tarántula — **tarantula**

f
[ta.ˈrãn̪.tu.la]

Tendré que ver a esa tarántula para creérmelo.
-I'll have to see that tarantula before I believe it.

9514 concurrir — **attend**

	vb	Su padre dice que ella iba a encontrarse con él aquí para concurrir al evento.
	[kõŋ.ku.ˈrir]	-Her father says she was meeting him here to attend the event.
9515	**expansivo**	**expansive**
	adj	El mortero expansivo hizo el resto del daño.
	[ɛks.pãn.ˈsi.βo]	-Expansive mortar did the rest of this damage.
9516	**risueño**	**smiling**
	adj	Vaya, que lujo verte aquí, chico risueño.
	[ri.ˈswe.ɲo]	-Well, fancy seeing you here, laughing boy.
9517	**glorieta**	**roundabout**
	f	En la primera glorieta, tome la segunda salida.
	[glo.ˈrjɛ.ta]	-In the first roundabout, take the second exit out.
9518	**reacio**	**reluctant**
	adj	Eres reacio a dejarme a cargo.
	[re.ˈa.sjo]	-You're reluctant to leave me in charge.
9519	**consolación**	**consolation**
	f	Esa es una consolación increíble.
	[kõn.so.la.ˈsjõn]	-That is a tremendous consolation.
9520	**urticaria**	**hives**
	f	El hombre tenía urticaria en el cuello. La he visto.
	[ur.ti.ˈka.rja]	-The man had hives on his neck. I saw them.
9521	**follaje**	**foliage**
	m	Además, se presta especial atención a la gestión del follaje.
	[fo.ˈja.xe]	-Furthermore, particular care is taken to manage the foliage.
9522	**renal**	**renal**
	adj	A menudo indican algún tipo de insuficiencia renal.
	[re.ˈnal]	-They typically indicate renal failure of some kind.
9523	**calentura**	**fever, cold sore**
	f	Es que una vez me picaron y me dio calentura.
	[ka.lɛ̃n.ˈtu.ra]	-Because they stung me once and gave me a fever.
9524	**desmantelar**	**dismantle**
	vb	Tendríamos que desmantelar la mina completa.
	[dɛs.mãn.te.ˈlar]	-We'd have to dismantle the entire mine.
9525	**yacimiento**	**deposit, field**
	m	No, lo mejor será que vaya al yacimiento.
	[ɟja.si.ˈmjẽn.to]	-No, I better run out to the field.
9526	**cajetilla**	**pack**
	f	Ni siquiera tengo una cajetilla de tabaco.
	[ka.xɛ.ˈti.ja]	-I don't even got a pack of cigarettes.
9527	**garbanzo**	**chickpea**
	m	Habría preferido un garbanzo o un tomate cherry.
	[gar.ˈβãn.so]	-I would have preferred a chickpea or a cherry tomato.
9528	**utilización**	**utilization**
	f	La tabla muestra un incremento estable de la utilización de esos servicios.
	[u.ti.li.sa.ˈsjõn]	-The table shows a steady increase in the utilization of the above services.
9529	**brillantez**	**brilliance**

f
[bri.ˈʝãn̯.tes]

Necesitamos producir brillantez en esta competición.
-We need to produce brilliance in this competition.

9530 calzar — **wear**

vb
[kal.ˈsar]

Bueno, supongo que podría calzar ese número.
-Well, I guess he might wear that size.

9531 parco — **frugal**

adj
[ˈpar.ko]

Él es muy parco al tratar con la gente.
-He's very economical in how he deals with people.

9532 ensamblaje — **assembly**

m
[ɛ̃n.sãm.ˈbla.xe]

Si no aguanta, desviaremos todo el ensamblaje.
-If it doesn't hold, we'll bypass the entire assembly.

9533 afroamericano — **Afro-American; African-American person**

adj; m
[a.fro.a.mɛ.ri.ˈka.no]

Estoy recaudando fondos para el festival afroamericano.
-I'm raising some cash for the Afro-American festival.

9534 traumatizar — **traumatize**

vb
[tra̯u.ma.ti.ˈsar]

Eso debería traumatizar bien a Henry.
-That should traumatize Henry nicely.

9535 inseminación — **insemination**

f
[ĩn.se.mi.na.ˈsjõn]

El caro proceso de inseminación valdrá la pena.
-It'll be worth the expensive insemination process.

9536 obesidad — **obesity**

f
[o.βe.si.ˈðað]

Tienen epidemias simultáneas de obesidad y hambre.
-You've got simultaneous epidemics of obesity and starvation.

9537 patín — **skate**

m
[pa.ˈtĩn]

Ya recuerdo donde dejé mi otro patín.
-Now I remember where I left my other skate.

9538 legionario — **legionary; legionnaire**

adj; m
[le.xjo.ˈna.rjo]

Arturo lleva puesta la vestimenta de un legionario romano.
-Arthur's wearing the equipment of a Roman legionnaire.

9539 cayado — **crook**

m
[ka.ˈʝa.ðo]

Lleva un cayado y un mayal.
-He's carrying a crook and flail.

9540 boreal — **boreal**

adj
[bo.re.ˈal]

La falta de precipitaciones en verano afecta a la productividad forestal en todas las zonas menos la boreal.
-Lack of summer precipitation is affecting forest productivity in all zones but the Boreal.

9541 doctrina — **doctrine**

f
[dok̚.ˈtri.na]

Tal opinión existe en la doctrina.
-Such a viewpoint is encountered in the doctrine.

9542 especulador — **speculator**

m
[ɛs.pe.ku.la.ˈðor]

¡Así que el millonario especulador se vuelve respetable!
-So the millionaire speculator is turning respectable!

9543 impresor — **printing; printer**

adj; m
[ĩm.pre.ˈsor]

Su impresor, un artesano rural, también ha sido condenado.
-His printer, a rural craftsman, has also been sentenced.

9544 apetitoso — **appetizing**

adj
[a.pɛ.ti.ˈto.so]

Este salami parece apetitoso, voy a probarlo.
-This salami looks appetizing, let me give it a try.

9545 chillón — **gaudy**
adj
[ʧi.ˈʝõn]
Espero que no sea muy chillón.
-I hope it's not too gaudy.

9546 tinglado — **racket**
m
[tĩŋ.ˈgla.ðo]
Se gana mucho dinero en ese tinglado.
-There's a good buck in that racket.

9547 contrariar — **cross, antagonize**
vb
[kõn.tra.ˈrjar]
El castigo llegaba rápido para quien se atreviera a contrariar al jefe.
-The punishment was swift for anyone who dared cross the boss.

9548 cédula — **document**
f
[ˈse.ðu.la]
Necesitábamos la cédula de ocupación.
-We needed to get the certificate of occupancy.

9549 omitir — **skip**
vb
[o.mi.ˈtir]
He optado por omitir esa parte.
-I chose to skip that part.

9550 derrochar — **waste**
vb
[dɛ.ro.ˈʧar]
Sin embargo, hay maneras de derrochar menos.
-But there are ways to waste less.

9551 cauto — **cautious**
adj
[ˈkau̯.to]
Hay motivos para un optimismo cauto.
-There are reasons for cautious optimism.

9552 avellana — **hazelnut; hazelnut**
adj; f
[a.βe.ˈʝa.na]
Solía hacer el mejor latte de avellana.
-He used to make the best hazelnut latte.

9553 exclamación — **exclamation**
f
[ɛkş.la.ma.ˈsjõn]
Hay una pequeña exclamación de color rojo delante de algunos eventos.
-There is a small red exclamation in front of some events.

9554 catéter — **catheter**
m
[ka.ˈtɛ.tɛr]
No sé cómo pusieron ese catéter ahí.
-I didn't know how they got that catheter in there.

9555 dramatismo — **drama**
m
[dra.ma.ˈtiş.mo]
Estoy intentando darle algo más de dramatismo.
-I'm trying to add a little drama.

9556 cañada — **glen**
f
[ka.ˈɲa.ða]
La familia lleva siglos viviendo en esta cañada.
-The family has lived in this glen for centuries.

9557 aclaración — **clarification**
f
[a.kla.ra.ˈsjõn]
Las normas actuales precisan de simplificación y aclaración.
-The current rules are in need of simplification and clarification.

9558 unilateral — **unilateral**
adj
[u.ni.la.tɛ.ˈral]
Tomaste una decisión unilateral para hundirnos.
-You took a unilateral action to sink us.

9559 bolero — **liar (coll); bolero**
adj; m
[bo.ˈlɛ.ro]
Baila muy bien samba, bolero, hasta el chachachá.
-He dances very well samba, bolero, even the cha-cha-chá.

9560 denominador — **denominator**
m
[de.no.mi.na.ˈðor]
Pero también debería preocuparnos el denominador.
-But we should also be concerned about the denominator.

9561 **compulsión**
f
[kõm.pul.ˈsjõn]
compulsion
La música es una compulsión, una obsesión.
-Music is a compulsion, an obsession.

9562 **efectividad**
f
[e.fek̚.ti.βi.ˈðað]
effectiveness
Debe respetarse la efectividad de dichos plazos.
-The effectiveness of these time limits should be respected.

9563 **sofisticar**
vb
[so.fis.ti.ˈkar]
sophisticate
Fuimos capaces de sofisticar y mejorar estos procedimientos.
-We were able to sophisticate and improve these procedures.

9564 **napolitano**
adj; m
[na.po.li.ˈta.no]
Neapolitan; Neapolitan person
A decir verdad me siento más romano que napolitano.
-As a matter of fact, I feel more Roman than Neapolitan.

9565 **disidente**
adj; m
[di.si.ˈðẽn̪.te]
dissident; dissident
Hoy he visto a un disidente sirio.
-Today, I saw a Syrian dissident.

9566 **agujerear**
vb
[a.ɣu.xɛ.re.ˈar]
make holes in
Esas mandíbulas son lo suficientemente poderosas para agujerear un dedo humano.
-Those powerful jaws are strong enough to pierce a man's finger.

9567 **suculento**
adj
[su.ku.ˈlẽn̪.to]
succulent
Y dile a la cocina que lo quiero delicioso y suculento.
-And tell the kitchen I want it rich and succulent.

9568 **celo**
m
[ˈse.lo]
zeal, tape
Quizás he sido cegado por mi celo.
-Perhaps I have been blinded by my zeal.

9569 **biotecnología**
f
[bjo.tek̚.no.lo.ˈxi.a]
biotechnology
Tiene experiencia en biotecnología y armas genéticas.
-He has a background in biotechnology and genetic weaponry.

9570 **dueto**
m
[ˈdwɛ.to]
duet
No puedo hacer un dueto contigo.
-I can't do a duet with you.

9571 **sifón**
m
[si.ˈfõn]
siphon
Se ha terminado el sifón, señora.
-You have finished your siphon, madam.

9572 **irregularidad**
f
[i.re.ɣu.la.ri.ˈðað]
irregularity
Un alto funcionario no detectó ni corrigió esta irregularidad.
-A senior staff member failed to identify and correct this irregularity.

9573 **perseguidor**
m
[pɛr.se.ɣi.ˈðor]
pursuer
Nuestro perseguidor me quiere matar, pero no va a arriesgar su vida por ello.
-Our pursuer wants to kill me, but he won't risk his life for it.

9574 **magnificencia**
f
[maɣ.ni.fi.ˈsẽn.sja]
magnificence
Hay magnificencia en ti, Tracy.
-There's a magnificence in you, Tracy.

9575 **deslumbrar**
vb
[dɛṣ.lũm.ˈbrar]
dazzle
Si quieres deslumbrar, tienes que dar la nota.
-If you want to dazzle, you got to take razzles.

9576 **magenta**
magenta

adj
[ma.ˈxẽn̪.ta]

No puedo creer que plantara azaleas magenta cuando sabía que Ana quería blancas.
-I can't believe she planted magenta azaleas when she knew Ana wanted white.

9577 **endurecer**

harden

vb
[ẽn̪.du.re.ˈsɛr]

Si la sal funciona, debería endurecerse bastante rápido.
-If the salt works, it should harden pretty quick.

9578 **predilecto**

favorite

adj
[pre.ði.ˈlek̚.to]

Ahora, tú has pasado a ser el hijo predilecto.
-Now you are the favorite son.

9579 **desagrado**

displeasure

m
[de.sa.ˈɣra.ðo]

Veo sorpresa y desagrado en tus ojos.
-I see surprise and displeasure in your eyes.

9580 **enlatar**

can

vb
[ẽn.la.ˈtar]

Comeremos lo que podamos, y enlataremos lo que no.
-We will eat what we can, and can what we can't.

9581 **cordel**

string

m
[kor.ˈðɛl]

Es solo un cordel para sacarlo.
-It's just a string to pull it out.

9582 **inmerso**

immersed

adj
[ĩm.ˈmɛr.so]

Él estaba inmerso en el rompecabezas.
-He was immersed in the puzzle.

9583 **envidiable**

enviable

adj
[ẽm.bi.ˈðja.βle]

Era una ciudad de una belleza envidiable.
-It was a city of enviable beauty.

9584 **guinda**

cherry, final touch

f
[ˈgĩn̪.da]

Incluso puedes ponerme una guinda encima.
-You can even put a cherry on top.

9585 **disponibilidad**

availability

f
[dis.po.ni.βi.li.ˈðað]

En varias ocasiones he oído mencionar la palabra disponibilidad.
-On a number of occasions, I have heard the word availability mentioned.

9586 **catapulta**

catapult

f
[ka.ta.ˈpul̪.ta]

El instrumento que usaba se convirtió en una catapulta.
-The instrument that I used turned into a catapult.

9587 **circuncidar**

circumcise

vb
[sir.kũn.si.ˈðar]

No voy a circuncidar a mi hijo.
-I will not circumcise my son.

9588 **disimulo**

disguise

m
[di.si.ˈmu.lo]

Sin quererlo, nos convertimos en maestros del disimulo.
-Without meaning to, we become masters of disguise.

9589 **cúmulo**

cluster

m
[ˈku.mu.lo]

Contiene un cúmulo de estrella jóvenes.
-It contains a cluster of young stars.

9590 **cómoda**

chest of drawers

f
[ˈko.mo.ða]

Me dijiste que consiguiera una cómoda.
-You told me to get a chest of drawers.

9591 **exención**

exemption

f
[ɛk.sɛ̃n.ˈsjõn]
Por consiguiente, puede concedérsele una exención a esta empresa.
-Accordingly, an exemption to this company can be granted.

9592 **lapsus** — **lapse**
m
[ˈlap.sus]
Seguro que ha sido un lapsus.
-I'm sure it was just a lapse.

9593 **papelería** — **stationery**
f
[pa.pe.lɛ.ˈri.a]
Bueno, involucra algo de papelería.
-Well, there's a bit of stationery involved.

9594 **tripular** — **crew**
vb
[tri.pu.ˈlar]
Necesitas a alguien para tripular esa cosa.
-You need someone to crew that thing.

9595 **imperceptible** — **imperceptible**
adj
[ĩm.pɛr.sep̚.ˈti.βle]
Aquí, esta aterradora velocidad es imperceptible.
-Here, this terrifying speed is imperceptible.

9596 **trilogía** — **trilogy**
f
[tri.lo.ˈxi.a]
Esperábamos poder ver aquí la trilogía.
-We were hoping we could watch the trilogy here.

9597 **egresar** — **graduate**
vb
[e.ɣre.ˈsar]
Y no veré a Adam egresar de la secundaria.
-And I won't get to see Adam graduate from high school.

9598 **antidroga** — **antidrug**
adj
[ãn̪.ti.ˈðro.ɣa]
Se trata de un control antidroga muy minucioso.
-It is a very meticulous antidrug control.

9599 **bulimia** — **bulimia**
f
[bu.ˈli.mja]
Los ejemplos más obvios son la anorexia y la bulimia.
-Anorexia and bulimia are obvious examples of this.

9600 **lentitud** — **slowness**
f
[lɛ̃n̪.ti.ˈtuð]
Se han hecho progresos pero con bastante lentitud.
-Progress has been made but it is quite slow.

9601 **drenar** — **drain**
vb
[dre.ˈnar]
Necesitamos drenar el hematoma y reparar el vaso sanguíneo.
-We need to drain the hematoma and repair the bleeding vessel.

9602 **extirpar** — **remove**
vb
[ɛks.tir.ˈpar]
Tu cirujano puede extirpar los ganglios linfáticos.
-Your surgeon may remove the lymph nodes.

9603 **repeler** — **repel**
vb
[re.pe.ˈlɛr]
Estoy preparado para repeler a quien me aborde.
-I'm ready to repel all boarders.

9604 **sintaxis** — **syntax**
f
[sĩn̪.ˈtak.sis]
La sintaxis de este archivo es simple.
-The syntax of this file is simple.

9605 **inverosímil** — **implausible**
adj
[ĩm.bɛ.ro.ˈsi.mil]
Esto hace que toda la carta suene totalmente inverosímil.
-It makes the whole letter sound totally implausible.

9606 **rocoso** — **rocky**
adj
[ro.ˈko.so]
Este es el fin de un camino rocoso.
-This is the end of a rocky road.

9607 **compañerismo** — **fellowship**

m
[kõm.pa.ɲɛ.ˈriʂ.mo]
Malinterpreta la naturaleza de nuestro compañerismo.
-You misunderstand the nature of our fellowship.

9608 **explanada**

f
[ɛks.pla.ˈna.ða]

esplanade

Puede que ya estén en la explanada.
-They might be on the esplanade already.

9609 **kiosco**

m
[ˈkjos.ko]

kiosk

Y me subí a un kiosco.
-And I got up on top of this kiosk.

9610 **diurno**

adj
[ˈdjur.no]

daytime

Los cursos de pago solo se ofrecen en régimen diurno.
-Fee-paying courses are offered during the daytime only.

9611 **destapar**

vb
[dɛs.ta.ˈpar]

uncover

No sé qué secreto estás buscando destapar.
-I don't know what secret you're looking to uncover.

9612 **recíproco**

adj
[re.ˈsi.pro.ko]

reciprocal

Las visitas también suponen una oportunidad de enriquecimiento
recíproco.
-In situ visits also represent an opportunity for reciprocal enrichment.

9613 **prodigioso**

adj
[pro.ði.ˈxjo.so]

prodigious

Mi invitado de esta noche es un prodigioso mago.
-My guest tonight is a prodigious magician.

9614 **desintegración**

f
[de.sĩn̪.te.ɣra.ˈsjõn]

disintegration

La desintegración de Georgia no beneficia a nadie.
-The disintegration of Georgia is in no one's interest.

9615 **desengaño**

m
[de.sẽŋ.ˈga.ɲo]

disappointment

Cinco años más tarde, la situación es un cruel desengaño.
-Five years later, the situation is a cruel disappointment.

9616 **aerodinámico**

adj
[a.ɛ.ro.ði.ˈna.mi.ko]

aerodynamic

No es tan aerodinámico como esperaba.
-It's not as aerodynamic as I'd hoped.

9617 **trasfondo**

m
[tras.ˈfõn̪.do]

background

Examinemos el trasfondo familiar del donante.
-Let's examine the family background of the donor.

9618 **efigie**

f
[e.ˈfi.xje]

effigy

Sus seguidores querían usar su efigie para destruir el mundo.
-Her followers intended to use her effigy to destroy the world.

9619 **alboroto**

m
[al.βo.ˈro.to]

fuss

Es algo que debería haber pasado sin mucho alboroto.
-It's something that should have happened without much fuss.

9620 **tráquea**

f
[ˈtra.ke.a]

trachea

Tenía graves daños en la tráquea.
-There was pretty intense damage to the trachea.

9621 **contentar**

vb
[kõn̪.tẽn̪.ˈtar]

please

Su padre parecía alguien difícil de contentar.
-His father sounded like a hard man to please.

9622 **etiquetar**

vb
[ɛ.ti.kɛ.ˈtar]

label

No sentimos la necesidad de etiquetar todo.
-We don't feel the need to label everything.

9623	**prepucio**	**foreskin**
	m	No olvides lavarte bajo el prepucio.
	[pre.ˈpu.sjo]	-Don't forget to wash under your foreskin.
9624	**amputación**	**amputation**
	f	Nunca he ayudado en ninguna amputación.
	[ãm.pu.ta.ˈsjõn]	-I've never even assisted in an amputation.
9625	**parroquial**	**parochial**
	adj	Fui a la escuela parroquial, Sr. Holmes.
	[pa.ro.ˈkjal]	-I went to parochial school, Mr. Holmes.
9626	**alucinar**	**hallucinate**
	vb	Esto te hace alucinar y disociarte por completo de tu cuerpo.
	[a.lu.si.ˈnar]	-This makes you hallucinate and totally dissociate from your body.
9627	**pulsación**	**pulse**
	f	Las tasas de pulsación suben otra vez.
	[pul.sa.ˈsjõn]	-The pulse rates are spiking again.
9628	**ramificación**	**branch**
	f	Una ramificación de la misma coalición desarrollaba actividades en Hawaii.
	[ra.mi.fi.ka.ˈsjõn]	-A branch of the same coalition was active in Hawaii.
9629	**litigio**	**litigation**
	m	En todo caso, ahora el litigio tiene que volver a empezar.
	[li.ˈti.xjo]	-In any case, the litigation now has to begin again.
9630	**dietético**	**dietary**
	adj	No, es un suplemento dietético.
	[djɛ.ˈtɛ.ti.ko]	-No, it's a dietary supplement.
9631	**privatización**	**privatization**
	f	En Portugal cada privatización entraña diversas medidas, incluso instrumentos legislativos concretos.
	[pri.βa.ti.sa.ˈsjõn]	-In Portugal, each privatization involves a number of steps, including specific legislative acts.
9632	**aguar**	**water down, spoil (coll)**
	vb	Lo último que quiero hacer es aguar una fiesta.
	[a.ˈɣwar]	-The last thing I want to do is to spoil a party.
9633	**quitanieves**	**snowplow**
	m	Bueno, al menos no es un quitanieves.
	[ki.ta.ˈnje.βes]	-Well, at least it's not a snowplow.
9634	**cuadrícula**	**grid**
	f	Usaremos esta zona como una cuadrícula.
	[kwa.ˈðri.ku.la]	-We'll treat this area as a grid.
9635	**rectal**	**rectal**
	adj	Ese fue mi primer termómetro rectal.
	[rek̚.ˈtal]	-That was my first rectal thermometer.
9636	**reiniciar**	**reboot**
	vb	Tuvo que reiniciar manualmente el firmware.
	[rei̯.ni.ˈsjar]	-She had to manually reboot the firmware herself.
9637	**higuera**	**fig tree**
	f	La higuera ya no tiene higos.
	[i.ˈɣɛ.ɾa]	-The fig tree no longer has figs.
9638	**confección**	**making, clothing**

f
[kõɱ.fɛk.ˈsjõn]

Europa es el segundo exportador mundial de textil y confección.
-Europe is the world's second largest textile and clothing exporter.

9639 **doblegar**

vb
[do.βle.ˈɣar]

crush

Nunca pueden doblegar mi espíritu.
-They can never crush the spirit.

9640 **absorción**

f
[aβ.sor.ˈsjõn]

absorption

Esto maximiza la superficie de absorción de fotones.
-This maximizes the photon absorption area.

9641 **edicto**

m
[e.ˈðik̚.to]

edict

No puedes cambiar eso con un edicto.
-You can't change that with an edict.

9642 **deshabitar**

vb
[de.sa.βi.ˈtar]

vacate

Tenemos que deshabitar este sitio ahora.
-We have to leave this place now.

9643 **espectral**

adj
[ɛs.pek̚.ˈtral]

spectral

Eres más que una alteración espectral común.
-You're more than a common spectral disturbance.

9644 **lírico**

adj
[ˈli.ɾi.ko]

lyrical

Ella hubiera preferido tener un lema más lírico.
-She would rather have had a more lyrical slogan.

9645 **untar**

vb
[ũn̪.ˈtar]

spread

No tiene nada en lo que untar el queso.
-She doesn't have anything to spread his cheese on.

9646 **endemoniado**

adj; m
[ɛ̃n̪.de.mo.ˈnja.ðo]

possessed; devil

Ese viejo endemoniado está haciendo de las suyas otra vez.
-That old devil is doing something again.

9647 **sima**

f
[ˈsi.ma]

chasm

La mariposa está en la sima de delante.
-The butterfly is in the chasm ahead.

9648 **amueblar**

vb
[a.mwe.ˈβlar]

furnish

No pensé que tuvieras tiempo para amueblar una oficina.
-I didn't think you had time to furnish an office.

9649 **regio**

adj
[ˈre.xjo]

royal

Mi regio nombre es respetado.
-My royal name is respected.

9650 **emigrante**

adj; m/f
[e.mi.ˈɣɾã̪n.te]

emigrant; emigrant

Era lo que se llamaba un emigrante.
-He was what's known as an immigrant.

9651 **modernidad**

f
[mo.ðɛɾ.ni.ˈðað]

modernity

Las vidrieras de esta capilla combinan antigüedad y modernidad.
-The stained glass windows of this chapel combine antiquity and modernity.

9652 **boquiabierto**

adj
[bo.kja.ˈβjɛr.to]

dumbstruck

Me giré hacia Frank, que estaba tan boquiabierto como yo.
-And I turned to Frank, who looked just as dumbstruck as I did.

9653 **mazorca**

f
[ma.ˈsor.ka]

corncob

Ya terminé mi disfraz de mazorca.
-I already finished my corncob costume.

9654 contraespionaje — counterintelligence
m
[kõn̪.tra.ɛs.pjo.ˈna.xe]
El contraespionaje de Dorota no es lo que era.
-Dorota's counterintelligence isn't what it used to be.

9655 loable — laudable
adj
[lo.ˈa.βle]
Se trata de una ambición loable y necesaria.
-That is a laudable and necessary ambition.

9656 invariable — unchanging; unchanged
adj; m
[ĩm.ba.ˈrja.βle]
Sin embargo, la legislación sobre nombres sigue invariable.
-However, the law on names remains unchanged.

9657 rapar — shave
vb
[ra.ˈpar]
¿Siempre te tienes que rapar la cabeza así?
-Do you always have to shave your hair like this?

9658 leño — log
m
[ˈle.ɲo]
Ponga otro leño en el fuego, reverendo.
-Put another log on the fire, reverend.

9659 tenista — tennis player
m/f
[te.ˈnis.ta]
Dicen que eres un excelente tenista.
-So I hear you're quite a tennis player.

9660 factoría — factory
f
[fak̚.to.ˈri.a]
Dime quién está dentro de esa factoría.
-Tell me who's inside that factory.

9661 inmutable — immutable
adj
[ĩm.mu.ˈta.βle]
Esta es la verdad inmutable que enseña la historia.
-This is the immutable truth taught by history.

9662 ranking — ranking
m
[rãŋ.ˈkĩŋg]
Estas victorias lo ponen arriba en los ranking.
-These victories do move him to the top of the rankings.

9663 meollo — crux
m
[me.ˈo.ʝo]
Ese es el meollo de la paradoja que mencioné anteriormente.
-That is the crux of the paradox I mentioned earlier.

9664 monografía — monograph
f
[mo.no.ɣra.ˈfi.a]
Podré terminar mi monografía sin distracciones.
-I'll be able to finish my monograph without any distractions.

9665 prerrogativa — prerogative
f
[prɛ.ro.ɣa.ˈti.βa]
Es prerrogativa del legislador actuar así.
-It is the legislator's prerogative to do so.

9666 cobalto — cobalt
m
[ko.ˈβal̪.to]
Esto es un anillo de átomos de cobalto.
-This is a ring of cobalt atoms.

9667 cabrito — lousy (coll); young goat
adj; m
[ka.ˈβri.to]
Un cabrito me ha dado una paliza.
-I got beat up by a goat.

9668 reorganización — reorganization
f
[re.or.ɣa.ni.sa.ˈsjõn]
La reorganización puede revestir diversas formas.
-Reorganization may take a number of different forms.

9669 slip — briefs (LA)
m
[ˈʂ.lip]
Con el traje de la orquesta, tengo que llevar un slip.
-I have to wear briefs with my orchestra outfit.

9670 forcejear — **struggle, wrestle**
vb
[for.se.xe.ˈar]
Cuando éramos niños, solíamos forcejear todo el tiempo.
-When we were kids, we used to wrestle all the time.

9671 apropiarse — **take over, pocket**
vbr
[a.pro.ˈpjar.se]
Pensó que podría apropiarse del negocio.
-He thought he could take over the business.

9672 preámbulo — **preamble**
m
[pre.ˈãm.bu.lo]
Esa propuesta se incluiría en el preámbulo del protocolo.
-That proposal would be included in the preamble to the protocol.

9673 repatriación — **repatriation**
f
[re.pa.trja.ˈsjõn]
Esperamos la repatriación de nuestros ciudadanos.
-We look forward to the repatriation of our citizens.

9674 bélico — **warlike**
adj
[ˈbe.li.ko]
Nuestro período bélico finalizó hace decenas de generaciones.
-Our warlike period ended dozens of generations ago.

9675 encerar — **wax**
vb
[ẽn.sɛ.ˈrar]
Voy a encerar mi coche mañana por la tarde.
-I'm going to wax my car tomorrow afternoon.

9676 laúd — **lute**
m
[la.ˈuð]
He preparado una pieza para laúd.
-I have prepared a song for the lute.

9677 almacenaje — **storage**
m
[al.ma.se.ˈna.xe]
Además hay mucho espacio para almacenaje.
-Plus there's plenty of room for storage.

9678 atribuir — **attribute**
vb
[a.tri.ˈβwir]
Puedo atribuir cinco tiroteos a nuestro tipo.
-I can attribute five shootings to our guy.

9679 catear — **flunk (ES) (coll)**
vb
[ka.te.ˈar]
No puedo catear mis cursos.
-I can't flunk my courses.

9680 insostenible — **untenable**
adj
[ĩn.sos.te.ˈni.βle]
Esto es insostenible a largo plazo.
-This is untenable in the long run.

9681 desigualdad — **inequality**
f
[de.si.ɣwal̩.ˈdað]
Le preocupaba especialmente la inmensa desigualdad social.
-She was particularly concerned about the immense social inequality.

9682 sinfín — **myriad**
m
[sĩɱ.ˈfĩn]
Hay un sinfín de diferencias, créame.
-There are a myriad of differences, believe me.

9683 emparejar — **match**
vb
[ẽm.pa.re.ˈxar]
Creo que podemos emparejar huellas dactilares.
-I think we can match fingerprints.

9684 doblaje — **dubbing**
m
[do.ˈβla.xe]
Hice el mismo doblaje hace un año.
-I did the same dubbing a year ago.

9685 reguero — **trail**
m
[re.ˈɣɛ.ro]
Hay un reguero de sangre en el pavimento.
-There's a blood trail on the pavement.

9686 **sondar**　　　　　　　　　**probe**

vb　　　　　　　　　　　¿Alguien quiere sondar la herida?
[sõn̪.ˈdar]　　　　　　　　　-Anyone care to probe the wound?

9687 **surgimiento**　　　　　　**appearance**

m　　　　　　　　　　　Otros factores que propician el surgimiento del racismo son
[sur.xi.ˈmjẽn̪.to]　　　　　económicos.
　　　　　　　　　　　　-Other factors conducive to the emergence of racism are economic.

9688 **inexorable**　　　　　　　**inexorable**

adj　　　　　　　　　　La mundialización es un proceso imperfecto y, sin embargo, inexorable.
[i.nɛk.so.ˈra.βle]　　　　　-Globalization was an incomplete yet inexorable process.

9689 **racimo**　　　　　　　　　**bunch**

m　　　　　　　　　　　Siempre terminan pareciendo un racimo de plátanos.
[ra.ˈsi.mo]　　　　　　　-They always end up looking like a bunch of bananas.

9690 **encaminar**　　　　　　　**route**

vb　　　　　　　　　　　Creo que podemos encaminar a la dama.
[ẽŋ.ka.mi.ˈnar]　　　　　-I think we can route the lady.

9691 **comité**　　　　　　　　　**committee**

m　　　　　　　　　　　Informaré al comité de la ciudad.
[ko.mi.ˈte]　　　　　　　-I'll inform the town committee.

9692 **rompimiento**　　　　　　**breakup**

m　　　　　　　　　　　El rompimiento con Stephanie fue muy doloroso.
[rõm.pi.ˈmjẽn̪.to]　　　　-The breakup with Stephanie was extremely painful.

9693 **genoma**　　　　　　　　　**genome**

m　　　　　　　　　　　La secuencia del genoma es demasiado perfecta.
[xe.ˈno.ma]　　　　　　　-The genome sequence, it's just too neat.

9694 **neural**　　　　　　　　　**neural**

adj　　　　　　　　　　Pero este implante neural en particular tiene algunos efectos
[neu̯.ˈral]　　　　　　　secundarios.
　　　　　　　　　　　　-But this particular neural implant has some side-effects.

9695 **arqueológico**　　　　　　**archaeological**

adj　　　　　　　　　　El proyecto arqueológico finalizará a finales del año 2007.
[ar.ke.o.ˈlo.xi.ko]　　　　-The archaeological project will finalize at the end of the year 2007.

9696 **acarrear**　　　　　　　　**entail**

vb　　　　　　　　　　　El no cumplimiento de esta exigencia podrá acarrear graves
[a.ka.re.ˈar]　　　　　　consecuencias.
　　　　　　　　　　　　-Failure to take such action can entail the risk of serious consequences.

9697 **diligente**　　　　　　　　**diligent**

adj　　　　　　　　　　Él no es menos diligente que ella.
[di.li.ˈxẽn̪.te]　　　　　　-He is no less diligent than she.

9698 **reivindicación**　　　　　**demand**

f　　　　　　　　　　　Nuestra reivindicación es modesta y simple.
[rei̯.βĩn̪.di.ka.ˈsjõn]　　　-Our demand is modest and simple.

9699 **desahogarse**　　　　　　**blow off steam**

vbr　　　　　　　　　　Está usando a su muñeco para desahogarse.
[de.sa.o.ˈɣar.se]　　　　-He's using the dummy to blow off steam.

9700 **desembarque**　　　　　　**unloading**

m　　　　　　　　　　　Debe registrarse el peso real en el momento del desembarque.
[de.sẽm.ˈbar.ke]　　　　-Actual weight at the time of unloading should be recorded.

9701 **mensualidad**　　　　　　**monthly wage**

	f	Él tiene su mensualidad, yo no.
	[mẽn.swa.li.ˈðað]	-He has your monthly payment, not me.
9702	**ávido**	**avid**
	adj	Soy un lector ávido de biografías.
	[ˈa.βi.ðo]	-I'm an avid reader of biographies.
9703	**merendar**	**have a snack**
	vb	Pero el sastre se ha ido a merendar.
	[mɛ.rẽn̪.ˈdar]	-But the tailor went to have a snack.
9704	**asbesto**	**asbestos**
	m	El asbesto es una sustancia notablemente peligrosa.
	[aṣ.ˈβɛs.to]	-Asbestos is a notoriously dangerous material.
9705	**humorista**	**humorist**
	m/f	Cuando quiera chistes llamaré a un humorista.
	[u.mo.ˈris.ta]	-If I need jokes, I'll hire a comedian.
9706	**estipular**	**stipulate**
	vb	La ley debería estipular claramente que toda persona tiene derecho a la objeción de conciencia al servicio militar.
	[ɛs.ti.pu.ˈlar]	-The law should clearly stipulate that individuals have the right to conscientious objection to military service.
9707	**tótem**	**totem**
	m	Quiero una toma de ti con el tótem.
	[ˈto.tɛm]	-I want a shot of you with the totem.
9708	**tarima**	**stage**
	f	Harvey, deberías subir a la tarima.
	[ta.ˈri.ma]	-Harvey, you should get to the stage.
9709	**deslealtad**	**disloyalty**
	f	Nadie podría acusarlos de deslealtad al otro.
	[dɛṣ.le.al̩.ˈtað]	-No one could accuse either of you of disloyalty to the other.
9710	**tozudo**	**stubborn**
	adj	Es más tozudo que una mula.
	[to.ˈsu.ðo]	-He's as stubborn as an old mule.
9711	**ingerir**	**ingest**
	vb	No ingerir, su ingesta es perjudicial.
	[ĩŋ.xɛ.ˈrir]	-Do not ingest, its ingestion is harmful.
9712	**obsoleto**	**obsolete**
	adj	Durante años he dicho que nuestro equipo está obsoleto.
	[oβ.so.ˈlɛ.to]	-I've been saying for years that our equipment is obsolete.
9713	**autocar**	**coach**
	m	Esto conlleva un viaje agotador en autocar de dos horas y media.
	[au̯.to.ˈkar]	-This means an exhausting two and a half hour coach trip.
9714	**perforación**	**drilling**
	f	Usamos un método de perforación completamente diferente.
	[pɛr.fo.ra.ˈsjõn]	-We use a totally different method of drilling.
9715	**toronja**	**grapefruit**
	f	Siempre comienzo mi desayuno con media toronja.
	[to.ˈrõŋ.xa]	-I always start my breakfast with half a grapefruit.
9716	**frazada**	**blanket**
	f	Ven y métete bajo mi frazada, chiquilla.
	[fra.ˈsa.ða]	-Come on and get under this blanket, girlie.

9717 emporio — emporium
m
[ɛ̃m.ˈpo.rjo]
Tendrán una receta en el emporio de los caracoles.
-They will have a recipe at the snail emporium.

9718 respiratorio — respiratory
adj
[rɛs.pi.ra.ˈto.rjo]
Mi bebita nació con un problema respiratorio.
-My baby girl was born with a respiratory problem.

9719 intuitivo — intuitive
adj
[ĩn.twi.ˈti.βo]
No es tan intuitivo como creía.
-It's not as intuitive as I thought.

9720 lumbar — lumbar
adj
[lũm.ˈbar]
Ningún soporte lumbar puede compensar eso.
-No amount of lumbar support can compensate for that.

9721 argumentar — argue
vb
[ar.ɣu.mɛ̃n.ˈtar]
Gracias, nos gustaría argumentar nuestro propio caso.
-Thank you, we'd like to argue our own case.

9722 exento — exempt
adj
[ɛk.ˈsɛ̃n.to]
Ningún país está exento de esta obligación.
-No country is exempt from this obligation.

9723 rezagarse — fall behind
vbr
[re.sa.ˈɣar.se]
Ellos no se están rezagando.
-They are not falling behind.

9724 turbulento — turbulent
adj
[tur.βu.ˈlɛ̃n.to]
En el último año, el panorama económico mundial ha sido muy turbulento.
-The world economic landscape has been quite turbulent over the past year.

9725 incredulidad — disbelief
f
[ĩn.kre.ðu.li.ˈðað]
Todos estamos todavía en una situación de conmoción e incredulidad.
-We are all still in a state of shock and disbelief.

9726 descompresión — decompression
f
[dɛs.kõm.pre.ˈsjõn]
Tienes que disminuir tu metabolismo antes de que empecemos con la descompresión.
-You need to lower your metabolism before we start the decompression.

9727 referéndum — referendum
m
[re.fɛ.ˈrɛ̃n.dũm]
Por último, estamos acercándonos al referéndum.
-Finally, we are coming close to the referendum.

9728 mogollón — lots of (coll); loads
m; adv
[mo.ɣo.ˈjõn]
Quiero decir, haría un mogollón de cosas por ti, hombre.
-I mean, I would do a lot of things for you, man.

9729 comercialización — marketing
f
[ko.mɛr.sja.li.sa.ˈsjõn]
Solamente se prohíbe la comercialización de nuevos dispositivos.
-It is only the marketing of new devices that are prohibited.

9730 residual — residual
adj
[re.si.ˈðwal]
Es la radiación residual del resplandor.
-It's the residual radiation from the flash.

9731 desocupar — vacate
vb
[de.so.ku.ˈpar]
Tienen hasta la puesta del sol para desocupar la casa.
-You've got until sunset to vacate the premises.

9732	**adolorido**	**in pain**
	adj	Bueno, él se ve adolorido, vale.
	[a.ðo.lo.ˈri.ðo]	-Well, he looks pained, all right.

9733	**chiquitito**	**tiny**
	adj	Dicen que es demasiado chiquitito.
	[ʧi.ki.ˈti.to]	-They say it's too small.

9734	**penalti**	**penalty**
	m	Quiero escuchar todo sobre ese penalti.
	[pe.ˈnal̪.ti]	-I want to hear all about that penalty.

9735	**estría**	**stretch mark**
	f	Se merece cada estría que le salga.
	[ɛs.ˈtri.a]	-She deserves every stretch mark she gets.

9736	**evolutivo**	**evolutionary**
	adj	En un sentido evolutivo estamos demasiado lejos.
	[e.βo.lu.ˈti.βo]	-In an evolutionary sense, we're too far ahead.

9737	**legitimidad**	**legitimacy**
	f	Solo así garantizaremos la legitimidad de esta reforma.
	[le.xi.ti.mi.ˈðað]	-Only in so doing will we ensure the legitimacy of that reform.

9738	**neurocirugía**	**neurosurgery**
	f	Es profesor de neurocirugía en Harvard.
	[neu̯.ro.si.ru.ˈxi.a]	-He's a professor of neurosurgery at Harvard.

9739	**impulsor**	**active; booster**
	adj; m	Un impulsor más y podría derribar un tanque.
	[ĩm.pul.ˈsor]	-One more booster and I could take out a tank.

9740	**izquierdista**	**leftist; leftist**
	adj; m/f	Uno de sus poemas fue publicado por un periódico izquierdista.
	[is.kjɛr.ˈðis.ta]	-One of your poems was published by a leftist newspaper.

9741	**incubación**	**incubation**
	m/f	La duración de la incubación debe ser como mínimo de 7 días.
	[ĩn.ku.βa.ˈsjõn]	-The duration of incubation should be at least 7 days.

9742	**norcoreano**	**North Korean; North Korean person**
	adj; m	No tienes ninguna información de este supuesto agente norcoreano.
	[nor.ko.re.ˈa.no]	-You've got no information on this supposed North Korean agent.

9743	**sostenible**	**sustainable**
	adj	Simplemente tenemos que reconstruir de una forma sostenible.
	[sos.te.ˈni.βle]	-We simply have to rebuild in a sustainable way.

9744	**narcisismo**	**narcissism**
	m	Lamentablemente, eso resultó en su narcisismo.
	[nar.si.ˈsis̬.mo]	-Unfortunately, that resulted in his narcissism.

9745	**simplista**	**simplistic**
	adj	No podemos responderle con una interpretación simplista.
	[sĩm.ˈplis.ta]	-We cannot respond to it with a simplistic interpretation.

9746	**compresor**	**compressor**
	m	Si el fuego alcanza el compresor, estamos fritos.
	[kõm.pre.ˈsor]	-If that fire reaches the compressor, we're stuffed.

9747	**fechar**	**date**
	vb	Podemos fechar esto hace 700 años.
	[fe.ˈʧar]	-We can date it 700 years ago.

9748 **papeleta** — **ballot**
f
[pa.pe.ˈlɛ.ta]
En cada papeleta escribiréis dos nombres.
-On each ballot, you'll write two names.

9749 **tribulación** — **tribulation**
f
[tri.βu.la.ˈsjõn]
Comienza un período de gran tribulación.
-It begins a period of great tribulation.

9750 **ablandar** — **soften**
vb
[a.βlãn̪.ˈdar]
Lo usan para ablandar el plástico.
-They use it to soften plastic.

9751 **soto** — **grove**
m
[ˈso.to]
Os conduciré a un soto sagrado.
-I'll take you to a sacred grove.

9752 **ojal** — **buttonhole**
m
[o.ˈxal]
Parece que he perdido mi ojal.
-I seem to have misplaced my buttonhole.

9753 **estocada** — **thrust**
f
[ɛs.to.ˈka.ða]
Él paró la estocada y contraatacó sin reconocerme.
-He parried and thrust without recognizing me.

9754 **aureola** — **halo**
f
[au̯.re.ˈo.la]
Entonces siéntate y endereza tu aureola.
-Then sit down and straighten your halo.

9755 **rebelarse** — **rebel**
vbr
[re.βe.ˈlar.se]
Los jóvenes nobles decidieron rebelarse y huir.
-The noble youths decided to rebel and to escape.

9756 **antesala** — **anteroom**
f
[ãn̪.te.ˈsa.la]
Esta es la antesala donde encontramos algunas piezas importantes.
-This is the anteroom where we found a few important pieces.

9757 **solomillo** — **sirloin**
m
[so.lo.ˈmi.jo]
Tráigame un filete de solomillo grande.
-I'll have a great big sirloin steak.

9758 **liquidez** — **liquidity**
f
[li.ˈki.ðes]
En particular, ponen de manifiesto un alto nivel de liquidez.
-In particular, they reveal a high level of liquidity.

9759 **reseco** — **arid**
adj
[re.ˈse.ko]
¿No puedes ver este paisaje reseco?
-Can't you see this arid landscape?

9760 **sinusitis** — **sinusitis**
f
[si.nu.ˈsi.tis]
Soy una vieja sirvienta con sinusitis.
-I'm an old maid with sinusitis.

9761 **bloc** — **pad**
m
[ˈblok]
Los forenses hallaron una chaqueta en el coche con un bloc y dos bolígrafos.
-Forensics found a jacket in his car with a notepad and two pens.

9762 **dialogar** — **talk**
vb
[dja.lo.ˈɣar]
La verdad es que todas las partes deben dialogar.
-The truth is that all parties should talk.

9763 **bagre** — **catfish**

	m	Sacaré a mi bagre de la bañera.
	[ˈba.ɣre]	-I'll get my catfish out of the tub.

9764 alhaja — jewel

f

[a.ˈla.xa]

Jamás ha visto una alhaja tan hermosa como esta.
-You've never seen a jewel as beautiful as this.

9765 hincapié — emphasis

m

[ĩŋ.ka.ˈpje]

Debemos aprovechar esta oportunidad para hacer especial hincapié en ello.
-We should take this opportunity to place particular emphasis on this point.

9766 certificación — certification

f

[sɛr.ti.fi.ka.ˈsjõn]

Es necesario exigir una certificación en este ámbito.
-There needs to be a certification requirement in this area.

9767 desencadenar — trigger, unchain

vb

[de.sɛ̃ŋ.ka.ðe.ˈnar]

Eso va a desencadenar algún tipo de protección.
-That's going to trigger some kind of protection.

9768 omisión — omission

f

[o.mi.ˈsjõn]

Es muy importante corregir esta omisión.
-It is very important to correct this omission.

9769 profesionalismo — professionalism

m

[pro.fe.sjo.na.ˈliṣ.mo]

Confiamos plenamente en su objetividad y profesionalismo.
-We have full confidence in their objectivity and professionalism.

9770 rapaz — predatory; kid

adj; m

[ˈra.pas]

Siempre me ha cautivado su ingenio rapaz.
-I've always been captivated by your rapacious wit.

9771 culinario — culinary

adj

[ku.li.ˈna.rjo]

Tú eres un genio culinario.
-You are a culinary genius.

9772 reconocible — recognizable

adj

[re.ko.no.ˈsi.βle]

Digamos que tenían un acento reconocible.
-Let's say they had a recognizable accent.

9773 ion — ion

m

[ˈɟjõn]

Esta mezcla contiene el ion metóxido.
-This mixture contains the methoxide ion.

9774 redimir — redeem

vb

[re.ði.ˈmir]

Y usted quiere redimir su nombre entrenando a este equipo.
-And you wish to redeem your name by coaching this team.

9775 intranquilo — uneasy

adj

[ĩṇ.trãŋ.ˈki.lo]

Estoy muy intranquilo respecto a esto.
-I'm very uneasy about this.

9776 capitulación — capitulation

f

[ka.pi.tu.la.ˈsjõn]

Creo que tu capitulación es sincera.
-I believe that your capitulation is sincere.

9777 radiología — radiology

f

[ra.ðjo.lo.ˈxi.a]

Solo me he perdido yendo a radiología.
-I just got lost on my way to radiology.

9778 perpetrar — perpetrate

vb

[pɛr.pɛ.ˈtrar]

Ningún gobierno puede atreverse a perpetrar tales actos.
-No government could dare perpetrate such acts.

9779 colorear — color
vb
[ko.lo.re.ˈar]
El autor ha aplicado este método para colorear una foto de una joven.
-The author applied this technique to colorize a photo of a young girl.

9780 procreación — procreation
f
[pro.kre.a.ˈsjõn]
Queremos libre acceso a los métodos y medios de procreación responsable.
-We want free access to methods and means of conscious procreation.

9781 hipotecar — mortgage
vb
[i.po.te.ˈkar]
Al banco le encantaría hipotecar su rancho.
-The bank'd be happy to mortgage his spread.

9782 diferencial — differential; gap
adj; f
[di.fɛ.rẽn.ˈsjal]
El vehículo no dispone de diferencial.
-The vehicle does not have a differential.

9783 geológico — geological
adj
[xe.o.ˈlo.xi.ko]
También se está actualizando el mapa geológico de la costa meridional.
-The geological map of the south side is also being updated.

9784 verídico — true
adj
[bɛ.ˈri.ði.ko]
¿Cómo sabes que el artículo de Maurice no puede ser verídico?
-How do you know that Maurice's story couldn't be true?

9785 iguana — iguana
f
[i.ˈɣwa.na]
Malas noticias, la iguana se comió el papel origami.
-Bad news, the iguana ate the origami paper.

9786 enfisema — emphysema
m
[ẽɱ.fi.ˈse.ma]
Le operaron hace años de un enfisema pulmonar.
-He was operated on a few years ago for pulmonary emphysema.

9787 lingüístico — linguistic
adj
[lĩŋ.ˈgwis.ti.ko]
La situación resulta especialmente problemática en el sector lingüístico.
-The situation appears to be especially problematic in the linguistic sector.

9788 geriátrico — geriatric; nursing home
adj; m
[xɛ.ˈrja.tri.ko]
Están viviendo en el mismo geriátrico.
-You're living in the same nursing home.

9789 magistral — masterly
adj
[ma.xis.ˈtral]
Tan osadas pinceladas de brocha, tan magistral control.
-Such bold strokes of the brush, such masterly control.

9790 alberca — swimming
f
[al.ˈβer.ka]
Ella perdió la llave de su taquilla mientras nadaba en la alberca.
-While swimming in the pool, she lost her locker key.

9791 mensajería — messaging
f
[mẽn.sa.xɛ.ˈri.a]
Tenemos que definir una nueva estrategia de mensajería y colaboración.
-We have to define a new messaging and collaboration strategy.

9792 ondear — wave
vb
[õn̪.de.ˈar]
Es hora de ondear la varita mágica.
-Time to wave that magic wand.

9793 eventual — eventual
adj
[e.βẽn̪.ˈtwal]
Estos debates fueron esenciales para el eventual éxito de dichas negociaciones.
-Those discussions were crucial to the eventual success of those negotiations.

9794 **antifaz** **mask**

m
[ãn̪.ˈti.fas]

Bueno, primero necesitas un antifaz y una capa.
-Well, first you need a mask and a cape.

9795 **adepto** **adept; follower**

adj; m
[a.ˈðep̚.to]

Alcancé el nivel de maestro adepto.
-I achieved the rank of master adept.

9796 **extinto** **extinct**

adj
[ɛks.ˈtĩn̪.to]

Pensé que estaba extinto hasta hace poco.
-I thought that was extinct until recently.

9797 **estupor** **stupor**

m
[ɛs.tu.ˈpor]

Siempre está en una especie de estupor de ebriedad.
-You're always in some sort of a drunken stupor.

9798 **pentagrama** **pentagram**

m
[pẽn̪.ta.ˈɣra.ma]

El hombre tenía un pentagrama en su espalda, Tony.
-The man had a pentagram on his back, Tony.

9799 **redundante** **redundant**

adj
[re.ðũn̪.ˈdãn̪.te]

Cuando algo es redundante es eliminado.
-When a thing is redundant, it is eliminated.

9800 **contemplación** **contemplation**

f
[kõn̪.tẽm.ˈpla.sjõn]

Estaba buscando algunos momentos de contemplación.
-I was seeking a few moments of contemplation.

9801 **abecedario** **alphabet**

m
[a.βe.se.ˈða.rjo]

En el abecedario B viene después de A.
-In the alphabet, B comes after A.

9802 **irreprochable** **irreproachable**

adj
[i.re.pro.ˈʧa.βle]

Fui huésped en una buena casa en donde la hospitalidad fue irreprochable.
-I was a guest in a fine home where the hospitality was irreproachable.

9803 **lira** **lyre**

f
[ˈli.ra]

Su estructura tiene forma de lira.
-Its structure is shaped like a lyre.

9804 **maquinilla** **razor**

f
[ma.ki.ˈni.ja]

Solo quiero ser capaz de utilizar tu maquinilla de afeitar.
-I just want to be able to use your razor.

9805 **transatlántico** **transatlantic; ocean liner**

adj; m
[trãn.sat̚.ˈlãn̪.ti.ko]

No cabe duda de que el abismo transatlántico se agranda cada vez más.
-It is clear that the transatlantic gap is becoming wider.

9806 **compatibilidad** **compatibility**

f
[kõm.pa.ti.βi.li.ˈðað]

Tú eras quien quería hablar sobre compatibilidad.
-You were the one who wanted to talk about compatibility.

9807 **recostar(se)** **lie down**

vb
[re.kos.ˈtar]

¿Te quieres recostar en el sofá?
-Would you like to lie down on the couch?

9808 **insípido** **tasteless**

adj
[ĩn.ˈsi.pi.ðo]

Puede parecer un poco insípido, eso es todo.
-It might seem a little tasteless, that's all.

9809 **filoso** **sharp**

adj
[fi.'lo.so]

Necesitaré una bolsa y algo filoso.
-I'll need a sack and something sharp.

9810 mandolina — **mandolin**

f
[mãn̪.do.'li.na]

Hace mucho tiempo tocaba la mandolina.
-A long time ago, I played the mandoline.

9811 albacea — **executor**

m/f
[al.βa.'se.a]

He sido designado albacea por un tribunal.
-I have been appointed executor by a court.

9812 desaprobar — **disapprove**

vb
[de.sa.pro.'βar]

Mamá parece desaprobar que la use.
-Mother seems to disapprove of me using it at all.

9813 retoque — **finishing touch**

m
[rɛ.'to.ke]

Ven y hazme el retoque final.
-Come and do the final touch-up.

9814 tomillo — **thyme**

m
[to.'mi.jo]

Está adobada en aceite de oliva y tomillo.
-It's marinated in a little olive oil and thyme.

9815 trivialidad — **triviality**

f
[tri.βja.li.'ðað]

Sin esto nos queda solo la trivialidad y la banalidad.
-Without this, we are left to triviality and the mundane.

9816 accionar — **trigger**

vb
[ak.sjo.'nar]

Solo tenías que accionar la palanca.
-All you had to do was pull the lever.

9817 terraplén — **embankment**

m
[tɛ.rap̚.'lẽn]

El autobús se deslizó en un terraplén.
-The bus slid down an embankment.

9818 subyacente — **underlying**

adj
[suβ.ja.'sẽn̪.te]

Pero el mensaje subyacente es muy positivo.
-But the underlying message is a very positive one.

9819 estabilizador — **stabilising; stabilizer**

adj; m
[ɛs.ta.βi.li.sa.'ðor]

Tenemos un estabilizador atorado o algo.
-We've got a jammed stabilizer or something.

9820 viscoso — **viscous**

adj
[bis.'ko.so]

Parece que segrega una especie de líquido viscoso.
-It seems to be secreting some sort of viscous fluid.

9821 denominar — **call**

vb
[de.no.mi.'nar]

Vacilo en denominar fracasos a esas operaciones.
-I hesitate to call those operations failures.

9822 capilar — **capillary; hair**

adj; m
[ka.pi.'lar]

Este producto capilar es adecuado para el tratamiento y cuidado del cabello.
-This inventive hair product is suitable for hair care and treatment.

9823 desfalco — **embezzlement**

m
[dɛs.'fal.ko]

Disfruta tus cinco años en prisión por desfalco.
-Enjoy your five years in the can for embezzlement.

9824 arriendo — **rent**

m
[a.'rjẽn̪.do]

Debería ahorrar para poder pagar todo el arriendo.
-I should be saving so I can pay full rent.

9825	**temido**	**feared**
	adj	Me han hecho rico, temido y respetado.
	[te.ˈmi.ðo]	-It's made me rich, feared and respected.
9826	**meridional**	**southern**
	adj	Instalaremos los generadores en el continente meridional.
	[mɛ.ri.ðjo.ˈnal]	-We're going to install the generators in the southern continent.
9827	**colector**	**collector**
	m	El dispositivo incluye una carcasa, una red de plancton y un colector.
	[ko.lek̚.ˈtor]	-The device includes a casing, a plankton net, and a collector.
9828	**coherencia**	**coherence**
	f	Debemos infundir más coherencia a nuestra acción.
	[ko.ɛ.ˈrẽn.sja]	-We need to instill more coherence to our action.
9829	**mímica**	**mime**
	f	Podrían tan solo hacer mímica de la canción.
	[ˈmi.mi.ka]	-They could just mime the song.
9830	**fleco**	**fringe**
	m	¿Para qué son esas toallitas con fleco dorado?
	[ˈfle.ko]	-What are those little towels with the gold fringe for?
9831	**separatista**	**separatist; separatist**
	adj; m/f	Tenía un pasado sospechoso y separatista.
	[se.pa.ra.ˈtis.ta]	-He did have a separatist and suspicious past.
9832	**anticongelante**	**antifreeze**
	adj	Sacó todo el anticongelante del radiador.
	[ãn̪.ti.kõŋ.xe.ˈlãn̪.te]	-She sucked out all the antifreeze from the radiator.
9833	**sintetizador**	**synthesizer**
	m	Vine a calibrar el sintetizador para las pruebas matutinas.
	[sĩn̪.tɛ.ti.sa.ˈðor]	-I come in to calibrate the synthesizer for the morning tests.
9834	**lumbago**	**lumbago**
	m	Tenía el lado izquierdo debilitado, un lumbago.
	[lũm.ˈba.ɣo]	-He had a left-side weakness, lumbago.
9835	**partición**	**allocation, partition**
	f	La partición de Siam ha comenzado.
	[par.ti.ˈsjõn]	-The partition of Siam, it has begun.
9836	**ganado**	**cattle**
	m	El país exporta algodón y ganado vivo.
	[ga.ˈna.ðo]	-The country exports cotton and cattle on the hoof.
9837	**dominicano**	**Dominican; Dominican person**
	adj; m	Esta es una novela breve del escritor dominicano Pedro Camilo.
	[do.mi.ni.ˈka.no]	-This is a short novel by the Dominican writer Pedro Camilo.
9838	**pretexto**	**pretext**
	m	Ningún pretexto puede justificar tales agresiones.
	[prɛ.ˈtɛks.to]	-There is no pretext that could justify such acts of aggression.
9839	**regañar**	**scold**
	vb	Tengo que ir a regañar a Zoe.
	[re.ɣa.ˈɲar]	-I need to go and scold Zoe.
9840	**salvaguardar**	**safeguard**
	vb	Es tu responsabilidad salvaguardar las pruebas.
	[sal.βa.ɣwar.ˈðar]	-It's your responsibility to safeguard the evidence.

9841 **secesión**
f
[se.se.ˈsjõn]
secession
El riesgo de secesión es muy real.
-The risk of secession is very real.

9842 **divisa**
f
[di.ˈβi.sa]
currency
Pero fue insuficiente para estabilizar la divisa.
-But it was not enough to stabilize the currency.

9843 **incumplimiento**
m
[ĩŋ.kũm.pli.ˈmjẽn̪.to]
breach
Cualquier demora constituye un incumplimiento del contrato.
-Any delivery at a later time constitutes a breach of contract.

9844 **sadismo**
m
[sa.ˈðiş.mo]
sadism
Fuimos testigos de escenas de sadismo muy personal.
-We witnessed scenes of very personal sadism.

9845 **introvertido**
adj; m
[ĩn̪.tro.βɛr.ˈti.ðo]
introverted; introvert
Giacomo quizás era más guapo, pero más introvertido.
-Perhaps Giacomo was better looking but too introverted.

9846 **axila**
f
[ak.ˈsi.la]
armpit
Perdona, tenía una erupción en la axila.
-Excuse me, there was a bull's-eye in my armpit.

9847 **escalador**
m
[ɛs.ka.la.ˈðor]
climber
Tu hijo es nuestro mejor escalador.
-Your son is the best climber we have.

9848 **catar**
vb
[ka.ˈtar]
taste
Estoy bastante seguro de que catar bebidas con cafeína no es hereditario.
-I'm pretty sure taste in coffee drinks isn't hereditary.

9849 **hendidura**
f
[ẽn̪.di.ˈðu.ra]
indent
Me he percatado de varias fracturas aquí y una hendidura.
-I noticed some fracturing here and an indentation.

9850 **bombazo**
m
[bõm.ˈba.so]
bomb
¿Están preparados para un bombazo?
-Are you guys ready for a bombshell?

9851 **metodología**
f
[mɛ.to.ðo.lo.ˈxi.a]
methodology
La metodología empleada se explicará en una nota correspondiente.
-The methodology employed will be disclosed in a corresponding note.

9852 **agudeza**
f
[a.ɣu.ˈðe.sa]
sharpness
Van a disminuir mi agudeza de la visión.
-They'll decrease my sharpness of vision.

9853 **maquillar(se)**
vb
[ma.ki.ˈjar]
make up
Estamos esperando para maquillar a la novia.
-We're waiting to do the makeup for the bride.

9854 **henchir(se)**
vb
[ẽn̪.ˈʧir]
fill
Nuestros patriotas estaban henchidos de indignación y valor.
-Our patriots were filled with indignation and valor.

9855 **bandolero**
m
[bãn̪.do.ˈlɛ.ro]
bandit
¡Hemos atrapado a un famoso bandolero!
-We've caught a famous bandit!

9856 **estiramiento**
stretching

m

[ɛs.ti.ra.ˈmjẽn̪.to]

Hay ejercicios de estiramiento que usted puede hacer.
-There are stretching exercises you can do.

9857 transpirar · **sweat**

vb

[trãns.pi.ˈrar]

No creí que pudiera transpirar, pero sí.
-I didn't think I could sweat, but I can.

9858 atrayente **attractive**

adj

[a.tra.ˈjẽn̪.te]

Se trata de un proyecto maravilloso y atrayente.
-It is a wonderful and attractive project.

9859 exasperante **infuriating**

adj

[ɛk.sas.pɛ.ˈrãn̪.te]

De alguna manera, todo esto es más liberador que exasperante.
-Somehow, all this is liberating rather than infuriating.

9860 bostezo **yawn**

m

[bos.ˈte.so]

El bostezo tiene una cualidad infecciosa de ser copiado.
-Yawning has an infectious quality of being copied.

9861 variante **alternative; variant**

adj; f

[ba.ˈrjãn̪.te]

Su delegación consideró que la segunda variante era preferible.
-His delegation considered that the second variant was preferable.

9862 agrandar **enlarge**

vb

[a.ɣrãn̪.ˈdar]

Puedes agrandar las páginas para ver más detalles o leer su contenido.
-You can enlarge the pages to view more details or read its contents.

9863 edema **edema**

m

[e.ˈðe.ma]

Tenías un edema en la tráquea superior.
-You had an edema of the upper tracheal track.

9864 cartílago **cartilage**

m

[kar.ˈti.la.ɣo]

Eso es porque no tiene cartílago en la rodilla.
-That's because there is no cartilage in your knee.

9865 inhalación **inhalation**

f

[i.na.la.ˈsjõn]

Los gases se ensayarán por inhalación.
-Gases should be tested by inhalation.

9866 marrano **disgusting (coll); pig**

adj; m

[ma.ˈra.no]

Mi hermano es un marrano.
-My brother is a pig.

9867 pucha **wow (LA)**

int

[ˈpu.tʃa]

Pucha, hermano. Gracias, en serio, ¿vale?
-Gosh, bro. Thanks, I mean it, OK?

9868 sumidero **sink**

m

[su.mi.ˈðɛ.ro]

En todos los casos esta subcategoría constituía un sumidero.
-In all cases, this subcategory constituted a sink.

9869 contingencia **contingency**

f

[kõn̪.tĩŋ.ˈxẽn.sja]

Lo mejor será que nos encarguemos de esa contingencia.
-We'd better take care of that contingency.

9870 rítmico **rhythmic**

adj

[ˈrit̚.mi.ko]

Y pensamos que puede ser suficientemente rítmico para tocar.
-And we thought that might be rhythmic enough to play to.

9871 reestructuración **restructuring**

f

[re.ɛs.truk̚.tu.ra.ˈsjõn]

A continuación se inició una reestructuración.
-A restructuring process was subsequently initiated.

9872 liberalismo **liberalism**

m
[li.βɛ.ra.ˈliṣ.mo]

Los enemigos del liberalismo son lo suficientemente reales.
-Liberalism's enemies are real enough.

9873 **semántico**

adj
[se.ˈmãn̪.ti.ko]

semantic

Un caso clásico de ruido semántico.
-A classic case of semantic noise.

9874 **fecal**

adj
[fe.ˈkal]

fecal

Raras veces se requiere cirugía para tratar una retención fecal.
-Surgery is rarely needed to treat a fecal impaction.

9875 **reunificación**

f
[reṷ.ni.fi.ka.ˈsjõn]

reunification

Ya hemos establecido los principios para la reunificación nacional.
-We have already established national reunification principles.

9876 **defensiva**

m
[de.fẽn.ˈsi.βa]

defensive

Habría sido peor aparentar ser defensiva.
-It would have looked worse to be defensive.

9877 **destinatario**

m
[dɛs.ti.na.ˈta.rjo]

recipient

Puede actuar como agente del expedidor o del destinatario.
-He can act as an agent for the shipper or the consignee.

9878 **indecisión**

f
[ĩn̪.de.si.ˈsjõn]

indecision

Los ganaderos británicos están sufriendo las consecuencias de la indecisión.
-British farmers are suffering as a result of indecision.

9879 **equidad**

f
[e.ki.ˈðað]

equity

Queremos construir sociedades marcadas por el desarrollo y equidad.
-We want to build societies marked by development and equity.

9880 **vislumbrar**

vb
[biṣ.lũm.ˈbrar]

glimpse

Creo que acaban de vislumbrar el futuro de la educación.
-I think you just got a glimpse of the future of education.

9881 **facturación**

f
[fak̚.tu.ra.ˈsjõn]

billing

Estoy bajando al departamento de facturación.
-I'm just going down to the billing department.

9882 **astronómico**

f
[as.tro.ˈno.mi.ko]

astronomical

El impacto sobre la economía es astronómico.
-The impact on the economy is astronomical.

9883 **burocrático**

adj
[bu.ro.ˈkra.ti.ko]

bureaucratic

Además, es burocrático y provoca grandes retrasos.
-What is more, it is bureaucratic and leads to long delays.

9884 **borrego**

m
[bo.ˈre.ɣo]

lamb, simple-minded (coll)

A donde sea que fuera Mary el borrego la seguiría.
-Everywhere that Mary went the lamb was sure to go.

9885 **terminante**

adj
[tɛr.mi.ˈnãn̪.te]

final

Todo lo que dices suena muy terminante.
-Everything you're saying sounds so final.

9886 **esclarecer**

vb
[ɛs.kla.re.ˈsɛr]

clarify

Pudieron ayudarnos a esclarecer ciertos detalles.
-They were able to help us clarify certain details.

9887 **temática**

adj; f
[te.ˈma.ti.ka]

thematic; theme

Cada una de estas conferencias tuvo su propia unidad temática.
-Each of those conferences had its own thematic unity.

9888 economizar — **economize**
vb
[e.ko.no.mi.ˈsar]
Bueno, es una manera maravillosa para economizar.
-Well, what a wonderful way to economize.

9889 agravar — **aggravate**
vb
[a.ɣra.ˈβar]
No quiero a agravar la situación.
-I don't want to aggravate the situation.

9890 pulpa — **pulp**
f
[ˈpul.pa]
La pulpa puede inflamarse o infectarse.
-The pulp can become inflamed or infected.

9891 desprendimiento — **detachment, open-handedness, landslide**
m
[des.prẽn.di.ˈmjẽn.to]
Hubo un desprendimiento hace una hora o así.
-There was a landslide an hour or so ago.

9892 parafernalia — **paraphernalia**
f
[pa.ra.fɛr.ˈna.lja]
Nada de parafernalia, nada de distribuir folletos.
-No paraphernalia, no literature being circulated.

9893 já — **ha**
int
[ˈxa]
¡Já! ¡Te dije que podía hacerlo!
-Ha! I told you I could do it!

9894 aminorar — **slow down**
vb
[a.mi.no.ˈrar]
Lo mejor es no hacerle caso y aminorar.
-Let's just ignore him, and slow down.

9895 acueducto — **aqueduct**
m
[a.kwe.ˈðuk.to]
El acueducto está terminado y es bueno.
-The aqueduct is completed, and it is good.

9896 contradictorio — **contradictory**
adj
[kõn.tra.ðik.ˈto.rjo]
Me parece muy contradictorio y completamente equivocado.
-I find that so contradictory and so utterly wrong.

9897 ocurrente — **witty**
adj
[o.ku.ˈrẽn.te]
Ella era excepcionalmente ocurrente y encantadora.
-She was uncommonly witty and charming.

9898 descomunal — **huge**
adj
[des.ko.mu.ˈnal]
Por lo visto la financiación ha sido una estafa descomunal.
-Apparently, the funding has been a huge scam.

9899 cosmopolita — **cosmopolitan; cosmopolitan**
adj; m
[kos.mo.po.ˈli.ta]
Por supuesto, una clase cosmopolita no tiene nada de nuevo.
-Of course, a cosmopolitan class is hardly new.

9900 barroco — **baroque**
adj
[ba.ˈro.ko]
Es el primer templo barroco con columnas salomónicas.
-It is the first Baroque temple with wreathed columns.

9901 ocasionar — **cause**
vb
[o.ka.sjo.ˈnar]
Va a ocasionar un buen revuelo.
-It's bound to cause a lot of talk.

9902 quintal — **hundredweight**
m
[kĩn.ˈtal]
Mi padre nos dejó un quintal.
-My father left us a hundredweight.

9903 menospreciar — **underestimate**
vb
[me.nos.pre.ˈsjar]
No debes menospreciar a un buen colega.
-You shouldn't underestimate a good colleague.

9904 **quiebra**
f
['kje.βra]

bankruptcy
En ocasiones puede llevarlas a la quiebra.
-Sometimes, it can lead to bankruptcy.

9905 **profesorado**
m
[pro.fe.so.'ra.ðo]

faculty
Algunos miembros del profesorado desean hacerte algunas preguntas.
-Certain members of the faculty wish to ask you some questions.

9906 **individualismo**
m
[ĩn̪.di.βi.ðwa.'lis̩.mo]

individualism
Es cierto que el individualismo tendía a ganar terreno.
-It was true that individualism was tending to gain ground.

9907 **erizo**
m
[ε.'ri.so]

hedgehog
A Poly el erizo le encantan los desafíos.
-Poly the hedgehog likes a challenge.

9908 **costra**
f
['kos.tra]

scab
Tiene una costra en la cara.
-There's a scab on her face.

9909 **antiséptico**
adj; m
[ãn̪.'ti.sep̚.ti.ko]

antiseptic; antiseptic
Estaba intentando hacer un antiséptico para el centro médico.
-I was trying to make antiseptic for the med center.

9910 **transeúnte**
m
[trãn.'se.ũn̪.te]

passerby
Una vez gritó a un transeúnte.
-Once he shouted to a passerby.

9911 **efímero**
adj
[e.'fi.mε.ro]

ephemeral
En este mundo terrenal, todo es efímero.
-In this earthly world, all is ephemeral.

9912 **inducción**
f
[ĩn̪.duk.'sjõn]

induction
Intentaré provocar un estado de inducción.
-I will try to provoke a state of induction.

9913 **desempate**
m
[de.sẽm.'pa.te]

tiebreaker
Todo lo que tiene que hacer es perder este desempate.
-All you have to do is lose this tiebreaker.

9914 **reingreso**
m
[rei̯n̪.'gre.so]

re-entry
Programemos esta cosa para el reingreso.
-Let's get this thing programmed for re-entry.

9915 **espátula**
f
[εs.'pa.tu.la]

spatula
Esta espátula es nuestra última esperanza.
-This spatula is our last hope.

9916 **taquicardia**
f
[ta.ki.'kar.ðja]

tachycardia
Tiene fiebre, taquicardia y taquipnea.
-He has a fever, tachycardia, and tachypnea.

9917 **fetal**
adj
[fε.'tal]

fetal
Lo encontré llorando en posición fetal.
-I found him crying in the fetal position.

9918 **peruano**
adj; m
[pε.'rwa.no]

Peruvian; Peruvian person
Vendrá ese chico peruano del gimnasio.
-I have that Peruvian boy coming over from the gym.

9919 **convergencia**
f
[kõm.bεr.'xẽn.sja]

convergence
No queremos relajar los criterios de convergencia.
-We do not wish to relax the convergence criteria.

9920	**arbitraje**	**arbitration**
	m	Ordeno que el arbitraje se reabra.
	[ar.βi.ˈtra.xe]	-I'm ordering that the arbitration be reopened.
9921	**placebo**	**placebo**
	m	Debe haberlas cambiado por placebo o algo.
	[pla.ˈse.βo]	-She must have switched them out for a placebo or something.
9922	**negatividad**	**negativity**
	f	Escucha, no me gusta toda esta negatividad, viejo.
	[ne.ɣa.ti.βi.ˈðað]	-Listen, I don't like all this negativity, man.
9923	**marcapasos**	**pacemaker**
	m	Tiene un marcapasos y su corazón funciona perfectamente.
	[mar.ka.ˈpa.sos]	-He has a pacemaker, and his heart works perfectly.
9924	**algoritmo**	**algorithm**
	m	No necesito un algoritmo para encontrar mujeres.
	[al.ɣo.ˈrit̚.mo]	-I don't need an algorithm to meet women.
9925	**orina**	**urine**
	f	Ya sabes que el doctor me volvió a encontrar nicotina en la orina.
	[o.ˈri.na]	-You know the doctor found nicotine in my urine again.
9926	**anormalidad**	**abnormality**
	f	Eres muy normal dentro de tu anormalidad.
	[a.nor.ma.li.ˈðað]	-You're very normal in your abnormality.
9927	**fluctuación**	**fluctuation**
	f	Detecto la fluctuación en sus escudos.
	[fluk̚.twa.ˈsjõn]	-I am detecting the fluctuation in their shields.
9928	**barbitúrico**	**barbiturate; barbiturate**
	m; adj	Es el barbitúrico que le hace dormirse.
	[bar.βi.ˈtu.ri.ko]	-It's the barbiturate to put him to sleep.
9929	**basílica**	**basilica**
	f	El edificio actual es una cruz basílica con tres altares.
	[ba.ˈsi.li.ka]	-The present building is a cross basilica with three altars.
9930	**pontífice**	**pontiff**
	m	Si voy a ser pontífice, debo familiarizarme con su jerga risible.
	[põn̪.ˈti.fi.se]	-If I am to be a pontiff, I must be familiar with their ludicrous jargon.
9931	**regocijar(se)**	**rejoice**
	vb	Y me regocijaré cuando ella esté bien.
	[re.ɣo.si.ˈxar]	-And I'll rejoice when she is well.
9932	**desnutrición**	**malnutrition**
	f	La desnutrición provoca retraso en el crecimiento de los niños.
	[dɛs̠.nu.tri.ˈsjõn]	-Malnutrition leads to the stunted growth of children.
9933	**batallar**	**battle**
	vb	En estos días he pensado que podría batallar contra ti en igualdad.
	[ba.ta.ˈjar]	-In these last days, I thought I could battle against you as an equal.
9934	**acallar**	**silence**
	vb	Viniste a este sitio solo para acallar las voces.
	[a.ka.ˈjar]	-You entered this place only to silence the voices.
9935	**esquí**	**ski**
	m	Aquí usted puede depositar su esquí o trineo.
	[ɛs.ˈki]	-Here you can deposit your ski or sled.

9936 **alcantarillado**   **sewerage**

m

[al.kã̠n.ta.ri.ˈja.ðo]

Tenemos que incorporar los proyectos de alcantarillado necesarios en el plan de desarrollo.
-We have to incorporate the necessary sewerage projects in the development plan.

9937 **anteanoche**   **the night before last**

adv

[ã̠n.te.a.ˈno.tʃe]

Richard y yo nos casamos anteanoche en Reno.
-Richard and I were married the night before last in Reno.

9938 **proscribir**   **outlaw**

vb

[pros.kri.ˈβir]

Debemos proscribir, desmantelar y desarmar a esos grupos.
-We must outlaw, dismantle, and disarm these groups.

9939 **helecho**   **fern**

m

[e.ˈle.tʃo]

Traigo lavanda y helecho para desinfectar la herida.
-I bring lavender and fern to disinfect the wound.

9940 **penúltimo**   **penultimate**

adj

[pe.ˈnul̠.ti.mo]

Estuve jugando, llegué al penúltimo nivel.
-I'm playing, I've got to the penultimate level.

9941 **oratorio**   **oratory**

m

[o.ra.ˈto.rjo]

Puedo reducir la amplitud del oratorio.
-I can scale down the oratory.

9942 **masilla**   **putty**

f

[ma.ˈsi.ja]

Parece un tipo de masilla adhesiva.
-It looks like a type of adhesive putty.

9943 **inactividad**   **inactivity**

f

[i.nak̚.ti.βi.ˈðað]

La inactividad física afecta al desarrollo físico y mental de los niños.
-Physical inactivity affects the physical and mental development of children.

9944 **autoritario**   **authoritarian; authoritarian**

adj; m

[au̯.to.ri.ˈta.rjo]

Votaré en contra de este último movimiento autoritario.
-I shall be voting against this latest authoritarian move.

9945 **canasto**   **basket**

m

[ka.ˈnas.to]

Mi canasto está debajo de la mesa.
-My basket is under the table.

9946 **modalidad**   **mode**

f

[mo.ða.li.ˈðað]

Ninguna modalidad de transporte debe quedar fuera del programa.
-No mode of transport should be excluded from the programme.

9947 **concordia**   **concord**

f

[kõŋ.ˈkor.ðja]

Necesitamos concordia para ganar esta guerra.
-We need concord to win this war.

9948 **profesionalidad**   **professionalism**

f

[pro.fe.sjo.na.li.ˈðað]

Creo que su profesionalidad durante la situación merece ser reconocida.
-I think their professionalism in the situation deserves much credit.

9949 **enigmático**   **enigmatic**

adj

[e.niɣ.ˈma.ti.ko]

A Leone le encanta ese tipo de diálogo enigmático.
-Leone likes that sort of enigmatic dialogue.

9950 **alterno**   **alternate**

adj

[al̠.ˈtɛr.no]

Tengo que cruzar hasta el universo alterno.
-I need to cross over into the alternate universe.

9951 **entereza**   **strength**

f
[ɛ̃n̪.tɛ.ˈre.sa]

Ha llevado esta estación con entereza, dignidad y compasión.
-You've run this station with strength, dignity, and compassion.

9952 **checar** — **check**

vb
[ʧe.ˈkar]

Hay algo que quiero checar cuando regresemos.
-There's something I want to check out when we get back.

9953 **dispensar** — **dispense**

vb
[dis.pɛ̃n.ˈsar]

No se me permite dispensar antibióticos.
-I'm not allowed to dispense antibiotics.

9954 **opcional** — **optional**

adj
[op.sjo.ˈnal]

Allí pararemos para el almuerzo opcional.
-There we will stop for the optional lunch.

9955 **puercoespín** — **porcupine**

m
[pwɛr.ko.ɛs.ˈpĩn]

Tu cabello parece el de puercoespín.
-Your hair looks like a porcupine.

9956 **artificio** — **artifice**

m
[ar.ti.ˈfi.sjo]

Esa es la diferencia entre artificio y realidad.
-That is the difference between artifice and reality.

9957 **replicar** — **replicate**

vb
[rep̚.li.ˈkar]

Siempre estamos tratando de replicar esos efectos.
-We're always trying to replicate those effects.

9958 **fundido** — **molten**

adj
[fũn̪.ˈdi.ðo]

No esperen hallar pepitas de oro fundido.
-Don't expect to find nuggets of molten gold.

9959 **nutrir** — **nourish**

vb
[nu.ˈtrir]

Ni un centavo para nutrir mi talento.
-Not a dime to nourish my talent.

9960 **cántaro** — **pitcher**

m
[ˈkãn̪.ta.ro]

Me reñiste por tropezar con un cántaro.
-You scolded me for bumping into a pitcher.

9961 **determinante** — **determinant; determinant**

adj; m
[dɛ.tɛr.mi.ˈnãn̪.te]

La solidaridad entre nuestras mujeres será un determinante vital del progreso.
-Solidarity among our women will be a vital determinant of progress.

9962 **discernir** — **discern**

vb
[dis.sɛr.ˈnir]

Trataba de discernir un patrón en sus decisiones.
-I was trying to discern a pattern to his choices.

9963 **eucalipto** — **eucalyptus**

m
[eu̯.ka.ˈlip̚.to]

Estas cifras mostraron el creciente interés en exportar eucalipto, pino y soja.
-These figures showed the increasing interest in exporting eucalyptus, pine, and soybean.

9964 **extinguidor** — **extinguisher**

m
[ɛks.tĩŋ.gi.ˈðor]

Podríamos romper el cristal con un extinguidor.
-We could break the glass with a fire extinguisher.

9965 **nivelar** — **level**

vb
[ni.βe.ˈlar]

Nos las arreglamos para nivelar el avión.
-We managed to level the plane out.

9966 **capacitación** — **training**

	f	Han recibido esa capacitación casi 800 organizaciones.
	[ka.pa.si.ta.ˈsjõn]	-This training has been given to almost 800 organizations.
9967	**desorientación**	**disorientation**
	f	La desorientación le ayudará a creer que todo fue un sueño.
	[de.so.rjẽn̪.ta.ˈsjõn]	-Disorientation will help convince her it was a dream.
9968	**prieto**	**tight**
	adj	¡Lo que quieres es algo bonito y prieto, pero flexible!
	[ˈprjɛ.to]	-What you want is something nice and tight, but flexible!
9969	**ultrasonido**	**ultrasound**
	m	No me puedo permitir un ultrasonido pero...
	[ul̪.tra.so.ˈni.ðo]	-I can't really afford an ultrasound, but...
9970	**coexistir**	**coexist**
	vb	Esta situación es insostenible y no se puede coexistir con ella.
	[ko.ɛk.sis.ˈtir]	-This situation is untenable and impossible to coexist with.
9971	**tintero**	**inkwell**
	m	Me hace pensar en un tintero.
	[tĩn̪.ˈtɛ.ro]	-It makes me think of an inkwell.
9972	**cascanueces**	**nutcracker**
	m	No debe usarse como un cascanueces.
	[kas.ka.ˈnwe.ses]	-It should not be used as a nutcracker.
9973	**sulfato**	**sulfate**
	m	El sulfato de magnesio, no lo encuentro.
	[sul.ˈfa.to]	-The magnesium sulfate, I can't find it.
9974	**apaciguar**	**appease**
	vb	No vamos a apaciguar al agresor.
	[a.pa.si.ˈɣwar]	-We are not going to appease the aggressor.
9975	**fumigar**	**fumigate**
	vb	Quizá deberíamos cerrar para fumigar o algo.
	[fu.mi.ˈɣar]	-Maybe we should close to fumigate or something.
9976	**ilícito**	**illicit**
	adj	Asumes que he hecho algo ilícito.
	[i.ˈli.si.to]	-You're assuming I've done something illicit.
9977	**largometraje**	**feature film**
	m	Krister Larsson actuó en un largometraje.
	[lar.ɣo.mɛ.ˈtra.xe]	-Krister Larsson was cast in a feature film.
9978	**cotillear**	**gossip**
	vb	Si quieres cotillear con nosotras entonces baja aquí.
	[ko.ti.je.ˈar]	-If you want to gossip with us then come down here.
9979	**desgarro**	**tear**
	m	Hubo un desgarro en su traje, pero lo arreglamos en el campo.
	[dɛṣ.ˈɣa.ro]	-There was a tear in his suit, but we fixed it in the field.
9980	**espinazo**	**spine**
	m	Otro hijo se cayó de un camión, se rompió el espinazo.
	[ɛs.pi.ˈna.so]	-Another son fell from a truck, broke his spine.
9981	**incuestionable**	**unquestionable**
	adj	El documento es de incuestionable interés.
	[ĩn.kwɛs.tjo.ˈna.βle]	-The document is of unquestionable interest.
9982	**talar**	**cut down**

vb
[ta.ˈlar]

Quiero talar este árbol para que no esté en medio.
-I want to cut down this tree so it doesn't get in my way.

9983 desembocar   **lead**

vb
[de.sẽm.bo.ˈkar]

Tales protestas podrían desembocar en nuevos derramamientos de sangre.
-Such protests could lead to further bloodshed.

9984 undécimo   **eleventh**

num
[ũn̩.ˈde.si.mo]

Celebrarán su undécima reunión en 2003.
-They will hold its eleventh meeting in 2003.

9985 ventilar   **ventilate**

vb
[bẽn̩.ti.ˈlar]

Te permiten respirar mecánicamente o ventilar mecánicamente.
-They allow you to mechanically breathe or mechanically ventilate.

9986 exaltación   **exaltation**

f
[ɛk.sal̩.ta.ˈsjõn]

Sin embargo, también hubo períodos de exaltación.
-But then there were also periods of exaltation.

9987 muñón   **stump**

m
[mu.ˈɲõn]

Podría abrir esa cerradura con mi muñón.
-I could pick that lock with my stump.

9988 hiriente   **hurtful**

adj
[i.ˈrjẽn̩.te]

Joey, nunca escribiría algo hiriente sobre ti.
-Joey, I would never write anything hurtful about you.

9989 suplementario   **supplementary**

adj
[sup̚.le.mẽn̩.ˈta.rjo]

Las actividades requerirían apoyo del fondo suplementario.
-These activities would require support from the supplementary fund.

9990 tórtola   **turtledove**

f
[ˈtor.to.la]

Comparada con ellas, soy como una tórtola.
-Compared to them, I'm like a turtledove.

9991 respectivo   **respective**

adj
[rɛs.pek̚.ˈti.βo]

La decisión de jubilación de un juez pertenece a su respectivo alto tribunal.
-The decision to retire judges is taken by their respective courts.

9992 arraigar   **take root**

vb
[a.rai̯.ˈɣar]

¡No tiene ningún lugar donde arraigar!
-It has nowhere to take root!

9993 expectación   **expectation**

f
[ɛks.pek̚.ta.ˈsjõn]

Y me llené de esperanza y expectación.
-And I was filled with hope and expectation.

9994 consecuente   **consistent**

adj
[kõn.se.ˈkwẽn̩.te]

Esto es consecuente con las definiciones internacionales de discriminación.
-This is consistent with the international definitions on discrimination.

9995 falange   **phalange**

f
[fa.ˈlãŋ.xe]

Yo tengo una falange rota.
-I have a broken phalange.

9996 pactar   **agree**

vb
[pak̚.ˈtar]

Si ella sabe algo, tendremos que pactar las condiciones con su abogado.
-If she knows anything at all, we have to agree on terms with the lawyer.

9997 desalentador   **discouraging**

adj
[de.sa.lẽn̪.ta.ˈðor]

Los resultados son desalentadores y preocupantes.
-The findings are discouraging and alarming.

9998 **diferir**   **differ**

vb
[di.fɛ.ˈrir]

El método auxiliar podrá diferir del de primer uso.
-The backup method may differ from that first used.

9999 **encarnar**   **embody**

vb
[ẽŋ.kar.ˈnar]

No había posibilidad de encarnar todas los aspectos que él retrataba.
-There was no way he could possibly embody all the facets that he portrayed.

10000 **acuchillar**   **slash**

vb
[a.ku.tʃi.ˈjar]

Destrozar y acuchillar no es suficiente.
-Smashing and slashing aren't enough.

10001 **inconsciencia**   **unconsciousness**

f
[ĩŋ.kõns.ˈsjẽn.sja]

No podrás alegar inconsciencia de nuevo.
-You won't be able to plead unconsciousness again.

10002 **compresa**   **compress**

f
[kõm.ˈpre.sa]

Entremos a ponerte una compresa.
-Let's go inside to put on a compress.

10003 **mayorista**   **wholesale**

adj
[ma.jo.ˈris.ta]

Esto resulta en una variación extrema de los costes a nivel mayorista.
-This results in an extreme variation in wholesale costs.

10004 **galgo**   **greyhound**

m
[ˈgal.ɣo]

Ha estado entrenando durante meses, es como un galgo.
-He's been training for months, he's like a greyhound.

10005 **irremediable**   **irremediable**

adj
[i.re.me.ˈðja.βle]

Lo que hicimos sigue siendo irremediable.
-What we really did is still irremediable.

10006 **indivisible**   **indivisible**

adj
[ĩn̪.di.βi.ˈsi.βle]

El movimiento hacia la paz es un todo indivisible.
-The movement towards peace is an indivisible whole.

10007 **altruista**   **altruistic; altruist**

adj; m/f
[al̪.ˈtrwis.ta]

No se trata solamente de un movimiento altruista y generoso.
-This is not solely a generous and altruistic move.

10008 **poblador**   **villager**

m
[po.βla.ˈðor]

Es el único poblador que vive aquí.
-He is the only villager that lives here.

10009 **deformación**   **deformation**

f
[de.for.ma.ˈsjõn]

Tiene una fractura o deformación grave.
-It has a serious fracture or deformation.

10010 **arañar**   **scratch**

vb
[a.ra.ˈɲar]

El gato empezó a arañar la alfombra.
-The cat started to scratch the carpet.

10011 **elasticidad**   **elasticity**

f
[e.las.ti.si.ˈðað]

Estamos hablando de fibras con una elasticidad muy alta.
-We're talking here about fibers with extremely high elasticity.

10012 **apilar**   **stack**

vb
[a.pi.ˈlar]

Entonces ayúdame a apilar la madera.
-Then help me stack the wood.

10013 **materialismo**　　**materialism**

m

[ma.tɛ.rja.ˈliş.mo]

Uno de los problemas del dinero es el materialismo.

-One of the problems with money is materialism.

10014 **atrofia**　　**atrophy**

f

[a.ˈtro.fja]

Este proceso de pérdida de masa muscular se denomina atrofia.

-This process of muscle loss is called atrophy.

10015 **terminología**　　**terminology**

f

[tɛr.mi.no.lo.ˈxi.a]

Se propuso que todos los comités normalizasen su terminología.

-It was suggested that all committees should standardize their technical terminology.

10016 **retraer**　　**retract**

vb

[rɛ.tra.ˈɛr]

Tiene que haber una forma de retraer el mecanismo manualmente.

-Maybe there's a way to manually retract the mechanism.

10017 **puerro**　　**leek**

m

[ˈpwɛ.ro]

La sopa es de puerro y papa.

-The soup is leek and potato.

10018 **encestar**　　**dunk**

vb

[ɛ̃n.sɛs.ˈtar]

Es escocés, sabe encestar, es perfecto.

-He's Scottish, he can dunk, he's perfect.

10019 **palpable**　　**palpable**

adj

[pal.ˈpa.βle]

Entre los músicos, el racismo es menos palpable que en otros entornos.

-Among musicians, racism is less palpable than in other milieus.

10020 **dilatación**　　**dilation**

f

[di.la.ta.ˈsjõn]

El movimiento de ojos y la dilatación de pupilas a menudo nos delatan.

-Eye movement and dilation are often dead giveaways.

10021 **vascular**　　**vascular**

adj

[bas.ku.ˈlar]

Repararon los tendones y el flujo vascular.

-They've repaired the tendons and the vascular supply.

10022 **subjetivo**　　**subjective**

adj

[suβ.xɛ.ˈti.βo]

No debe basarse en un sentimiento subjetivo.

-It should not be based on a subjective feeling.

10023 **silicio**　　**silicon**

m

[si.ˈli.sjo]

También se ha logrado hacer un uso más eficaz del silicio.

-It has also become more efficient in its use of silicon.

10024 **mariguana**　　**marijuana**

f

[ma.ri.ˈɣwa.na]

La mariguana es una puerta a más drogas peligrosas.

-Marijuana is a gateway to more dangerous drugs.

10025 **escrutinio**　　**scrutiny**

m

[ɛs.kru.ˈti.njo]

Lo averiguaré antes del siguiente escrutinio.

-I will find out before the next scrutiny.

Adjectives

Rank	Spanish-PoS	Translation(s)
7503	**bestial**-*adj*	brutal
7509	**finalista**-*adj; m/f*	finalist; finalist
7513	**indignante**-*adj*	outrageous
7514	**catastrófico**-*adj*	catastrophic
7515	**canino**-*adj; m*	canine; canine tooth
7517	**radial**-*adj; f*	radio; circular saw
7521	**intermitente**-*adj; m*	intermittent; blinker
7530	**estudioso**-*adj; m*	studious; scholar
7531	**innato**-*adj*	innate
7535	**rutinario**-*adj*	routine
7538	**ilógico**-*adj*	illogical
7540	**esquizofrénico**-*adj*	schizophrenic
7541	**retrospectivo**-*adj*	retrospective
7554	**salino**-*adj*	saline
7558	**inca**-*m/f; adj*	Inca; Incan
7560	**sigiloso**-*adj*	stealthy
7561	**informático**-*adj; m*	computer; computer expert
7568	**candente**-*adj*	red-hot
7569	**lucrativo**-*adj*	lucrative
7572	**insuficiente**-*adj; m*	insufficient; unsatisfactory
7575	**afectuoso**-*adj*	affectionate
7578	**angular**-*adj*	angular
7580	**abrumador**-*adj*	overwhelming
7582	**tecnológico**-*adj*	technological
7583	**servicial**-*adj*	helpful
7587	**paternal**-*adj*	fatherly
7593	**estratégico**-*adj*	strategic
7596	**vaginal**-*adj*	vaginal
7599	**saliente**-*adj; m*	outgoing; projection
7602	**indeciso**-*adj*	indecisive
7616	**diabético**-*adj; m*	diabetic; diabetic
7620	**minúsculo**-*adj*	tiny
7623	**imperativo**-*adj; m*	imperative; imperative
7624	**textil**-*adj; m*	textile; textile
7626	**pacifista**-*adj; m/f*	pacifist; pacifist
7629	**indeseable**-*adj; m/f*	undesirable; undesirable
7631	**épico**-*adj*	epic
7632	**lúcido**-*adj*	lucid
7633	**triunfal**-*adj*	triumphal
7635	**pedante**-*adj; m/f*	pedantic; pedant
7637	**benigno**-*adj*	benign
7641	**ocupante**-*adj; m/f*	occupying; occupant
7648	**inalcanzable**-*adj*	unattainable
7654	**intensivo**-*adj*	intensive
7655	**colegial**-*adj; m*	school; schoolboy
7661	**fronterizo**-*m; adj*	border; frontier
7667	**amplificador**-*adj; m*	amplifying; amplifier
7678	**incendiario**-*adj; m*	incendiary; arsonist
7679	**factible**-*adj*	feasible
7692	**paterno**-*adj*	paternal
7708	**inmaculado**-*adj*	immaculate
7710	**negociable**-*adj*	negotiable
7714	**maloliente**-*adj*	stinking
7717	**lúgubre**-*adj*	grim
7719	**inaccesible**-*adj*	inaccessible
7725	**consecutivo**-*adj*	consecutive
7730	**deficiente**-*adj*	deficient
7734	**ejecutor**-*adj; m*	executing; executor
7735	**inflamable**-*adj*	flammable
7739	**furtivo**-*adj; m*	furtive; poacher
7746	**exaltado**-*adj; m*	frenzied; hothead
7749	**resbaladizo**-*adj*	slippery
7755	**depresivo**-*adj*	depressing
7759	**sintético**-*adj*	synthetic
7760	**colateral**-*adj*	collateral
7765	**tenue**-*adj*	faint
7772	**irreversible**-*adj*	irreversible
7773	**cívico**-*adj*	civic
7775	**antidepresivo**-*adj*	antidepressant
7788	**afgano**-*adj; m*	Afghan; Afghan person
7789	**paramédico**-*adj; m*	paramedical; paramedic
7796	**triunfante**-*adj*	triumphant
7797	**cautivo**-*adj; m*	captive; captivity
7798	**israelita**-*adj; m*	Israelite; Israelite person
7810	**tosco**-*adj; m*	crude; rough
7811	**acústico**-*adj*	acoustic
7818	**aconsejable**-*adj*	advisable
7822	**lisiado**-*adj; m*	disabled; disabled person
7824	**invicto**-*adj*	unbeaten
7825	**latente**-*adj*	latent
7831	**neurótico**-*adj; m*	neurotic; neurotic
7832	**caótico**-*adj*	chaotic

7835	**iraní**-*adj; m/f*	Iranian; Iranian person	7987	**fraternal**-*adj*	fraternal
7837	**amenazante**-*adj*	threatening	7989	**mongol**-*adj; m*	Mongolian; Mongol
7840	**agrio**-*adj*	sour	7993	**perjudicado**-*adj*	harmed
7843	**deudor**-*adj; m*	in debt; debtor	7994	**flagrante**-*adj*	flagrant
7844	**anexo**-*adj; m*	attached; annex	7999	**hereditario**-*adj*	hereditary
7846	**doblado**-*adj*	dubbed in, bent	8002	**comestible**-*adj*	edible
7850	**sindical**-*adj*	union	8008	**engañoso**-*adj*	misleading
7851	**intravenoso**-*adj*	intravenous	8011	**medicinal**-*adj*	medicinal
7855	**equilibrado**-*adj*	well-balanced	8012	**ceremonial**-*adj*	ceremonial
7857	**ofendido**-*adj*	offended	8018	**supersticioso**-*adj*	superstitious
7864	**ferviente**-*adj*	fervent	8025	**meticuloso**-*adj*	meticulous
7867	**conmocionado**-*adj*	shocked	8038	**hospitalario**-*adj*	hospitable
7869	**sustancial**-*adj*	substantial	8046	**propicio**-*adj*	conductive
7874	**pomposo**-*adj*	pompous	8048	**macabro**-*adj*	macabre
7878	**marroquí**-*adj; m/f*	Moroccan; Moroccan person	8056	**subversivo**-*adj*	subversive
7880	**dañino**-*adj*	harmful	8072	**bravucón**-*adj; m*	cocky; bully
7884	**aborigen**-*adj; m/f*	indigenous; aboriginal	8075	**municipal**-*adj*	municipal
7885	**televisivo**-*adj*	television	8076	**comparable**-*adj*	comparable
7887	**esquivo**-*adj*	elusive	8077	**jurídico**-*adj*	legal
7896	**distintivo**-*adj; m*	distinctive; emblem	8079	**rotundo**-*adj*	resounding
7900	**presunto**-*adj*	alleged	8080	**parejo**-*adj*	even
7902	**postiza**-*adj*	fake	8084	**bucal**-*adj*	oral
7903	**inquebrantable**-*adj*	unwavering	8086	**flamante**-*adj*	brand-new
7911	**riguroso**-*adj*	rigorous	8089	**afable**-*adj*	affable
7919	**desprevenido**-*adj*	unprepared	8091	**previsible**-*adj*	foreseeable
7921	**enérgico**-*adj*	energetic	8096	**deseoso**-*adj*	keen
7926	**desesperante**-*adj*	desperate, maddening	8106	**venerable**-*adj*	venerable
7935	**botánico**-*adj; m*	botanical; botanist	8107	**contiguo**-*adj*	adjacent
7939	**antisemita**-*adj; m/f*	anti-Semitic; anti-Semite	8112	**preventivo**-*adj*	preventive
7940	**procesador**-*adj; m*	processing; processor	8115	**indiscutible**-*adj*	indisputable
7943	**despegado**-*adj*	taken off	8116	**melodramático**-*adj*	melodramatic
7951	**decepcionado**-*adj*	disappointed	8117	**novedoso**-*adj*	novel
7953	**sistemático**-*adj*	systematic	8121	**hispano**-*adj; m*	Hispanic; Hispanic
7961	**regulador**-*m; adj*	regulator; regulating	8122	**espinal**-*adj*	spinal
7962	**chévere**-*int; adj*	great (LA) (coll); cool (LA) (coll)	8125	**planetario**-*adj; m*	planetary; planetarium
7966	**forjado**-*adj*	wrought	8140	**aplastante**-*adj*	overwhelming
7967	**nacionalista**-*adj; m/f*	nationalist; nationalist	8141	**venidero**-*adj*	coming
			8142	**trópico**-*adj; m*	tropic; tropic
7974	**armenio**-*adj; m*	Armenian; Armenian person	8143	**causante**-*adj; m*	responsible; cause
			8151	**desocupado**-*adj*	unoccupied
7977	**marítimo**-*adj*	maritime	8152	**pectoral**-*adj; m*	chest; chest
7978	**invernal**-*adj*	wintry	8155	**imperfecto**-*adj*	imperfect
7983	**antiaéreo**-*adj*	anti-aircraft	8157	**imaginativo**-*adj*	imaginative
7985	**panorámico**-*adj*	panoramic	8158	**infrarrojo**-*adj*	infrared
			8163	**inepto**-*adj*	inept

8166	**concluyente**-*adj*	conclusive	8333	**frívolo**-*adj*	frivolous
8167	**malicioso**-*adj*	malicious	8338	**encubierto**-*adj*	undercover
8168	**servil**-*adj*	servile	8352	**caritativo**-*adj*	charitable
8174	**domiciliario**-*adj*	home	8353	**nómada**-*adj; m/f*	nomadic; Nomad
8180	**emisor**-*m; adj*	sender; emitting	8356	**callado**-*adj*	quiet
8181	**beneficioso**-*adj*	beneficial	8361	**liberador**-*adj*	liberating
8184	**atormentado**-*adj*	tormented	8362	**indoloro**-*adj*	painless
8187	**hidráulico**-*adj*	hydraulic	8368	**bioquímico**-*adj; m*	biochemical; biochemist
8195	**yugular**-*adj*	jugular			
8196	**nebuloso**-*adj*	foggy	8370	**antisocial**-*adj*	anti-social
8198	**imaginable**-*adj*	imaginable	8373	**contemporáneo**-*adj; m*	contemporary; contemporary
8206	**instrumental**-*adj; m*	instrumental; instrument	8375	**disperso**-*adj*	dispersed
8213	**irrefutable**-*adj*	irrefutable	8376	**monótono**-*adj*	monotonous
8215	**oportunista**-*adj; m/f*	opportunistic; opportunist	8380	**respirador**-*adj; m*	inhaling; respirator
			8384	**propenso**-*adj*	prone
8217	**ultravioleta**-*adj*	ultraviolet	8385	**analfabeto**-*adj; m*	illiterate; illiterate
8223	**manso**-*adj*	tame	8387	**pertinente**-*adj*	relevant
8226	**vibrante**-*adj*	vibrant	8389	**reaccionario**-*adj; m*	reactionary; reactionary
8233	**impropio**-*adj*	inappropriate			
8236	**estructural**-*adj*	structural	8390	**craneal**-*adj*	cranial
8238	**oval**-*adj*	oval	8393	**radioactivo**-*adj*	radioactive
8239	**imperialista**-*adj; m/f*	imperialistic; imperialist	8394	**térmico**-*adj*	thermal
			8400	**mísero**-*adj*	measly
8240	**casto**-*adj*	chaste	8401	**corpulento**-*adj*	corpulent
8247	**filial**-*f; adj*	subsidiary; filial	8402	**férreo**-*adj*	iron
8248	**inexperto**-*adj*	inexperienced	8403	**narrativo**-*adj; f*	narrative; narrative
8259	**polémico**-*adj*	controversial	8414	**insurgente**-*adj; m/f*	insurgent; rebel
8261	**innegable**-*adj*	undeniable	8419	**miope**-*adj*	short-sighted
8267	**integrado**-*adj*	integrated	8422	**mordaz**-*adj*	scathing
8271	**epiléptico**-*adj; m*	epileptic; epileptic	8423	**aneurisma**-*adj*	aneurysm
8272	**austriaco**-*adj; m*	Austrian; Austrian person	8424	**caucásico**-*adj; m*	Caucasian; Caucasian person
8277	**perito**-*m/f; adj*	expert; expert	8425	**operacional**-*adj*	operational
8292	**filosófico**-*adj*	philosophical	8429	**maya**-*adj; m*	Mayan; Mayan person
8293	**prestigioso**-*adj*	prestigious	8432	**ilegítimo**-*adj*	illegitimate
8297	**alfabético**-*adj*	alphabetical	8436	**ficticio**-*adj*	fictional
8298	**progresista**-*adj; m/f*	progressive; progressive	8443	**íntegro**-*adj*	entire
			8448	**anestésico**-*adj*	anesthetic
8306	**rancio**-*adj*	rancid	8452	**marxista**-*adj; m/f*	marxist; Marxist
8307	**caballeroso**-*adj*	gentlemanly	8465	**islamista**-*adj*	Islamist
8311	**bellaco**-*adj*	coward	8472	**aislante**-*adj; m*	insulation; insulator
8314	**incalculable**-*adj*	incalculable	8475	**irrazonable**-*adj*	unreasonable
8318	**finlandés**-*adj; m*	Finnish; Finnish person	8481	**irreparable**-*adj*	unrepairable
			8491	**disciplinado**-*adj*	disciplined
8320	**autista**-*adj; m/f*	autistic; autistic person	8493	**recurrente**-*adj*	recurrent
8324	**forzoso**-*adj*	forced	8495	**minucioso**-*adj*	thorough

8497	**cúbico**-*adj*	cubic
8499	**notorio**-*adj*	notorious
8503	**discutible**-*adj*	questionable
8504	**controversial**-*adj*	controversial
8508	**simpatizante**-*adj; m/f*	sympathetic to; sympathizer
8509	**caoba**-*adj*	mahogany
8514	**gustoso**-*adj*	delicious, gladly
8516	**inactivo**-*adj*	inactive
8522	**incansable**-*adj*	tireless
8525	**inerte**-*adj*	inert
8532	**docente**-*adj; m/f*	educational; teacher
8533	**traumático**-*adj*	traumatic
8537	**pelón**-*adj*	bald (coll)
8539	**tibetano**-*adj; m*	Tibetan; Tibetan person
8542	**tortillera**-*adj*	dyke (coll)
8546	**agridulce**-*adj*	bittersweet
8549	**sagaz**-*adj*	sharp
8557	**dedicatoria**-*adj; f*	dedicatory; dedication
8558	**inherente**-*adj*	inherent
8559	**terapéutico**-*adj*	therapeutic
8566	**glotón**-*m; adj*	glutton; gluttonous
8569	**penetrante**-*adj*	penetrating
8571	**merecedor**-*adj*	worthy
8573	**compasivo**-*adj*	compassionate
8575	**jovial**-*adj*	jovial
8580	**quirúrgico**-*adj*	surgical
8585	**finito**-*adj*	finite
8587	**pueblerino**-*adj*	hick (coll)
8588	**atónito**-*adj*	stunned
8589	**varonil**-*adj*	manly
8592	**vivaz**-*adj*	vivacious
8598	**grupal**-*adj*	group
8602	**absorto**-*adj*	absorbed
8604	**abusivo**-*adj*	abusive
8606	**marginal**-*adj*	marginal
8608	**instruido**-*adj*	instructed
8614	**territorial**-*adj*	territorial
8627	**profano**-*adj*	profane
8629	**conocedor**-*adj; m*	knowledgeable; connoisseur
8630	**triunfador**-*m; adj*	winner; winning
8631	**gallardo**-*adj; m*	dashing; gallant
8633	**sinfónico**-*adj*	symphonic
8643	**libertino**-*adj; m*	licentious; libertine
8646	**converso**-*adj; m*	converted; convert
8664	**inexistente**-*adj*	nonexistent
8665	**patológico**-*adj*	pathological
8671	**vigente**-*adj*	existing
8679	**carismático**-*adj; m*	charismatic; charismatic
8680	**ambiguo**-*adj*	ambiguous
8682	**reparador**-*adj; m*	comforting; repairman
8684	**reluciente**-*adj*	shiny
8687	**ascendente**-*adj*	rising
8689	**atenuante**-*adj*	mitigating
8694	**correspondiente**-*adj*	corresponding
8701	**alimentario**-*adj*	food
8707	**aleatorio**-*adj*	random
8709	**sensorial**-*adj*	sensory
8710	**provincial**-*adj*	provincial
8718	**fortuito**-*adj*	fortuitous
8721	**renombrado**-*adj*	renowned
8727	**contingente**-*m; adj*	contingent; possible
8730	**interino**-*adj; m*	interim; caretaker
8735	**multinacional**-*f; adj*	multinational; multinational
8736	**provechoso**-*adj*	fruitful
8739	**insuperable**-*adj*	unbeatable
8750	**provocador**-*adj; m*	provocative; troublemaker
8752	**tardío**-*adj*	late
8754	**elástico**-*m; adj*	elastic; elastic
8756	**categórico**-*adj*	categorical
8758	**centenario**-*adj; m*	centenary; centennial
8761	**diagonal**-*adj; f*	diagonal; diagonal
8767	**mundano**-*adj*	mundane
8768	**póstumo**-*adj*	posthumous
8773	**majestuoso**-*adj*	majestic
8774	**aeronáutica**-*adj; f*	aerospace; aviation
8775	**glacial**-*adj*	glacial
8778	**impersonal**-*adj*	impersonal
8781	**recomendable**-*adj*	advisable
8785	**descerebrado**-*adj*	brainless
8791	**albanés**-*adj; m*	Albanian; Albanian person
8793	**libanés**-*adj; m*	Lebanese; Lebanese person
8794	**moralista**-*m/f; adj*	moralist; moralistic
8797	**precario**-*adj*	precarious
8798	**mítico**-*adj*	mythical
8801	**desigual**-*adj*	unequal

8816	**anfibio**-*adj; m*	amphibious; amphibian
8818	**giratorio**-*adj*	rotating
8821	**autónomo**-*adj; m*	autonomous; independent
8822	**incinerador**-*adj; m*	incinerating; incinerator
8823	**obeso**-*adj*	obese
8824	**soportable**-*adj*	bearable
8827	**plástica**-*adj; f*	acrylic; plastic
8828	**volátil**-*adj; m*	volatile; volatility
8836	**frenético**-*adj*	frantic
8847	**certero**-*adj*	accurate
8853	**instructivo**-*adj*	instructive
8854	**termal**-*adj*	thermal
8855	**mixto**-*adj*	mixed
8858	**semental**-*adj; m*	stud; stallion
8859	**clarividente**-*adj; m/f*	clairvoyant; psychic
8861	**frustrado**-*adj*	frustrated
8862	**materialista**-*adj; m/f*	materialistic; materialist
8864	**tridimensional**-*adj*	three-dimensional
8865	**anticonceptivo**-*adj; m*	contraceptive; birth control
8866	**bipolar**-*adj*	bipolar
8867	**diminutivo**-*adj; m*	diminutive; diminutive
8872	**austríaco**-*adj; m*	Austrian; Austrian person
8876	**trascendental**-*adj*	momentous
8883	**inoxidable**-*adj*	stainless
8888	**sumario**-*adj; m*	summary; investigation
8890	**insatisfecho**-*adj*	dissatisfied
8891	**constructivo**-*adj*	constructive
8892	**conmemorativo**-*adj*	memorial
8901	**metafórico**-*adj*	metaphorical
8903	**pornográfico**-*adj*	pornographic
8904	**curador**-*adj; m*	healing; curator
8909	**triangular**-*adj; vb*	triangular; triangulate
8911	**circunstancial**-*adj*	circumstantial
8916	**plebeyo**-*m; adj*	commoner; peasant
8919	**libertador**-*m; adj*	liberator; liberator
8922	**letrado**-*m; adj*	counsel; learned
8929	**ecológico**-*adj*	ecological
8946	**pecaminoso**-*adj*	sinful
8947	**satánico**-*adj; m*	satanic; satanist

8952	**pastoral**-*adj*	pastoral
8953	**ucraniano**-*adj; m*	Ukrainian; Ukrainian person
8964	**fundamentalista**-*adj; m/f*	fundamentalist; fundamentalist
8965	**ocioso**-*adj*	idle
8970	**neutro**-*adj*	neutral
8975	**eufórico**-*adj*	euphoric
8977	**inmunológico**-*adj*	immune
8981	**étnico**-*adj*	ethnic
8982	**discográfico**-*adj*	recording
8983	**física**-*adj; f*	physical; physics
8986	**prolongado**-*adj*	prolonged
8988	**inestimable**-*adj*	invaluable
8990	**torácico**-*adj; m*	thoracic; thoracic duct
8994	**filtrado**-*adj; m*	filtering; filter
8997	**neurológico**-*adj*	neurological
9001	**fornido**-*adj*	strapping
9015	**instintivo**-*adj*	instinctive
9018	**promiscuo**-*adj*	promiscuous
9024	**tembloroso**-*adj*	trembling
9030	**isleño**-*adj; m*	island; islander
9032	**rencoroso**-*adj*	spiteful
9033	**vigoroso**-*adj*	vigorous
9036	**cuestionable**-*adj*	questionable
9043	**sumiso**-*adj*	submissive
9047	**incompatible**-*adj*	incompatible
9048	**minusválido**-*adj; m*	disabled; disabled person
9049	**viral**-*adj*	viral
9052	**saudí**-*adj; m/f*	Saudi; Saudi person
9053	**carnívoro**-*adj*	carnivore
9055	**legislador**-*adj; m*	legislative; legislator
9057	**encantado**-*adj*	delighted
9060	**dolido**-*adj*	hurt
9063	**fantasmal**-*adj*	ghostly
9067	**impuro**-*adj*	impure
9070	**irrevocable**-*adj*	irrevocable
9074	**carente**-*adj*	lacking
9077	**rústico**-*adj*	rustic
9088	**sindicalista**-*adj; m/f*	union; trade unionist
9089	**prioritario**-*adj*	critical
9090	**puertorriqueño**-*adj; m*	Puerto Rican; Puerto Rican person
9091	**islámico**-*adj*	Islamic
9093	**feudal**-*adj*	feudal

9094	**voraz**-*adj*	voracious
9098	**argelino**-*adj; m*	Algerian; Algerian person
9100	**domesticado**-*adj*	domesticated
9102	**incesante**-*adj*	incessant
9104	**báltico**-*adj*	Baltic
9106	**atmosférico**-*adj*	atmospheric
9107	**secular**-*adj*	secular
9117	**intestinal**-*adj*	intestinal
9122	**momentáneo**-*adj*	momentary
9125	**laborista**-*adj; m*	Labour; Labor Party member
9129	**progresivo**-*adj*	progressive
9135	**bengalí**-*adj; m/f*	Bengali; Bengali person
9136	**lineal**-*adj*	linear
9137	**existencial**-*adj*	existential
9140	**prehistórico**-*adj*	prehistoric
9144	**energético**-*adj*	energetic
9149	**debutante**-*adj; m/f*	debut; debutante
9154	**metodista**-*adj; m/f*	Methodist; Methodist
9156	**poblado**-*adj; m*	populated; village
9160	**iluso**-*adj*	gullible, deluded
9161	**hormonal**-*adj*	hormonal
9163	**fatídico**-*adj*	fateful
9165	**digestivo**-*adj*	digestive
9166	**periodístico**-*adj*	journalistic
9168	**amoníaco**-*m; adj*	ammonia; ammonia
9169	**exhaustivo**-*adj*	comprehensive
9174	**penitenciario**-*adj; m*	penitentiary; prison
9176	**posgrado**-*m; adj*	postgraduate degree; postgraduate
9179	**integrante**-*adj; m/f*	integral; member
9180	**genealógico**-*adj*	genealogical
9192	**preferente**-*adj*	preferential
9193	**prepotente**-*adj*	arrogant
9194	**cristalino**-*adj*	crystalline
9196	**tópico**-*m; adj*	cliche; topical
9199	**hipotético**-*adj*	hypothetical
9200	**burdo**-*adj*	crude
9207	**binario**-*adj*	binary
9208	**chileno**-*adj; m*	Chilean; Chilean person
9212	**kurdo**-*adj; m*	Kurdish; Kurdish person
9216	**alzado**-*adj*	raised
9220	**punzante**-*adj*	sharp
9228	**disciplinario**-*adj*	disciplinary
9232	**pulcro**-*adj*	neat
9235	**nauseabundo**-*adj*	nauseating
9238	**metafísico**-*adj*	metaphysical
9248	**exagerado**-*adj*	exaggerated
9250	**radiactivo**-*adj*	radioactive
9252	**centígrado**-*adj*	centigrade
9253	**febril**-*adj*	febrile
9254	**superfluo**-*adj*	superfluous
9279	**inadvertido**-*adj*	unnoticed
9281	**venéreo**-*adj*	venereal
9282	**jesuita**-*adj; m/f*	Jesuit; Jesuit
9290	**papal**-*adj*	papal
9297	**escénico**-*adj*	scenic
9306	**idóneo**-*adj*	suitable
9310	**incoherente**-*adj*	incoherent
9311	**ventajoso**-*adj*	advantageous
9316	**troyano**-*adj; m*	Trojan; Trojan horse
9317	**colocado**-*adj*	placed, stoned
9321	**intencionado**-*adj*	deliberate
9325	**portuario**-*adj*	port
9326	**floral**-*adj*	floral
9331	**inconstante**-*adj*	inconstant
9332	**mosaico**-*adj; m*	mosaic; mosaic
9336	**arbitrario**-*adj*	arbitrary
9339	**indebido**-*adj*	improper
9341	**pegajoso**-*adj*	sticky
9344	**reservado**-*adj*	reserved
9346	**comunal**-*adj*	communal
9355	**disfuncional**-*adj*	dysfunctional
9366	**selectivo**-*adj*	selective
9368	**concienzudo**-*adj*	conscientious
9369	**explícito**-*adj*	explicit
9371	**sumergible**-*adj*	submersible
9375	**recio**-*adj*	tough
9376	**croata**-*adj; m/f*	Croatian; Croatian person
9379	**temporario**-*adj*	temporary
9382	**hermético**-*adj*	airtight
9384	**nutritivo**-*adj*	nutritious
9385	**oceánico**-*adj*	oceanic
9389	**ecologista**-*m/f; adj*	ecologist; environmental
9392	**fulminante**-*adj*	fulminant
9394	**plausible**-*adj*	plausible
9403	**árido**-*adj*	arid

9407	**felino**-*adj; m*	feline; feline
9411	**impasible**-*adj*	impassive
9418	**dimensional**-*adj*	dimensional
9422	**norteño**-*adj; m*	northern; northerner
9423	**justiciero**-*adj; m*	tough; vigilante
9424	**provinciano**-*adj; m*	provincial; provincial
9425	**mortífero**-*adj*	lethal
9431	**reglamentario**-*adj*	regulation
9434	**despampanante**-*adj*	stunning
9440	**tolerable**-*adj*	tolerable
9448	**contaminante**-*adj; m*	pollutant; contaminant
9459	**parlamentario**-*adj; m*	parliamentary; Member of Parliament
9460	**presumible**-*adj*	likely, alleged
9466	**lastimoso**-*adj*	pitiful
9471	**censor**-*adj; m*	censorial; censor
9474	**conciso**-*adj*	concise
9476	**fogoso**-*adj*	ardent
9482	**estanco**-*adj; m*	watertight; shop
9487	**mercantil**-*adj*	commercial
9490	**recreativo**-*adj*	recreational
9497	**abrupto**-*adj*	abrupt
9498	**interestelar**-*adj*	interstellar
9505	**inagotable**-*adj*	inexhaustible
9510	**inexcusable**-*adj*	inexcusable
9515	**expansivo**-*adj*	expansive
9516	**risueño**-*adj*	smiling
9518	**reacio**-*adj*	reluctant
9522	**renal**-*adj*	renal
9531	**parco**-*adj*	frugal
9533	**afroamericano**-*adj; M*	Afro-American; African-American person
9538	**legionario**-*adj; m*	legionary; legionnaire
9540	**boreal**-*adj*	boreal
9543	**impresor**-*adj; m*	printing; printer
9544	**apetitoso**-*adj*	appetizing
9545	**chillón**-*adj*	gaudy
9551	**cauto**-*adj*	cautious
9552	**avellana**-*adj; f*	hazelnut; hazelnut
9558	**unilateral**-*adj*	unilateral
9559	**bolero**-*adj; m*	liar (coll); bolero
9564	**napolitano**-*adj; m*	Neapolitan; Neapolitan person
9565	**disidente**-*adj; m*	dissident; dissident
9567	**suculento**-*adj*	succulent
9576	**magenta**-*adj*	magenta
9578	**predilecto**-*adj*	favorite
9582	**inmerso**-*adj*	immersed
9583	**envidiable**-*adj*	enviable
9595	**imperceptible**-*adj*	imperceptible
9598	**antidroga**-*adj*	antidrug
9605	**inverosímil**-*adj*	implausible
9606	**rocoso**-*adj*	rocky
9610	**diurno**-*adj*	daytime
9612	**recíproco**-*adj*	reciprocal
9613	**prodigioso**-*adj*	prodigious
9616	**aerodinámico**-*adj*	aerodynamic
9625	**parroquial**-*adj*	parochial
9630	**dietético**-*adj*	dietary
9635	**rectal**-*adj*	rectal
9643	**espectral**-*adj*	spectral
9644	**lírico**-*adj*	lyrical
9646	**endemoniado**-*adj; m*	possessed; devil
9649	**regio**-*adj*	royal
9650	**emigrante**-*adj; m/f*	emigrant; emigrant
9652	**boquiabierto**-*adj*	dumbstruck
9655	**loable**-*adj*	laudable
9656	**invariable**-*adj; m*	unchanging; unchanged
9661	**inmutable**-*adj*	immutable
9667	**cabrito**-*adj; m*	lousy (coll); young goat
9674	**bélico**-*adj*	warlike
9680	**insostenible**-*adj*	untenable
9688	**inexorable**-*adj*	inexorable
9694	**neural**-*adj*	neural
9695	**arqueológico**-*adj*	archaeological
9697	**diligente**-*adj*	diligent
9702	**ávido**-*adj*	avid
9710	**tozudo**-*adj*	stubborn
9712	**obsoleto**-*adj*	obsolete
9718	**respiratorio**-*adj*	respiratory
9719	**intuitivo**-*adj*	intuitive
9720	**lumbar**-*adj*	lumbar
9722	**exento**-*adj*	exempt
9724	**turbulento**-*adj*	turbulent
9730	**residual**-*adj*	residual
9732	**adolorido**-*adj*	in pain
9733	**chiquitito**-*adj*	tiny
9736	**evolutivo**-*adj*	evolutionary

9739	**impulsor**-*adj; m*	active; booster
9740	**izquierdista**-*adj; m/f*	leftist; leftist
9742	**norcoreano**-*adj; m*	North Korean; North Korean person
9743	**sostenible**-*adj*	sustainable
9745	**simplista**-*adj*	simplistic
9759	**reseco**-*adj*	arid
9770	**rapaz**-*adj; m*	predatory; kid
9771	**culinario**-*adj*	culinary
9772	**reconocible**-*adj*	recognizable
9775	**intranquilo**-*adj*	uneasy
9782	**diferencial**-*adj; f*	differential; gap
9783	**geológico**-*adj*	geological
9784	**verídico**-*adj*	true
9787	**lingüístico**-*adj*	linguistic
9788	**geriátrico**-*adj; m*	geriatric; nursing home
9789	**magistral**-*adj*	masterly
9793	**eventual**-*adj*	eventual
9795	**adepto**-*adj; m*	adept; follower
9796	**extinto**-*adj*	extinct
9799	**redundante**-*adj*	redundant
9802	**irreprochable**-*adj*	irreproachable
9805	**transatlántico**-*adj; m*	transatlantic; ocean liner
9808	**insípido**-*adj*	tasteless
9809	**filoso**-*adj*	sharp
9818	**subyacente**-*adj*	underlying
9819	**estabilizador**-*adj; m*	stabilising; stabilizer
9820	**viscoso**-*adj*	viscous
9822	**capilar**-*adj; m*	capillary; hair
9825	**temido**-*adj*	feared
9826	**meridional**-*adj*	southern
9831	**separatista**-*adj; m/f*	separatist; separatist
9832	**anticongelante**-*adj*	antifreeze
9837	**dominicano**-*adj; m*	Dominican; Dominican person
9845	**introvertido**-*adj; m*	introverted; introvert
9858	**atrayente**-*adj*	attractive
9859	**exasperante**-*adj*	infuriating
9861	**variante**-*adj; f*	alternative; variant
9866	**marrano**-*adj; m*	disgusting (coll); pig
9870	**rítmico**-*adj*	rhythmic
9873	**semántico**-*adj*	semantic
9874	**fecal**-*adj*	fecal
9883	**burocrático**-*adj*	bureaucratic
9885	**terminante**-*adj*	final
9887	**temática**-*adj; f*	thematic; theme
9896	**contradictorio**-*adj*	contradictory
9897	**ocurrente**-*adj*	witty
9898	**descomunal**-*adj*	huge
9899	**cosmopolita**-*adj; m*	cosmopolitan; cosmopolitan
9900	**barroco**-*adj*	baroque
9909	**antiséptico**-*adj; m*	antiseptic; antiseptic
9911	**efímero**-*adj*	ephemeral
9917	**fetal**-*adj*	fetal
9918	**peruano**-*adj; m*	Peruvian; Peruvian person
9928	**barbitúrico**-*m; adj*	barbiturate; barbiturate
9940	**penúltimo**-*adj*	penultimate
9944	**autoritario**-*adj; m*	authoritarian; authoritarian
9949	**enigmático**-*adj*	enigmatic
9950	**alterno**-*adj*	alternate
9954	**opcional**-*adj*	optional
9958	**fundido**-*adj*	molten
9961	**determinante**-*adj; m*	determinant; determinant
9968	**prieto**-*adj*	tight
9976	**ilícito**-*adj*	illicit
9981	**incuestionable**-*adj*	unquestionable
9988	**hiriente**-*adj*	hurtful
9989	**suplementario**-*adj*	supplementary
9991	**respectivo**-*adj*	respective
9994	**consecuente**-*adj*	consistent
9997	**desalentador**-*adj*	discouraging
10003	**mayorista**-*adj*	wholesale
10005	**irremediable**-*adj*	irremediable
10006	**indivisible**-*adj*	indivisible
10007	**altruista**-*adj; m/f*	altruistic; altruist
10019	**palpable**-*adj*	palpable
10021	**vascular**-*adj*	vascular
10022	**subjetivo**-*adj*	subjective

Adverbs

Rank	Spanish-*PoS*	Translation(s)
7888	**siquiera**-*adv*	at least
7917	**bis**-*adv; m*	bis; encore
8028	**hipotéticamente**-*adv*	hypothetically
8228	**asimismo**-*adv*	also
9225	**inusualmente**-*adv*	unusually
9442	**ídem**-*prn; adv*	likewise; ditto
9728	**mogollón**-*m; adv*	lots of (coll); loads
9937	**anteanoche**-*adv*	the night before last

Nouns

Rank	Spanish-PoS	Translation(s)
7504	renombre-*m*	renown
7505	frenesí-*m*	frenzy
7506	heces-*fpl*	dregs, feces
7507	atletismo-*m*	athletics
7509	finalista-*adj; m/f*	finalist; finalist
7512	poro-*m*	pore
7515	canino-*adj; m*	canine; canine tooth
7516	dote-*f*	dowry
7517	radial-*adj; f*	radio; circular saw
7518	podio-*m*	podium
7520	burócrata-*m/f*	bureaucrat
7521	intermitente-*adj; m*	intermittent; blinker
7522	helio-*m*	helium
7523	elixir-*m*	elixir
7524	autonomía-*f*	autonomy
7525	furor-*m*	fury
7527	frialdad-*f*	coldness
7528	barandilla-*f*	handrail
7530	estudioso-*adj; m*	studious; scholar
7532	municipalidad-*f*	municipality
7533	encarnación-*f*	incarnation
7536	mausoleo-*m*	mausoleum
7537	cerezo-*m*	cherry tree
7539	sodio-*m*	sodium
7542	asentamiento-*m*	settlement
7543	contusión-*f*	contusion
7544	crematorio-*m*	crematorium
7545	trampolín-*m*	springboard
7546	sociología-*f*	sociology
7548	embrión-*m*	embryo
7549	activación-*f*	activation
7551	renacuajo-*m*	tadpole, little kid
7552	olmo-*m*	elm
7555	acné-*m*	acne
7557	nitrato-*m*	nitrate
7558	inca-*m/f; adj*	Inca; Incan
7561	informático-*adj; m*	computer; computer expert
7562	batuta-*f*	baton
7563	gasa-*f*	chiffon
7565	suspense-*m*	suspense
7566	sarta-*f*	bunch
7567	abordaje-*m*	approach, boarding
7570	voleibol-*m*	volleyball
7571	puñetero-*m*	annoyance, damn (coll)
7572	insuficiente-*adj; m*	insufficient; unsatisfactory
7573	cacerola-*f*	pan
7574	bandada-*f*	flock
7576	mejoría-*f*	improvement
7577	cobijo-*m*	shelter
7579	sencillez-*f*	simplicity
7581	caperuza-*f*	hood
7584	frescura-*f*	freshness
7586	legua-*f*	league
7588	gangrena-*f*	gangrene
7591	parentesco-*m*	kinship
7592	boina-*f*	beret
7595	diapositiva-*f*	slide
7597	encubrimiento-*m*	concealment
7599	saliente-*adj; m*	outgoing; projection
7600	riel-*m*	rail
7603	súplica-*f*	plea
7605	mordedura-*f*	bite
7609	peña-*f*	rock, club
7611	fatalidad-*f*	fatality
7612	tala-*f*	felling
7613	parto-*m*	childbirth
7614	bulevar-*m*	boulevard
7615	negociador-*m*	negotiator
7616	diabético-*adj; m*	diabetic; diabetic
7617	averiguación-*f*	inquiry
7619	vecindad-*f*	neighborhood
7622	soldado-*m/f*	soldier
7623	imperativo-*adj; m*	imperative; imperative
7624	textil-*adj; m*	textile; textile
7626	pacifista-*adj; m/f*	pacifist; pacifist
7627	especificación-*f*	specification
7628	albatros-*m*	albatross
7629	indeseable-*adj; m/f*	undesirable; undesirable
7634	sobrenombre-*m*	nickname
7635	pedante-*adj; m/f*	pedantic; pedant
7638	contrincante-*m/f*	opponent
7639	portería-*f*	goal
7641	ocupante-*adj; m/f*	occupying; occupant
7643	astrología-*f*	astrology
7644	espasmo-*m*	spasm
7645	crucifixión-*f*	crucifixion

7646	**deterioro**-*m*	deterioration	
7647	**asaltante**-*m/f*	robber	
7649	**inferioridad**-*f*	inferiority	
7650	**hinchazón**-*f*	swelling	
7651	**perejil**-*m*	parsley	
7652	**hilera**-*f*	row	
7653	**consorcio**-*m*	consortium	
7655	**colegial**-*adj; m*	school; schoolboy	
7656	**presunción**-*f*	presumption	
7659	**chichón**-*m*	bump	
7660	**pavor**-*m*	dread	
7661	**fronterizo**-*m; adj*	border; frontier	
7664	**insistencia**-*f*	insistence	
7665	**rebeldía**-*f*	rebellion	
7667	**amplificador**-*adj; m*	amplifying; amplifier	
7668	**ascensión**-*f*	ascension	
7669	**novillo**-*m*	heifer, steer	
7674	**maleante**-*m/f*	criminal	
7676	**maceta**-*f*	pot	
7677	**mutilación**-*f*	mutilation	
7678	**incendiario**-*adj; m*	incendiary; arsonist	
7680	**perdiz**-*f*	partridge	
7682	**dibujante**-*m/f*	cartoonist	
7684	**recolección**-*f*	collection	
7685	**tampón**-*m*	tampon	
7686	**narcotraficante**-*m/f*	drug dealer	
7687	**desesperanza**-*f*	despair	
7690	**devastación**-*f*	devastation	
7693	**sonata**-*f*	sonata	
7694	**firmamento**-*m*	firmament	
7695	**encarcelamiento**-*m*	imprisonment	
7697	**arañazo**-*m*	scratch	
7698	**sentimentalismo**-*m*	sentimentality	
7700	**afán**-*m*	eagerness	
7701	**matorral**-*m*	bush	
7703	**fricción**-*f*	friction	
7707	**ruedo**-*m*	arena	
7709	**nutrición**-*f*	nutrition	
7711	**consenso**-*m*	consensus	
7712	**carbohidrato**-*m*	carbohydrate	
7715	**yugo**-*m*	yoke	
7716	**apogeo**-*m*	peak	
7721	**quiosco**-*m*	kiosk	
7723	**mecedora**-*f*	rocking chair	
7726	**cronómetro**-*m*	stopwatch	
7728	**prótesis**-*f*	prosthesis	

7729	**previsión**-*f*	forecast
7731	**patinador**-*m*	skater
7732	**mole**-*f*	mass
7733	**bajista**-*m/f*	bass player
7734	**ejecutor**-*adj; m*	executing; executor
7736	**merengue**-*m*	meringue
7737	**quijada**-*f*	jaw
7738	**rareza**-*f*	rarity
7739	**furtivo**-*adj; m*	furtive; poacher
7740	**penumbra**-*f*	gloom
7741	**alquimia**-*f*	alchemy
7742	**trapecio**-*m*	trapeze
7744	**atributo**-*m*	attribute
7745	**arnés**-*m*	harness
7746	**exaltado**-*adj; m*	frenzied; hothead
7747	**derechazo**-*m*	right
7748	**redada**-*f*	raid
7750	**ilustración**-*f*	illustration
7751	**tablón**-*m*	plank
7752	**coloso**-*m*	colossus
7754	**fideicomiso**-*m*	trust
7756	**varicela**-*f*	chickenpox
7757	**bragueta**-*f*	fly
7758	**altibajos**-*mpl*	ups and downs
7761	**escroto**-*m*	scrotum
7763	**mejillón**-*m*	mussel
7764	**soldador**-*m*	welder
7767	**hijastro**-*m*	stepson
7768	**perilla**-*f*	goatee
7770	**condecoración**-*f*	award
7771	**jeta**-*f*	face (coll)
7774	**alameda**-*f*	avenue
7776	**regatear**-*vb; m*	haggle; haggling
7777	**peseta**-*f*	peseta
7779	**pelvis**-*f*	pelvis
7780	**almacenamiento**-*m*	storage
7782	**afección**-*f*	condition
7786	**parkinson**-*m*	parkinson's disease
7788	**afgano**-*adj; m*	Afghan; Afghan person
7789	**paramédico**-*adj; m*	paramedical; paramedic
7790	**articulación**-*f*	joint
7791	**gotera**-*f*	leak
7792	**lapso**-*m*	period of time
7793	**infortunio**-*m*	misfortune

7795	**prólogo**-*m*	prologue
7797	**cautivo**-*adj; m*	captive; captivity
7798	**israelita**-*adj; m*	Israelite; Israelite person
7799	**conciudadano**-*m*	fellow citizen
7800	**quimera**-*f*	chimera
7802	**insurrección**-*f*	insurrection
7804	**inflamación**-*f*	inflammation
7806	**censo**-*m*	census
7809	**racionamiento**-*m*	rationing
7810	**tosco**-*adj; m*	crude; rough
7812	**tracción**-*f*	traction
7813	**telenovela**-*f*	soap opera
7814	**desalojo**-*m*	eviction
7815	**estirpe**-*f*	lineage
7820	**difusión**-*f*	diffusion
7822	**lisiado**-*adj; m*	disabled; disabled person
7823	**garabato**-*m*	doodle
7826	**peatón**-*m*	pedestrian
7827	**estimación**-*f*	estimation
7828	**licenciatura**-*f*	degree
7829	**impresora**-*f*	printer
7831	**neurótico**-*adj; m*	neurotic; neurotic
7833	**marcación**-*f*	marking
7834	**disentería**-*f*	dysentery
7835	**iraní**-*adj; m/f*	Iranian; Iranian person
7836	**degradación**-*f*	degradation
7838	**seudónimo**-*m*	pseudonym
7839	**engranaje**-*m*	gear
7841	**sondeo**-*m*	survey
7842	**jonrón**-*m*	home run
7843	**deudor**-*adj; m*	in debt; debtor
7844	**anexo**-*adj; m*	attached; annex
7847	**bonificación**-*f*	bonus
7848	**pericia**-*f*	expertise
7849	**lejía**-*f*	bleach
7852	**labrador**-*m/f*	farmer, lab
7853	**coordinador**-*m*	coordinator
7858	**desequilibrio**-*m*	imbalance
7859	**hormigueo**-*m*	tingling
7860	**simulador**-*m*	simulator
7861	**relajación**-*f*	relaxation
7862	**cancelación**-*f*	cancellation
7863	**magnetismo**-*m*	magnetism
7865	**asesoramiento**-*m*	advice
7866	**cuenca**-*f*	basin
7871	**purificación**-*m*	purification
7872	**pincho**-*m*	spike
7873	**tobogán**-*m*	slide
7875	**artesano**-*m*	craftsman
7876	**envejecimiento**-*m*	aging
7877	**trasplante**-*m*	transplant
7878	**marroquí**-*adj; m/f*	Moroccan; Moroccan person
7881	**nerviosismo**-*m*	nervousness
7883	**brea**-*f*	pitch
7884	**aborigen**-*adj; m/f*	indigenous; aboriginal
7886	**dramaturgo**-*m*	playwright
7892	**prescripción**-*f*	prescription
7893	**carabina**-*f*	carbine
7894	**hospicio**-*m*	hospice
7895	**mediocridad**-*m/f; f*	mediocre; mediocrity
7896	**distintivo**-*adj; m*	distinctive; emblem
7897	**clavícula**-*f*	clavicle
7898	**imperialismo**-*m*	imperialism
7901	**peregrinación**-*f*	pilgrimage
7904	**carpintería**-*f*	carpentry
7905	**augurio**-*m*	omen
7906	**fallecimiento**-*m*	death
7907	**plenitud**-*f*	fullness
7908	**tapiz**-*m*	tapestry
7912	**diván**-*m*	divan
7913	**oleaje**-*m*	surf
7916	**auge**-*m*	boom
7917	**bis**-*adv; m*	bis; encore
7918	**ranura**-*f*	groove
7923	**cota**-*f*	peak
7924	**escarabajo**-*m*	beetle
7928	**contagio**-*m*	contagion
7930	**masculinidad**-*f*	masculinity
7931	**desliz**-*m*	slip
7933	**noticiario**-*m*	news
7934	**lince**-*m*	lynx
7935	**botánico**-*adj; m*	botanical; botanist
7936	**espuela**-*f*	spur
7937	**codorniz**-*m/f*	quail
7938	**tesorería**-*f*	treasury
7939	**antisemita**-*adj; m/f*	anti-Semitic; anti-Semite

7940	**procesador**-*adj; m*	processing; processor		8020	**comillas**-*fpl*	quotation marks
7945	**preservación**-*f*	preservation		8021	**prosa**-*f*	prose
7946	**estimulación**-*f*	stimulation		8023	**autocontrol**-*m*	self-control
7948	**tapia**-*f*	wall		8024	**aberración**-*f*	aberration
7949	**pitido**-*m*	whistle		8029	**aparador**-*m*	sideboard
7952	**tatarabuelo**-*m*	Great-great-grandfather		8030	**electrón**-*m*	electron
				8033	**antropología**-*f*	anthropology
7955	**intimidación**-*f*	intimidation		8034	**currículum**-*m*	curriculum vitae
7957	**labia**-*f*	gift of the gab		8035	**retrovisor**-*m*	rear-view mirror
7958	**hernia**-*f*	hernia		8036	**apego**-*m*	attachment
7959	**mueca**-*f*	grin		8037	**suplemento**-*m*	supplement
7960	**avioneta**-*f*	plane		8039	**ampliación**-*f*	extension
7961	**regulador**-*m; adj*	regulator; regulating		8040	**contienda**-*f*	contest
7963	**quehacer**-*m*	chore		8041	**galera**-*f*	galley
7964	**bazo**-*m*	spleen		8042	**caballerosidad**-*f*	chivalry
7967	**nacionalista**-*adj; m/f*	nationalist; nationalist		8043	**limpiaparabrisas**-*m*	wiper
				8044	**anemia**-*f*	anemia
7968	**rosca**-*f*	thread		8047	**balanceo**-*m*	rocking
7972	**estrofa**-*f*	stanza		8049	**torniquete**-*m*	tourniquet
7973	**trazado**-*m*	outline		8050	**obscenidad**-*f*	obscenity
7974	**armenio**-*adj; m*	Armenian; Armenian person		8051	**disminución**-*f*	decrease
				8052	**masón**-*m*	mason
7975	**despecho**-*m*	spite		8053	**afinidad**-*f*	affinity
7976	**cepa**-*f*	strain		8055	**configuración**-*f*	configuration
7979	**validez**-*f*	validity		8057	**camaleón**-*m*	chameleon
7980	**espesor**-*m*	thickness		8058	**cómic**-*m*	comic
7982	**privación**-*f*	deprivation		8059	**lagartija**-*f*	lizard
7984	**cristiandad**-*f*	Christianity		8060	**espiritualidad**-*f*	spirituality
7989	**mongol**-*adj; m*	Mongolian; Mongol		8061	**analogía**-*f*	analogy
7990	**proeza**-*f*	feat		8062	**desmayo**-*m*	fainting
7991	**flexibilidad**-*f*	flexibility		8063	**distorsión**-*f*	distortion
7996	**incomodidad**-*f*	discomfort		8064	**rosal**-*m*	rosebush
7997	**camaradería**-*f*	camaraderie		8066	**girasol**-*m*	sunflower
8000	**vulgaridad**-*f*	vulgarity		8067	**metamorfosis**-*f*	metamorphosis
8001	**ocurrencia**-*f*	idea		8068	**ciclón**-*m*	cyclone
8003	**narcotráfico**-*m*	drug trafficking		8070	**financiamiento**-*m*	financing
8004	**posteridad**-*f*	posterity		8072	**bravucón**-*adj; m*	cocky; bully
8005	**turbina**-*f*	turbine		8073	**funda**-*f*	cover
8006	**toma**-*f*	socket		8078	**sílaba**-*f*	syllable
8007	**deportación**-*f*	deportation		8081	**audífono**-*m*	hearing aid
8009	**premisa**-*f*	premise		8083	**refrigeración**-*f*	refrigeration
8010	**dispersión**-*f*	dispersion		8085	**congelación**-*f*	freezing
8014	**listado**-*m*	list		8088	**inmensidad**-*f*	immensity
8015	**afrenta**-*f*	affront		8090	**hundimiento**-*m*	sinking
8017	**parrillada**-*f*	barbecue		8092	**locutor**-*m*	announcer
8019	**reclusión**-*f*	imprisonment		8093	**catalizador**-*m*	catalyst

8094	declive-*m*	decline	8176	neutrón-*f*	neutron
8095	vándalo-*m/f*	vandal	8178	similitud-*f*	similarity
8098	borrón-*m*	smudge	8179	cacho-*m*	piece
8099	relatividad-*f*	relativity	8180	emisor-*m; adj*	sender; emitting
8100	preservativo-*m*	condom	8183	timonel-*m/f*	helmsperson
8101	retina-*f*	retina	8185	percusión-*f*	percussion
8102	elector-*m*	elector	8186	crisma-*f*	neck (coll)
8103	celibato-*m*	celibacy	8188	criadero-*m*	hatchery
8109	salvoconducto-*m*	pass	8189	catecismo-*m*	Catechism
8110	insensatez-*f*	folly	8190	objetividad-*f*	objectivity
8111	aeroplano-*m*	airplane	8191	cancillería-*f*	chancellery
8113	utensilio-*m*	utensil	8192	reuma-*m*	rheumatism
8114	zapatería-*f*	shoe shop	8193	cesárea-*f*	C-section
8121	hispano-*adj; m*	Hispanic; Hispanic	8194	recolector-*m*	collector
8123	subsuelo-*m*	subsoil	8197	oficinista-*m/f*	office worker
8124	discapacidad-*f*	disability	8200	inestabilidad-*f*	instability
8125	planetario-*adj; m*	planetary; planetarium	8201	retroceso-*m*	setback
			8202	innovación-*f*	innovation
8126	pediatra-*m/f*	pediatrician	8203	monogamia-*f*	monogamy
8127	televidente-*m/f*	viewer	8204	nailon-*m*	nylon
8130	astrónomo-*m*	astronomer	8206	instrumental-*adj; m*	instrumental; instrument
8131	lentejuela-*f*	sequin			
8132	frac-*m*	tuxedo	8208	laptop-*f*	laptop
8134	féretro-*m*	coffin	8209	riego-*m*	irrigation
8136	destierro-*m*	exile	8210	clamor-*m*	cry
8137	peldaño-*m*	step	8211	canibalismo-*m*	cannibalism
8139	ganadero-*m*	farmer	8212	beneficiario-*m*	beneficiary
8142	trópico-*adj; m*	tropic; tropic	8214	localidad-*f*	town
8143	causante-*adj; m*	responsible; cause	8215	oportunista-*adj; m/f*	opportunistic; opportunist
8144	idealismo-*m*	idealism			
8145	lenteja-*f*	lentil	8218	horquilla-*f*	hairpin
8146	tez-*f*	complexion	8219	enfriamiento-*m*	cooling
8147	franela-*f*	flannel	8220	minería-*f*	mining
8148	envoltorio-*m*	wrapper	8221	tacho-*m*	container (LA)
8152	pectoral-*adj; m*	chest; chest	8222	alarde-*m*	boast
8153	manzanilla-*f*	chamomile	8225	laca-*f*	lacquer
8154	atajo-*m*	shortcut	8227	escama-*f*	scale
8156	diócesis-*f*	diocese	8229	festejo-*m*	feast
8160	manjar-*m*	delicacy	8231	casaca-*f*	coat
8161	ajuar-*m*	trousseau	8232	libreto-*m*	script
8162	meseta-*f*	plateau	8234	movilidad-*f*	mobility
8164	magnesio-*m*	magnesium	8235	radioactividad-*f*	radioactivity
8165	brasa-*f*	ember	8237	pasa-*f*	raisin
8170	irritación-*f*	irritation	8239	imperialista-*adj; m/f*	imperialistic; imperialist
8172	verruga-*f*	wart			
8175	sátira-*f*	satire	8241	sacerdocio-*m*	priesthood
			8242	dolencia-*f*	disease

8243	**remolcador**-*m*	tugboat
8244	**mediador**-*m*	mediator
8245	**desarme**-*m*	disarmament
8246	**oca**-*f*	goose
8247	**filial**-*f; adj*	subsidiary; filial
8249	**unanimidad**-*f*	unanimity
8250	**insolación**-*f*	sunstroke
8251	**reparo**-*m*	objection
8252	**cutis**-*m*	skin
8253	**mecenas**-*m/f*	patron
8256	**manzano**-*m*	apple tree
8257	**procedencia**-*f*	origin
8260	**geología**-*f*	geology
8263	**camada**-*f*	litter
8265	**enganche**-*m*	coupling
8266	**alegación**-*f*	allegation
8268	**sicario**-*m*	hitman
8269	**hipotermia**-*f*	hypothermia
8271	**epiléptico**-*adj; m*	epileptic; epileptic
8272	**austriaco**-*adj; m*	Austrian; Austrian person
8273	**canon**-*m*	canon
8274	**canoa**-*f*	canoe
8275	**calvario**-*m*	ordeal (coll)
8276	**agüero**-*m*	omen
8277	**perito**-*m/f; adj*	expert; expert
8278	**consistencia**-*f*	consistency
8279	**ratero**-*m*	pickpocket
8283	**apreciación**-*f*	appreciation
8284	**autobiografía**-*f*	autobiography
8285	**traste**-*m*	fret
8286	**sutileza**-*f*	subtlety
8291	**cala**-*f*	cove
8294	**desplazamiento**-*m*	displacement
8295	**coraza**-*f*	shell
8296	**discordia**-*f*	discord
8298	**progresista**-*adj; m/f*	progressive; progressive
8299	**monotonía**-*f*	monotony
8300	**artimaña**-*f*	trick
8301	**irrigación**-*f*	irrigation
8304	**desenlace**-*m*	outcome
8305	**ardid**-*m*	scheme
8310	**legalidad**-*f*	legality
8312	**sanción**-*f*	sanction
8313	**autismo**-*m*	autism

8315	**artesanía**-*f*	craftwork
8316	**emancipación**-*f*	emancipation
8317	**embolia**-*f*	embolism
8318	**finlandés**-*adj; m*	Finnish; Finnish person
8319	**mercadeo**-*m*	marketing
8320	**autista**-*adj; m/f*	autistic; autistic person
8321	**finalidad**-*f*	purpose
8323	**recambio**-*m*	replacement
8325	**envoltura**-*f*	wrapper
8326	**fragata**-*f*	frigate
8327	**linchamiento**-*m*	lynching
8328	**artilugio**-*m*	gadget
8329	**ciclista**-*m/f*	cyclist
8330	**simetría**-*f*	symmetry
8331	**acidez**-*f*	heartburn
8332	**desgaste**-*m*	wear
8334	**setiembre**-*m*	September
8335	**brío**-*m*	verve
8337	**damisela**-*f*	damsel
8339	**fisura**-*f*	fissure
8340	**polución**-*f*	pollution
8341	**globalización**-*f*	globalization
8342	**infinidad**-*f*	infinity
8343	**catolicismo**-*m*	Catholicism
8344	**baranda**-*f*	railing
8347	**puf**-*m; int*	beanbag; ugh
8349	**grosor**-*m*	thickness
8351	**armazón**-*m*	frame
8353	**nómada**-*adj; m/f*	nomadic; Nomad
8355	**barniz**-*m*	varnish
8358	**bobina**-*f*	coil
8359	**confidencia**-*f*	confidence
8360	**bíceps**-*m*	biceps
8363	**hardware**-*m*	hardware
8365	**fardo**-*m*	bundle
8366	**paréntesis**-*m*	parentheses
8367	**nazismo**-*m*	Nazism
8368	**bioquímico**-*adj; m*	biochemical; biochemist
8369	**promiscuidad**-*f*	promiscuity
8371	**biopsia**-*f*	biopsy
8373	**contemporáneo**-*adj; m*	contemporary; contemporary
8374	**cazuela**-*f*	pot
8378	**ímpetu**-*m*	impetus

8379	**fonógrafo**-*m*	phonograph	8450	**embudo**-*m*	funnel
8380	**respirador**-*adj; m*	inhaling; respirator	8451	**refinería**-*f*	refinery
8381	**crecida**-*f*	flood	8452	**marxista**-*adj; m/f*	marxist; Marxist
8385	**analfabeto**-*adj; m*	illiterate; illiterate	8453	**logística**-*f*	logistics
8386	**perjuicio**-*m*	damage	8454	**intercepción**-*f*	interception
8388	**síntesis**-*f*	synthesis	8455	**menstruación**-*f*	menstruation
8389	**reaccionario**-*adj; m*	reactionary; reactionary	8456	**enzima**-*f*	enzyme
			8457	**óvulo**-*m*	ovum
8391	**disfunción**-*f*	dysfunction	8458	**coliflor**-*f*	cauliflower
8392	**realizador**-*m*	producer	8459	**vid**-*f*	vine
8395	**menopausia**-*f*	menopause	8460	**adiestramiento**-*m*	training
8396	**clonación**-*f*	cloning	8461	**suscripción**-*f*	subscription
8397	**ligereza**-*f*	lightness	8462	**sota**-*f*	jack
8398	**prórroga**-*f*	extension	8464	**bombo**-*m*	bass drum
8403	**narrativo**-*adj; f*	narrative; narrative	8466	**capote**-*m*	cape
8404	**polizón**-*m/f*	stowaway	8467	**compresión**-*f*	compression
8405	**complexión**-*f*	complexion	8468	**coartada**-*f*	alibi
8406	**residencia**-*f*	residence	8470	**escolta**-*m/f*	bodyguard
8408	**dorso**-*m*	back	8472	**aislante**-*adj; m*	insulation; insulator
8411	**glóbulo**-*m*	globule	8474	**boquilla**-*f*	mouthpiece
8412	**azulejo**-*m*	tile	8476	**resina**-*f*	resin
8413	**conformidad**-*f*	accordance	8478	**contrabajo**-*m*	double bass
8414	**insurgente**-*adj; m/f*	insurgent; rebel	8480	**planeador**-*m*	glider
8415	**fluidez**-*f*	fluency	8483	**coacción**-*f*	coercion
8416	**brevedad**-*f*	brevity	8486	**llamamiento**-*m*	call
8417	**esterilización**-*f*	sterilization	8487	**golondrina**-*f*	swallow
8418	**fichero**-*m*	filing cabinet	8488	**espino**-*m*	hawthorn
8420	**sacacorchos**-*m*	corkscrew	8490	**cordillera**-*f*	mountain range
8421	**péndulo**-*m*	pendulum	8492	**gratificación**-*f*	gratification
8424	**caucásico**-*adj; m*	Caucasian; Caucasian person	8494	**inhibición**-*f*	inhibition
			8500	**bujía**-*f*	spark plug
8426	**reciclaje**-*m*	recycling	8501	**electrodoméstico**-*m*	domestic appliance
8427	**cercanía**-*f*	closeness	8502	**retención**-*f*	retention
8428	**lucidez**-*f*	lucidity	8506	**faceta**-*f*	facet
8429	**maya**-*adj; m*	Mayan; Mayan person	8507	**resignación**-*f*	resignation
			8508	**simpatizante**-*adj; m/f*	sympathetic to; sympathizer
8430	**savia**-*f*	sap			
8433	**butaca**-*f*	armchair	8510	**preludio**-*m*	prelude
8435	**clandestinidad**-*f*	underground	8511	**intemperie**-*f*	weather
8437	**programador**-*m*	programmer	8512	**apoplejía**-*f*	stroke
8439	**croqueta**-*f*	croquette	8513	**regata**-*f*	regatta
8440	**camarote**-*m*	cabin	8515	**hidalgo**-*m*	nobleman
8442	**clarín**-*m*	bugle	8517	**maza**-*f*	mace
8445	**patrocinio**-*m*	patronage	8519	**lumbre**-*f*	fire
8446	**apatía**-*f*	apathy	8520	**caballeriza**-*f*	stable
8447	**supremacía**-*f*	supremacy	8521	**cabida**-*f*	room
8449	**hoz**-*f*	sickle			

8523	**velorio**-*m*	wake	
8524	**enema**-*m*	enema	
8526	**individualidad**-*f*	individuality	
8527	**simbolismo**-*m*	symbolism	
8528	**posguerra**-*f*	post-war era	
8529	**severidad**-*f*	severity	
8532	**docente**-*adj; m/f*	educational; teacher	
8534	**sutura**-*f*	stitch	
8535	**risco**-*m*	crag	
8538	**urbanización**-*f*	urbanisation	
8539	**tibetano**-*adj; m*	Tibetan; Tibetan person	
8540	**secuela**-*f*	sequel	
8541	**paradigma**-*m*	paradigm	
8544	**dividendo**-*m*	dividend	
8547	**erotismo**-*m*	eroticism	
8548	**agilidad**-*f*	agility	
8550	**cátedra**-*f*	professorship	
8551	**óleo**-*m*	oil painting	
8553	**regadera**-*f*	watering can, shower (LA)	
8554	**gruñido**-*m*	growl	
8555	**amapola**-*f*	poppy	
8556	**toldo**-*m*	awning	
8557	**dedicatoria**-*adj; f*	dedicatory; dedication	
8560	**vivero**-*m*	nursery	
8561	**epicentro**-*m*	epicenter	
8562	**ecografía**-*f*	ultrasound	
8564	**camillero**-*m*	stretcher-bearer	
8565	**archiduque**-*m*	archduke	
8566	**glotón**-*m; adj*	glutton; gluttonous	
8568	**estigma**-*m*	stigma	
8579	**derroche**-*m*	waste	
8581	**deficiencia**-*f*	deficiency	
8582	**destrozo**-*m*	heavy damage	
8583	**asignatura**-*f*	subject	
8584	**alcázar**-*m*	fortress	
8590	**haba**-*f*	bean	
8591	**colibrí**-*m*	hummingbird	
8593	**rubor**-*m*	blush	
8594	**jarro**-*m*	mug	
8595	**monzón**-*m*	monsoon	
8596	**adición**-*f*	addition	
8597	**glucosa**-*f*	glucose	
8600	**despojo**-*m*	dispossession	
8601	**logotipo**-*m*	logo	

8605	**coágulo**-*m*	clot	
8609	**reverso**-*m*	reverse	
8610	**productividad**-*f*	productivity	
8611	**canapé**-*m*	canape	
8613	**olivo**-*m*	olive tree	
8615	**panteón**-*m*	pantheon	
8618	**autodefensa**-*f*	self-defence	
8619	**golfista**-*m/f*	golfer	
8620	**lámina**-*f*	sheet	
8621	**carencia**-*f*	lack	
8622	**parpadeo**-*m*	blink	
8623	**remolque**-*m*	trailer	
8624	**estereotipo**-*m*	stereotype	
8625	**marxismo**-*m*	Marxism	
8626	**espontaneidad**-*f*	spontaneity	
8628	**dicción**-*f*	diction	
8629	**conocedor**-*adj; m*	knowledgeable; connoisseur	
8630	**triunfador**-*m; adj*	winner; winning	
8631	**gallardo**-*adj; m*	dashing; gallant	
8632	**disolución**-*f*	dissolution	
8634	**pana**-*f*	corduroy	
8635	**pagaré**-*m*	promissory note	
8636	**contorno**-*m*	contour	
8638	**nicho**-*m*	niche	
8639	**unificación**-*f*	unification	
8640	**fármaco**-*m*	drug	
8641	**delator**-*m*	informer	
8642	**imperfección**-*f*	imperfection	
8643	**libertino**-*adj; m*	licentious; libertine	
8644	**regeneración**-*f*	regeneration	
8646	**converso**-*adj; m*	converted; convert	
8647	**zinc**-*m*	zinc	
8648	**monóxido**-*m*	monoxide	
8649	**epitafio**-*m*	epitaph	
8650	**pistón**-*m*	piston	
8652	**sobriedad**-*f*	sobriety	
8653	**exclusividad**-*f*	exclusivity	
8654	**libido**-*f*	libido	
8655	**quejido**-*m*	whimper	
8658	**cataclismo**-*m*	cataclysm	
8660	**relicario**-*m*	reliquary	
8661	**paria**-*m/f*	outcast	
8662	**talonario**-*m*	checkbook	
8663	**neurólogo**-*m*	neurologist	
8667	**cúspide**-*f*	top	

8668	**atraco**-*m*	robbery		8741	**exterminación**-*f*	extermination
8669	**pronunciación**-*f*	pronunciation		8742	**saltador**-*m*	jumper
8670	**escarcha**-*f*	frost		8743	**vulnerabilidad**-*f*	vulnerability
8673	**góndola**-*f*	gondola		8744	**flautista**-*m/f*	flutist
8674	**bolos**-*mpl*	bowling		8746	**colación**-*f*	collation
8677	**erosión**-*f*	erosion		8748	**víscera**-*f*	entrails
8678	**semifinal**-*f*	semi-final		8749	**inmueble**-*m*	building
8679	**carismático**-*adj; m*	charismatic; charismatic		8750	**provocador**-*adj; m*	provocative; troublemaker
8681	**columnista**-*m/f*	columnist		8751	**bellota**-*f*	acorn
8682	**reparador**-*adj; m*	comforting; repairman		8753	**pasador**-*m*	pin
				8754	**elástico**-*m; adj*	elastic; elastic
8683	**retribución**-*f*	payment		8755	**polluelo**-*m*	chick
8685	**disección**-*f*	dissection		8757	**eliminatoria**-*f*	heat
8686	**tórax**-*m*	thorax		8758	**centenario**-*adj; m*	centenary; centennial
8690	**contrata**-*f*	contract				
8691	**desintoxicación**-*f*	detoxification		8759	**polio**-*f*	polio
8693	**reseña**-*f*	review		8761	**diagonal**-*adj; f*	diagonal; diagonal
8695	**estratega**-*m/f*	strategist		8763	**betún**-*m*	shoe polish
8696	**almidón**-*m*	starch		8764	**colonización**-*f*	colonization
8697	**subvención**-*f*	grant		8765	**refrigerio**-*m*	snack
8698	**prestación**-*f*	provision		8766	**acusador**-*m*	prosecutor
8699	**convivencia**-*f*	coexistence		8769	**margarina**-*f*	margarine
8700	**abolición**-*f*	abolition		8770	**ahijado**-*m*	godson
8703	**matiz**-*m*	nuance		8771	**neutralidad**-*f*	neutrality
8705	**infiltración**-*f*	infiltration		8772	**batidora**-*m*	blender
8706	**protón**-*m*	proton		8774	**aeronáutica**-*adj; f*	aerospace; aviation
8711	**economista**-*m/f*	economist		8776	**disquete**-*m*	diskette
8712	**escenografía**-*f*	scenography		8777	**boludez**-*f*	nonsense (LA) (coll)
8713	**farola**-*f*	lamppost		8779	**barbarie**-*f*	barbarism
8714	**ferocidad**-*f*	ferocity		8780	**cartelera**-*f*	billboard
8716	**acompañamiento**-*m*	accompanying		8782	**mica**-*f*	mica
8717	**progresión**-*f*	progression		8783	**chasis**-*m*	chassis
8722	**biólogo**-*m*	biologist		8784	**centralita**-*f*	switchboard
8723	**palpitación**-*f*	pounding		8788	**estupefaciente**-*m*	narcotic
8724	**bastión**-*m*	bastion		8789	**acumulación**-*f*	accumulation
8725	**bronquitis**-*f*	bronchitis		8791	**albanés**-*adj; m*	Albanian; Albanian person
8727	**contingente**-*m; adj*	contingent; possible				
8728	**piquete**-*m*	picket		8792	**acoplamiento**-*m*	coupling
8729	**sobrepeso**-*m*	overweight		8793	**libanés**-*adj; m*	Lebanese; Lebanese person
8730	**interino**-*adj; m*	interim; caretaker				
8733	**vinilo**-*m*	vinyl		8794	**moralista**-*m/f; adj*	moralist; moralistic
8734	**ovario**-*m*	ovary		8795	**descarte**-*m*	discard
8735	**multinacional**-*f; adj*	multinational; multinational		8796	**ovación**-*f*	ovation
				8800	**fauces**-*fpl*	maw
8737	**marimacho**-*m*	tomboy (coll)		8802	**enemistad**-*f*	enmity
8740	**requerimiento**-*m*	requirement		8803	**estepa**-*f*	steppe

8804	**pita**-*f*	pita
8805	**parienta**-*f*	wife (coll)
8807	**mote**-*m*	nickname
8809	**operario**-*m*	operator
8810	**originalidad**-*f*	originality
8811	**terminación**-*f*	termination
8812	**pupitre**-*m*	desk
8813	**gaita**-*f*	bagpipe
8815	**ápice**-*m*	apex
8816	**anfibio**-*adj; m*	amphibious; amphibian
8817	**teorema**-*m*	theorem
8819	**conjunción**-*f*	conjunction
8820	**remolacha**-*f*	beet
8821	**autónomo**-*adj; m*	autonomous; independent
8822	**incinerador**-*adj; m*	incinerating; incinerator
8825	**regresión**-*f*	regression
8827	**plástica**-*adj; f*	acrylic; plastic
8828	**volátil**-*adj; m*	volatile; volatility
8829	**segregación**-*f*	segregation
8830	**páncreas**-*m*	pancreas
8831	**ecosistema**-*m*	ecosystem
8832	**descontaminación**-*f*	decontamination
8833	**contestación**-*f*	reply
8837	**brebaje**-*m*	concoction
8838	**agitador**-*m*	agitator
8839	**caudillo**-*m*	leader
8840	**obstinación**-*f*	obstinacy
8842	**arrendamiento**-*m*	lease
8844	**rigidez**-*f*	rigidity
8845	**gaceta**-*f*	gazette
8846	**esguince**-*m*	sprain
8848	**bifurcación**-*f*	fork
8849	**jauría**-*f*	pack
8850	**anfiteatro**-*m*	amphitheater
8852	**natalidad**-*f*	birth rate
8856	**meteorólogo**-*m*	meteorologist
8857	**triciclo**-*m*	tricycle
8858	**semental**-*adj; m*	stud; stallion
8859	**clarividente**-*adj; m/f*	clairvoyant; psychic
8860	**trituradora**-*f*	crusher
8862	**materialista**-*adj; m/f*	materialistic; materialist
8863	**primate**-*m*	primate
8865	**anticonceptivo**-*adj; m*	contraceptive; birth control
8867	**diminutivo**-*adj; m*	diminutive; diminutive
8868	**baza**-*f*	asset
8870	**anticuario**-*m*	antique dealer
8871	**infusión**-*f*	infusion
8872	**austríaco**-*adj; m*	Austrian; Austrian person
8873	**huelguista**-*m/f*	striker
8874	**navegador**-*m*	browser, navigator
8877	**jacinto**-*m*	hyacinth
8878	**magnolia**-*f*	magnolia
8880	**cauce**-*m*	channel
8881	**gardenia**-*f*	gardenia
8882	**quid**-*m*	crux
8885	**narciso**-*m*	daffodil
8886	**insuficiencia**-*f*	insufficiency
8887	**poderío**-*m*	power
8888	**sumario**-*adj; m*	summary; investigation
8889	**cuña**-*f*	wedge
8894	**vértebra**-*f*	vertebra
8895	**traumatismo**-*m*	trauma
8896	**ascendencia**-*f*	ancestry
8897	**anticuerpo**-*m*	antibody
8898	**azafrán**-*m*	saffron
8899	**cachetada**-*f*	slap
8900	**tartamudo**-*m/f*	stutterer
8902	**abridor**-*m*	opener
8904	**curador**-*adj; m*	healing; curator
8905	**plática**-*f*	talk (LA)
8906	**decodificador**-*m*	decoder
8907	**fotocopiadora**-*f*	photocopier
8908	**rectoría**-*f*	rectory
8910	**festividad**-*f*	festivity
8913	**fanatismo**-*m*	fanaticism
8915	**proclamación**-*f*	proclamation
8916	**plebeyo**-*m; adj*	commoner; peasant
8917	**percance**-*m*	mishap
8919	**libertador**-*m; adj*	liberator; liberator
8920	**pirueta**-*f*	pirouette
8921	**costal**-*m*	bag
8922	**letrado**-*m; adj*	counsel; learned
8923	**donativo**-*m*	donation
8924	**pliegue**-*m*	crease
8925	**lucero**-*m*	bright star

8926	cacique-*m/f*	cacique
8927	yema-*f*	yolk
8928	charca-*f*	pond
8930	culminación-*f*	culmination
8931	comentarista-*m/f*	commentator
8932	garza-*f*	heron
8933	inercia-*f*	inertia
8934	embalaje-*m*	packaging
8935	cardiólogo-*m*	cardiologist
8936	irresponsabilidad-*f*	irresponsibility
8937	placenta-*f*	placenta
8938	orégano-*m*	oregano
8939	casete-*m/f*	cassette
8941	tilde-*f*	accent
8943	pesticida-*m*	pesticide
8947	satánico-*adj; m*	satanic; satanist
8948	asador-*m*	grill
8949	elegía-*f*	elegy
8950	cántico-*m*	chant
8951	perdigón-*m*	pellet
8953	ucraniano-*adj; m*	Ukrainian; Ukrainian person
8954	marejada-*f*	tidal wave
8955	feligrés-*m*	parishioner
8956	parra-*f*	vine
8957	taquigrafía-*f*	shorthand
8958	tanda-*f*	batch
8959	estampa-*f*	stamp
8960	brocha-*f*	brush
8961	quinina-*f*	quinine
8962	edredón-*m*	quilt
8963	nacionalismo-*m*	nationalism
8964	fundamentalista-*adj; m/f*	fundamentalist; fundamentalist
8971	nexo-*m*	nexus
8976	empanada-*f*	pie
8978	espermatozoide-*m*	spermatozoon
8979	cromosoma-*m*	chromosome
8980	telecomunicaciones-*fpl*	telecommunications
8983	física-*adj; f*	physical; physics
8984	cinematografía-*f*	cinematography
8987	cepo-*m*	trap
8989	superhombre-*m*	superman
8990	torácico-*adj; m*	thoracic; thoracic duct
8991	junco-*m*	reed

8993	pancarta-*f*	banner
8994	filtrado-*adj; m*	filtering; filter
9000	mirlo-*m*	blackbird
9005	balde-*m*	bucket
9006	perturbación-*f*	disturbance
9007	remisión-*f*	remission
9008	imposición-*f*	imposition
9009	permanencia-*f*	permanence
9011	níquel-*m*	nickel
9012	bidón-*m*	drum
9013	condimento-*m*	seasoning
9016	dogma-*m*	dogma
9017	culebra-*f*	snake
9020	curvatura-*f*	curvature
9021	inmigración-*f*	immigration
9022	quilombo-*m*	mess
9025	alfalfa-*f*	alfalfa
9026	epílogo-*f*	epilogue
9029	patriarca-*m*	patriarch
9030	isleño-*adj; m*	island; islander
9034	barítono-*m*	baritone
9035	aval-*m*	guarantee
9037	nogal-*m*	walnut
9038	acequia-*f*	ditch
9039	zanja-*f*	ditch
9040	bochorno-*m*	embarrassment
9041	aparejo-*m*	rig
9042	bilis-*f*	bile
9044	habichuela-*f*	bean
9045	andamio-*m*	scaffold
9048	minusválido-*adj; m*	disabled; disabled person
9050	prefijo-*m*	prefix
9051	ecología-*f*	ecology
9052	saudí-*adj; m/f*	Saudi; Saudi person
9054	abrelatas-*f*	can opener
9055	legislador-*adj; m*	legislative; legislator
9056	cupo-*m*	quota
9059	sedición-*f*	sedition
9064	vestigio-*m*	vestige
9065	periferia-*f*	periphery
9066	enagua-*f*	petticoat
9068	pamplinas-*fpl*	nonsense
9069	anaconda-*f*	anaconda
9071	electrodo-*m*	electrode
9072	auditoría-*f*	audit

9073	**relajo**-*m*	relax	
9075	**frutilla**-*f*	strawberry (LA)	
9076	**espora**-*f*	spore	
9079	**clausura**-*f*	closing	
9080	**anotador**-*m*	notepad (LA)	
9081	**opositor**-*m*	opponent	
9082	**laringe**-*f*	larynx	
9084	**planeamiento**-*m*	planning	
9085	**desperfecto**-*m*	flaw	
9087	**paladín**-*m*	paladin	
9088	**sindicalista**-*adj; m/f*	union; trade unionist	
9090	**puertorriqueño**-*adj; m*	Puerto Rican; Puerto Rican person	
9092	**interfaz**-*f*	interface	
9096	**penuria**-*f*	hardship	
9098	**argelino**-*adj; m*	Algerian; Algerian person	
9099	**ducado**-*m*	duchy	
9101	**estaño**-*m*	tin	
9105	**cónyuge**-*m/f*	spouse	
9110	**fiambre**-*m*	meat	
9111	**quilla**-*f*	keel	
9112	**conjuro**-*m*	spell	
9114	**fontanería**-*f*	plumbing	
9115	**banqueta**-*f*	stool	
9120	**cojera**-*f*	limp	
9121	**carabinero**-*m*	policeman	
9124	**albornoz**-*m*	bathrobe	
9125	**laborista**-*adj; m*	Labour; Labor Party member	
9126	**propagación**-*f*	spreading	
9127	**bisagra**-*f*	hinge	
9128	**estrangulación**-*f*	strangulation	
9131	**amplitud**-*f*	extent	
9132	**gimnasta**-*m/f*	gymnast	
9133	**criminalidad**-*f*	criminality	
9134	**bombeo**-*m*	pumping	
9135	**bengalí**-*adj; m/f*	Bengali; Bengali person	
9138	**asesoría**-*f*	advice	
9142	**ciudadela**-*f*	citadel	
9143	**fechoría**-*f*	piece of mischief	
9146	**esbozo**-*m*	outline	
9147	**mirador**-*m*	viewpoint	
9149	**debutante**-*adj; m/f*	debut; debutante	
9150	**voltereta**-*f*	somersault	
9152	**difteria**-*f*	diphtheria	
9153	**ricachón**-*f*	rich man (coll)	
9154	**metodista**-*adj; m/f*	Methodist; Methodist	
9155	**conmemoración**-*f*	commemoration	
9156	**poblado**-*adj; m*	populated; village	
9157	**aguacate**-*m*	avocado	
9158	**bonanza**-*f*	bonanza	
9168	**amoníaco**-*m; adj*	ammonia; ammonia	
9170	**concesionario**-*m*	concessionaire	
9171	**afiche**-*m*	poster	
9172	**albahaca**-*f*	basil	
9173	**transportación**-*f*	transportation	
9174	**penitenciario**-*adj; m*	penitentiary; prison	
9175	**transformador**-*m*	transformer	
9176	**posgrado**-*m; adj*	postgraduate degree; postgraduate	
9177	**atrio**-*m*	atrium	
9179	**integrante**-*adj; m/f*	integral; member	
9181	**bocanada**-*f*	breath	
9182	**persistencia**-*f*	persistence	
9186	**varilla**-*f*	rod	
9189	**deshielo**-*m*	thaw	
9191	**rodillo**-*m*	roller	
9196	**tópico**-*m; adj*	cliche; topical	
9197	**trazo**-*m*	stroke	
9198	**complemento**-*m*	complement	
9201	**hule**-*m*	oilcloth	
9202	**envergadura**-*f*	scale	
9203	**enjuague**-*m*	rinse	
9205	**imposibilidad**-*f*	impossibility	
9206	**exclusión**-*f*	exclusion	
9208	**chileno**-*adj; m*	Chilean; Chilean person	
9209	**transparencia**-*f*	transparency	
9210	**garrapata**-*f*	tick	
9211	**cabezazo**-*m*	header	
9212	**kurdo**-*adj; m*	Kurdish; Kurdish person	
9213	**piropo**-*m*	compliment	
9214	**revestimiento**-*m*	coating	
9217	**esmero**-*m*	care	
9221	**folclore**-*m*	folklore	
9222	**supresión**-*f*	suppression	
9223	**náufrago**-*m/f*	castaway	
9227	**boicot**-*m*	boycott	
9229	**comitiva**-*f*	motorcade	

9233	**emplazamiento**-*m*	site
9236	**encuadre**-*m*	framing
9239	**cazatalentos**-*m/f*	talent scout
9240	**navegante**-*m/f*	navigator
9241	**fisiología**-*f*	physiology
9242	**esternón**-*m*	sternum
9243	**acupuntura**-*f*	acupuncture
9244	**simposio**-*m*	symposium
9245	**urbanismo**-*m*	town planning
9247	**magma**-*m*	magma
9249	**subsecretario**-*m*	undersecretary
9255	**despilfarro**-*m*	waste
9256	**valoración**-*f*	assessment
9258	**degeneración**-*f*	degeneration
9259	**inmoralidad**-*f*	immorality
9260	**tenencia**-*f*	possession
9261	**celuloide**-*m*	celluloid
9262	**escepticismo**-*m*	skepticism
9263	**catedral**-*f*	cathedral
9265	**escaramuza**-*f*	skirmish
9266	**coreógrafo**-*m*	choreographer
9267	**calza**-*f*	wedge
9269	**galeón**-*m*	galleon
9270	**berenjena**-*f*	eggplant
9271	**tablilla**-*f*	clipboard
9272	**alusión**-*f*	allusion
9273	**presentimiento**-*m*	feeling
9274	**pescadería**-*f*	fish market
9277	**panal**-*m*	honeycomb
9278	**surco**-*m*	groove
9282	**jesuita**-*adj; m/f*	Jesuit; Jesuit
9284	**aorta**-*f*	aorta
9285	**comadre**-*f*	close friend (coll) (LA), midwife (coll) (ES)
9287	**experimentación**-*f*	experimentation
9289	**tríada**-*f*	triad
9291	**lactosa**-*f*	lactose
9292	**maña**-*f*	skill
9293	**cuaresma**-*f*	Lent
9295	**púlpito**-*m*	pulpit
9296	**ultramar**-*m*	overseas
9298	**esclerosis**-*f*	sclerosis
9299	**tintura**-*f*	dye
9300	**traspaso**-*m*	transfer
9301	**fragilidad**-*f*	fragility

9302	**purga**-*f*	purge
9303	**lamentación**-*f*	lamentation
9305	**carretero**-*m*	chimney
9307	**pesimismo**-*m*	pessimism
9308	**microchip**-*m*	microchip
9312	**repugnancia**-*f*	disgust
9314	**ego**-*m*	ego
9315	**flotación**-*f*	flotation
9316	**troyano**-*adj; m*	Trojan; Trojan horse
9318	**aleación**-*f*	alloy
9319	**bronceador**-*m*	tanning lotion
9320	**anterioridad**-*f*	previous
9322	**alejamiento**-*m*	removal
9323	**diana**-*f*	target
9324	**legislatura**-*f*	legislature
9327	**recelo**-*m*	suspicion
9328	**veracidad**-*f*	veracity
9329	**oruga**-*f*	caterpillar
9330	**morro**-*m*	snout
9332	**mosaico**-*adj; m*	mosaic; mosaic
9333	**ciclismo**-*m*	cycling
9334	**estratagema**-*f*	stratagem
9335	**subsistencia**-*f*	subsistence
9337	**vocalista**-*m/f*	vocalist
9340	**pantorrilla**-*f*	calf
9342	**deposición**-*f*	deposition
9343	**tendón**-*m*	tendon
9345	**perico**-*m*	parakeet
9348	**sangría**-*f*	indentation, sangria
9349	**reanimación**-*f*	revival
9350	**candela**-*f*	candle
9351	**látex**-*m*	latex
9352	**diálisis**-*f*	dialysis
9353	**sinapsis**-*f*	synapse
9356	**vaivén**-*m*	swinging
9357	**designio**-*m*	plan
9358	**fulgor**-*m*	brightness
9362	**sustitución**-*f*	substitution
9363	**biombo**-*m*	screen
9364	**yunque**-*m*	anvil
9367	**discrepancia**-*f*	discrepancy
9370	**arrebato**-*m*	outburst
9372	**meteorología**-*f*	meteorology
9373	**precipitación**-*f*	precipitation
9374	**malversación**-*f*	embezzlement

9376	**croata**-*adj; m/f*	Croatian; Croatian person	
9377	**sabandija**-*f*	bug, scoundrel (coll)	
9380	**relieve**-*m*	importance, topography	
9387	**rating**-*m*	rating	
9388	**remodelación**-*f*	remodeling	
9389	**ecologista**-*m/f; adj*	ecologist; environmental	
9390	**ambigüedad**-*f*	ambiguity	
9397	**malabarista**-*m/f*	juggler	
9398	**incubadora**-*f*	incubator	
9400	**losa**-*f*	slab	
9401	**carrocería**-*f*	bodywork	
9404	**índole**-*f*	nature	
9406	**reclutador**-*m*	recruiter	
9407	**felino**-*adj; m*	feline; feline	
9408	**agrupación**-*f*	group	
9412	**oleoducto**-*m*	pipeline	
9413	**directriz**-*f*	guideline	
9415	**guijarro**-*m*	pebble	
9416	**meningitis**-*f*	meningitis	
9417	**saturación**-*f*	saturation	
9419	**ebriedad**-*f*	drunkenness	
9421	**tedio**-*m*	tedium	
9422	**norteño**-*adj; m*	northern; northerner	
9423	**justiciero**-*adj; m*	tough; vigilante	
9424	**provinciano**-*adj; m*	provincial; provincial	
9427	**evangelista**-*m/f*	evangelist	
9428	**asunción**-*f*	assumption	
9430	**flotador**-*m*	float	
9433	**gala**-*f*	gala	
9437	**especialización**-*f*	specialization	
9439	**forraje**-*m*	forage	
9441	**puchero**-*m*	pot	
9445	**feudo**-*m*	fief	
9446	**langostino**-*m*	prawn	
9447	**vencimiento**-*m*	expiration	
9448	**contaminante**-*adj; m*	pollutant; contaminant	
9450	**dialéctica**-*f*	dialectic	
9452	**fémur**-*m*	femur	
9455	**examinador**-*m*	examiner	
9457	**congestión**-*f*	congestion	
9458	**liposucción**-*f*	liposuction	

9459	**parlamentario**-*adj; m*	parliamentary; Member of Parliament	
9461	**convocatoria**-*f*	call	
9462	**boticario**-*m*	apothecary	
9467	**contratación**-*f*	recruitment	
9468	**barómetro**-*m*	barometer	
9469	**achicoria**-*f*	chicory	
9470	**intendencia**-*f*	quartermaster	
9471	**censor**-*adj; m*	censorial; censor	
9472	**referí**-*m*	referee	
9473	**predisposición**-*f*	predisposition	
9475	**medición**-*f*	measurement	
9477	**catedrático**-*m*	professor	
9478	**refinamiento**-*m*	refinement	
9479	**ascuas**-*fpl*	embers	
9482	**estanco**-*adj; m*	watertight; shop	
9488	**cronograma**-*m*	timeline	
9491	**antropólogo**-*m*	anthropologist	
9493	**sacristía**-*f*	sacristy	
9494	**mediación**-*f*	mediation	
9495	**membrana**-*f*	membrane	
9496	**colocación**-*f*	placement	
9499	**castración**-*f*	castration	
9501	**hebilla**-*f*	buckle	
9502	**inanición**-*f*	starvation	
9503	**cedro**-*m*	cedar	
9504	**sotavento**-*m*	leeward	
9506	**repulsión**-*f*	repulsion	
9508	**parábola**-*f*	parable	
9509	**jornalero**-*m*	day laborer	
9511	**deslizamiento**-*m*	slide	
9513	**tarántula**-*f*	tarantula	
9517	**glorieta**-*f*	roundabout	
9519	**consolación**-*f*	consolation	
9520	**urticaria**-*f*	hives	
9521	**follaje**-*m*	foliage	
9523	**calentura**-*f*	fever, cold sore	
9525	**yacimiento**-*m*	deposit, field	
9526	**cajetilla**-*f*	pack	
9527	**garbanzo**-*m*	chickpea	
9528	**utilización**-*f*	utilization	
9529	**brillantez**-*f*	brilliance	
9532	**ensamblaje**-*m*	assembly	
9533	**afroamericano**-*adj; M*	Afro-American; African-American person	

9535	**inseminación**-*f*	insemination
9536	**obesidad**-*f*	obesity
9537	**patín**-*m*	skate
9538	**legionario**-*adj; m*	legionary; legionnaire
9539	**cayado**-*m*	crook
9541	**doctrina**-*f*	doctrine
9542	**especulador**-*m*	speculator
9543	**impresor**-*adj; m*	printing; printer
9546	**tinglado**-*m*	racket
9548	**cédula**-*f*	document
9552	**avellana**-*adj; f*	hazelnut; hazelnut
9553	**exclamación**-*f*	exclamation
9554	**catéter**-*m*	catheter
9555	**dramatismo**-*m*	drama
9556	**cañada**-*f*	glen
9557	**aclaración**-*f*	clarification
9559	**bolero**-*adj; m*	liar (coll); bolero
9560	**denominador**-*m*	denominator
9561	**compulsión**-*f*	compulsion
9562	**efectividad**-*f*	effectiveness
9564	**napolitano**-*adj; m*	Neapolitan; Neapolitan person
9565	**disidente**-*adj; m*	dissident; dissident
9568	**celo**-*m*	zeal, tape
9569	**biotecnología**-*f*	biotechnology
9570	**dueto**-*m*	duet
9571	**sifón**-*m*	siphon
9572	**irregularidad**-*f*	irregularity
9573	**perseguidor**-*m*	pursuer
9574	**magnificencia**-*f*	magnificence
9579	**desagrado**-*m*	displeasure
9581	**cordel**-*m*	string
9584	**guinda**-*f*	cherry, final touch
9585	**disponibilidad**-*f*	availability
9586	**catapulta**-*f*	catapult
9588	**disimulo**-*m*	disguise
9589	**cúmulo**-*m*	cluster
9590	**cómoda**-*f*	chest of drawers
9591	**exención**-*f*	exemption
9592	**lapsus**-*m*	lapse
9593	**papelería**-*f*	stationery
9596	**trilogía**-*f*	trilogy
9599	**bulimia**-*f*	bulimia
9600	**lentitud**-*f*	slowness
9604	**sintaxis**-*f*	syntax
9607	**compañerismo**-*m*	fellowship
9608	**explanada**-*f*	esplanade
9609	**kiosco**-*m*	kiosk
9614	**desintegración**-*f*	disintegration
9615	**desengaño**-*m*	disappointment
9617	**trasfondo**-*m*	background
9618	**efigie**-*f*	effigy
9619	**alboroto**-*m*	fuss
9620	**tráquea**-*f*	trachea
9623	**prepucio**-*m*	foreskin
9624	**amputación**-*f*	amputation
9627	**pulsación**-*f*	pulse
9628	**ramificación**-*f*	branch
9629	**litigio**-*m*	litigation
9631	**privatización**-*f*	privatization
9633	**quitanieves**-*m*	snowplow
9634	**cuadrícula**-*f*	grid
9637	**higuera**-*f*	fig tree
9638	**confección**-*f*	making, clothing
9640	**absorción**-*f*	absorption
9641	**edicto**-*m*	edict
9646	**endemoniado**-*adj; m*	possessed; devil
9647	**sima**-*f*	chasm
9650	**emigrante**-*adj; m/f*	emigrant; emigrant
9651	**modernidad**-*f*	modernity
9653	**mazorca**-*f*	corncob
9654	**contraespionaje**-*m*	counterintelligence
9656	**invariable**-*adj; m*	unchanging; unchanged
9658	**leño**-*m*	log
9659	**tenista**-*m/f*	tennis player
9660	**factoría**-*f*	factory
9662	**ranking**-*m*	ranking
9663	**meollo**-*m*	crux
9664	**monografía**-*f*	monograph
9665	**prerrogativa**-*f*	prerogative
9666	**cobalto**-*m*	cobalt
9667	**cabrito**-*adj; m*	lousy (coll); young goat
9668	**reorganización**-*f*	reorganization
9669	**slip**-*m*	briefs (LA)
9672	**preámbulo**-*m*	preamble
9673	**repatriación**-*f*	repatriation
9676	**laúd**-*m*	lute
9677	**almacenaje**-*m*	storage
9681	**desigualdad**-*f*	inequality

9682	**sinfín**-*m*	myriad	
9684	**doblaje**-*m*	dubbing	
9685	**reguero**-*m*	trail	
9687	**surgimiento**-*m*	appearance	
9689	**racimo**-*m*	bunch	
9691	**comité**-*m*	committee	
9692	**rompimiento**-*m*	breakup	
9693	**genoma**-*m*	genome	
9698	**reivindicación**-*f*	demand	
9700	**desembarque**-*m*	unloading	
9701	**mensualidad**-*f*	monthly wage	
9704	**asbesto**-*m*	asbestos	
9705	**humorista**-*m/f*	humorist	
9707	**tótem**-*m*	totem	
9708	**tarima**-*f*	stage	
9709	**deslealtad**-*f*	disloyalty	
9713	**autocar**-*m*	coach	
9714	**perforación**-*f*	drilling	
9715	**toronja**-*f*	grapefruit	
9716	**frazada**-*f*	blanket	
9717	**emporio**-*m*	emporium	
9725	**incredulidad**-*f*	disbelief	
9726	**descompresión**-*f*	decompression	
9727	**referéndum**-*m*	referendum	
9728	**mogollón**-*m; adv*	lots of (coll); loads	
9729	**comercialización**-*f*	marketing	
9734	**penalti**-*m*	penalty	
9735	**estría**-*f*	stretch mark	
9737	**legitimidad**-*f*	legitimacy	
9738	**neurocirugía**-*f*	neurosurgery	
9739	**impulsor**-*adj; m*	active; booster	
9740	**izquierdista**-*adj; m/f*	leftist; leftist	
9741	**incubación**-*m/f*	incubation	
9742	**norcoreano**-*adj; m*	North Korean; North Korean person	
9744	**narcisismo**-*m*	narcissism	
9746	**compresor**-*m*	compressor	
9748	**papeleta**-*f*	ballot	
9749	**tribulación**-*f*	tribulation	
9751	**soto**-*m*	grove	
9752	**ojal**-*m*	buttonhole	
9753	**estocada**-*f*	thrust	
9754	**aureola**-*f*	halo	
9756	**antesala**-*f*	anteroom	
9757	**solomillo**-*m*	sirloin	
9758	**liquidez**-*f*	liquidity	
9760	**sinusitis**-*f*	sinusitis	
9761	**bloc**-*m*	pad	
9763	**bagre**-*m*	catfish	
9764	**alhaja**-*f*	jewel	
9765	**hincapié**-*m*	emphasis	
9766	**certificación**-*f*	certification	
9768	**omisión**-*f*	omission	
9769	**profesionalismo**-*m*	professionalism	
9770	**rapaz**-*adj; m*	predatory; kid	
9773	**ion**-*m*	ion	
9776	**capitulación**-*f*	capitulation	
9777	**radiología**-*f*	radiology	
9780	**procreación**-*f*	procreation	
9782	**diferencial**-*adj; f*	differential; gap	
9785	**iguana**-*f*	iguana	
9786	**enfisema**-*m*	emphysema	
9788	**geriátrico**-*adj; m*	geriatric; nursing home	
9790	**alberca**-*f*	swimming	
9791	**mensajería**-*f*	messaging	
9794	**antifaz**-*m*	mask	
9795	**adepto**-*adj; m*	adept; follower	
9797	**estupor**-*m*	stupor	
9798	**pentagrama**-*m*	pentagram	
9800	**contemplación**-*f*	contemplation	
9801	**abecedario**-*m*	alphabet	
9803	**lira**-*f*	lyre	
9804	**maquinilla**-*f*	razor	
9805	**transatlántico**-*adj; m*	transatlantic; ocean liner	
9806	**compatibilidad**-*f*	compatibility	
9810	**mandolina**-*f*	mandolin	
9811	**albacea**-*m/f*	executor	
9813	**retoque**-*m*	finishing touch	
9814	**tomillo**-*m*	thyme	
9815	**trivialidad**-*f*	triviality	
9817	**terraplén**-*m*	embankment	
9819	**estabilizador**-*adj; m*	stabilising; stabilizer	
9822	**capilar**-*adj; m*	capillary; hair	
9823	**desfalco**-*m*	embezzlement	
9824	**arriendo**-*m*	rent	
9827	**colector**-*m*	collector	
9828	**coherencia**-*f*	coherence	
9829	**mímica**-*f*	mime	
9830	**fleco**-*m*	fringe	
9831	**separatista**-*adj; m/f*	separatist; separatist	

9833	**sintetizador**-*m*	synthesizer
9834	**lumbago**-*m*	lumbago
9835	**partición**-*f*	allocation, partition
9836	**ganado**-*m*	cattle
9837	**dominicano**-*adj; m*	Dominican; Dominican person
9838	**pretexto**-*m*	pretext
9841	**secesión**-*f*	secession
9842	**divisa**-*f*	currency
9843	**incumplimiento**-*m*	breach
9844	**sadismo**-*m*	sadism
9845	**introvertido**-*adj; m*	introverted; introvert
9846	**axila**-*f*	armpit
9847	**escalador**-*m*	climber
9849	**hendidura**-*f*	indent
9850	**bombazo**-*m*	bomb
9851	**metodología**-*f*	methodology
9852	**agudeza**-*f*	sharpness
9855	**bandolero**-*m*	bandit
9856	**estiramiento**-*m*	stretching
9860	**bostezo**-*m*	yawn
9861	**variante**-*adj; f*	alternative; variant
9863	**edema**-*m*	edema
9864	**cartílago**-*m*	cartilage
9865	**inhalación**-*f*	inhalation
9866	**marrano**-*adj; m*	disgusting (coll); pig
9868	**sumidero**-*m*	sink
9869	**contingencia**-*f*	contingency
9871	**reestructuración**-*f*	restructuring
9872	**liberalismo**-*m*	liberalism
9875	**reunificación**-*f*	reunification
9876	**defensiva**-*m*	defensive
9877	**destinatario**-*m*	recipient
9878	**indecisión**-*f*	indecision
9879	**equidad**-*f*	equity
9881	**facturación**-*f*	billing
9882	**astronómico**-*f*	astronomical
9884	**borrego**-*m*	lamb, simple-minded (coll)
9887	**temática**-*adj; f*	thematic; theme
9890	**pulpa**-*f*	pulp
9891	**desprendimiento**-*m*	detachment, openhandedness, landslide
9892	**parafernalia**-*f*	paraphernalia
9895	**acueducto**-*m*	aqueduct
9899	**cosmopolita**-*adj; m*	cosmopolitan; cosmopolitan
9902	**quintal**-*m*	hundredweight
9904	**quiebra**-*f*	bankruptcy
9905	**profesorado**-*m*	faculty
9906	**individualismo**-*m*	individualism
9907	**erizo**-*m*	hedgehog
9908	**costra**-*f*	scab
9909	**antiséptico**-*adj; m*	antiseptic; antiseptic
9910	**transeúnte**-*m*	passerby
9912	**inducción**-*f*	induction
9913	**desempate**-*m*	tiebreaker
9914	**reingreso**-*m*	re-entry
9915	**espátula**-*f*	spatula
9916	**taquicardia**-*f*	tachycardia
9918	**peruano**-*adj; m*	Peruvian; Peruvian person
9919	**convergencia**-*f*	convergence
9920	**arbitraje**-*m*	arbitration
9921	**placebo**-*m*	placebo
9922	**negatividad**-*f*	negativity
9923	**marcapasos**-*m*	pacemaker
9924	**algoritmo**-*m*	algorithm
9925	**orina**-*f*	urine
9926	**anormalidad**-*f*	abnormality
9927	**fluctuación**-*f*	fluctuation
9928	**barbitúrico**-*m; adj*	barbiturate; barbiturate
9929	**basílica**-*f*	basilica
9930	**pontífice**-*m*	pontiff
9932	**desnutrición**-*f*	malnutrition
9935	**esquí**-*m*	ski
9936	**alcantarillado**-*m*	sewerage
9939	**helecho**-*m*	fern
9941	**oratorio**-*m*	oratory
9942	**masilla**-*f*	putty
9943	**inactividad**-*f*	inactivity
9944	**autoritario**-*adj; m*	authoritarian; authoritarian
9945	**canasto**-*m*	basket
9946	**modalidad**-*f*	mode
9947	**concordia**-*f*	concord
9948	**profesionalidad**-*f*	professionalism
9951	**entereza**-*f*	strength
9955	**puercoespín**-*m*	porcupine
9956	**artificio**-*m*	artifice
9960	**cántaro**-*m*	pitcher

9961	**determinante-**_adj; m_	determinant; determinant
9963	**eucalipto-**_m_	eucalyptus
9964	**extinguidor-**_m_	extinguisher
9966	**capacitación-**_f_	training
9967	**desorientación-**_f_	disorientation
9969	**ultrasonido-**_m_	ultrasound
9971	**tintero-**_m_	inkwell
9972	**cascanueces-**_m_	nutcracker
9973	**sulfato-**_m_	sulfate
9977	**largometraje-**_m_	feature film
9979	**desgarro-**_m_	tear
9980	**espinazo-**_m_	spine
9986	**exaltación-**_f_	exaltation
9987	**muñón-**_m_	stump
9990	**tórtola-**_f_	turtledove
9993	**expectación-**_f_	expectation
9995	**falange-**_f_	phalange
10001	**inconsciencia-**_f_	unconsciousness
10002	**compresa-**_f_	compress
10004	**galgo-**_m_	greyhound
10007	**altruista-**_adj; m/f_	altruistic; altruist
10008	**poblador-**_m_	villager
10009	**deformación-**_f_	deformation
10011	**elasticidad-**_f_	elasticity
10013	**materialismo-**_m_	materialism
10014	**atrofia-**_f_	atrophy
10015	**terminología-**_f_	terminology
10017	**puerro-**_m_	leek
10020	**dilatación-**_f_	dilation
10023	**silicio-**_m_	silicon
10024	**mariguana-**_f_	marijuana
10025	**escrutinio-**_m_	scrutiny

Numerals

Rank	Spanish-*PoS*	Translation(s)
7995	**veintiséis**-*num*	twenty-six
8262	**ochocientos**-*num*	eight hundred
8282	**setecientos**-*num*	seven hundred
8345	**vigésimo**-*num*	twentieth
8407	**veintinueve**-*num*	twenty-nine
9984	**undécimo**-*num*	eleventh

Verbs

Rank	Spanish-PoS	Translation(s)
7501	urgir-*vb*	press
7502	chantajear-*vb*	blackmail
7508	zurrar-*vb*	spank
7510	alegar-*vb*	claim
7511	estrenar-*vb*	use for the first time
7519	relevar-*vb*	relieve, substitute
7526	alistar(se)-*vb*	enlist
7529	tumbar(se)-*vb*	knock down; lay down
7534	aferrarse-*vbr*	cling to
7553	invocar-*vb*	invoke
7556	desatar-*vb*	untie
7559	exiliar-*vb*	exile
7564	engendrar-*vb*	engender
7585	anhelar-*vb*	yearn for
7589	desorientar-*vb*	disorient
7590	redactar-*vb*	write
7594	pasmar-*vb*	astound
7598	ayunar-*vb*	fast
7601	comparecer-*vb*	appear
7604	persistir-*vb*	persist
7606	horrorizar(se)-*vb*	horrify
7607	multiplicar(se)-*vb*	multiply
7608	excluir-*vb*	exclude
7610	adelgazar-*vb*	lose weight
7618	uniformar-*vb*	standardize
7621	enganchar-*vb*	hook
7625	deportar-*vb*	deport
7630	formular-*vb*	formulate
7636	calar-*vb*	seep through, sink in
7640	influenciar-*vb*	influence
7642	equilibrar-*vb*	balance
7657	respaldar-*vb*	support
7658	debilitar-*vb*	weaken
7662	desordenar-*vb*	make a mess of
7663	pitar-*vb*	whistle
7666	machacar-*vb*	crush
7671	alargar-*vb*	lengthen
7672	platicar-*vb*	talk (LA)
7673	confinar-*vb*	confine
7675	desfilar-*vb*	parade
7681	desmoronar(se)-*vb*	collapse
7683	subordinar-*vb*	subordinate
7688	abarcar-*vb*	encompass
7689	divulgar-*vb*	divulge
7691	consagrar-*vb*	enshrine
7696	errar-*vb*	err
7699	regir-*vb*	govern
7702	figurar-*vb*	include
7704	frotar-*vb*	rub
7705	disolver-*vb*	dissolve
7706	refrescar-*vb*	refresh
7713	deparar-*vb*	bring
7718	agachar(se)-*vb*	duck
7720	lesionar-*vb*	injure
7722	desconfiar-*vb*	distrust
7724	incapacitar-*vb*	incapacitate
7727	maniobrar-*vb*	maneuver
7743	moler-*vb*	grind
7753	recaer-*vb*	relapse
7762	moderar-*vb*	moderate
7766	aniquilar-*vb*	annihilate
7769	volcar-*vb*	dump
7776	regatear-*vb; m*	haggle; haggling
7778	estornudar-*vb*	sneeze
7781	intrigar-*vb*	intrigue
7783	neutralizar-*vb*	neutralize
7784	originar-*vb*	originate
7785	duchar(se)-*vb*	shower
7787	conciliar-*vb*	reconcile
7794	aplazar-*vb*	postpone
7801	arar-*vb*	plow
7803	alentar-*vb*	encourage
7805	escarmentar-*vb*	punish severely
7807	hornear-*vb*	bake
7808	retardar-*vb*	slow down
7816	vacilar-*vb*	tease, hesitate
7817	colapsar-*vb*	collapse
7819	comprimir-*vb*	compress
7821	alojar-*vb*	accommodate
7830	emborrachar(se)-*vb*	get drunk
7845	acortar-*vb*	shorten
7854	pulsar-*vb*	press
7856	profundizar-*vb*	deepen
7868	ejercitar-*vb*	exercise
7870	roncar-*vb*	snore
7879	desquiciar-*vb*	make to despair
7882	sobrevolar-*vb*	fly over
7889	exhibir-*vb*	display

7890	**desplomar(se)**-*vb*	collapse	8105	**verter**-*vb*	pour
7891	**tintar**-*vb*	dye	8108	**inaugurar**-*vb*	inaugurate
7899	**potar**-*vb*	puke (coll)	8118	**contagiar**-*vb*	infect
7909	**desgarrar**-*vb*	tear	8119	**triplicar**-*vb*	triple
7910	**atenerse a**-*vbr*	abide by	8120	**reabrir**-*vb*	reopen
7914	**deliberar**-*vb*	deliberate	8128	**fatigar**-*vb*	exhaust
7915	**rayar**-*vb*	scratch	8129	**exceptuar**-*vb*	exclude
7920	**parpadear**-*vb*	blink	8133	**extinguir**-*vb*	extinguish
7922	**desanimar**-*vb*	discourage	8135	**indagar**-*vb*	investigate
7925	**asimilar**-*vb*	assimilate	8138	**reconfortar**-*vb*	comfort
7927	**despistar**-*vb*	mislead	8149	**cojear**-*vb*	limp
7929	**resonar**-*vb*	resonate	8150	**perdurar**-*vb*	endure
7932	**inscribir**-*vb*	register	8159	**contradecir**-*vb*	contradict
7941	**abundar**-*vb*	be plentiful, elaborate	8169	**enrollar**-*vb*	roll
7942	**vincular**-*vb*	link	8171	**cablear**-*vb*	wire
7944	**documentar**-*vb*	document	8173	**conmemorar**-*vb*	commemorate
7947	**detestar**-*vb*	loathe	8177	**concretar**-*vb*	specify
7950	**excusar**-*vb*	excuse	8182	**transcurrir**-*vb*	elapse
7954	**erradicar**-*vb*	eradicate	8199	**desequilibrar**-*vb*	unbalance
7956	**envasar**-*vb*	package	8205	**contraatacar**-*vb*	fight back
7965	**entablar**-*vb*	enter into	8207	**masticar**-*vb*	chew
7969	**consumar**-*vb*	consummate	8216	**predestinar**-*vb*	predestine
7970	**suavizar**-*vb*	soften	8224	**exceder**-*vb*	exceed
7971	**brotar**-*vb*	sprout	8230	**rebotar**-*vb*	bounce
7981	**almacenar**-*vb*	store	8254	**medicar**-*vb*	medicate
7986	**desplegar**-*vb*	deploy	8255	**babear**-*vb*	drool
7988	**idear**-*vb*	devise	8258	**aparear**-*vb*	mate
7992	**nominar**-*vb*	nominate	8264	**arribar**-*vb*	arrive
7998	**sepultar**-*vb*	bury	8270	**desempeñar**-*vb*	perform
8013	**duplicar**-*vb*	double	8280	**arrodillar(se)**-*vb*	kneel
8016	**degradar**-*vb*	degrade	8281	**enjaular**-*vb*	cage
8022	**encariñarse**-*vbr*	grow fond of	8287	**podrir**-*vb*	rot
8026	**rentar**-*vb*	rent	8288	**aderezar**-*vb*	season
8027	**ensuciar(se)**-*vb*	mess	8289	**balancear(se)**-*vb*	balance
8031	**subestimar**-*vb*	underestimate	8290	**obrar**-*vb*	act
8032	**perfeccionar**-*vb*	perfect	8302	**fotocopiar**-*vb*	photocopy
8045	**planificar**-*vb*	plan	8303	**suspirar**-*vb*	sigh
8054	**acontecer**-*vb*	happen	8308	**suministrar**-*vb*	supply
8065	**costear**-*vb*	finance	8309	**hospitalizar**-*vb*	hospitalize
8069	**entrometerse**-*vbr*	interfere	8322	**corretear**-*vb*	run around
8071	**reescribir**-*vb*	rewrite	8336	**brincar**-*vb*	jump
8074	**estancar(se)**-*vb*	stall	8346	**entrometer(se)**-*vb*	interfere
8082	**bombear**-*vb*	pump	8348	**resaltar**-*vb*	highlight
8087	**notificar**-*vb*	notify	8350	**desalojar**-*vb*	evict
8097	**promocionar**-*vb*	promote	8354	**premiar**-*vb*	reward
8104	**conspirar**-*vb*	conspire	8357	**reprochar**-*vb*	reproach

8364	**peinar(se)**-*vb*	comb your hair	8612	**pisotear**-*vb*	trample
8372	**estereotipar**-*vb*	stereotype	8616	**fomentar**-*vb*	foster
8377	**conmocionar**-*vb*	shake profoundly	8617	**abolir**-*vb*	abolish
8382	**peligrar**-*vb*	endanger	8637	**rascar**-*vb*	scratch
8383	**resfriarse**-*vbr*	catch a cold	8645	**contrarrestar**-*vb*	counter
8399	**deambular**-*vb*	wander	8651	**gruñir**-*vb*	growl
8409	**solapar**-*vb*	overlap	8656	**purificar**-*vb*	purify
8410	**habituar(se)**-*vb*	get in the habit of	8657	**benévolo**-*vb*	benevolent
8431	**apresar**-*vb*	apprehend	8659	**enriquecer(se)**-*vb*	enrich
8434	**traspasar**-*vb*	cross, hand over	8666	**abarrotar**-*vb*	pack
8438	**abrigar(se)**-*vb*	shelter, keep warm	8672	**pastar**-*vb*	graze
8441	**pringar(se)**-*vb*	drizzle (LA), work hard (coll), stain	8675	**roer**-*vb*	gnaw
			8676	**agredir**-*vb*	assault
8444	**incorporar**-*vb*	incorporate	8688	**desnudar(se)**-*vb*	undress
8463	**incitar**-*vb*	incite	8692	**movilizar**-*vb*	mobilize
8469	**simplificar**-*vb*	simplify	8702	**afinar**-*vb*	tune
8471	**chinchar**-*vb*	tease	8704	**patrocinar**-*vb*	sponsor
8473	**amparar**-*vb*	protect	8708	**diagnosticar**-*vb*	diagnose
8477	**reanudar**-*vb*	resume	8715	**infestar**-*vb*	infest
8479	**albergar**-*vb*	host	8719	**desconcertar**-*vb*	perplex
8482	**descalificar**-*vb*	disqualify	8720	**tambalearse**-*vbr*	stagger
8484	**propagar**-*vb*	spread	8726	**asemejar(se)**-*vb*	resemble
8485	**clamar**-*vb*	clamour for	8731	**minimizar**-*vb*	minimise
8489	**sobresalir**-*vb*	excel	8732	**especializar**-*vb*	specialize
8496	**encoger**-*vb*	shrink	8738	**compactar**-*vb*	compact
8498	**rifar**-*vb*	raffle	8745	**derivar**-*vb*	derive
8518	**inyectar**-*vb*	inject	8747	**frecuentar**-*vb*	frequent
8530	**asentar(se)**-*vb*	settle	8760	**exprimir**-*vb*	squeeze
8531	**socializar**-*vb*	socialize	8762	**avistar**-*vb*	sight
8536	**plagiar**-*vb*	plagiarise	8786	**filtrar**-*vb*	filter
8543	**encomendar**-*vb*	entrust	8787	**protagonizar**-*vb*	star in
8545	**atestiguar**-*vb*	testify	8790	**matricular(se)**-*vb*	enroll
8552	**dificultar**-*vb*	hinder	8799	**sucumbir**-*vb*	succumb
8563	**murmurar**-*vb*	murmur	8806	**archivar**-*vb*	file
8567	**rebajar**-*vb*	reduce	8808	**bosquejar**-*vb*	sketch
8570	**desfigurar**-*vb*	disfigure	8814	**marginar**-*vb*	marginalize
8572	**tontear**-*vb*	flirt (coll), fool around (coll)	8826	**sobrellevar**-*vb*	endure
			8834	**despojar(se)**-*vb*	strip
8574	**actualizar**-*vb*	update	8835	**apremiar**-*vb*	hurry
8576	**menear**-*vb*	shake	8841	**atañer**-*vb*	concern
8577	**asfixiar**-*vb*	choke	8843	**despachar**-*vb*	dispatch
8578	**privar**-*vb*	deprive	8851	**empaquetar**-*vb*	pack
8586	**emigrar**-*vb*	emigrate	8869	**atestar**-*vb*	attest
8599	**precintar**-*vb*	seal	8875	**encabezar**-*vb*	lead
8603	**forjar**-*vb*	forge	8879	**desenmascarar**-*vb*	unmask
8607	**redoblar**-*vb*	redouble	8884	**desguazar**-*vb*	scrap

8893	**deteriorar**-*vb*	deteriorate	
8909	**triangular**-*adj; vb*	triangular; triangulate	
8912	**estremecer(se)**-*vb*	shudder	
8914	**desprender**-*vb*	detach, release	
8918	**anclar**-*vb*	anchor	
8940	**desechar**-*vb*	discard	
8942	**caducar**-*vb*	expire	
8944	**surtir(se)**-*vb*	supply	
8945	**destituir**-*vb*	remove	
8966	**estabilizar(se)**-*vb*	stabilize	
8967	**emanar**-*vb*	emanate	
8968	**rasgar**-*vb*	rip	
8969	**capar**-*vb*	castrate	
8972	**integrar**-*vb*	integrate	
8973	**escayolar**-*vb*	put in a cast	
8974	**desacreditar**-*vb*	discredit	
8985	**escasear**-*vb*	be scarce	
8992	**desplazar**-*vb*	displace	
8995	**revocar**-*vb*	revoke	
8996	**prevalecer**-*vb*	prevail	
8998	**entonar**-*vb*	sing	
8999	**sintonizar**-*vb*	tune	
9002	**acatar**-*vb*	abide by	
9003	**agobiar(se)**-*vb*	overwhelm	
9004	**amputar**-*vb*	amputate	
9010	**trotar**-*vb*	trot	
9014	**arbitrar**-*vb*	arbitrate	
9019	**cifrar**-*vb*	encrypt	
9023	**modelar**-*vb*	model	
9027	**venerar**-*vb*	worship	
9028	**inquietar**-*vb*	unsettle	
9031	**reorganizar**-*vb*	reorganize	
9046	**chutar**-*vb*	shoot	
9058	**atemorizar**-*vb*	terrify	
9061	**inmovilizar**-*vb*	immobilize	
9062	**pirarse**-*vbr*	bait (ES) (coll)	
9078	**estampar**-*vb*	stamp	
9083	**embotellar**-*vb*	bottle	
9086	**refutar**-*vb*	refute	
9095	**sobrecargar**-*vb*	overburden	
9097	**apodar**-*vb*	nickname	
9103	**subsistir**-*vb*	subsist	
9108	**incinerar**-*vb*	incinerate	
9109	**procrear**-*vb*	procreate	
9113	**evocar**-*vb*	evoke	
9116	**recetar**-*vb*	prescribe	

9118	**levar**-*vb*	weigh
9119	**abreviar**-*vb*	shorten
9123	**sulfurar(se)**-*vb*	get angry
9130	**rehabilitar**-*vb*	rehabilitate
9139	**corroborar**-*vb*	corroborate
9141	**inducir**-*vb*	induce
9145	**caracterizar**-*vb*	characterize
9148	**apalear**-*vb*	beat
9151	**escarbar**-*vb*	dig
9159	**rectificar**-*vb*	rectify
9162	**obstruir**-*vb*	obstruct
9164	**incomunicar**-*vb*	isolate
9167	**noquear**-*vb*	knock out
9178	**alinear**-*vb*	align
9183	**ilustrar**-*vb*	illustrate
9184	**infringir**-*vb*	infringe
9185	**mellar**-*vb*	chip
9187	**silenciar**-*vb*	silence
9188	**adjudicar**-*vb*	award
9190	**evaporar**-*vb*	evaporate
9195	**quebrantar**-*vb*	break
9204	**visualizar**-*vb*	visualize
9215	**sumir**-*vb*	plunge
9218	**vagabundear**-*vb*	roam
9219	**relatar**-*vb*	recount
9224	**apañar**-*vb*	fix
9226	**conferir**-*vb*	confer
9230	**camuflar**-*vb*	camouflage
9231	**adornar**-*vb*	decorate
9234	**consolidar**-*vb*	consolidate
9237	**rematar**-*vb*	conclude
9246	**reciclar**-*vb*	recycle
9251	**reconciliar**-*vb*	reconcile
9257	**degollar**-*vb*	cut someone's throat
9264	**desbordar**-*vb*	overflow
9268	**inflar**-*vb*	inflate
9275	**canalizar**-*vb*	channel
9276	**comandar**-*vb*	command
9280	**arrollar**-*vb*	run down
9283	**decaer**-*vb*	decay
9286	**especificar**-*vb*	specify
9288	**vegetar**-*vb*	vegetate
9294	**aplacar**-*vb*	placate
9304	**abastecer**-*vb*	supply
9309	**empalmar(se)**-*vb; vbr*	connect; overlap (LA), get a hard-on (ES) (coll)

9313	**sofocar(se)**-*vb; vbr*	suffocate; get embarrassed, get upset
9338	**dislocar(se)**-*vb*	dislocate
9347	**implementar**-*vb*	implement
9359	**descontar**-*vb*	discount
9360	**perecer**-*vb*	perish
9361	**decretar**-*vb*	decree
9365	**tachar**-*vb*	cross out
9378	**confrontar**-*vb*	confront
9381	**tiritar**-*vb*	shiver
9383	**acuñar**-*vb*	coin
9386	**distorsionar**-*vb*	distort
9391	**embriagar**-*vb*	get drunk
9393	**simpatizar**-*vb*	sympathize
9395	**enfatizar**-*vb*	emphasize
9396	**salpicar**-*vb*	splash
9399	**veranear**-*vb*	spend the summer in
9402	**insertar**-*vb*	insert
9405	**trascender**-*vb*	transcend
9409	**retar**-*vb*	challenge
9410	**desenterrar**-*vb*	dig up
9414	**dispersar**-*vb*	disperse
9420	**expirar**-*vb*	expire
9426	**retratar**-*vb*	portray
9429	**entrelazar**-*vb*	weave together, interlock
9432	**desgastar**-*vb*	wear out
9435	**saturar**-*vb*	saturate
9436	**acalorar**-*vb; vbr*	heat up; get worked up
9438	**esclavizar**-*vb*	enslave
9443	**descolgar**-*vb*	take down
9444	**corroer**-*vb*	corrode
9449	**remontar**-*vb; vbr*	overcome; date back
9451	**unificar**-*vb*	unify
9453	**reprobar**-*vb*	fail
9454	**deshidratar**-*vb*	dehydrate
9456	**interactuar**-*vb*	interact
9463	**purgar**-*vb*	purge
9464	**consternar**-*vb*	shock
9465	**marchitar**-*vb*	wither
9480	**canjear**-*vb*	exchange
9481	**cautivar**-*vb*	captivate
9483	**afiliar**-*vb*	enrol
9484	**lanzar**-*vb*	throw
9485	**optar**-*vb*	choose
9486	**disecar**-*vb*	dissect
9489	**aclamar**-*vb*	hail
9492	**recluir**-*vb*	detain
9500	**laburar**-*vb*	work (LA)
9507	**perpetuar**-*vb*	perpetuate
9512	**alumbrar**-*vb*	light
9514	**concurrir**-*vb*	attend
9524	**desmantelar**-*vb*	dismantle
9530	**calzar**-*vb*	wear
9534	**traumatizar**-*vb*	traumatize
9547	**contrariar**-*vb*	cross, antagonize
9549	**omitir**-*vb*	skip
9550	**derrochar**-*vb*	waste
9563	**sofisticar**-*vb*	sophisticate
9566	**agujerear**-*vb*	make holes in
9575	**deslumbrar**-*vb*	dazzle
9577	**endurecer**-*vb*	harden
9580	**enlatar**-*vb*	can
9587	**circuncidar**-*vb*	circumcise
9594	**tripular**-*vb*	crew
9597	**egresar**-*vb*	graduate
9601	**drenar**-*vb*	drain
9602	**extirpar**-*vb*	remove
9603	**repeler**-*vb*	repel
9611	**destapar**-*vb*	uncover
9621	**contentar**-*vb*	please
9622	**etiquetar**-*vb*	label
9626	**alucinar**-*vb*	hallucinate
9632	**aguar**-*vb*	water down, spoil (coll)
9636	**reiniciar**-*vb*	reboot
9639	**doblegar**-*vb*	crush
9642	**deshabitar**-*vb*	vacate
9645	**untar**-*vb*	spread
9648	**amueblar**-*vb*	furnish
9657	**rapar**-*vb*	shave
9670	**forcejear**-*vb*	struggle, wrestle
9671	**apropiarse**-*vbr*	take over, pocket
9675	**encerar**-*vb*	wax
9678	**atribuir**-*vb*	attribute
9679	**catear**-*vb*	flunk (ES) (coll)
9683	**emparejar**-*vb*	match
9686	**sondar**-*vb*	probe
9690	**encaminar**-*vb*	route
9696	**acarrear**-*vb*	entail
9699	**desahogarse**-*vbr*	blow off steam
9703	**merendar**-*vb*	have a snack
9706	**estipular**-*vb*	stipulate

9711	**ingerir**-*vb*	ingest		9982	**talar**-*vb*	cut down
9721	**argumentar**-*vb*	argue		9983	**desembocar**-*vb*	lead
9723	**rezagarse**-*vbr*	fall behind		9985	**ventilar**-*vb*	ventilate
9731	**desocupar**-*vb*	vacate		9992	**arraigar**-*vb*	take root
9747	**fechar**-*vb*	date		9996	**pactar**-*vb*	agree
9750	**ablandar**-*vb*	soften		9998	**diferir**-*vb*	differ
9755	**rebelarse**-*vbr*	rebel		9999	**encarnar**-*vb*	embody
9762	**dialogar**-*vb*	talk		10000	**acuchillar**-*vb*	slash
9767	**desencadenar**-*vb*	trigger, unchain		10010	**arañar**-*vb*	scratch
9774	**redimir**-*vb*	redeem		10012	**apilar**-*vb*	stack
9778	**perpetrar**-*vb*	perpetrate		10016	**retraer**-*vb*	retract
9779	**colorear**-*vb*	color		10018	**encestar**-*vb*	dunk
9781	**hipotecar**-*vb*	mortgage				
9792	**ondear**-*vb*	wave				
9807	**recostar(se)**-*vb*	lie down				
9812	**desaprobar**-*vb*	disapprove				
9816	**accionar**-*vb*	trigger				
9821	**denominar**-*vb*	call				
9839	**regañar**-*vb*	scold				
9840	**salvaguardar**-*vb*	safeguard				
9848	**catar**-*vb*	taste				
9853	**maquillar(se)**-*vb*	make up				
9854	**henchir(se)**-*vb*	fill				
9857	**transpirar**-*vb*	sweat				
9862	**agrandar**-*vb*	enlarge				
9880	**vislumbrar**-*vb*	glimpse				
9886	**esclarecer**-*vb*	clarify				
9888	**economizar**-*vb*	economize				
9889	**agravar**-*vb*	aggravate				
9894	**aminorar**-*vb*	slow down				
9901	**ocasionar**-*vb*	cause				
9903	**menospreciar**-*vb*	underestimate				
9931	**regocijar(se)**-*vb*	rejoice				
9933	**batallar**-*vb*	battle				
9934	**acallar**-*vb*	silence				
9938	**proscribir**-*vb*	outlaw				
9952	**checar**-*vb*	check				
9953	**dispensar**-*vb*	dispense				
9957	**replicar**-*vb*	replicate				
9959	**nutrir**-*vb*	nourish				
9962	**discernir**-*vb*	discern				
9965	**nivelar**-*vb*	level				
9970	**coexistir**-*vb*	coexist				
9974	**apaciguar**-*vb*	appease				
9975	**fumigar**-*vb*	fumigate				
9978	**cotillear**-*vb*	gossip				

Alphabetical Order

Rank	Spanish-*PoS*	Translation(s)
	A	
7688	**abarcar**-*vb*	encompass
8666	**abarrotar**-*vb*	pack
9304	**abastecer**-*vb*	supply
9801	**abecedario**-*m*	alphabet
8024	**aberración**-*f*	aberration
9750	**ablandar**-*vb*	soften
8700	**abolición**-*f*	abolition
8617	**abolir**-*vb*	abolish
7567	**abordaje**-*m*	approach, boarding
7884	**aborigen**-*adj; m/f*	indigenous; aboriginal
9054	**abrelatas**-*f*	can opener
9119	**abreviar**-*vb*	shorten
8902	**abridor**-*m*	opener
8438	**abrigar(se)**-*vb*	shelter, keep warm
7580	**abrumador**-*adj*	overwhelming
9497	**abrupto**-*adj*	abrupt
9640	**absorción**-*f*	absorption
8602	**absorto**-*adj*	absorbed
7941	**abundar**-*vb*	be plentiful, elaborate
8604	**abusivo**-*adj*	abusive
9934	**acallar**-*vb*	silence
9436	**acalorar**-*vb; vbr*	heat up; get worked up
9696	**acarrear**-*vb*	entail
9002	**acatar**-*vb*	abide by
9816	**accionar**-*vb*	trigger
9038	**acequia**-*f*	ditch
9469	**achicoria**-*f*	chicory
8331	**acidez**-*f*	heartburn
9489	**aclamar**-*vb*	hail
9557	**aclaración**-*f*	clarification
7555	**acné**-*m*	acne
8716	**acompañamiento**-*m*	accompanying
7818	**aconsejable**-*adj*	advisable
8054	**acontecer**-*vb*	happen
8792	**acoplamiento**-*m*	coupling
7845	**acortar**-*vb*	shorten
7549	**activación**-*f*	activation
8574	**actualizar**-*vb*	update
10000	**acuchillar**-*vb*	slash
9895	**acueducto**-*m*	aqueduct
8789	**acumulación**-*f*	accumulation
9383	**acuñar**-*vb*	coin
9243	**acupuntura**-*f*	acupuncture
8766	**acusador**-*m*	prosecutor
7811	**acústico**-*adj*	acoustic
7610	**adelgazar**-*vb*	lose weight
9795	**adepto**-*adj; m*	adept; follower
8288	**aderezar**-*vb*	season
8596	**adición**-*f*	addition
8460	**adiestramiento**-*m*	training
9188	**adjudicar**-*vb*	award
9354	**ADN**-*abr*	DNA
9732	**adolorido**-*adj*	in pain
9231	**adornar**-*vb*	decorate
9616	**aerodinámico**-*adj*	aerodynamic
8774	**aeronáutica**-*adj; f*	aerospace; aviation
8111	**aeroplano**-*m*	airplane
8089	**afable**-*adj*	affable
7700	**afán**-*m*	eagerness
7782	**afección**-*f*	condition
7575	**afectuoso**-*adj*	affectionate
7534	**aferrarse**-*vbr*	cling to
7788	**afgano**-*adj; m*	Afghan; Afghan person
9171	**afiche**-*m*	poster
9483	**afiliar**-*vb*	enrol
8702	**afinar**-*vb*	tune
8053	**afinidad**-*f*	affinity
8015	**afrenta**-*f*	affront
9533	**afroamericano**-*adj; m*	Afro-American; African-American person
7718	**agachar(se)**-*vb*	duck
8548	**agilidad**-*f*	agility
8838	**agitador**-*m*	agitator
9003	**agobiar(se)**-*vb*	overwhelm
9862	**agrandar**-*vb*	enlarge
9889	**agravar**-*vb*	aggravate
8676	**agredir**-*vb*	assault
8546	**agridulce**-*adj*	bittersweet
7840	**agrio**-*adj*	sour
9408	**agrupación**-*f*	group
9157	**aguacate**-*m*	avocado
9632	**aguar**-*vb*	water down, spoil (coll)

9852	**agudeza**-*f*	sharpness	8555	**amapola**-*f*	poppy
8276	**agüero**-*m*	omen	9390	**ambigüedad**-*f*	ambiguity
9566	**agujerear**-*vb*	make holes in	8680	**ambiguo**-*adj*	ambiguous
8770	**ahijado**-*m*	godson	7837	**amenazante**-*adj*	threatening
8472	**aislante**-*adj; m*	insulation; insulator	9894	**aminorar**-*vb*	slow down
8161	**ajuar**-*m*	trousseau	9168	**amoníaco**-*m; adj*	ammonia; ammonia
7774	**alameda**-*f*	avenue	8473	**amparar**-*vb*	protect
8222	**alarde**-*m*	boast	8039	**ampliación**-*f*	extension
7671	**alargar**-*vb*	lengthen	7667	**amplificador**-*adj; m*	amplifying; amplifier
9811	**albacea**-*m/f*	executor	9131	**amplitud**-*f*	extent
9172	**albahaca**-*f*	basil	9624	**amputación**-*f*	amputation
8791	**albanés**-*adj; m*	Albanian; Albanian person	9004	**amputar**-*vb*	amputate
7628	**albatros**-*m*	albatross	9648	**amueblar**-*vb*	furnish
9790	**alberca**-*f*	swimming	9069	**anaconda**-*f*	anaconda
8479	**albergar**-*vb*	host	8385	**analfabeto**-*adj; m*	illiterate; illiterate
9124	**albornoz**-*m*	bathrobe	8061	**analogía**-*f*	analogy
9619	**alboroto**-*m*	fuss	8918	**anclar**-*vb*	anchor
9936	**alcantarillado**-*m*	sewerage	9045	**andamio**-*m*	scaffold
8584	**alcázar**-*m*	fortress	8044	**anemia**-*f*	anemia
9318	**aleación**-*f*	alloy	8448	**anestésico**-*adj*	anesthetic
8707	**aleatorio**-*adj*	random	8423	**aneurisma**-*adj*	aneurysm
8266	**alegación**-*f*	allegation	7844	**anexo**-*adj; m*	attached; annex
7510	**alegar**-*vb*	claim	8816	**anfibio**-*adj; m*	amphibious; amphibian
9322	**alejamiento**-*m*	removal	8850	**anfiteatro**-*m*	amphitheater
7803	**alentar**-*vb*	encourage	7578	**angular**-*adj*	angular
8297	**alfabético**-*adj*	alphabetical	7585	**anhelar**-*vb*	yearn for
9025	**alfalfa**-*f*	alfalfa	7766	**aniquilar**-*vb*	annihilate
9924	**algoritmo**-*m*	algorithm	9926	**anormalidad**-*f*	abnormality
9764	**alhaja**-*f*	jewel	9080	**anotador**-*m*	notepad (LA)
8701	**alimentario**-*adj*	food	9937	**anteanoche**-*adv*	the night before last
9178	**alinear**-*vb*	align	9320	**anterioridad**-*f*	previous
7526	**alistar(se)**-*vb*	enlist	9756	**antesala**-*f*	anteroom
9677	**almacenaje**-*m*	storage	7983	**antiaéreo**-*adj*	anti-aircraft
7780	**almacenamiento**-*m*	storage	8865	**anticonceptivo**-*adj; m*	contraceptive; birth control
7981	**almacenar**-*vb*	store	9832	**anticongelante**-*adj*	antifreeze
8696	**almidón**-*m*	starch	8870	**anticuario**-*m*	antique dealer
7821	**alojar**-*vb*	accommodate	8897	**anticuerpo**-*m*	antibody
7741	**alquimia**-*f*	alchemy	7775	**antidepresivo**-*adj*	antidepressant
9950	**alterno**-*adj*	alternate	9598	**antidroga**-*adj*	antidrug
7758	**altibajos**-*mpl*	ups and downs	9794	**antifaz**-*m*	mask
10007	**altruista**-*adj; m/f*	altruistic; altruist	7939	**antisemita**-*adj; m/f*	anti-Semitic; anti-Semite
9626	**alucinar**-*vb*	hallucinate			
9512	**alumbrar**-*vb*	light	9909	**antiséptico**-*adj; m*	antiseptic; antiseptic
9272	**alusión**-*f*	allusion	8370	**antisocial**-*adj*	anti-social
9216	**alzado**-*adj*	raised	8033	**antropología**-*f*	anthropology

9491	**antropólogo**-*m*	anthropologist	8280	**arrodillar(se)**-*vb*	kneel
9284	**aorta**-*f*	aorta	9280	**arrollar**-*vb*	run down
9974	**apaciguar**-*vb*	appease	8315	**artesanía**-*f*	craftwork
9148	**apalear**-*vb*	beat	7875	**artesano**-*m*	craftsman
9224	**apañar**-*vb*	fix	7790	**articulación**-*f*	joint
8029	**aparador**-*m*	sideboard	9956	**artificio**-*m*	artifice
8258	**aparear**-*vb*	mate	8328	**artilugio**-*m*	gadget
9041	**aparejo**-*m*	rig	8300	**artimaña**-*f*	trick
8446	**apatía**-*f*	apathy	8948	**asador**-*m*	grill
8036	**apego**-*m*	attachment	7647	**asaltante**-*m/f*	robber
9544	**apetitoso**-*adj*	appetizing	9704	**asbesto**-*m*	asbestos
8815	**ápice**-*m*	apex	8896	**ascendencia**-*f*	ancestry
10012	**apilar**-*vb*	stack	8687	**ascendente**-*adj*	rising
9294	**aplacar**-*vb*	placate	7668	**ascensión**-*f*	ascension
8140	**aplastante**-*adj*	overwhelming	9479	**ascuas**-*fpl*	embers
7794	**aplazar**-*vb*	postpone	8726	**asemejar(se)**-*vb*	resemble
9097	**apodar**-*vb*	nickname	7542	**asentamiento**-*m*	settlement
7716	**apogeo**-*m*	peak	8530	**asentar(se)**-*vb*	settle
8512	**apoplejía**-*f*	stroke	7865	**asesoramiento**-*m*	advice
8283	**apreciación**-*f*	appreciation	9138	**asesoría**-*f*	advice
8835	**apremiar**-*vb*	hurry	8577	**asfixiar**-*vb*	choke
8431	**apresar**-*vb*	apprehend	8583	**asignatura**-*f*	subject
9671	**apropiarse**-*vbr*	take over, pocket	7925	**asimilar**-*vb*	assimilate
10010	**arañar**-*vb*	scratch	8228	**asimismo**-*adv*	also
7697	**arañazo**-*m*	scratch	7643	**astrología**-*f*	astrology
7801	**arar**-*vb*	plow	9882	**astronómico**-*f*	astronomical
9920	**arbitraje**-*m*	arbitration	8130	**astrónomo**-*m*	astronomer
9336	**arbitrario**-*adj*	arbitrary	9428	**asunción**-*f*	assumption
9014	**arbitrar**-*vb*	arbitrate	8154	**atajo**-*m*	shortcut
8565	**archiduque**-*m*	archduke	8841	**atañer**-*vb*	concern
8806	**archivar**-*vb*	file	9058	**atemorizar**-*vb*	terrify
8305	**ardid**-*m*	scheme	7910	**atenerse a**-*vbr*	abide by
9098	**argelino**-*adj; m*	Algerian; Algerian person	8689	**atenuante**-*adj*	mitigating
			8869	**atestar**-*vb*	attest
9721	**argumentar**-*vb*	argue	8545	**atestiguar**-*vb*	testify
9403	**árido**-*adj*	arid	7507	**atletismo**-*m*	athletics
8351	**armazón**-*m*	frame	9106	**atmosférico**-*adj*	atmospheric
7974	**armenio**-*adj; m*	Armenian; Armenian person	8588	**atónito**-*adj*	stunned
			8184	**atormentado**-*adj*	tormented
7745	**arnés**-*m*	harness	8668	**atraco**-*m*	robbery
9695	**arqueológico**-*adj*	archaeological	9858	**atrayente**-*adj*	attractive
9992	**arraigar**-*vb*	take root	9678	**atribuir**-*vb*	attribute
9370	**arrebato**-*m*	outburst	7744	**atributo**-*m*	attribute
8842	**arrendamiento**-*m*	lease	9177	**atrio**-*m*	atrium
8264	**arribar**-*vb*	arrive	10014	**atrofia**-*f*	atrophy
9824	**arriendo**-*m*	rent	8081	**audífono**-*m*	hearing aid

9072	**auditoría**-*f*	audit
7916	**auge**-*m*	boom
7905	**augurio**-*m*	omen
9754	**aureola**-*f*	halo
8272	**austriaco**-*adj; m*	Austrian; Austrian person
8872	**austríaco**-*adj; m*	Austrian; Austrian person
8313	**autismo**-*m*	autism
8320	**autista**-*adj; m/f*	autistic; autistic person
8284	**autobiografía**-*f*	autobiography
9713	**autocar**-*m*	coach
8023	**autocontrol**-*m*	self-control
8618	**autodefensa**-*f*	self-defence
7524	**autonomía**-*f*	autonomy
8821	**autónomo**-*adj; m*	autonomous; independent
9944	**autoritario**-*adj; m*	authoritarian; authoritarian
9035	**aval**-*m*	guarantee
9552	**avellana**-*adj; f*	hazelnut; hazelnut
7617	**averiguación**-*f*	inquiry
9702	**ávido**-*adj*	avid
7960	**avioneta**-*f*	plane
8762	**avistar**-*vb*	sight
9846	**axila**-*f*	armpit
7598	**ayunar**-*vb*	fast
8898	**azafrán**-*m*	saffron
8412	**azulejo**-*m*	tile

B

8255	**babear**-*vb*	drool
9763	**bagre**-*m*	catfish
7733	**bajista**-*m/f*	bass player
8289	**balancear(se)**-*vb*	balance
8047	**balanceo**-*m*	rocking
9005	**balde**-*m*	bucket
9104	**báltico**-*adj*	Baltic
7574	**bandada**-*f*	flock
9855	**bandolero**-*m*	bandit
9115	**banqueta**-*f*	stool
8344	**baranda**-*f*	railing
7528	**barandilla**-*f*	handrail
8779	**barbarie**-*f*	barbarism

9928	**barbitúrico**-*m; adj*	barbiturate; barbiturate
9034	**barítono**-*m*	baritone
8355	**barniz**-*m*	varnish
9468	**barómetro**-*m*	barometer
9900	**barroco**-*adj*	baroque
9929	**basílica**-*f*	basilica
8724	**bastión**-*m*	bastion
9933	**batallar**-*vb*	battle
8772	**batidora**-*m*	blender
7562	**batuta**-*f*	baton
8868	**baza**-*f*	asset
7964	**bazo**-*m*	spleen
9674	**bélico**-*adj*	warlike
8311	**bellaco**-*adj*	coward
8751	**bellota**-*f*	acorn
8212	**beneficiario**-*m*	beneficiary
8181	**beneficioso**-*adj*	beneficial
8657	**benévolo**-*vb*	benevolent
9135	**bengalí**-*adj; m/f*	Bengali; Bengali person
7637	**benigno**-*adj*	benign
9270	**berenjena**-*f*	eggplant
7503	**bestial**-*adj*	brutal
8763	**betún**-*m*	shoe polish
8360	**bíceps**-*m*	biceps
9012	**bidón**-*m*	drum
8848	**bifurcación**-*f*	fork
9042	**bilis**-*f*	bile
9207	**binario**-*adj*	binary
8722	**biólogo**-*m*	biologist
9363	**biombo**-*m*	screen
8371	**biopsia**-*f*	biopsy
8368	**bioquímico**-*adj; m*	biochemical; biochemist
9569	**biotecnología**-*f*	biotechnology
8866	**bipolar**-*adj*	bipolar
7917	**bis**-*adv; m*	bis; encore
9127	**bisagra**-*f*	hinge
9761	**bloc**-*m*	pad
8358	**bobina**-*f*	coil
9181	**bocanada**-*f*	breath
9040	**bochorno**-*m*	embarrassment
9227	**boicot**-*m*	boycott
7592	**boina**-*f*	beret
9559	**bolero**-*adj; m*	liar (coll); bolero
8674	**bolos**-*mpl*	bowling

8777	**boludez**-*f*	nonsense (LA) (coll)	
9850	**bombazo**-*m*	bomb	
8082	**bombear**-*vb*	pump	
9134	**bombeo**-*m*	pumping	
8464	**bombo**-*m*	bass drum	
9158	**bonanza**-*f*	bonanza	
7847	**bonificación**-*f*	bonus	
9652	**boquiabierto**-*adj*	dumbstruck	
8474	**boquilla**-*f*	mouthpiece	
9540	**boreal**-*adj*	boreal	
9884	**borrego**-*m*	lamb, simple-minded (coll)	
8098	**borrón**-*m*	smudge	
8808	**bosquejar**-*vb*	sketch	
9860	**bostezo**-*m*	yawn	
7935	**botánico**-*adj; m*	botanical; botanist	
9462	**boticario**-*m*	apothecary	
7757	**bragueta**-*f*	fly	
8165	**brasa**-*f*	ember	
8072	**bravucón**-*adj; m*	cocky; bully	
7883	**brea**-*f*	pitch	
8837	**brebaje**-*m*	concoction	
8416	**brevedad**-*f*	brevity	
9529	**brillantez**-*f*	brilliance	
8336	**brincar**-*vb*	jump	
8335	**brío**-*m*	verve	
8960	**brocha**-*f*	brush	
9319	**bronceador**-*m*	tanning lotion	
8725	**bronquitis**-*f*	bronchitis	
7971	**brotar**-*vb*	sprout	
8084	**bucal**-*adj*	oral	
8500	**bujía**-*f*	spark plug	
7614	**bulevar**-*m*	boulevard	
9599	**bulimia**-*f*	bulimia	
9200	**burdo**-*adj*	crude	
7520	**burócrata**-*m/f*	bureaucrat	
9883	**burocrático**-*adj*	bureaucratic	
8433	**butaca**-*f*	armchair	

C

8520	**caballeriza**-*f*	stable	
8042	**caballerosidad**-*f*	chivalry	
8307	**caballeroso**-*adj*	gentlemanly	
9211	**cabezazo**-*m*	header	
8521	**cabida**-*f*	room	

8171	**cablear**-*vb*	wire	
9667	**cabrito**-*adj; m*	lousy (coll); young goat	
7573	**cacerola**-*f*	pan	
8899	**cachetada**-*f*	slap	
8179	**cacho**-*m*	piece	
8926	**cacique**-*m/f*	cacique	
8942	**caducar**-*vb*	expire	
9526	**cajetilla**-*f*	pack	
8291	**cala**-*f*	cove	
7636	**calar**-*vb*	seep through, sink in	
9523	**calentura**-*f*	fever, cold sore	
8356	**callado**-*adj*	quiet	
8275	**calvario**-*m*	ordeal (coll)	
9267	**calza**-*f*	wedge	
9530	**calzar**-*vb*	wear	
8263	**camada**-*f*	litter	
8057	**camaleón**-*m*	chameleon	
7997	**camaradería**-*f*	camaraderie	
8440	**camarote**-*m*	cabin	
8564	**camillero**-*m*	stretcher-bearer	
9230	**camuflar**-*vb*	camouflage	
9556	**cañada**-*f*	glen	
9275	**canalizar**-*vb*	channel	
8611	**canapé**-*m*	canape	
9945	**canasto**-*m*	basket	
7862	**cancelación**-*f*	cancellation	
8191	**cancillería**-*f*	chancellery	
9350	**candela**-*f*	candle	
7568	**candente**-*adj*	red-hot	
8211	**canibalismo**-*m*	cannibalism	
7515	**canino**-*adj; m*	canine; canine tooth	
9480	**canjear**-*vb*	exchange	
8274	**canoa**-*f*	canoe	
8273	**canon**-*m*	canon	
9960	**cántaro**-*m*	pitcher	
8950	**cántico**-*m*	chant	
8509	**caoba**-*adj*	mahogany	
7832	**caótico**-*adj*	chaotic	
9966	**capacitación**-*f*	training	
8969	**capar**-*vb*	castrate	
7581	**caperuza**-*f*	hood	
9822	**capilar**-*adj; m*	capillary; hair	
9776	**capitulación**-*f*	capitulation	
8466	**capote**-*m*	cape	
7893	**carabina**-*f*	carbine	

9121	**carabinero**-*m*	policeman	8103	**celibato**-*m*	celibacy
9145	**caracterizar**-*vb*	characterize	9568	**celo**-*m*	zeal, tape
7712	**carbohidrato**-*m*	carbohydrate	9261	**celuloide**-*m*	celluloid
8935	**cardiólogo**-*m*	cardiologist	7806	**censo**-*m*	census
8621	**carencia**-*f*	lack	9471	**censor**-*adj; m*	censorial; censor
9074	**carente**-*adj*	lacking	8758	**centenario**-*adj; m*	centenary; centennial
8679	**carismático**-*adj; m*	charismatic; charismatic	9252	**centígrado**-*adj*	centigrade
8352	**caritativo**-*adj*	charitable	8784	**centralita**-*f*	switchboard
9053	**carnívoro**-*adj*	carnivore	7976	**cepa**-*f*	strain
7904	**carpintería**-*f*	carpentry	8987	**cepo**-*m*	trap
9305	**carretero**-*m*	chimney	8427	**cercanía**-*f*	closeness
9401	**carrocería**-*f*	bodywork	8012	**ceremonial**-*adj*	ceremonial
8780	**cartelera**-*f*	billboard	7537	**cerezo**-*m*	cherry tree
9864	**cartílago**-*m*	cartilage	8847	**certero**-*adj*	accurate
8231	**casaca**-*f*	coat	9766	**certificación**-*f*	certification
9972	**cascanueces**-*m*	nutcracker	8193	**cesárea**-*f*	C-section
8939	**casete**-*m/f*	cassette	7502	**chantajear**-*vb*	blackmail
8240	**casto**-*adj*	chaste	8928	**charca**-*f*	pond
9499	**castración**-*f*	castration	8783	**chasis**-*m*	chassis
8658	**cataclismo**-*m*	cataclysm	9952	**checar**-*vb*	check
8093	**catalizador**-*m*	catalyst	7962	**chévere**-*int; adj*	great (LA) (coll); cool (LA) (coll)
9586	**catapulta**-*f*	catapult	7659	**chichón**-*m*	bump
9848	**catar**-*vb*	taste	9208	**chileno**-*adj; m*	Chilean; Chilean person
7514	**catastrófico**-*adj*	catastrophic			
9679	**catear**-*vb*	flunk (ES) (coll)	9545	**chillón**-*adj*	gaudy
8189	**catecismo**-*m*	Catechism	8471	**chinchar**-*vb*	tease
8550	**cátedra**-*f*	professorship	9733	**chiquitito**-*adj*	tiny
9263	**catedral**-*f*	cathedral	9046	**chutar**-*vb*	shoot
9477	**catedrático**-*m*	professor	9333	**ciclismo**-*m*	cycling
8756	**categórico**-*adj*	categorical	8329	**ciclista**-*m/f*	cyclist
9554	**catéter**-*m*	catheter	8068	**ciclón**-*m*	cyclone
8343	**catolicismo**-*m*	Catholicism	9019	**cifrar**-*vb*	encrypt
8424	**caucásico**-*adj; m*	Caucasian; Caucasian person	8984	**cinematografía**-*f*	cinematography
8880	**cauce**-*m*	channel	9587	**circuncidar**-*vb*	circumcise
8839	**caudillo**-*m*	leader	8911	**circunstancial**-*adj*	circumstantial
8143	**causante**-*adj; m*	responsible; cause	9142	**ciudadela**-*f*	citadel
9481	**cautivar**-*vb*	captivate	7773	**cívico**-*adj*	civic
7797	**cautivo**-*adj; m*	captive; captivity	8485	**clamar**-*vb*	clamour for
9551	**cauto**-*adj*	cautious	8210	**clamor**-*m*	cry
9539	**cayado**-*m*	crook	8435	**clandestinidad**-*f*	underground
9239	**cazatalentos**-*m/f*	talent scout	8442	**clarín**-*m*	bugle
8374	**cazuela**-*f*	pot	8859	**clarividente**-*adj; m/f*	clairvoyant; psychic
9503	**cedro**-*m*	cedar	9079	**clausura**-*f*	closing
9548	**cédula**-*f*	document	7897	**clavícula**-*f*	clavicle
			8396	**clonación**-*f*	cloning

8483	**coacción**-*f*	coercion
8605	**coágulo**-*m*	clot
8468	**coartada**-*f*	alibi
9666	**cobalto**-*m*	cobalt
7577	**cobijo**-*m*	shelter
7937	**codorniz**-*m/f*	quail
9970	**coexistir**-*vb*	coexist
9828	**coherencia**-*f*	coherence
8149	**cojear**-*vb*	limp
9120	**cojera**-*f*	limp
8746	**colación**-*f*	collation
7817	**colapsar**-*vb*	collapse
7760	**colateral**-*adj*	collateral
9827	**colector**-*m*	collector
7655	**colegial**-*adj; m*	school; schoolboy
8591	**colibrí**-*m*	hummingbird
8458	**coliflor**-*f*	cauliflower
9496	**colocación**-*f*	placement
9317	**colocado**-*adj*	placed, stoned
8764	**colonización**-*f*	colonization
9779	**colorear**-*vb*	color
7752	**coloso**-*m*	colossus
8681	**columnista**-*m/f*	columnist
9285	**comadre**-*f*	close friend (coll) (LA), midwife (coll) (ES)
9276	**comandar**-*vb*	command
8931	**comentarista**-*m/f*	commentator
9729	**comercialización**-*f*	marketing
8002	**comestible**-*adj*	edible
8058	**cómic**-*m*	comic
8020	**comillas**-*fpl*	quotation marks
9691	**comité**-*m*	committee
9229	**comitiva**-*f*	motorcade
9590	**cómoda**-*f*	chest of drawers
8738	**compactar**-*vb*	compact
9607	**compañerismo**-*m*	fellowship
8076	**comparable**-*adj*	comparable
7601	**comparecer**-*vb*	appear
8573	**compasivo**-*adj*	compassionate
9806	**compatibilidad**-*f*	compatibility
9198	**complemento**-*m*	complement
8405	**complexión**-*f*	complexion
10002	**compresa**-*f*	compress
8467	**compresión**-*f*	compression
9746	**compresor**-*m*	compressor
7819	**comprimir**-*vb*	compress
9561	**compulsión**-*f*	compulsion
9346	**comunal**-*adj*	communal
9170	**concesionario**-*m*	concessionaire
9368	**concienzudo**-*adj*	conscientious
7787	**conciliar**-*vb*	reconcile
9474	**conciso**-*adj*	concise
7799	**conciudadano**-*m*	fellow citizen
8166	**concluyente**-*adj*	conclusive
9947	**concordia**-*f*	concord
8177	**concretar**-*vb*	specify
9514	**concurrir**-*vb*	attend
7770	**condecoración**-*f*	award
9013	**condimento**-*m*	seasoning
9638	**confección**-*f*	making, clothing
9226	**conferir**-*vb*	confer
8359	**confidencia**-*f*	confidence
8055	**configuración**-*f*	configuration
7673	**confinar**-*vb*	confine
8413	**conformidad**-*f*	accordance
9378	**confrontar**-*vb*	confront
8085	**congelación**-*f*	freezing
9457	**congestión**-*f*	congestion
8819	**conjunción**-*f*	conjunction
9112	**conjuro**-*m*	spell
9155	**conmemoración**-*f*	commemoration
8173	**conmemorar**-*vb*	commemorate
8892	**conmemorativo**-*adj*	memorial
7867	**conmocionado**-*adj*	shocked
8377	**conmocionar**-*vb*	shake profoundly
8629	**conocedor**-*adj; m*	knowledgeable; connoisseur
7691	**consagrar**-*vb*	enshrine
9994	**consecuente**-*adj*	consistent
7725	**consecutivo**-*adj*	consecutive
7711	**consenso**-*m*	consensus
8278	**consistencia**-*f*	consistency
9519	**consolación**-*f*	consolation
9234	**consolidar**-*vb*	consolidate
7653	**consorcio**-*m*	consortium
8104	**conspirar**-*vb*	conspire
9464	**consternar**-*vb*	shock
8891	**constructivo**-*adj*	constructive
7969	**consumar**-*vb*	consummate
8118	**contagiar**-*vb*	infect
7928	**contagio**-*m*	contagion

9448	**contaminante**-*adj; m*	pollutant; contaminant	
9800	**contemplación**-*f*	contemplation	
8373	**contemporáneo**-*adj; m*	contemporary; contemporary	
9621	**contentar**-*vb*	please	
8833	**contestación**-*f*	reply	
8040	**contienda**-*f*	contest	
8107	**contiguo**-*adj*	adjacent	
9869	**contingencia**-*f*	contingency	
8727	**contingente**-*m; adj*	contingent; possible	
8636	**contorno**-*m*	contour	
8205	**contraatacar**-*vb*	fight back	
8478	**contrabajo**-*m*	double bass	
8159	**contradecir**-*vb*	contradict	
9896	**contradictorio**-*adj*	contradictory	
9654	**contraespionaje**-*m*	counterintelligence	
9547	**contrariar**-*vb*	cross, antagonize	
8645	**contrarrestar**-*vb*	counter	
9467	**contratación**-*f*	recruitment	
8690	**contrata**-*f*	contract	
7638	**contrincante**-*m/f*	opponent	
8504	**controversial**-*adj*	controversial	
7543	**contusión**-*f*	contusion	
9919	**convergencia**-*f*	convergence	
8646	**converso**-*adj; m*	converted; convert	
8699	**convivencia**-*f*	coexistence	
9461	**convocatoria**-*f*	call	
9105	**cónyuge**-*m/f*	spouse	
7853	**coordinador**-*m*	coordinator	
8295	**coraza**-*f*	shell	
9581	**cordel**-*m*	string	
8490	**cordillera**-*f*	mountain range	
9266	**coreógrafo**-*m*	choreographer	
8401	**corpulento**-*adj*	corpulent	
8694	**correspondiente**-*adj*	corresponding	
8322	**corretear**-*vb*	run around	
9139	**corroborar**-*vb*	corroborate	
9444	**corroer**-*vb*	corrode	
9899	**cosmopolita**-*adj; m*	cosmopolitan; cosmopolitan	
8921	**costal**-*m*	bag	
8065	**costear**-*vb*	finance	
9908	**costra**-*f*	scab	
7923	**cota**-*f*	peak	
9978	**cotillear**-*vb*	gossip	
8390	**craneal**-*adj*	cranial	

8381	**crecida**-*f*	flood
7544	**crematorio**-*m*	crematorium
8188	**criadero**-*m*	hatchery
9133	**criminalidad**-*f*	criminality
8186	**crisma**-*f*	neck (coll)
9194	**cristalino**-*adj*	crystalline
7984	**cristiandad**-*f*	Christianity
9376	**croata**-*adj; m/f*	Croatian; Croatian person
8979	**cromosoma**-*m*	chromosome
9488	**cronograma**-*m*	timeline
7726	**cronómetro**-*m*	stopwatch
8439	**croqueta**-*f*	croquette
7645	**crucifixión**-*f*	crucifixion
9634	**cuadrícula**-*f*	grid
9293	**cuaresma**-*f*	Lent
8497	**cúbico**-*adj*	cubic
7866	**cuenca**-*f*	basin
9036	**cuestionable**-*adj*	questionable
9017	**culebra**-*f*	snake
9771	**culinario**-*adj*	culinary
8930	**culminación**-*f*	culmination
9589	**cúmulo**-*m*	cluster
8889	**cuña**-*f*	wedge
9056	**cupo**-*m*	quota
8904	**curador**-*adj; m*	healing; curator
8034	**currículum**-*m*	curriculum vitae
9020	**curvatura**-*f*	curvature
8667	**cúspide**-*f*	top
8252	**cutis**-*m*	skin

D

8337	**damisela**-*f*	damsel
7880	**dañino**-*adj*	harmful
8399	**deambular**-*vb*	wander
7658	**debilitar**-*vb*	weaken
9149	**debutante**-*adj; m/f*	debut; debutante
9283	**decaer**-*vb*	decay
7951	**decepcionado**-*adj*	disappointed
8094	**declive**-*m*	decline
8906	**decodificador**-*m*	decoder
9361	**decretar**-*vb*	decree
8557	**dedicatoria**-*adj; f*	dedicatory; dedication
9876	**defensiva**-*m*	defensive

8581	**deficiencia**-*f*	deficiency	9767	**desencadenar**-*vb*	trigger, unchain
7730	**deficiente**-*adj*	deficient	9615	**desengaño**-*m*	disappointment
10009	**deformación**-*f*	deformation	8304	**desenlace**-*m*	outcome
9258	**degeneración**-*f*	degeneration	8879	**desenmascarar**-*vb*	unmask
9257	**degollar**-*vb*	cut someone's throat	9410	**desenterrar**-*vb*	dig up
7836	**degradación**-*f*	degradation	8096	**deseoso**-*adj*	keen
8016	**degradar**-*vb*	degrade	8199	**desequilibrar**-*vb*	unbalance
8641	**delator**-*m*	informer	7858	**desequilibrio**-*m*	imbalance
7914	**deliberar**-*vb*	deliberate	7926	**desesperante**-*adj*	desperate, maddening
9560	**denominador**-*m*	denominator			
9821	**denominar**-*vb*	call	7687	**desesperanza**-*f*	despair
7713	**deparar**-*vb*	bring	9823	**desfalco**-*m*	embezzlement
8007	**deportación**-*f*	deportation	8570	**desfigurar**-*vb*	disfigure
7625	**deportar**-*vb*	deport	7675	**desfilar**-*vb*	parade
9342	**deposición**-*f*	deposition	7909	**desgarrar**-*vb*	tear
7755	**depresivo**-*adj*	depressing	9979	**desgarro**-*m*	tear
7747	**derechazo**-*m*	right	9432	**desgastar**-*vb*	wear out
8745	**derivar**-*vb*	derive	8332	**desgaste**-*m*	wear
9550	**derrochar**-*vb*	waste	8884	**desguazar**-*vb*	scrap
8579	**derroche**-*m*	waste	9642	**deshabitar**-*vb*	vacate
8974	**desacreditar**-*vb*	discredit	9454	**deshidratar**-*vb*	dehydrate
9579	**desagrado**-*m*	displeasure	9189	**deshielo**-*m*	thaw
9699	**desahogarse**-*vbr*	blow off steam	9357	**designio**-*m*	plan
9997	**desalentador**-*adj*	discouraging	8801	**desigual**-*adj*	unequal
8350	**desalojar**-*vb*	evict	9681	**desigualdad**-*f*	inequality
7814	**desalojo**-*m*	eviction	9614	**desintegración**-*f*	disintegration
7922	**desanimar**-*vb*	discourage	8691	**desintoxicación**-*f*	detoxification
9812	**desaprobar**-*vb*	disapprove	9709	**deslealtad**-*f*	disloyalty
8245	**desarme**-*m*	disarmament	9511	**deslizamiento**-*m*	slide
7556	**desatar**-*vb*	untie	7931	**desliz**-*m*	slip
9264	**desbordar**-*vb*	overflow	9575	**deslumbrar**-*vb*	dazzle
8482	**descalificar**-*vb*	disqualify	9524	**desmantelar**-*vb*	dismantle
8795	**descarte**-*m*	discard	8062	**desmayo**-*m*	fainting
8785	**descerebrado**-*adj*	brainless	7681	**desmoronar(se)**-*vb*	collapse
9443	**descolgar**-*vb*	take down	8688	**desnudar(se)**-*vb*	undress
9726	**descompresión**-*f*	decompression	9932	**desnutrición**-*f*	malnutrition
9898	**descomunal**-*adj*	huge	8151	**desocupado**-*adj*	unoccupied
8719	**desconcertar**-*vb*	perplex	9731	**desocupar**-*vb*	vacate
7722	**desconfiar**-*vb*	distrust	7662	**desordenar**-*vb*	make a mess of
8832	**descontaminación**-*f*	decontamination	9967	**desorientación**-*f*	disorientation
9359	**descontar**-*vb*	discount	7589	**desorientar**-*vb*	disorient
8940	**desechar**-*vb*	discard	8843	**despachar**-*vb*	dispatch
9700	**desembarque**-*m*	unloading	9434	**despampanante**-*adj*	stunning
9983	**desembocar**-*vb*	lead	7975	**despecho**-*m*	spite
9913	**desempate**-*m*	tiebreaker	7943	**despegado**-*adj*	taken off
8270	**desempeñar**-*vb*	perform	9085	**desperfecto**-*m*	flaw

9255	despilfarro-*m*	waste
7927	despistar-*vb*	mislead
8294	desplazamiento-*m*	displacement
8992	desplazar-*vb*	displace
7986	desplegar-*vb*	deploy
7890	desplomar(se)-*vb*	collapse
8834	despojar(se)-*vb*	strip
8600	despojo-*m*	dispossession
8914	desprender-*vb*	detach, release
9891	desprendimiento-*m*	detachment, open-handedness, landslide
7919	desprevenido-*adj*	unprepared
7879	desquiciar-*vb*	make to despair
9611	destapar-*vb*	uncover
8136	destierro-*m*	exile
9877	destinatario-*m*	recipient
8945	destituir-*vb*	remove
8582	destrozo-*m*	heavy damage
8893	deteriorar-*vb*	deteriorate
7646	deterioro-*m*	deterioration
9961	determinante-*adj; m*	determinant; determinant
7947	detestar-*vb*	loathe
7843	deudor-*adj; m*	in debt; debtor
7690	devastación-*f*	devastation
7616	diabético-*adj; m*	diabetic; diabetic
8708	diagnosticar-*vb*	diagnose
8761	diagonal-*adj; f*	diagonal; diagonal
9450	dialéctica-*f*	dialectic
9352	diálisis-*f*	dialysis
9762	dialogar-*vb*	talk
9323	diana-*f*	target
7595	diapositiva-*f*	slide
7682	dibujante-*m/f*	cartoonist
8628	dicción-*f*	diction
9630	dietético-*adj*	dietary
9782	diferencial-*adj; f*	differential; gap
9998	diferir-*vb*	differ
8552	dificultar-*vb*	hinder
9152	difteria-*f*	diphtheria
7820	difusión-*f*	diffusion
9165	digestivo-*adj*	digestive
10020	dilatación-*f*	dilation
9697	diligente-*adj*	diligent
9418	dimensional-*adj*	dimensional

8867	diminutivo-*adj; m*	diminutive; diminutive
8156	diócesis-*f*	diocese
9413	directriz-*f*	guideline
8124	discapacidad-*f*	disability
9962	discernir-*vb*	discern
8491	disciplinado-*adj*	disciplined
9228	disciplinario-*adj*	disciplinary
8982	discográfico-*adj*	recording
8296	discordia-*f*	discord
9367	discrepancia-*f*	discrepancy
8503	discutible-*adj*	questionable
9486	disecar-*vb*	dissect
8685	disección-*f*	dissection
7834	disentería-*f*	dysentery
9355	disfuncional-*adj*	dysfunctional
8391	disfunción-*f*	dysfunction
9565	disidente-*adj; m*	dissident; dissident
9588	disimulo-*m*	disguise
9338	dislocar(se)-*vb*	dislocate
8051	disminución-*f*	decrease
8632	disolución-*f*	dissolution
7705	disolver-*vb*	dissolve
9953	dispensar-*vb*	dispense
9414	dispersar-*vb*	disperse
8010	dispersión-*f*	dispersion
8375	disperso-*adj*	dispersed
9585	disponibilidad-*f*	availability
8776	disquete-*m*	diskette
7896	distintivo-*adj; m*	distinctive; emblem
9386	distorsionar-*vb*	distort
8063	distorsión-*f*	distortion
9610	diurno-*adj*	daytime
7912	diván-*m*	divan
8544	dividendo-*m*	dividend
9842	divisa-*f*	currency
7689	divulgar-*vb*	divulge
8505	DNI-*abr*	identity card
7846	doblado-*adj*	dubbed in, bent
9684	doblaje-*m*	dubbing
9639	doblegar-*vb*	crush
8532	docente-*adj; m/f*	educational; teacher
9541	doctrina-*f*	doctrine
7944	documentar-*vb*	document
9016	dogma-*m*	dogma
8242	dolencia-*f*	disease

9060	dolido-*adj*	hurt	
9100	domesticado-*adj*	domesticated	
8174	domiciliario-*adj*	home	
9837	dominicano-*adj; m*	Dominican; Dominican person	
8923	donativo-*m*	donation	
8408	dorso-*m*	back	
7516	dote-*f*	dowry	
9555	dramatismo-*m*	drama	
7886	dramaturgo-*m*	playwright	
9601	drenar-*vb*	drain	
9099	ducado-*m*	duchy	
7785	duchar(se)-*vb*	shower	
9570	dueto-*m*	duet	
8013	duplicar-*vb*	double	

E

9419	ebriedad-*f*	drunkenness
8562	ecografía-*f*	ultrasound
9051	ecología-*f*	ecology
8929	ecológico-*adj*	ecological
9389	ecologista-*m/f; adj*	ecologist; environmental
8711	economista-*m/f*	economist
9888	economizar-*vb*	economize
8831	ecosistema-*m*	ecosystem
9863	edema-*m*	edema
9641	edicto-*m*	edict
8962	edredón-*m*	quilt
9562	efectividad-*f*	effectiveness
9618	efigie-*f*	effigy
9911	efímero-*adj*	ephemeral
9314	ego-*m*	ego
9597	egresar-*vb*	graduate
7734	ejecutor-*adj; m*	executing; executor
7868	ejercitar-*vb*	exercise
10011	elasticidad-*f*	elasticity
8754	elástico-*m; adj*	elastic; elastic
8102	elector-*m*	elector
9071	electrodo-*m*	electrode
8501	electrodoméstico-*m*	domestic appliance
8030	electrón-*m*	electron
8949	elegía-*f*	elegy
8757	eliminatoria-*f*	heat
7523	elixir-*m*	elixir

8967	emanar-*vb*	emanate
8316	emancipación-*f*	emancipation
8934	embalaje-*m*	packaging
8317	embolia-*f*	embolism
7830	emborrachar(se)-*vb*	get drunk
9083	embotellar-*vb*	bottle
9391	embriagar-*vb*	get drunk
7548	embrión-*m*	embryo
8450	embudo-*m*	funnel
9650	emigrante-*adj; m/f*	emigrant; emigrant
8586	emigrar-*vb*	emigrate
8180	emisor-*m; adj*	sender; emitting
9309	empalmar(se)-*vb; vbr*	connect; overlap (LA), get a hard-on (ES) (coll)
8976	empanada-*f*	pie
8851	empaquetar-*vb*	pack
9683	emparejar-*vb*	match
9233	emplazamiento-*m*	site
9717	emporio-*m*	emporium
9066	enagua-*f*	petticoat
8875	encabezar-*vb*	lead
9690	encaminar-*vb*	route
9057	encantado-*adj*	delighted
7695	encarcelamiento-*m*	imprisonment
8022	encariñarse-*vbr*	grow fond of
7533	encarnación-*f*	incarnation
9999	encarnar-*vb*	embody
9675	encerar-*vb*	wax
10018	encestar-*vb*	dunk
8496	encoger-*vb*	shrink
8543	encomendar-*vb*	entrust
9236	encuadre-*m*	framing
8338	encubierto-*adj*	undercover
7597	encubrimiento-*m*	concealment
9646	endemoniado-*adj; m*	possessed; devil
9577	endurecer-*vb*	harden
8524	enema-*m*	enema
8802	enemistad-*f*	enmity
9144	energético-*adj*	energetic
7921	enérgico-*adj*	energetic
9395	enfatizar-*vb*	emphasize
9786	enfisema-*m*	emphysema
8219	enfriamiento-*m*	cooling
7621	enganchar-*vb*	hook
8265	enganche-*m*	coupling

8008	**engañoso**-*adj*	misleading	8985	**escasear**-*vb*	be scarce
7564	**engendrar**-*vb*	engender	8973	**escayolar**-*vb*	put in a cast
7839	**engranaje**-*m*	gear	9297	**escénico**-*adj*	scenic
9949	**enigmático**-*adj*	enigmatic	8712	**escenografía**-*f*	scenography
8281	**enjaular**-*vb*	cage	9262	**escepticismo**-*m*	skepticism
9203	**enjuague**-*m*	rinse	9886	**esclarecer**-*vb*	clarify
9580	**enlatar**-*vb*	can	9438	**esclavizar**-*vb*	enslave
8659	**enriquecer(se)**-*vb*	enrich	9298	**esclerosis**-*f*	sclerosis
8169	**enrollar**-*vb*	roll	8470	**escolta**-*m/f*	bodyguard
9532	**ensamblaje**-*m*	assembly	7761	**escroto**-*m*	scrotum
8027	**ensuciar(se)**-*vb*	mess	10025	**escrutinio**-*m*	scrutiny
7965	**entablar**-*vb*	enter into	8846	**esguince**-*m*	sprain
9951	**entereza**-*f*	strength	9217	**esmero**-*m*	care
8998	**entonar**-*vb*	sing	7644	**espasmo**-*m*	spasm
9429	**entrelazar**-*vb*	weave together, interlock	9915	**espátula**-*f*	spatula
8346	**entrometer(se)**-*vb*	interfere	9437	**especialización**-*f*	specialization
8069	**entrometerse**-*vbr*	interfere	8732	**especializar**-*vb*	specialize
7956	**envasar**-*vb*	package	7627	**especificación**-*f*	specification
7876	**envejecimiento**-*m*	aging	9286	**especificar**-*vb*	specify
9202	**envergadura**-*f*	scale	9643	**espectral**-*adj*	spectral
9583	**envidiable**-*adj*	enviable	9542	**especulador**-*m*	speculator
8148	**envoltorio**-*m*	wrapper	8978	**espermatozoide**-*m*	spermatozoon
8325	**envoltura**-*f*	wrapper	7980	**espesor**-*m*	thickness
8456	**enzima**-*f*	enzyme	8122	**espinal**-*adj*	spinal
8561	**epicentro**-*m*	epicenter	9980	**espinazo**-*m*	spine
7631	**épico**-*adj*	epic	8488	**espino**-*m*	hawthorn
8271	**epiléptico**-*adj; m*	epileptic; epileptic	8060	**espiritualidad**-*f*	spirituality
9026	**epílogo**-*f*	epilogue	8626	**espontaneidad**-*f*	spontaneity
8649	**epitafio**-*m*	epitaph	9076	**espora**-*f*	spore
9879	**equidad**-*f*	equity	7936	**espuela**-*f*	spur
7855	**equilibrado**-*adj*	well-balanced	9935	**esquí**-*m*	ski
7642	**equilibrar**-*vb*	balance	7887	**esquivo**-*adj*	elusive
9907	**erizo**-*m*	hedgehog	7540	**esquizofrénico**-*adj*	schizophrenic
8677	**erosión**-*f*	erosion	9819	**estabilizador**-*adj; m*	stabilising; stabilizer
8547	**erotismo**-*m*	eroticism	8966	**estabilizar(se)**-*vb*	stabilize
7954	**erradicar**-*vb*	eradicate	8959	**estampa**-*f*	stamp
7696	**errar**-*vb*	err	9078	**estampar**-*vb*	stamp
9146	**esbozo**-*m*	outline	8074	**estancar(se)**-*vb*	stall
9847	**escalador**-*m*	climber	9482	**estanco**-*adj; m*	watertight; shop
8227	**escama**-*f*	scale	9101	**estaño**-*m*	tin
7924	**escarabajo**-*m*	beetle	8803	**estepa**-*f*	steppe
9265	**escaramuza**-*f*	skirmish	8372	**estereotipar**-*vb*	stereotype
9151	**escarbar**-*vb*	dig	8624	**estereotipo**-*m*	stereotype
8670	**escarcha**-*f*	frost	8417	**esterilización**-*f*	sterilization
7805	**escarmentar**-*vb*	punish severely	9242	**esternón**-*m*	sternum
			8568	**estigma**-*m*	stigma

7827	**estimación**-*f*	estimation	
7946	**estimulación**-*f*	stimulation	
9706	**estipular**-*vb*	stipulate	
9856	**estiramiento**-*m*	stretching	
7815	**estirpe**-*f*	lineage	
9753	**estocada**-*f*	thrust	
7778	**estornudar**-*vb*	sneeze	
9128	**estrangulación**-*f*	strangulation	
9334	**estratagema**-*f*	stratagem	
8695	**estratega**-*m/f*	strategist	
7593	**estratégico**-*adj*	strategic	
8912	**estremecer(se)**-*vb*	shudder	
7511	**estrenar**-*vb*	use for the first time	
9735	**estría**-*f*	stretch mark	
7972	**estrofa**-*f*	stanza	
8236	**estructural**-*adj*	structural	
7530	**estudioso**-*adj; m*	studious; scholar	
8788	**estupefaciente**-*m*	narcotic	
9797	**estupor**-*m*	stupor	
9622	**etiquetar**-*vb*	label	
8981	**étnico**-*adj*	ethnic	
9963	**eucalipto**-*m*	eucalyptus	
8975	**eufórico**-*adj*	euphoric	
9427	**evangelista**-*m/f*	evangelist	
9190	**evaporar**-*vb*	evaporate	
9793	**eventual**-*adj*	eventual	
9113	**evocar**-*vb*	evoke	
9736	**evolutivo**-*adj*	evolutionary	
9248	**exagerado**-*adj*	exaggerated	
9986	**exaltación**-*f*	exaltation	
7746	**exaltado**-*adj; m*	frenzied; hothead	
9455	**examinador**-*m*	examiner	
9859	**exasperante**-*adj*	infuriating	
8224	**exceder**-*vb*	exceed	
8129	**exceptuar**-*vb*	exclude	
9553	**exclamación**-*f*	exclamation	
7608	**excluir**-*vb*	exclude	
9206	**exclusión**-*f*	exclusion	
8653	**exclusividad**-*f*	exclusivity	
7950	**excusar**-*vb*	excuse	
9591	**exención**-*f*	exemption	
9722	**exento**-*adj*	exempt	
9169	**exhaustivo**-*adj*	comprehensive	
7889	**exhibir**-*vb*	display	
7559	**exiliar**-*vb*	exile	
9137	**existencial**-*adj*	existential	

9515	**expansivo**-*adj*	expansive
9993	**expectación**-*f*	expectation
9287	**experimentación**-*f*	experimentation
7550	**ex**-*pfx*	ex
9420	**expirar**-*vb*	expire
9608	**explanada**-*f*	esplanade
9369	**explícito**-*adj*	explicit
8760	**exprimir**-*vb*	squeeze
8741	**exterminación**-*f*	extermination
9964	**extinguidor**-*m*	extinguisher
8133	**extinguir**-*vb*	extinguish
9796	**extinto**-*adj*	extinct
9602	**extirpar**-*vb*	remove

F

8506	**faceta**-*f*	facet
7679	**factible**-*adj*	feasible
9660	**factoría**-*f*	factory
9881	**facturación**-*f*	billing
9995	**falange**-*f*	phalange
7906	**fallecimiento**-*m*	death
8913	**fanatismo**-*m*	fanaticism
9063	**fantasmal**-*adj*	ghostly
8365	**fardo**-*m*	bundle
8640	**fármaco**-*m*	drug
8713	**farola**-*f*	lamppost
7611	**fatalidad**-*f*	fatality
9163	**fatídico**-*adj*	fateful
8128	**fatigar**-*vb*	exhaust
8800	**fauces**-*fpl*	maw
9253	**febril**-*adj*	febrile
9874	**fecal**-*adj*	fecal
9747	**fechar**-*vb*	date
9143	**fechoría**-*f*	piece of mischief
8955	**feligrés**-*m*	parishioner
9407	**felino**-*adj; m*	feline; feline
9452	**fémur**-*m*	femur
8134	**féretro**-*m*	coffin
8714	**ferocidad**-*f*	ferocity
8402	**férreo**-*adj*	iron
7864	**ferviente**-*adj*	fervent
8229	**festejo**-*m*	feast
8910	**festividad**-*f*	festivity
9917	**fetal**-*adj*	fetal
9093	**feudal**-*adj*	feudal

9445	feudo-*m*	fief	8302	fotocopiar-*vb*	photocopy
9110	fiambre-*m*	meat	8132	frac-*m*	tuxedo
8418	fichero-*m*	filing cabinet	8326	fragata-*f*	frigate
8436	ficticio-*adj*	fictional	9301	fragilidad-*f*	fragility
7754	fideicomiso-*m*	trust	8147	franela-*f*	flannel
7702	figurar-*vb*	include	7987	fraternal-*adj*	fraternal
8247	filial-*f; adj*	subsidiary; filial	9716	frazada-*f*	blanket
9809	filoso-*adj*	sharp	8747	frecuentar-*vb*	frequent
8292	filosófico-*adj*	philosophical	7505	frenesí-*m*	frenzy
8994	filtrado-*adj; m*	filtering; filter	8836	frenético-*adj*	frantic
8786	filtrar-*vb*	filter	7584	frescura-*f*	freshness
8321	finalidad-*f*	purpose	7527	frialdad-*f*	coldness
7509	finalista-*adj; m/f*	finalist; finalist	7703	fricción-*f*	friction
8070	financiamiento-*m*	financing	8333	frívolo-*adj*	frivolous
8585	finito-*adj*	finite	7661	fronterizo-*m; adj*	border; frontier
8318	finlandés-*adj; m*	Finnish; Finnish person	7704	frotar-*vb*	rub
7694	firmamento-*m*	firmament	8861	frustrado-*adj*	frustrated
8983	física-*adj; f*	physical; physics	9075	frutilla-*f*	strawberry (LA)
9241	fisiología-*f*	physiology	9358	fulgor-*m*	brightness
8339	fisura-*f*	fissure	9392	fulminante-*adj*	fulminant
7994	flagrante-*adj*	flagrant	9975	fumigar-*vb*	fumigate
8086	flamante-*adj*	brand-new	8073	funda-*f*	cover
8744	flautista-*m/f*	flutist	8964	fundamentalista-*adj; m/f*	fundamentalist; fundamentalist
9830	fleco-*m*	fringe	9958	fundido-*adj*	molten
7991	flexibilidad-*f*	flexibility	7525	furor-*m*	fury
9326	floral-*adj*	floral	7739	furtivo-*adj; m*	furtive; poacher
9315	flotación-*f*	flotation			
9430	flotador-*m*	float			
9927	fluctuación-*f*	fluctuation		**G**	
8415	fluidez-*f*	fluency			
9476	fogoso-*adj*	ardent	8845	gaceta-*f*	gazette
9221	folclore-*m*	folklore	8813	gaita-*f*	bagpipe
9521	follaje-*m*	foliage	9433	gala-*f*	gala
8616	fomentar-*vb*	foster	9269	galeón-*m*	galleon
8379	fonógrafo-*m*	phonograph	8041	galera-*f*	galley
9114	fontanería-*f*	plumbing	10004	galgo-*m*	greyhound
9670	forcejear-*vb*	struggle, wrestle	8631	gallardo-*adj; m*	dashing; gallant
7966	forjado-*adj*	wrought	8139	ganadero-*m*	farmer
8603	forjar-*vb*	forge	9836	ganado-*m*	cattle
7630	formular-*vb*	formulate	7588	gangrena-*f*	gangrene
9001	fornido-*adj*	strapping	7823	garabato-*m*	doodle
9439	forraje-*m*	forage	9527	garbanzo-*m*	chickpea
8718	fortuito-*adj*	fortuitous	8881	gardenia-*f*	gardenia
8324	forzoso-*adj*	forced	9210	garrapata-*f*	tick
8907	fotocopiadora-*f*	photocopier	8932	garza-*f*	heron
			7563	gasa-*f*	chiffon

9180	**genealógico**-*adj*	genealogical	7767	**hijastro**-*m*	stepson
9693	**genoma**-*m*	genome	7652	**hilera**-*f*	row
8260	**geología**-*f*	geology	9765	**hincapié**-*m*	emphasis
9783	**geológico**-*adj*	geological	7650	**hinchazón**-*f*	swelling
9788	**geriátrico**-*adj; m*	geriatric; nursing home	9781	**hipotecar**-*vb*	mortgage
			8269	**hipotermia**-*f*	hypothermia
9132	**gimnasta**-*m/f*	gymnast	8028	**hipotéticamente**-*adv*	hypothetically
8066	**girasol**-*m*	sunflower			
8818	**giratorio**-*adj*	rotating	9199	**hipotético**-*adj*	hypothetical
8775	**glacial**-*adj*	glacial	9988	**hiriente**-*adj*	hurtful
8341	**globalización**-*f*	globalization	8121	**hispano**-*adj; m*	Hispanic; Hispanic
8411	**glóbulo**-*m*	globule	7859	**hormigueo**-*m*	tingling
9517	**glorieta**-*f*	roundabout	9161	**hormonal**-*adj*	hormonal
8566	**glotón**-*m; adj*	glutton; gluttonous	7807	**hornear**-*vb*	bake
8597	**glucosa**-*f*	glucose	8218	**horquilla**-*f*	hairpin
8619	**golfista**-*m/f*	golfer	7606	**horrorizar(se)**-*vb*	horrify
8487	**golondrina**-*f*	swallow	7894	**hospicio**-*m*	hospice
8673	**góndola**-*f*	gondola	8038	**hospitalario**-*adj*	hospitable
7791	**gotera**-*f*	leak	8309	**hospitalizar**-*vb*	hospitalize
8492	**gratificación**-*f*	gratification	8449	**hoz**-*f*	sickle
8349	**grosor**-*m*	thickness	8873	**huelguista**-*m/f*	striker
8554	**gruñido**-*m*	growl	9201	**hule**-*m*	oilcloth
8651	**gruñir**-*vb*	growl	9705	**humorista**-*m/f*	humorist
8598	**grupal**-*adj*	group	8090	**hundimiento**-*m*	sinking
9415	**guijarro**-*m*	pebble			
9584	**guinda**-*f*	cherry, final touch		**I**	
8514	**gustoso**-*adj*	delicious, gladly			

H

			8144	**idealismo**-*m*	idealism
8590	**haba**-*f*	bean	7988	**idear**-*vb*	devise
9044	**habichuela**-*f*	bean	9442	**ídem**-*prn; adv*	likewise; ditto
8410	**habituar(se)**-*vb*	get in the habit of	9306	**idóneo**-*adj*	suitable
8363	**hardware**-*m*	hardware	9785	**iguana**-*f*	iguana
9501	**hebilla**-*f*	buckle	8432	**ilegítimo**-*adj*	illegitimate
7506	**heces**-*fpl*	dregs, feces	9976	**ilícito**-*adj*	illicit
9939	**helecho**-*m*	fern	7538	**ilógico**-*adj*	illogical
7522	**helio**-*m*	helium	9160	**iluso**-*adj*	gullible, deluded
9854	**henchir(se)**-*vb*	fill	7750	**ilustración**-*f*	illustration
9849	**hendidura**-*f*	indent	9183	**ilustrar**-*vb*	illustrate
7999	**hereditario**-*adj*	hereditary	8198	**imaginable**-*adj*	imaginable
9382	**hermético**-*adj*	airtight	8157	**imaginativo**-*adj*	imaginative
7958	**hernia**-*f*	hernia	9411	**impasible**-*adj*	impassive
8515	**hidalgo**-*m*	nobleman	7623	**imperativo**-*adj; m*	imperative; imperative
8187	**hidráulico**-*adj*	hydraulic	9595	**imperceptible**-*adj*	imperceptible
9637	**higuera**-*f*	fig tree	8642	**imperfección**-*f*	imperfection
			8155	**imperfecto**-*adj*	imperfect

7898	**imperialismo-***m*	imperialism	7602	**indeciso-***adj*	indecisive
8239	**imperialista-***adj; m/f*	imperialistic; imperialist	7629	**indeseable-***adj; m/f*	undesirable; undesirable
8778	**impersonal-***adj*	impersonal	7513	**indignante-***adj*	outrageous
8378	**ímpetu-***m*	impetus	8115	**indiscutible-***adj*	indisputable
9347	**implementar-***vb*	implement	8526	**individualidad-***f*	individuality
9205	**imposibilidad-***f*	impossibility	9906	**individualismo-***m*	individualism
9008	**imposición-***f*	imposition	10006	**indivisible-***adj*	indivisible
9543	**impresor-***adj; m*	printing; printer	9404	**índole-***f*	nature
7829	**impresora-***f*	printer	8362	**indoloro-***adj*	painless
8233	**impropio-***adj*	inappropriate	9912	**inducción-***f*	induction
9739	**impulsor-***adj; m*	active; booster	9141	**inducir-***vb*	induce
9067	**impuro-***adj*	impure	8163	**inepto-***adj*	inept
7719	**inaccesible-***adj*	inaccessible	8933	**inercia-***f*	inertia
9943	**inactividad-***f*	inactivity	8525	**inerte-***adj*	inert
8516	**inactivo-***adj*	inactive	8200	**inestabilidad-***f*	instability
9279	**inadvertido-***adj*	unnoticed	8988	**inestimable-***adj*	invaluable
9505	**inagotable-***adj*	inexhaustible	9510	**inexcusable-***adj*	inexcusable
7648	**inalcanzable-***adj*	unattainable	8664	**inexistente-***adj*	nonexistent
9502	**inanición-***f*	starvation	9688	**inexorable-***adj*	inexorable
8108	**inaugurar-***vb*	inaugurate	8248	**inexperto-***adj*	inexperienced
8314	**incalculable-***adj*	incalculable	7649	**inferioridad-***f*	inferiority
7558	**inca-***m/f; adj*	Inca; Incan	8715	**infestar-***vb*	infest
8522	**incansable-***adj*	tireless	8705	**infiltración-***f*	infiltration
7724	**incapacitar-***vb*	incapacitate	8342	**infinidad-***f*	infinity
7678	**incendiario-***adj; m*	incendiary; arsonist	7735	**inflamable-***adj*	flammable
9102	**incesante-***adj*	incessant	7804	**inflamación-***f*	inflammation
8822	**incinerador-***adj; m*	incinerating; incinerator	9268	**inflar-***vb*	inflate
9108	**incinerar-***vb*	incinerate	7640	**influenciar-***vb*	influence
8463	**incitar-***vb*	incite	7561	**informático-***adj; m*	computer; computer expert
9310	**incoherente-***adj*	incoherent	7793	**infortunio-***m*	misfortune
7996	**incomodidad-***f*	discomfort	8158	**infrarrojo-***adj*	infrared
9047	**incompatible-***adj*	incompatible	9184	**infringir-***vb*	infringe
9164	**incomunicar-***vb*	isolate	8871	**infusión-***f*	infusion
10001	**inconsciencia-***f*	unconsciousness	9711	**ingerir-***vb*	ingest
9331	**inconstante-***adj*	inconstant	9865	**inhalación-***f*	inhalation
8444	**incorporar-***vb*	incorporate	8558	**inherente-***adj*	inherent
9725	**incredulidad-***f*	disbelief	8494	**inhibición-***f*	inhibition
9741	**incubación-***m/f*	incubation	7708	**inmaculado-***adj*	immaculate
9398	**incubadora-***f*	incubator	8088	**inmensidad-***f*	immensity
9981	**incuestionable-***adj*	unquestionable	9582	**inmerso-***adj*	immersed
9843	**incumplimiento-***m*	breach	9021	**inmigración-***f*	immigration
8135	**indagar-***vb*	investigate	9259	**inmoralidad-***f*	immorality
9339	**indebido-***adj*	improper	9061	**inmovilizar-***vb*	immobilize
9878	**indecisión-***f*	indecision	8749	**inmueble-***m*	building

8977	**inmunológico**-*adj*	immune
9661	**inmutable**-*adj*	immutable
7531	**innato**-*adj*	innate
8261	**innegable**-*adj*	undeniable
8202	**innovación**-*f*	innovation
8883	**inoxidable**-*adj*	stainless
7903	**inquebrantable**-*adj*	unwavering
9028	**inquietar**-*vb*	unsettle
8890	**insatisfecho**-*adj*	dissatisfied
7932	**inscribir**-*vb*	register
9535	**inseminación**-*f*	insemination
8110	**insensatez**-*f*	folly
9402	**insertar**-*vb*	insert
9808	**insípido**-*adj*	tasteless
7664	**insistencia**-*f*	insistence
8250	**insolación**-*f*	sunstroke
9680	**insostenible**-*adj*	untenable
9015	**instintivo**-*adj*	instinctive
8853	**instructivo**-*adj*	instructive
8608	**instruido**-*adj*	instructed
8206	**instrumental**-*adj; m*	instrumental; instrument
8886	**insuficiencia**-*f*	insufficiency
7572	**insuficiente**-*adj; m*	insufficient; unsatisfactory
8739	**insuperable**-*adj*	unbeatable
8414	**insurgente**-*adj; m/f*	insurgent; rebel
7802	**insurrección**-*f*	insurrection
8267	**integrado**-*adj*	integrated
9179	**integrante**-*adj; m/f*	integral; member
8972	**integrar**-*vb*	integrate
8443	**íntegro**-*adj*	entire
8511	**intemperie**-*f*	weather
9321	**intencionado**-*adj*	deliberate
9470	**intendencia**-*f*	quartermaster
7654	**intensivo**-*adj*	intensive
9456	**interactuar**-*vb*	interact
8454	**intercepción**-*f*	interception
9498	**interestelar**-*adj*	interstellar
9092	**interfaz**-*f*	interface
8730	**interino**-*adj; m*	interim; caretaker
7521	**intermitente**-*adj; m*	intermittent; blinker
9117	**intestinal**-*adj*	intestinal
7955	**intimidación**-*f*	intimidation
9775	**intranquilo**-*adj*	uneasy
7851	**intravenoso**-*adj*	intravenous

7781	**intrigar**-*vb*	intrigue
9845	**introvertido**-*adj; m*	introverted; introvert
9719	**intuitivo**-*adj*	intuitive
9225	**inusualmente**-*adv*	unusually
9656	**invariable**-*adj; m*	unchanging; unchanged
7978	**invernal**-*adj*	wintry
9605	**inverosímil**-*adj*	implausible
7824	**invicto**-*adj*	unbeaten
7553	**invocar**-*vb*	invoke
8518	**inyectar**-*vb*	inject
9773	**ion**-*m*	ion
7835	**iraní**-*adj; m/f*	Iranian; Iranian person
8475	**irrazonable**-*adj*	unreasonable
8213	**irrefutable**-*adj*	irrefutable
9572	**irregularidad**-*f*	irregularity
10005	**irremediable**-*adj*	irremediable
8481	**irreparable**-*adj*	unrepairable
9802	**irreprochable**-*adj*	irreproachable
8936	**irresponsabilidad**-*f*	irresponsibility
7772	**irreversible**-*adj*	irreversible
9070	**irrevocable**-*adj*	irrevocable
8301	**irrigación**-*f*	irrigation
8170	**irritación**-*f*	irritation
9091	**islámico**-*adj*	Islamic
8465	**islamista**-*adj*	Islamist
9030	**isleño**-*adj; m*	island; islander
7798	**israelita**-*adj; m*	Israelite; Israelite person
9740	**izquierdista**-*adj; m/f*	leftist; leftist

J

8877	**jacinto**-*m*	hyacinth
9893	**já**-*int*	ha
8594	**jarro**-*m*	mug
8849	**jauría**-*f*	pack
9282	**jesuita**-*adj; m/f*	Jesuit; Jesuit
7771	**jeta**-*f*	face (coll)
7842	**jonrón**-*m*	home run
9509	**jornalero**-*m*	day laborer
8575	**jovial**-*adj*	jovial
8991	**junco**-*m*	reed
8077	**jurídico**-*adj*	legal
9423	**justiciero**-*adj; m*	tough; vigilante

K

| 9609 | kiosco-*m* | kiosk |
| 9212 | kurdo-*adj; m* | Kurdish; Kurdish person |

L

7957	labia-*f*	gift of the gab
9125	laborista-*adj; m*	Labour; Labor Party member
7852	labrador-*m/f*	farmer, lab
9500	laburar-*vb*	work (LA)
8225	laca-*f*	lacquer
9291	lactosa-*f*	lactose
8059	lagartija-*f*	lizard
9303	lamentación-*f*	lamentation
8620	lámina-*f*	sheet
9446	langostino-*m*	prawn
9484	lanzar-*vb*	throw
7792	lapso-*m*	period of time
9592	lapsus-*m*	lapse
8208	laptop-*f*	laptop
9977	largometraje-*m*	feature film
9082	laringe-*f*	larynx
9466	lastimoso-*adj*	pitiful
7825	latente-*adj*	latent
9351	látex-*m*	latex
9676	laúd-*m*	lute
8310	legalidad-*f*	legality
9538	legionario-*adj; m*	legionary; legionnaire
9055	legislador-*adj; m*	legislative; legislator
9324	legislatura-*f*	legislature
9737	legitimidad-*f*	legitimacy
7586	legua-*f*	league
7849	lejía-*f*	bleach
9658	leño-*m*	log
8145	lenteja-*f*	lentil
8131	lentejuela-*f*	sequin
9600	lentitud-*f*	slowness
7720	lesionar-*vb*	injure
8922	letrado-*m; adj*	counsel; learned
9118	levar-*vb*	weigh
8793	libanés-*adj; m*	Lebanese; Lebanese person

8361	liberador-*adj*	liberating
9872	liberalismo-*m*	liberalism
8919	libertador-*m; adj*	liberator; liberator
8643	libertino-*adj; m*	licentious; libertine
8654	libido-*f*	libido
8232	libreto-*m*	script
7828	licenciatura-*f*	degree
8397	ligereza-*f*	lightness
8043	limpiaparabrisas-*m*	wiper
7934	lince-*m*	lynx
8327	linchamiento-*m*	lynching
9136	lineal-*adj*	linear
9787	lingüístico-*adj*	linguistic
9458	liposucción-*f*	liposuction
9758	liquidez-*f*	liquidity
9803	lira-*f*	lyre
9644	lírico-*adj*	lyrical
7822	lisiado-*adj; m*	disabled; disabled person
8014	listado-*m*	list
9629	litigio-*m*	litigation
8486	llamamiento-*m*	call
9655	loable-*adj*	laudable
8214	localidad-*f*	town
8092	locutor-*m*	announcer
8453	logística-*f*	logistics
8601	logotipo-*m*	logo
9400	losa-*f*	slab
8925	lucero-*m*	bright star
8428	lucidez-*f*	lucidity
7632	lúcido-*adj*	lucid
7569	lucrativo-*adj*	lucrative
7717	lúgubre-*adj*	grim
9834	lumbago-*m*	lumbago
9720	lumbar-*adj*	lumbar
8519	lumbre-*f*	fire

M

8048	macabro-*adj*	macabre
7676	maceta-*f*	pot
7666	machacar-*vb*	crush
9576	magenta-*adj*	magenta
9789	magistral-*adj*	masterly
9247	magma-*m*	magma
8164	magnesio-*m*	magnesium

7863	magnetismo-*m*	magnetism	
9574	magnificencia-*f*	magnificence	
8878	magnolia-*f*	magnolia	
8773	majestuoso-*adj*	majestic	
9397	malabarista-*m/f*	juggler	
7674	maleante-*m/f*	criminal	
8167	malicioso-*adj*	malicious	
7714	maloliente-*adj*	stinking	
9374	malversación-*f*	embezzlement	
9292	maña-*f*	skill	
9810	mandolina-*f*	mandolin	
7727	maniobrar-*vb*	maneuver	
8160	manjar-*m*	delicacy	
8223	manso-*adj*	tame	
8153	manzanilla-*f*	chamomile	
8256	manzano-*m*	apple tree	
9853	maquillar(se)-*vb*	make up	
9804	maquinilla-*f*	razor	
7833	marcación-*f*	marking	
9923	marcapasos-*m*	pacemaker	
9465	marchitar-*vb*	wither	
8954	marejada-*f*	tidal wave	
8769	margarina-*f*	margarine	
8606	marginal-*adj*	marginal	
8814	marginar-*vb*	marginalize	
10024	mariguana-*f*	marijuana	
8737	marimacho-*m*	tomboy (coll)	
7977	marítimo-*adj*	maritime	
9866	marrano-*adj; m*	disgusting (coll); pig	
7878	marroquí-*adj; m/f*	Moroccan; Moroccan person	
8625	marxismo-*m*	Marxism	
8452	marxista-*adj; m/f*	marxist; Marxist	
7930	masculinidad-*f*	masculinity	
9942	masilla-*f*	putty	
8052	masón-*m*	mason	
8207	masticar-*vb*	chew	
10013	materialismo-*m*	materialism	
8862	materialista-*adj; m/f*	materialistic; materialist	
8703	matiz-*m*	nuance	
7701	matorral-*m*	bush	
8790	matricular(se)-*vb*	enroll	
7536	mausoleo-*m*	mausoleum	
8429	maya-*adj; m*	Mayan; Mayan person	
10003	mayorista-*adj*	wholesale	

8517	maza-*f*	mace	
9653	mazorca-*f*	corncob	
7723	mecedora-*f*	rocking chair	
8253	mecenas-*m/f*	patron	
9494	mediación-*f*	mediation	
8244	mediador-*m*	mediator	
8254	medicar-*vb*	medicate	
8011	medicinal-*adj*	medicinal	
9475	medición-*f*	measurement	
7895	mediocridad-*m/f; f*	mediocre; mediocrity	
7763	mejillón-*m*	mussel	
7576	mejoría-*f*	improvement	
9185	mellar-*vb*	chip	
8116	melodramático-*adj*	melodramatic	
9495	membrana-*f*	membrane	
8576	menear-*vb*	shake	
9416	meningitis-*f*	meningitis	
8395	menopausia-*f*	menopause	
9903	menospreciar-*vb*	underestimate	
9791	mensajería-*f*	messaging	
8455	menstruación-*f*	menstruation	
9701	mensualidad-*f*	monthly wage	
9663	meollo-*m*	crux	
8319	mercadeo-*m*	marketing	
9487	mercantil-*adj*	commercial	
8571	merecedor-*adj*	worthy	
9703	merendar-*vb*	have a snack	
7736	merengue-*m*	meringue	
9826	meridional-*adj*	southern	
8162	meseta-*f*	plateau	
9238	metafísico-*adj*	metaphysical	
8901	metafórico-*adj*	metaphorical	
8067	metamorfosis-*f*	metamorphosis	
9372	meteorología-*f*	meteorology	
8856	meteorólogo-*m*	meteorologist	
8025	meticuloso-*adj*	meticulous	
9154	metodista-*adj; m/f*	Methodist; Methodist	
9851	metodología-*f*	methodology	
8782	mica-*f*	mica	
9308	microchip-*m*	microchip	
9829	mímica-*f*	mime	
8220	minería-*f*	mining	
8731	minimizar-*vb*	minimise	
8495	minucioso-*adj*	thorough	
7620	minúsculo-*adj*	tiny	

9048	**minusválido**-*adj; m*	disabled; disabled person
8419	**miope**-*adj*	short-sighted
9147	**mirador**-*m*	viewpoint
9000	**mirlo**-*m*	blackbird
8400	**mísero**-*adj*	measly
8798	**mítico**-*adj*	mythical
8855	**mixto**-*adj*	mixed
9946	**modalidad**-*f*	mode
9023	**modelar**-*vb*	model
7762	**moderar**-*vb*	moderate
9651	**modernidad**-*f*	modernity
9728	**mogollón**-*m; adv*	lots of (coll); loads
7732	**mole**-*f*	mass
7743	**moler**-*vb*	grind
9122	**momentáneo**-*adj*	momentary
7989	**mongol**-*adj; m*	Mongolian; Mongol
8203	**monogamia**-*f*	monogamy
9664	**monografía**-*f*	monograph
8299	**monotonía**-*f*	monotony
8376	**monótono**-*adj*	monotonous
8648	**monóxido**-*m*	monoxide
8595	**monzón**-*m*	monsoon
8794	**moralista**-*m/f; adj*	moralist; moralistic
8422	**mordaz**-*adj*	scathing
7605	**mordedura**-*f*	bite
9330	**morro**-*m*	snout
9425	**mortífero**-*adj*	lethal
9332	**mosaico**-*adj; m*	mosaic; mosaic
8807	**mote**-*m*	nickname
8234	**movilidad**-*f*	mobility
8692	**movilizar**-*vb*	mobilize
7959	**mueca**-*f*	grin
8735	**multinacional**-*f; adj*	multinational; multinational
7607	**multiplicar(se)**-*vb*	multiply
8767	**mundano**-*adj*	mundane
8075	**municipal**-*adj*	municipal
7532	**municipalidad**-*f*	municipality
9987	**muñón**-*m*	stump
8563	**murmurar**-*vb*	murmur
7677	**mutilación**-*f*	mutilation

N

8963	**nacionalismo**-*m*	nationalism
7967	**nacionalista**-*adj; m/f*	nationalist; nationalist
8204	**nailon**-*m*	nylon
9564	**napolitano**-*adj; m*	Neapolitan; Neapolitan person
9744	**narcisismo**-*m*	narcissism
8885	**narciso**-*m*	daffodil
7686	**narcotraficante**-*m/f*	drug dealer
8003	**narcotráfico**-*m*	drug trafficking
8403	**narrativo**-*adj; f*	narrative; narrative
8852	**natalidad**-*f*	birth rate
9223	**náufrago**-*m/f*	castaway
9235	**nauseabundo**-*adj*	nauseating
8874	**navegador**-*m*	browser, navigator
9240	**navegante**-*m/f*	navigator
8367	**nazismo**-*m*	Nazism
8196	**nebuloso**-*adj*	foggy
9922	**negatividad**-*f*	negativity
7710	**negociable**-*adj*	negotiable
7615	**negociador**-*m*	negotiator
7881	**nerviosismo**-*m*	nervousness
9694	**neural**-*adj*	neural
9738	**neurocirugía**-*f*	neurosurgery
8997	**neurológico**-*adj*	neurological
8663	**neurólogo**-*m*	neurologist
7831	**neurótico**-*adj; m*	neurotic; neurotic
8771	**neutralidad**-*f*	neutrality
7783	**neutralizar**-*vb*	neutralize
8970	**neutro**-*adj*	neutral
8176	**neutrón**-*f*	neutron
8971	**nexo**-*m*	nexus
8638	**nicho**-*m*	niche
9011	**níquel**-*m*	nickel
7557	**nitrato**-*m*	nitrate
9965	**nivelar**-*vb*	level
9037	**nogal**-*m*	walnut
8353	**nómada**-*adj; m/f*	nomadic; Nomad
7992	**nominar**-*vb*	nominate
9167	**noquear**-*vb*	knock out
9742	**norcoreano**-*adj; m*	North Korean; North Korean person
9422	**norteño**-*adj; m*	northern; northerner
7933	**noticiario**-*m*	news
8087	**notificar**-*vb*	notify
8499	**notorio**-*adj*	notorious
8117	**novedoso**-*adj*	novel
7669	**novillo**-*m*	heifer, steer

7709	**nutrición**-*f*	nutrition
9959	**nutrir**-*vb*	nourish
9384	**nutritivo**-*adj*	nutritious

O

9536	**obesidad**-*f*	obesity
8823	**obeso**-*adj*	obese
8190	**objetividad**-*f*	objectivity
8290	**obrar**-*vb*	act
8050	**obscenidad**-*f*	obscenity
9712	**obsoleto**-*adj*	obsolete
8840	**obstinación**-*f*	obstinacy
9162	**obstruir**-*vb*	obstruct
8246	**oca**-*f*	goose
9901	**ocasionar**-*vb*	cause
9385	**oceánico**-*adj*	oceanic
8262	**ochocientos**-*num*	eight hundred
8965	**ocioso**-*adj*	idle
7641	**ocupante**-*adj; m/f*	occupying; occupant
8001	**ocurrencia**-*f*	idea
9897	**ocurrente**-*adj*	witty
7857	**ofendido**-*adj*	offended
8197	**oficinista**-*m/f*	office worker
9752	**ojal**-*m*	buttonhole
7913	**oleaje**-*m*	surf
9412	**oleoducto**-*m*	pipeline
8551	**óleo**-*m*	oil painting
8613	**olivo**-*m*	olive tree
7552	**olmo**-*m*	elm
9768	**omisión**-*f*	omission
9549	**omitir**-*vb*	skip
9792	**ondear**-*vb*	wave
9954	**opcional**-*adj*	optional
8425	**operacional**-*adj*	operational
8809	**operario**-*m*	operator
8215	**oportunista**-*adj; m/f*	opportunistic; opportunist
9081	**opositor**-*m*	opponent
9485	**optar**-*vb*	choose
9941	**oratorio**-*m*	oratory
8938	**orégano**-*m*	oregano
8810	**originalidad**-*f*	originality
7784	**originar**-*vb*	originate
9925	**orina**-*f*	urine
9329	**oruga**-*f*	caterpillar
8796	**ovación**-*f*	ovation
8238	**oval**-*adj*	oval
8734	**ovario**-*m*	ovary
8457	**óvulo**-*m*	ovum

P

7626	**pacifista**-*adj; m/f*	pacifist; pacifist
9996	**pactar**-*vb*	agree
8635	**pagaré**-*m*	promissory note
9087	**paladín**-*m*	paladin
10019	**palpable**-*adj*	palpable
8723	**palpitación**-*f*	pounding
9068	**pamplinas**-*fpl*	nonsense
8634	**pana**-*f*	corduroy
9277	**panal**-*m*	honeycomb
8993	**pancarta**-*f*	banner
8830	**páncreas**-*m*	pancreas
7985	**panorámico**-*adj*	panoramic
8615	**panteón**-*m*	pantheon
9340	**pantorrilla**-*f*	calf
9290	**papal**-*adj*	papal
9593	**papelería**-*f*	stationery
9748	**papeleta**-*f*	ballot
9508	**parábola**-*f*	parable
8541	**paradigma**-*m*	paradigm
9892	**parafernalia**-*f*	paraphernalia
7789	**paramédico**-*adj; m*	paramedical; paramedic
9531	**parco**-*adj*	frugal
8080	**parejo**-*adj*	even
7591	**parentesco**-*m*	kinship
8366	**paréntesis**-*m*	parentheses
8661	**paria**-*m/f*	outcast
8805	**parienta**-*f*	wife (coll)
7786	**parkinson**-*m*	parkinson's disease
9459	**parlamentario**-*adj; m*	parliamentary; Member of Parliament
7920	**parpadear**-*vb*	blink
8622	**parpadeo**-*m*	blink
8956	**parra**-*f*	vine
8017	**parrillada**-*f*	barbecue
9625	**parroquial**-*adj*	parochial
9835	**partición**-*f*	allocation, partition
7613	**parto**-*m*	childbirth
8753	**pasador**-*m*	pin

8237	**pasa**-*f*	raisin	
7594	**pasmar**-*vb*	astound	
8672	**pastar**-*vb*	graze	
8952	**pastoral**-*adj*	pastoral	
7587	**paternal**-*adj*	fatherly	
7692	**paterno**-*adj*	paternal	
7731	**patinador**-*m*	skater	
9537	**patín**-*m*	skate	
8665	**patológico**-*adj*	pathological	
9029	**patriarca**-*m*	patriarch	
8704	**patrocinar**-*vb*	sponsor	
8445	**patrocinio**-*m*	patronage	
7660	**pavor**-*m*	dread	
7826	**peatón**-*m*	pedestrian	
8946	**pecaminoso**-*adj*	sinful	
8152	**pectoral**-*adj; m*	chest; chest	
7635	**pedante**-*adj; m/f*	pedantic; pedant	
8126	**pediatra**-*m/f*	pediatrician	
9341	**pegajoso**-*adj*	sticky	
8364	**peinar(se)**-*vb*	comb your hair	
8137	**peldaño**-*m*	step	
8382	**peligrar**-*vb*	endanger	
8537	**pelón**-*adj*	bald (coll)	
7779	**pelvis**-*f*	pelvis	
7609	**peña**-*f*	rock, club	
9734	**penalti**-*m*	penalty	
8421	**péndulo**-*m*	pendulum	
8569	**penetrante**-*adj*	penetrating	
9174	**penitenciario**-*adj; m*	penitentiary; prison	
9798	**pentagrama**-*m*	pentagram	
9940	**penúltimo**-*adj*	penultimate	
7740	**penumbra**-*f*	gloom	
9096	**penuria**-*f*	hardship	
8917	**percance**-*m*	mishap	
8185	**percusión**-*f*	percussion	
8951	**perdigón**-*m*	pellet	
7680	**perdiz**-*f*	partridge	
8150	**perdurar**-*vb*	endure	
9360	**perecer**-*vb*	perish	
7901	**peregrinación**-*f*	pilgrimage	
7651	**perejil**-*m*	parsley	
8032	**perfeccionar**-*vb*	perfect	
9714	**perforación**-*f*	drilling	
7848	**pericia**-*f*	expertise	
9345	**perico**-*m*	parakeet	
9065	**periferia**-*f*	periphery	

7768	**perilla**-*f*	goatee	
9166	**periodístico**-*adj*	journalistic	
8277	**perito**-*m/f; adj*	expert; expert	
7993	**perjudicado**-*adj*	harmed	
8386	**perjuicio**-*m*	damage	
9009	**permanencia**-*f*	permanence	
9778	**perpetrar**-*vb*	perpetrate	
9507	**perpetuar**-*vb*	perpetuate	
9573	**perseguidor**-*m*	pursuer	
9182	**persistencia**-*f*	persistence	
7604	**persistir**-*vb*	persist	
8387	**pertinente**-*adj*	relevant	
9006	**perturbación**-*f*	disturbance	
9918	**peruano**-*adj; m*	Peruvian; Peruvian person	
9274	**pescadería**-*f*	fish market	
7777	**peseta**-*f*	peseta	
9307	**pesimismo**-*m*	pessimism	
8943	**pesticida**-*m*	pesticide	
7872	**pincho**-*m*	spike	
8728	**piquete**-*m*	picket	
9062	**pirarse**-*vbr*	bait (ES) (coll)	
9213	**piropo**-*m*	compliment	
8920	**pirueta**-*f*	pirouette	
8612	**pisotear**-*vb*	trample	
8650	**pistón**-*m*	piston	
8804	**pita**-*f*	pita	
7663	**pitar**-*vb*	whistle	
7949	**pitido**-*m*	whistle	
9921	**placebo**-*m*	placebo	
8937	**placenta**-*f*	placenta	
8536	**plagiar**-*vb*	plagiarise	
8480	**planeador**-*m*	glider	
9084	**planeamiento**-*m*	planning	
8125	**planetario**-*adj; m*	planetary; planetarium	
8045	**planificar**-*vb*	plan	
8827	**plástica**-*adj; f*	acrylic; plastic	
8905	**plática**-*f*	talk (LA)	
7672	**platicar**-*vb*	talk (LA)	
9394	**plausible**-*adj*	plausible	
8916	**plebeyo**-*m; adj*	commoner; peasant	
7907	**plenitud**-*f*	fullness	
8924	**pliegue**-*m*	crease	
9156	**poblado**-*adj; m*	populated; village	
10008	**poblador**-*m*	villager	

8887	**poderío**-*m*	power
7518	**podio**-*m*	podium
8287	**podrir**-*vb*	rot
8259	**polémico**-*adj*	controversial
8759	**polio**-*f*	polio
8404	**polizón**-*m/f*	stowaway
8755	**polluelo**-*m*	chick
8340	**polución**-*f*	pollution
7874	**pomposo**-*adj*	pompous
9930	**pontífice**-*m*	pontiff
8903	**pornográfico**-*adj*	pornographic
7512	**poro**-*m*	pore
7639	**portería**-*f*	goal
9325	**portuario**-*adj*	port
9176	**posgrado**-*m; adj*	postgraduate degree; postgraduate
8528	**posguerra**-*f*	post-war era
8004	**posteridad**-*f*	posterity
7902	**postiza**-*adj*	fake
8768	**póstumo**-*adj*	posthumous
7899	**potar**-*vb*	puke (coll)
9672	**preámbulo**-*m*	preamble
8797	**precario**-*adj*	precarious
8599	**precintar**-*vb*	seal
9373	**precipitación**-*f*	precipitation
8216	**predestinar**-*vb*	predestine
9578	**predilecto**-*adj*	favorite
9473	**predisposición**-*f*	predisposition
9192	**preferente**-*adj*	preferential
9050	**prefijo**-*m*	prefix
9140	**prehistórico**-*adj*	prehistoric
8510	**preludio**-*m*	prelude
8354	**premiar**-*vb*	reward
8009	**premisa**-*f*	premise
9193	**prepotente**-*adj*	arrogant
9623	**prepucio**-*m*	foreskin
9665	**prerrogativa**-*f*	prerogative
7892	**prescripción**-*f*	prescription
9273	**presentimiento**-*m*	feeling
7945	**preservación**-*f*	preservation
8100	**preservativo**-*m*	condom
8698	**prestación**-*f*	provision
8293	**prestigioso**-*adj*	prestigious
9460	**presumible**-*adj*	likely, alleged
7656	**presunción**-*f*	presumption

7900	**presunto**-*adj*	alleged
9838	**pretexto**-*m*	pretext
8996	**prevalecer**-*vb*	prevail
8112	**preventivo**-*adj*	preventive
8091	**previsible**-*adj*	foreseeable
7729	**previsión**-*f*	forecast
9968	**prieto**-*adj*	tight
8863	**primate**-*m*	primate
8441	**pringar(se)**-*vb*	drizzle (LA), work hard (coll), stain
9089	**prioritario**-*adj*	critical
7982	**privación**-*f*	deprivation
8578	**privar**-*vb*	deprive
9631	**privatización**-*f*	privatization
8257	**procedencia**-*f*	origin
7940	**procesador**-*adj; m*	processing; processor
8915	**proclamación**-*f*	proclamation
9780	**procreación**-*f*	procreation
9109	**procrear**-*vb*	procreate
9613	**prodigioso**-*adj*	prodigious
8610	**productividad**-*f*	productivity
7990	**proeza**-*f*	feat
8627	**profano**-*adj*	profane
9948	**profesionalidad**-*f*	professionalism
9769	**profesionalismo**-*m*	professionalism
9905	**profesorado**-*m*	faculty
7856	**profundizar**-*vb*	deepen
8437	**programador**-*m*	programmer
8717	**progresión**-*f*	progression
8298	**progresista**-*adj; m/f*	progressive; progressive
9129	**progresivo**-*adj*	progressive
7795	**prólogo**-*m*	prologue
8986	**prolongado**-*adj*	prolonged
8369	**promiscuidad**-*f*	promiscuity
9018	**promiscuo**-*adj*	promiscuous
8097	**promocionar**-*vb*	promote
8669	**pronunciación**-*f*	pronunciation
9126	**propagación**-*f*	spreading
8484	**propagar**-*vb*	spread
8384	**propenso**-*adj*	prone
8046	**propicio**-*adj*	conductive
8398	**prórroga**-*f*	extension
8021	**prosa**-*f*	prose
9938	**proscribir**-*vb*	outlaw
8787	**protagonizar**-*vb*	star in

7728	**prótesis**-*f*	prosthesis	
8706	**protón**-*m*	proton	
8736	**provechoso**-*adj*	fruitful	
8710	**provincial**-*adj*	provincial	
9424	**provinciano**-*adj; m*	provincial; provincial	
8750	**provocador**-*adj; m*	provocative; troublemaker	
9867	**pucha**-*int*	wow (LA)	
9441	**puchero**-*m*	pot	
8587	**pueblerino**-*adj*	hick (coll)	
9955	**puercoespín**-*m*	porcupine	
10017	**puerro**-*m*	leek	
9090	**puertorriqueño**-*adj; m*	Puerto Rican; Puerto Rican person	
8347	**puf**-*m; int*	beanbag; ugh	
9232	**pulcro**-*adj*	neat	
9890	**pulpa**-*f*	pulp	
9295	**púlpito**-*m*	pulpit	
9627	**pulsación**-*f*	pulse	
7854	**pulsar**-*vb*	press	
7571	**puñetero**-*m*	annoyance, damn (coll)	
9220	**punzante**-*adj*	sharp	
8812	**pupitre**-*m*	desk	
9302	**purga**-*f*	purge	
9463	**purgar**-*vb*	purge	
7871	**purificación**-*m*	purification	
8656	**purificar**-*vb*	purify	

Q

9195	**quebrantar**-*vb*	break
7963	**quehacer**-*m*	chore
8655	**quejido**-*m*	whimper
8882	**quid**-*m*	crux
9904	**quiebra**-*f*	bankruptcy
7737	**quijada**-*f*	jaw
9111	**quilla**-*f*	keel
9022	**quilombo**-*m*	mess
7800	**quimera**-*f*	chimera
8961	**quinina**-*f*	quinine
9902	**quintal**-*m*	hundredweight
7721	**quiosco**-*m*	kiosk
8580	**quirúrgico**-*adj*	surgical
9633	**quitanieves**-*m*	snowplow

R

9689	**racimo**-*m*	bunch
7809	**racionamiento**-*m*	rationing
9250	**radiactivo**-*adj*	radioactive
7517	**radial**-*adj; f*	radio; circular saw
8235	**radioactividad**-*f*	radioactivity
8393	**radioactivo**-*adj*	radioactive
9777	**radiología**-*f*	radiology
9628	**ramificación**-*f*	branch
8306	**rancio**-*adj*	rancid
9662	**ranking**-*m*	ranking
7918	**ranura**-*f*	groove
9657	**rapar**-*vb*	shave
9770	**rapaz**-*adj; m*	predatory; kid
7738	**rareza**-*f*	rarity
8637	**rascar**-*vb*	scratch
8968	**rasgar**-*vb*	rip
8279	**ratero**-*m*	pickpocket
9387	**rating**-*m*	rating
7915	**rayar**-*vb*	scratch
8120	**reabrir**-*vb*	reopen
8389	**reaccionario**-*adj; m*	reactionary; reactionary
9518	**reacio**-*adj*	reluctant
8392	**realizador**-*m*	producer
9349	**reanimación**-*f*	revival
8477	**reanudar**-*vb*	resume
8567	**rebajar**-*vb*	reduce
9755	**rebelarse**-*vbr*	rebel
7665	**rebeldía**-*f*	rebellion
8230	**rebotar**-*vb*	bounce
7753	**recaer**-*vb*	relapse
8323	**recambio**-*m*	replacement
9327	**recelo**-*m*	suspicion
9116	**recetar**-*vb*	prescribe
8426	**reciclaje**-*m*	recycling
9246	**reciclar**-*vb*	recycle
9375	**recio**-*adj*	tough
9612	**recíproco**-*adj*	reciprocal
9492	**recluir**-*vb*	detain
8019	**reclusión**-*f*	imprisonment
9406	**reclutador**-*m*	recruiter
7684	**recolección**-*f*	collection
8194	**recolector**-*m*	collector
8781	**recomendable**-*adj*	advisable
9251	**reconciliar**-*vb*	reconcile

8138	**reconfortar**-*vb*	comfort
9772	**reconocible**-*adj*	recognizable
9807	**recostar(se)**-*vb*	lie down
9490	**recreativo**-*adj*	recreational
9635	**rectal**-*adj*	rectal
9159	**rectificar**-*vb*	rectify
8908	**rectoría**-*f*	rectory
8493	**recurrente**-*adj*	recurrent
7590	**redactar**-*vb*	write
7748	**redada**-*f*	raid
9774	**redimir**-*vb*	redeem
8607	**redoblar**-*vb*	redouble
9799	**redundante**-*adj*	redundant
8071	**reescribir**-*vb*	rewrite
9871	**reestructuración**-*f*	restructuring
9727	**referéndum**-*m*	referendum
9472	**referí**-*m*	referee
9478	**refinamiento**-*m*	refinement
8451	**refinería**-*f*	refinery
7706	**refrescar**-*vb*	refresh
8083	**refrigeración**-*f*	refrigeration
8765	**refrigerio**-*m*	snack
9086	**refutar**-*vb*	refute
8553	**regadera**-*f*	watering can, shower (LA)
9839	**regañar**-*vb*	scold
8513	**regata**-*f*	regatta
7776	**regatear**-*vb; m*	haggle; haggling
8644	**regeneración**-*f*	regeneration
9649	**regio**-*adj*	royal
7699	**regir**-*vb*	govern
9431	**reglamentario**-*adj*	regulation
9931	**regocijar(se)**-*vb*	rejoice
8825	**regresión**-*f*	regression
9685	**reguero**-*m*	trail
7961	**regulador**-*m; adj*	regulator; regulating
9130	**rehabilitar**-*vb*	rehabilitate
9914	**reingreso**-*m*	re-entry
9636	**reiniciar**-*vb*	reboot
9698	**reivindicación**-*f*	demand
7861	**relajación**-*f*	relaxation
9073	**relajo**-*m*	relax
9219	**relatar**-*vb*	recount
8099	**relatividad**-*f*	relativity
7519	**relevar**-*vb*	relieve, substitute
8660	**relicario**-*m*	reliquary
9380	**relieve**-*m*	importance, topography
8684	**reluciente**-*adj*	shiny
9237	**rematar**-*vb*	conclude
9007	**remisión**-*f*	remission
9388	**remodelación**-*f*	remodeling
8820	**remolacha**-*f*	beet
8243	**remolcador**-*m*	tugboat
8623	**remolque**-*m*	trailer
9449	**remontar**-*vb; vbr*	overcome; date back
7551	**renacuajo**-*m*	tadpole, little kid
9522	**renal**-*adj*	renal
9032	**rencoroso**-*adj*	spiteful
8721	**renombrado**-*adj*	renowned
7504	**renombre**-*m*	renown
8026	**rentar**-*vb*	rent
9668	**reorganización**-*f*	reorganization
9031	**reorganizar**-*vb*	reorganize
8682	**reparador**-*adj; m*	comforting; repairman
8251	**reparo**-*m*	objection
9673	**repatriación**-*f*	repatriation
9603	**repeler**-*vb*	repel
9957	**replicar**-*vb*	replicate
9453	**reprobar**-*vb*	fail
8357	**reprochar**-*vb*	reproach
9312	**repugnancia**-*f*	disgust
9506	**repulsión**-*f*	repulsion
8740	**requerimiento**-*m*	requirement
8348	**resaltar**-*vb*	highlight
7749	**resbaladizo**-*adj*	slippery
9759	**reseco**-*adj*	arid
8693	**reseña**-*f*	review
9344	**reservado**-*adj*	reserved
8383	**resfriarse**-*vbr*	catch a cold
8406	**residencia**-*f*	residence
9730	**residual**-*adj*	residual
8507	**resignación**-*f*	resignation
8476	**resina**-*f*	resin
7929	**resonar**-*vb*	resonate
7657	**respaldar**-*vb*	support
9991	**respectivo**-*adj*	respective
8380	**respirador**-*adj; m*	inhaling; respirator
9718	**respiratorio**-*adj*	respiratory
7808	**retardar**-*vb*	slow down
9409	**retar**-*vb*	challenge

8502	**retención**-*f*	retention	
8101	**retina**-*f*	retina	
9813	**retoque**-*m*	finishing touch	
10016	**retraer**-*vb*	retract	
9426	**retratar**-*vb*	portray	
8683	**retribución**-*f*	payment	
8201	**retroceso**-*m*	setback	
7541	**retrospectivo**-*adj*	retrospective	
8035	**retrovisor**-*m*	rear-view mirror	
8192	**reuma**-*m*	rheumatism	
9875	**reunificación**-*f*	reunification	
8609	**reverso**-*m*	reverse	
9214	**revestimiento**-*m*	coating	
8995	**revocar**-*vb*	revoke	
9723	**rezagarse**-*vbr*	fall behind	
9153	**ricachón**-*f*	rich man (coll)	
8209	**riego**-*m*	irrigation	
7600	**riel**-*m*	rail	
8498	**rifar**-*vb*	raffle	
8844	**rigidez**-*f*	rigidity	
7911	**riguroso**-*adj*	rigorous	
8535	**risco**-*m*	crag	
9516	**risueño**-*adj*	smiling	
9870	**rítmico**-*adj*	rhythmic	
9606	**rocoso**-*adj*	rocky	
9191	**rodillo**-*m*	roller	
8675	**roer**-*vb*	gnaw	
9692	**rompimiento**-*m*	breakup	
7870	**roncar**-*vb*	snore	
8064	**rosal**-*m*	rosebush	
7968	**rosca**-*f*	thread	
8079	**rotundo**-*adj*	resounding	
8593	**rubor**-*m*	blush	
7707	**ruedo**-*m*	arena	
9077	**rústico**-*adj*	rustic	
7535	**rutinario**-*adj*	routine	

S

9377	**sabandija**-*f*	bug, scoundrel (coll)
8420	**sacacorchos**-*m*	corkscrew
8241	**sacerdocio**-*m*	priesthood
9493	**sacristía**-*f*	sacristy
9844	**sadismo**-*m*	sadism
8549	**sagaz**-*adj*	sharp
7599	**saliente**-*adj; m*	outgoing; projection

7554	**salino**-*adj*	saline
9396	**salpicar**-*vb*	splash
8742	**saltador**-*m*	jumper
9840	**salvaguardar**-*vb*	safeguard
8109	**salvoconducto**-*m*	pass
8312	**sanción**-*f*	sanction
9348	**sangría**-*f*	indentation, sangria
7566	**sarta**-*f*	bunch
8947	**satánico**-*adj; m*	satanic; satanist
8175	**sátira**-*f*	satire
9417	**saturación**-*f*	saturation
9435	**saturar**-*vb*	saturate
9052	**saudí**-*adj; m/f*	Saudi; Saudi person
8430	**savia**-*f*	sap
9841	**secesión**-*f*	secession
8540	**secuela**-*f*	sequel
9107	**secular**-*adj*	secular
9059	**sedición**-*f*	sedition
8829	**segregación**-*f*	segregation
9366	**selectivo**-*adj*	selective
9873	**semántico**-*adj*	semantic
8858	**semental**-*adj; m*	stud; stallion
8678	**semifinal**-*f*	semi-final
7547	**semi**-*pfx*	semi
7579	**sencillez**-*f*	simplicity
8709	**sensorial**-*adj*	sensory
7698	**sentimentalismo**-*m*	sentimentality
9831	**separatista**-*adj; m/f*	separatist; separatist
7998	**sepultar**-*vb*	bury
7583	**servicial**-*adj*	helpful
8168	**servil**-*adj*	servile
8282	**setecientos**-*num*	seven hundred
8334	**setiembre**-*m*	September
7838	**seudónimo**-*m*	pseudonym
8529	**severidad**-*f*	severity
8268	**sicario**-*m*	hitman
9571	**sifón**-*m*	siphon
7560	**sigiloso**-*adj*	stealthy
8078	**sílaba**-*f*	syllable
9187	**silenciar**-*vb*	silence
10023	**silicio**-*m*	silicon
9647	**sima**-*f*	chasm
8527	**simbolismo**-*m*	symbolism
8330	**simetría**-*f*	symmetry
8178	**similitud**-*f*	similarity

8508	simpatizante-*adj; m/f*	sympathetic to; sympathizer	7970	suavizar-*vb*	soften
9393	simpatizar-*vb*	sympathize	8031	subestimar-*vb*	underestimate
8469	simplificar-*vb*	simplify	10022	subjetivo-*adj*	subjective
9745	simplista-*adj*	simplistic	7683	subordinar-*vb*	subordinate
9244	simposio-*m*	symposium	9249	subsecretario-*m*	undersecretary
7860	simulador-*m*	simulator	9335	subsistencia-*f*	subsistence
9353	sinapsis-*f*	synapse	9103	subsistir-*vb*	subsist
7850	sindical-*adj*	union	8123	subsuelo-*m*	subsoil
9088	sindicalista-*adj; m/f*	union; trade unionist	8697	subvención-*f*	grant
9682	sinfín-*m*	myriad	8056	subversivo-*adj*	subversive
8633	sinfónico-*adj*	symphonic	9818	subyacente-*adj*	underlying
9604	sintaxis-*f*	syntax	9567	suculento-*adj*	succulent
8388	síntesis-*f*	synthesis	8799	sucumbir-*vb*	succumb
7759	sintético-*adj*	synthetic	9973	sulfato-*m*	sulfate
9833	sintetizador-*m*	synthesizer	9123	sulfurar(se)-*vb*	get angry
8999	sintonizar-*vb*	tune	8888	sumario-*adj; m*	summary; investigation
9760	sinusitis-*f*	sinusitis	9371	sumergible-*adj*	submersible
7888	siquiera-*adv*	at least	9868	sumidero-*m*	sink
7953	sistemático-*adj*	systematic	8308	suministrar-*vb*	supply
9669	slip-*m*	briefs (LA)	9215	sumir-*vb*	plunge
9095	sobrecargar-*vb*	overburden	9043	sumiso-*adj*	submissive
8826	sobrellevar-*vb*	endure	9254	superfluo-*adj*	superfluous
7634	sobrenombre-*m*	nickname	8989	superhombre-*m*	superman
8729	sobrepeso-*m*	overweight	8018	supersticioso-*adj*	superstitious
8489	sobresalir-*vb*	excel	9989	suplementario-*adj*	supplementary
7882	sobrevolar-*vb*	fly over	8037	suplemento-*m*	supplement
8652	sobriedad-*f*	sobriety	7603	súplica-*f*	plea
8531	socializar-*vb*	socialize	8447	supremacía-*f*	supremacy
7546	sociología-*f*	sociology	9222	supresión-*f*	suppression
7539	sodio-*m*	sodium	9278	surco-*m*	groove
9563	sofisticar-*vb*	sophisticate	9687	surgimiento-*m*	appearance
9313	sofocar(se)-*vb; vbr*	suffocate; get embarrassed, get upset	8944	surtir(se)-*vb*	supply
			8461	suscripción-*f*	subscription
8409	solapar-*vb*	overlap	7565	suspense-*m*	suspense
7622	soldado-*m/f*	soldier	8303	suspirar-*vb*	sigh
7764	soldador-*m*	welder	7869	sustancial-*adj*	substantial
9757	solomillo-*m*	sirloin	9362	sustitución-*f*	substitution
7693	sonata-*f*	sonata	8286	sutileza-*f*	subtlety
9686	sondar-*vb*	probe	8534	sutura-*f*	stitch
7841	sondeo-*m*	survey			
8824	soportable-*adj*	bearable		**T**	
9743	sostenible-*adj*	sustainable			
8462	sota-*f*	jack	9271	tablilla-*f*	clipboard
9504	sotavento-*m*	leeward	7751	tablón-*m*	plank
9751	soto-*m*	grove	9365	tachar-*vb*	cross out

8221	**tacho**-*m*	container (LA)	8183	**timonel**-*m/f*	helmsperson
7612	**tala**-*f*	felling	9546	**tinglado**-*m*	racket
9982	**talar**-*vb*	cut down	7891	**tintar**-*vb*	dye
8662	**talonario**-*m*	checkbook	9971	**tintero**-*m*	inkwell
8720	**tambalearse**-*vbr*	stagger	9299	**tintura**-*f*	dye
7685	**tampón**-*m*	tampon	9381	**tiritar**-*vb*	shiver
8958	**tanda**-*f*	batch	7873	**tobogán**-*m*	slide
7948	**tapia**-*f*	wall	8556	**toldo**-*m*	awning
7908	**tapiz**-*m*	tapestry	9440	**tolerable**-*adj*	tolerable
9916	**taquicardia**-*f*	tachycardia	8006	**toma**-*f*	socket
8957	**taquigrafía**-*f*	shorthand	9814	**tomillo**-*m*	thyme
9513	**tarántula**-*f*	tarantula	8572	**tontear**-*vb*	flirt (coll), fool around (coll)
8752	**tardío**-*adj*	late			
9708	**tarima**-*f*	stage	9196	**tópico**-*m; adj*	cliche; topical
8900	**tartamudo**-*m/f*	stutterer	8990	**torácico**-*adj; m*	thoracic; thoracic duct
7952	**tatarabuelo**-*m*	Great-great-grandfather			
			8686	**tórax**-*m*	thorax
7582	**tecnológico**-*adj*	technological	8049	**torniquete**-*m*	tourniquet
9421	**tedio**-*m*	tedium	9715	**toronja**-*f*	grapefruit
8980	**telecomunicaciones**-*fpl*	telecommunications	8542	**tortillera**-*adj*	dyke (coll)
			9990	**tórtola**-*f*	turtledove
7813	**telenovela**-*f*	soap opera	7810	**tosco**-*adj; m*	crude; rough
8127	**televidente**-*m/f*	viewer	9707	**tótem**-*m*	totem
7885	**televisivo**-*adj*	television	9710	**tozudo**-*adj*	stubborn
9887	**temática**-*adj; f*	thematic; theme	7812	**tracción**-*f*	traction
9024	**tembloroso**-*adj*	trembling	7545	**trampolín**-*m*	springboard
9825	**temido**-*adj*	feared	9805	**transatlántico**-*adj; m*	transatlantic; ocean liner
9379	**temporario**-*adj*	temporary			
9343	**tendón**-*m*	tendon	8182	**transcurrir**-*vb*	elapse
9260	**tenencia**-*f*	possession	9910	**transeúnte**-*m*	passerby
9659	**tenista**-*m/f*	tennis player	9175	**transformador**-*m*	transformer
7765	**tenue**-*adj*	faint	9209	**transparencia**-*f*	transparency
8817	**teorema**-*m*	theorem	9857	**transpirar**-*vb*	sweat
8559	**terapéutico**-*adj*	therapeutic	9173	**transportación**-*f*	transportation
8854	**termal**-*adj*	thermal	7742	**trapecio**-*m*	trapeze
8394	**térmico**-*adj*	thermal	9620	**tráquea**-*f*	trachea
8811	**terminación**-*f*	termination	8876	**trascendental**-*adj*	momentous
9885	**terminante**-*adj*	final	9405	**trascender**-*vb*	transcend
10015	**terminología**-*f*	terminology	9617	**trasfondo**-*m*	background
9817	**terraplén**-*m*	embankment	8434	**traspasar**-*vb*	cross, hand over
8614	**territorial**-*adj*	territorial	9300	**traspaso**-*m*	transfer
7938	**tesorería**-*f*	treasury	7877	**trasplante**-*m*	transplant
7624	**textil**-*adj; m*	textile; textile	8285	**traste**-*m*	fret
8146	**tez**-*f*	complexion	8533	**traumático**-*adj*	traumatic
8539	**tibetano**-*adj; m*	Tibetan; Tibetan person	8895	**traumatismo**-*m*	trauma
			9534	**traumatizar**-*vb*	traumatize
8941	**tilde**-*f*	accent	7973	**trazado**-*m*	outline

9197	**trazo**-*m*	stroke	
9289	**tríada**-*f*	triad	
8909	**triangular**-*adj; vb*	triangular; triangulate	
9749	**tribulación**-*f*	tribulation	
8857	**triciclo**-*m*	tricycle	
8864	**tridimensional**-*adj*	three-dimensional	
9596	**trilogía**-*f*	trilogy	
8119	**triplicar**-*vb*	triple	
9594	**tripular**-*vb*	crew	
8860	**trituradora**-*f*	crusher	
8630	**triunfador**-*m; adj*	winner; winning	
7633	**triunfal**-*adj*	triumphal	
7796	**triunfante**-*adj*	triumphant	
9815	**trivialidad**-*f*	triviality	
8142	**trópico**-*adj; m*	tropic; tropic	
9010	**trotar**-*vb*	trot	
9316	**troyano**-*adj; m*	Trojan; Trojan horse	
7529	**tumbar(se)**-*vb*	knock down; lay down	
8005	**turbina**-*f*	turbine	
9724	**turbulento**-*adj*	turbulent	

U

8953	**ucraniano**-*adj; m*	Ukrainian; Ukrainian person
9296	**ultramar**-*m*	overseas
9969	**ultrasonido**-*m*	ultrasound
8217	**ultravioleta**-*adj*	ultraviolet
8249	**unanimidad**-*f*	unanimity
9984	**undécimo**-*num*	eleventh
8639	**unificación**-*f*	unification
9451	**unificar**-*vb*	unify
7618	**uniformar**-*vb*	standardize
9558	**unilateral**-*adj*	unilateral
9645	**untar**-*vb*	spread
9245	**urbanismo**-*m*	town planning
8538	**urbanización**-*f*	urbanisation
7501	**urgir**-*vb*	press
9520	**urticaria**-*f*	hives
8113	**utensilio**-*m*	utensil
9528	**utilización**-*f*	utilization

V

7816	**vacilar**-*vb*	tease, hesitate

9218	**vagabundear**-*vb*	roam
7596	**vaginal**-*adj*	vaginal
9356	**vaivén**-*m*	swinging
7979	**validez**-*f*	validity
9256	**valoración**-*f*	assessment
8095	**vándalo**-*m/f*	vandal
9861	**variante**-*adj; f*	alternative; variant
7756	**varicela**-*f*	chickenpox
9186	**varilla**-*f*	rod
8589	**varonil**-*adj*	manly
10021	**vascular**-*adj*	vascular
7619	**vecindad**-*f*	neighborhood
9288	**vegetar**-*vb*	vegetate
8407	**veintinueve**-*num*	twenty-nine
7995	**veintiséis**-*num*	twenty-six
8523	**velorio**-*m*	wake
9447	**vencimiento**-*m*	expiration
8106	**venerable**-*adj*	venerable
9027	**venerar**-*vb*	worship
9281	**venéreo**-*adj*	venereal
8141	**venidero**-*adj*	coming
9311	**ventajoso**-*adj*	advantageous
9985	**ventilar**-*vb*	ventilate
9328	**veracidad**-*f*	veracity
9399	**veranear**-*vb*	spend the summer in
9784	**verídico**-*adj*	true
8172	**verruga**-*f*	wart
7670	**versus**-*prp*	versus
8894	**vértebra**-*f*	vertebra
8105	**verter**-*vb*	pour
9064	**vestigio**-*m*	vestige
8226	**vibrante**-*adj*	vibrant
8459	**vid**-*f*	vine
8671	**vigente**-*adj*	existing
8345	**vigésimo**-*num*	twentieth
9033	**vigoroso**-*adj*	vigorous
7942	**vincular**-*vb*	link
8733	**vinilo**-*m*	vinyl
9049	**viral**-*adj*	viral
8748	**víscera**-*f*	entrails
9820	**viscoso**-*adj*	viscous
9880	**vislumbrar**-*vb*	glimpse
9204	**visualizar**-*vb*	visualize
8592	**vivaz**-*adj*	vivacious
8560	**vivero**-*m*	nursery
9337	**vocalista**-*m/f*	vocalist

8828	**volátil**-*adj; m*	volatile; volatility
7769	**volcar**-*vb*	dump
7570	**voleibol**-*m*	volleyball
9150	**voltereta**-*f*	somersault
9094	**voraz**-*adj*	voracious
8000	**vulgaridad**-*f*	vulgarity
8743	**vulnerabilidad**-*f*	vulnerability

Y

9525	**yacimiento**-*m*	deposit, field
8927	**yema**-*f*	yolk
7715	**yugo**-*m*	yoke

| 8195 | **yugular**-*adj* | jugular |
| 9364 | **yunque**-*m* | anvil |

Z

9039	**zanja**-*f*	ditch
8114	**zapatería**-*f*	shoe shop
8647	**zinc**-*m*	zinc
7508	**zurrar**-*vb*	spank

Contact, Further Reading and Resources

For more tools, tips & tricks, please visit www.mostusedwords.com. We publish various language learning resources. If you have a great idea you want to pitch, please send an e-mail to info@mostusedwords.com.

Frequency Dictionaries

In this series:

Spanish Frequency Dictionary 1 – Essential Vocabulary – 2500 Most Common Spanish Words
Spanish Frequency Dictionary 2 - Intermediate Vocabulary – 2501-5000 Most Common Spanish Words
Spanish Frequency Dictionary 3 - Advanced Vocabulary – 5001-7500 Most Common Spanish Words
Spanish Frequency Dictionary 4 - Master Vocabulary – 7501-10000 Most Common Spanish Words

Our mission is to provide language learners worldwide with frequency dictionaries for every major and minor language. We are working hard to accomplish this goal. You can view our selection on https://store.mostusedwords.com/frequency-dictionaries

Bilingual books

We're creating a selection of parallel texts. We decided to rework timeless classics, such as Alice in Wonderland, Sherlock Holmes, Dracula, The Picture of Dorian Gray, and many more.

Our books are paragraph aligned: on the left side of the page you will find the English version of the story, and on the right side the Spanish version..

To help you in your language learning journey, all our bilingual books come with a dictionary included, created for that particular book.

Current bilingual books available are English, Spanish, Portuguese, Italian, German, and Spanish.

For more information, check https://store.mostusedwords.com/bilingual-books . Check back regularly for new books and languages.

Other language learning methods

You'll find reviews of other 3rd party language learning applications, software, audio courses, and apps. There are so many available, and some are (much) better than others.

Check out our reviews at www.mostusedwords.com/reviews.

Contact

If you have any questions, you can contact us through e-mail info@mostusedwords.com.

Printed in Great Britain
by Amazon

22384259R00132